London To Dublin

DUBLIN.

LONDON TO DUBLIN:

WITH

A TRIP TO THE IRISH LAKES

AND

THE MOUNTAINS OF CONNAMARA.

INTERSPERSED WITH PASSING GLANCES AT

NORTH WALES AND THE MANUFACTURING DISTRICTS OF ENGLAND.

WITH NUMEROUS ENGRAVINGS.

FLINT CASTLE.

LONDON:
WILLIAM S. ORR AND CO., AMEN CORNER;
AND JAMES McGLASHAN, 50, UPPER SACKVILLE STREET, DUBLIN.
1853.

CONTENTS.

LIST OF ILLUSTRATIONS.

DESIGNED AND EXECUTED BY THE FIRST ARTISTS.

ENGRAVINGS ON STEEL.

ENGRAVINGS ON WOOD.

*

LONDON TO DUBLIN.

———————◆———————

THE CAMDEN TOWN STATION.

As the London and North-western Railway, with its numerous branches, forms the great artery of communication with Wales and Ireland, we shall at once enter upon our route from London to Birmingham,—the metropolitan terminus of which is at Euston Square.

This station, including its dependency, Camden Town, which is also the terminus of the Blackwall branch line, is the greatest railway area in England, or perhaps in Europe. It is the principal gate through which flows and reflows traffic of a line which has cost more that twenty-two millions sterling; which annually earns more than two millions and a-half for the conveyance of passengers, and merchandise, and live stock; and which directly employs more than ten thousand servants, besides the tens of thousands to whom, in mills or mines, in ironworks, in steamboats and coasters, it gives indirect employment. What London is to the world, Euston is to Great Britain: there is no part of the country to which railway communication has extended, with the exception of the Dover and Southampton lines, which may not be reached by railway conveyance from Euston station. Originally the line was intended to have ended at Camden Town; but a favourable opportunity led to the purchase of fifteen acres, which has turned out most advantageous for the proprietors and the public. The propylæum, or great gateway, cost thirty thousand pounds in the erection, and certainly appears very imposing, although its practical utility is questionable.

The Mixed train on this North-western line holds an intermediate rank between the Parliamentary and the Express, consisting as it does of first and second-class carriages, at lower fares than the one and higher than the other, stopping at fewer stations than the Parliamentary, and at more than the Express; but the circumstance is worth mentioning, because it is by these trains only that horses and carriages are allowed to be conveyed. Carriages require very careful packing on a truck. At the principal stations this may be very well left to the practised porters, but at road-side stations it is a point deserving attention; for it has not unfrequently happened that the jogging and lateral motion of the railway has heated the axles of a carriage or truck, so that at the end of the journey the wheels have been found as fast as if they had been welded, and quite unfit to travel.

As we move slowly off, towards Camden Town, we emerge with light whirl along within sight of some rows of capital houses, whose gardens descend to the edge of the embankments. On arriving at Camden Town, the busy scene which presents itself on every side deserves a passing notice. The arrangements for building waggons and trucks, and conveying coals, merchandise, goods, and all live stock, present a wonderful scene of busy industry. On this railway the increase of the goods traffic has been of very recent date. At a very early period after the opening of the line, the merchandise department became the monopoly of the great carriers, who found it answer their purpose to divide the profits afforded by the discount allowed to carriers by the railway company, without seeking to develop an increase of occupation. Under this system, while carriers grew rich, the goods traffic remained stationary. But when the amalgamation with the Grand Junction, which had always been its own carrier, took place, a great reduction in rates was made, as well as arrangements for encouraging the conveyance of every kind of saleable article. The company became a common carrier, but employing Messrs. Pickford, and Chaplin and Horne to collect goods. The result was a marvellous increase, which has been progressing ever since. A regular trade is now carried on between London and the most remote parts of the kingdom in every conceivable thing that will bear moving. The carrying department is very conveniently situated close to the Regent's Canal, so as to have easy communication with inland as well as sea navigation. A series of sheds occupy an area of 135,000 superficial feet; and the platforms, to receive goods from railway trucks on one side and from waggons on the other, occupy 30,000 feet. The railway trucks and waggons are moved about by horses. It is amusing to see the activity with which the heavy brutes often bring a waggon up at a trot, jump out of the way just at the right moment, and allow the waggon to roll up to the right spot by its own momentum. Twenty-four steam waggon horses, or engines, for heavy loads, are kept in a circular engine-house, or stable, 160 feet in diameter, with an iron roof. This form renders every engine accessible at a moment's notice.

Camden station, under the alterations effected in 1848-9, has a double line, for goods waggons only, 2500 feet in length, entirely clear of the main line. The length of single lines, exclusive of the main line, exceeds twelve miles.

Leaving Camden Town, we rapidly pass KILBURN, WILLESDEN, and SUDBURY. The next station is within a mile of HARROW-ON-THE-HILL, with its beacon-like church spire. Harrow school is almost as much one of the institutions of England as Oxford and Cambridge Universities. It was founded by one John Lyon, a farmer of the parish, who died in 1592. Attached to it are four exhibitions of £20 each, and two scholarships of £50 each. The grand celebrity of the school rests upon the education of those who are not on the foundation. Among its illustrious scholars Harrow numbers Lord Byron and Sir Robert Peel. Since the palmy days when Dr. Drury was master, and Byron and Peel were pupils, Harrow has declined in importance; but by the abilities of Dr. Wordsworth it has been raised again.

PINNER station is about two miles from Harrow, where we pass from Middlesex into the county of Hertford.

HERTFORDSHIRE.

Passing Bushey we soon arrive at WATFORD, which is one of the principal stations of the county. It is within a mile of the town of that name, on the river Colne.

Cashiobury Park, a favourite spot for pic-nics, is close to the station. It was the opposition of the late proprietor, the Earl of Essex, that forced upon the engineer of the line the formidable tunnel, which was once considered an astonishing railway work.

KINGS LANGLEY is about four miles from Watford, and, though the parish is small, it was once a place of some historical importance. Here was a palace, in which Henry III. resided, and a celebrated priory, in which Piers Gaveston, a favourite of Henry II., was buried. In the church, the bodies of Richard II. and Edmund of Langley, fifth son of Edward III., were interred. Near Kings Langley we pass the Booksellers' Provident Retreat, erected on ground given by Mr. Dickenson, the great paper maker, who has seven mills on the neighbouring streams, and reach Boxmoor, only noticeable as the first station opened on the line.

The next station is BERKHAMPSTEAD. Cowper the poet was born here; his father was rector of the parish. Berkhampstead Castle is part of the hereditary property of the Prince of Wales and Duke of Cornwall. At this castle William the Conqueror, after the battle of Hastings, met the Abbot of St. Albans with a party of chiefs and prelates, who had prepared to oppose the Norman, and disarmed their hostility by swearing to rule according to the ancient laws and customs of the country. Having, of course, broken his oath, he bestowed the castle on his half-brother, Robert Moreton, Earl of Cornwall. King John strengthened the castle, which was afterwards besieged by the Dauphin of France. When Edward III. created the Black Prince Duke of Cornwall, the castle and manor of Berkhampstead were bestowed upon him " to hold to him, and the heirs of him, and the eldest sons of the kings of England, and the dukes of the said place;" and under these words have they been held through civil wars and revolutions, and changes from Plantagenet to Tudor, from Tudor to Stuart, with the interregnum of a republic, an abdication, and the installation of the Brunswick dynasty. The castle is now vested in Albert Prince of Wales.

The CHILTERN HILLS, including the Chiltern Hundreds, the only office under the crown always open to the acceptance of all without distinction of parties, lies within a short distance of Berkhampstead. Ashdridge Park, formerly the seat of the Duke of Bridgewater the originator and author, with the aid of Brindley and Telford, of our great canal system, lies about a mile to the eastward.　The scenery of the park and gardens is fine.　The house is modern.

TRING station, a mile and a half from the town, may be reached from London, 31½ miles, in less than an hour by the express train, and the traveller arrives in as wild a district as any in England.　This station is the highest point on the line, being 420 feet above the sea, 300 above Camden Town, and 52 above Birmingham.　Three miles north of Tring lies the town of IVINGHOE, which possesses a large cruciform church, with an old sculptured timber roof, and contains a tomb with a Norman-French inscription.　According to some it was the tomb of Henry de Blois, Bishop of Winchester, and brother of King Stephen.　Two miles from Tring we pass from Hertfordshire into Bucks.

BUCKINGHAMSHIRE.

The first station of importance, in this county, is AYLESBURY, which is connected by a short branch line.　This ancient town stands on a hill in the middle of one of the richest pasture lands in England; but the loss of the coaching trade, by the substitution of the railroad, has proved a serious blow to the leading interests of the town.　The Berry field, said to be the best field in England, lies in the Vale of Aylesbury.　But, with few exceptions, the farming around Aylesbury is as bad as it can be—the farmers miserably poor, and the labourers ignorant to the lowest degree.

Passing from the Aylesbury branch, and gliding out of the deep cutting over a fine open country, we soon arrive at LEIGHTON BUZZARD station, and see in the distance the lofty octagonal spire of its venerable cruciform church.　The town is about half a mile from the station.　The cross stands in an open area in the centre of the market-place, and is twenty-seven feet high above the basement, which is raised by rows of steps about five feet.　At Leighton Buzzard a branch line of seven miles communicates with DUNSTABLE, which is situated in the centre of the Dunstable Chalk Downs, where the celebrated Dunstable larks are caught, which are made mention of in one of Miss Edgeworth's pretty stories.　The manufactures are whiting and straw hats.　Of an ancient priory, founded in 1131 by Henry I., and endowed with the town, and the privileges of jurisdiction extending to life and death, nothing remains but the parish church, of which the interior is richly ornamented.　Over the altar-piece is a large painting representing the Lord's Supper, by Sir James Thornhill, the father-in-law of Hogarth.　In a charity school, founded in 1727, forty boys are clothed, educated, and apprenticed.　In twelve almshouses twelve poor widows are lodged; and in six houses near the church, called the Maidens' Lodge, six unmarried gentlewomen live and enjoy an income of £120 per annum.

At BLETCHLEY, the church (embowered in a grove of yews, planted perhaps when Henry VIII. issued his decrees for planting the archer's tree) contains an altar tomb of Lord Grey of Wilton, A.D. 1412.　The station has now become important, as from it diverge the Bedford line to the east, and the lines to Banbury and Oxford to the west.　A few miles from Bletchley is a forgotten but once celebrated spot, Denbigh Hall, over which the traveller whirls without notice, yet worthy of remembrance, because it affords a name and date for tracing the march of railway enterprise.

WOLVERTON, which is near six miles north of Bletchley, is the central manufacturing and repairing shop for the locomotives north of Birmingham, and the first specimen of a railway town built on a plan to order.　The population consists entirely of men employed in the company's service, as mechanics, guards, enginemen, stokers, porters, labourers, their wives and children, their superintendents, a clergyman, schoolmasters and schoolmistresses, the ladies engaged on the refreshment establishment, and the tradesmen attracted to Wolverton by the demand of the population.　Here may be seen collected together in companies, each under command of its captain or foremen, in separate workshops, some hundreds of the best handicraftsmen that Europe can produce.　Machinery, while superseding, has created manual labour.　In a steam-engine factory machinery is called upon to do what no amount of manual labour could effect.　To appreciate the extraordinary amount of intellect and mental and manual dexterity daily called into exercise, it would be necessary to have the origin, progress to construction, trial, and amendment of a locomotive engine.　But such a history would be a book itself. After seeing the operations of forging or of casting, we may take a walk round the shops of the turners and Smiths.　In some Whitworth's beautiful self-acting machines are planing, or polishing, or boring holes, under charge of an intelligent boy; in others lathes are ranged round the walls, and a double row of vices down the centre of the long rooms.　Solid masses of cast or forged metal are carved by keen and powerful lathe-tools like so much box-wood, and long shavings of iron and steel sweep off as easily as deal shavings from a carpenter's plane. The whole work of this vast establishment is carried on by dividing the workmen into small companies, under the superintendence of an officer responsible for the quantity and quality of the work of his men.

The two important lines leading from Bletchley station—the one into BEDFORDSHIRE and the other into OXFORDSHIRE—here present the opportunity of noting the chief attractions of these two important counties.

BEDFORDSHIRE.

WOBURN, on the Bedford line, is one of those dull places, neat, clean, and pretentious in public buildings, which are forced under the hot-house influence of a great political family. Woburn Abbey is the residence of the Russell family, with its extensive and magnificent gardens, its model farms, its picture gallery, and other accessories of a great nobleman's seat.

BEDFORD is distinguished for the number and wealth of its charities. The chief source of these charities is derived from an estate of thirteen acres of land in the parish of St. Andrew, Holborn, London, bequeathed by Sir William Harpur, an alderman of that city, in the reign of Edward VI., for founding a free school for instructing the children of the town in grammar and good manners. This land, now covered with valuable houses, produces some £16,000 per annum. On this fund there are supported—first, a grammar school, with eighty boys on the foundation, and as many private boarders; a commercial school, containing 100 to 150 boys; a national school, of 350 boys, where on the half-holidays 170 girls are received; a regular girls' school, and an infant school. The cheap and good education attainable as a matter of right in this borough has rendered it a favourite resort of half-pay officers, and unbeneficed clergymen, blessed with large families. The church of St. Paul is spacious, with a nave and a south aisle, divided by early English piers and arches. A stone pulpit, ornamented with gilt tracery, on a blue ground, has been removed in favour of an oak one, with the chancel. The church of St. Peter has an old Norman door, a fine antique font, and some curious stained glass in the windows. John Bunyan, author of the "Pilgrim's Progress," was co-pastor in a Baptist Meeting House, in Mill-lane, from 1671 until his death, in 1688. The chair in which he used to sit is still preserved in the vestry as a relic.

OXFORDSHIRE.

The extensive line which branches from Bletchley through Buckinghamshire diverges, at Winslow, by one line to BANBURY, and by the other to OXFORD.

BANBURY is considered by commercial travellers as one of the best towns in England, as it is a sort of metropolis to a great number of thriving villages. Banbury cakes are known wherever English children are bred; and to them, where not educated in too sensible a manner, the Homeric ballad of

> " Ride a cock horse
> To Banbury cross "

is sung. Unfortunately, the Puritans, in the time of Edward VI., pulled this famous cross down.

BICESTER, commonly pronounced Bister, is thirteen miles by the road from Oxford—a town as ancient as the Heptarchy; famous for a well once sacred, and dedicated to St. Edburgh, for its well-attended markets and cattle fairs, and especially for its excellent ale. It is in the centre of a capital hunting country.

Along the Bletchley line we now rapidly approach the fair city of OXFORD; and its glittering spires announce it at a distance. The entrance to this ancient seat of learning is of the most imposing character; and cannot fail to make a strong impression on the mind of the visitor. As we roll round a spacious semicircle, we sweep into sight of the dome of Ratcliffe Library, and the spire of St. Mary's Church; and passing through an inferior suburb, reach the head of High-street, of which a great German art critic declared, "that it had not its equal in the whole world." Wide, long, and gently curving, approached from either end, it presents in succession the colleges of Lincoln, Brazennose, University, All Souls, Queen's, St. Mary's Church, with peeps of gardens with private houses and shops, whch rather add to the dignity and weight of the grand old buildings.

J. Thom. del.

OXFORD FROM THE HENLEY ROAD.

OXFORD.

OXFORD is, indisputably, the most beautiful city in England. It contains a far larger and richer display of medieval and academic architecture than any other; and it yields to none in picturesque variety. And as it is the most beautiful, we doubt whether it be not also, at any rate to Englishmen, the most generally interesting of English cities. Indeed, apart from its attractions in point of taste, the place could hardly fail to be regarded with more than common interest, wherein so many of our greatest men laid the foundation of their greatness in that "culture and manurance of the mind," as Bacon terms it, which not alone prepared them to produce such abundant fruit in their season, but by its "forcible though unseen operation," conduced more than anything else to the formation and completion of their whole moral and mental character; wherein so many are being educated of those on whom the future virtue, and, therefore, honour of our country will depend; and that so abounds with recollections and associations which appeal to our loftiest feelings, and are connected with so much that is important in our history. Few who think of its fame, and recollect its associations, and recognize the dignity of its position, can approach it for the first time without some (it may be vague) excitement of feeling; and assuredly, none who do so approach it are disappointed. When even those come to visit it, who, from carelessness or prejudice, usually regard it with indifference or dislike, the genius of the place seldom fails to seize hold of them; gradually better and kindlier feelings supersede those which were before cherished; and the placid grandeur, the peaceful venerableness, of this ancient favourite of the Muses, is recognized and respected. A first visit to Oxford is a thing to remember.

The situation of Oxford is singularly fortunate. Scarcely could the noble city have been placed where its surpassing beauty would be more admirably displayed. It stands on a slight eminence between the rivers Isis and Cherwell, and near their confluence. Hills of gentle elevation surround it; from nearly all of which its matchless array of domes and spires is seen to great advantage. In the days of stage-coach travelling, the visitor, in whatever direction he came, as he drew near, obtained a glorious prospect of the good city;—and he seldom forgot that first view. Now that it is generally reached by the railway, little is seen of the city till it is entered:—and then the view from Folly Bridge is a poor substitute for the famous one from Magdalen. The visitor has now to seek after a general view of Oxford; but if he have any delight in the survey of what is beautiful, he will not fail to do so :—the general view of Oxford is in its way quite without a rival.

There are many places from which this view may be obtained. One of the best stations is a short distance up the Abingdon Road. From a point sufficiently elevated to command the whole town, the splendid series of buildings falls into a most picturesque composition, while a fertile and richly-wooded level tract, with the silver Thames winding through it, stretches between you and the city; and a line of softly-swelling uplands forms an agreeable back ground, and completes the picture: it is a view that always fills a painter's heart with delight, and might be transferred at once to the canvas, without changing a single feature. One of the finest of Turner's early pictures—the large engraving from which is probably known to many of our readers—is, indeed, a very faithful transcript of this scene. The other most celebrated views are those from Hinksey Hill, from Shotover Hill, and from the Henley Road. The former are very beautiful; but we have preferred giving an engraving of the latter, as that least known. The spot from which it is taken is some distance up the Henley Road, and about midway between the villages of Ifley and Cowley. The academic spires and pinnacles stretch across the view. As from most places the great dome of the Ratcliffe Library, and the magnificent spire of St. Mary's (the University Church) occupy the centre, and around them the loftier parts of the various colleges are seen ranging themselves in picturesque order. The tall pile on the extreme right is the famous tower of Magdalen College,—a prominent object from almost every part of Oxford and its vicinity; while, on the left, the cupola of the Tom Gateway, and the Cathedral steeple, indicate the site of Christ's Church College. The other buildings it is unnecessary to particularise. Another and very fine view of Oxford is thus described in the 'Rambles by Rivers'—("The Thames:")—"It is perhaps from the gentle slopes between Wytham and Binsey, that the best general view of Oxford is obtained. The broad sheet of water stretches beneath and before you, and the dark roofs and tall chimneys of the western suburb, which occupy the middle ground, serve to throw into a finer distance, and impart a more airy grace to the long range of towers, domes, and spires, that form the picture, and that mark, as we know, spots where have lived and laboured a succession of the noblest men that our country—so rich in noble men—has to boast of." The slopes here intended are probably those of Wytham Park, the property of the Earl of Abingdon; but the stranger had better not go there in search of the prospect:—admission is no longer granted to the wayfarer.

Our wood-engraving of Oxford (Cut, No. 1) is taken from the Thames near Binsey Green, just under Wytham Park. It is, perhaps, not so striking a prospect as some others, but we select it because it is less known, and has seldom, if ever before, been engraved. In this view, the city is seen from the opposite direction to that of the steel engraving.

We shall defer our examination of the interior of the city till we have glanced hastily over its history.

Like almost every ancient and every important city, Oxford has sought the aid of fable in order to extend its antiquity. It is, however, hardly worth our while to inquire whether it was a city in the shadowy era of the early British princes, or to search after the date of its foundation; nor need we stay to "consider curiously" into the origin of its name. It seems to be generally allowed that the name arose from there having been a ford across the Thames here; but Warton, and some other learned writers of late date have attempted to show that it was originally called Ousen-ford, or the Ford of the Ouse, a usual Saxon name for a river; and they think their hypothesis is supported by the preservation of the word in Ouseney, or Oseney Abbey, in the adjacent meadows; while the common opinion is, that Oxford owes its name to the ford being one chiefly used for oxen. This last is the favourite etymology of our older antiquaries, who found some pretty classical supports to strengthen it; and it is that adopted by the city itself, which carries as its arms "an ox *gules* passing through a ford"—an authority that surely ought to satisfy all reasonable people as to the sufficiency of this derivation. The name was written Oxnaford by the Saxons; in the Domesday Survey it is Oxeneford; and Oxenford it continued to be written down to a comparatively recent period.

Whatever was the date of its foundation, it was a place of some consequence in Saxon times, and was not unfrequently the seat of royalty. Alfred is said to have resided here; and some of his coins still exist, on which the name of the city is inscribed. In 1010 it was burned by the Danes, but it appears to have been quickly restored; for, not long after, it is spoken of as the residence of Edmund Ironsides, who died here, as was supposed, by unfair means, in 1016. During the reign of his successor, Canute, the great council of the nation was often held at Oxford. After the death of Canute, it was here that the Council met to decide on the rival claims of Harold and Hardicanute to the throne. In accordance with their decision, Harold was crowned at Oxford; and it was at Oxford that he died. At the Norman invasion the citizens of Oxford refused to submit to the Conqueror; and when, after his coronation, he marched into Oxfordshire, they resolutely denied him admittance into the city. But they paid dearly for their temerity. William stormed the walls, and wreaked a terrible vengeance on the inhabitants. The more effectually to keep them in subjection, he gave a considerable portion of land to one of his followers, named Robert D'Oilli, on condition of his erecting and maintaining a castle. The Domesday Survey, compiled about eighteen years after William's storming of the city, affords striking evidence of the effect of his violence, or of subsequent oppressive measures, or, perhaps, of both combined.

" In the town itself, as well within the walls as without, there are two hundred and forty-three houses paying the tax; and besides these, there are five hundred houses, save twenty-two, so waste and decayed that they cannot pay the tax." It deserves notice, too, as a proof of the king's resentment, that while other places, on account of their poverty, were rated at lower sums than in Edward's time (the survey being so drawn up as to show the present value as compared with that in the lifetime of the Confessor), Oxford was amerced at a far higher sum. " In the time of King Edward, Oxeneford paid for toll and gable, and all other customs, yearly to the king, twenty pounds and six sextaries of honey. But to Earl Algar ten pounds, his mill being added, which he had below the city. When the king went on an expedition, twenty burgesses went with him for all the others; or they paid twenty pounds to the king that all might be free. Now Oxeneford pays sixty pounds by tale, of twentypence in the ore." One other short passage is worth quoting, as an instance of the kind of tenure by which houses were held in walled towns:—" The king has twenty mural mansions, which were Earl Algar's in King Edward's time, paying then and now fourteen shillings save two-pence." And after enumerating other similar mansions of the king's, it adds, " They are called mural mansions, because, if it be necessary, and the king command it, they repair the walls." A list of those who hold mural mansions is then given, and it proceeds: " All these hold the aforesaid mansions free, because they repair the walls. All the mansions which are called mural were, in King Edward's time, free from all customary payments, except expedition and reparation of the walls. . . . And if, while the wall is necessary, it is not renewed by him who ought to do it, he shall either pay forty shillings to the king or lose his house." Some distance further the penalty for refusing to join an 'expedition' is also stated: " If he who is warned to go on an expedition do not go, he shall pay one hundred shillings to the king."

In the next reign Oxford was raised from its adversity by the presence and favour of the sovereign. Henry I. appears to have entertained considerable partiality for the town, perhaps, as Wood asserts, from his having been educated there. He built for himself a residence at Oxford, which was called Beaumont Palace, and was occasionally occupied by royalty down to the time of Edward II., who gave it to the society of Carmelite Friars for a monastery. A dilapidated fragment of it remained till 1830, when it was removed to make way for a new street, which, from its occupying the site of the palace, received the name of Beaumont-street. Henry also conferred upon the inhabitants of Oxford a charter of incorporation. Robert D'Oilli, the nephew of the Robert who built the castle, also contributed to the prosperity of the city by the foundation of the Abbey of Oseney.

Early in the following reign, Oxford witnessed the treacherous arrest of the bishops of Salisbury, Ely, and Lincoln; an event that had no small share in producing the calamities of the ensuing years. Stephen summoned a council at Oxford in 1139. Among the

1.—FROM THE THAMES, NEAR BINSEY-GREEN.

chief men of the nation who were called to take part in it, was Roger, bishop of Salisbury, one of the most powerful of the English prelates. Roger had been treasurer and justiciary to Henry I.; and though he held no office under Stephen, his general influence remained unimpaired. Roger was, indeed, no ordinary man. He was distinguished by learning and ability, and scarcely less by his almost unbounded wealth, and the manner in which he expended it. "With unrivalled magnificence in their construction," says William of Malmesbury, "he erected splendid mansions on all his estates; in merely maintaining which, the labour of his successors will toil in vain. His cathedral [which he rebuilt] he dignified to the utmost with matchless ornaments and buildings, on which no expense was spared. It was truly wonderful to behold in this man what abundant power attended him in every kind of dignity, and flowed as it were to his hand. How great was the glory, indeed what could exceed it, that he should have made his two nephews, by virtue of his education, men of noted learning and industry, bishops; and not of mean sees, but of Lincoln and Ely." Malmesbury adds: "He was sensible of his power, and somewhat more harshly than became such a character, abused the favours of heaven." The nobles and powerful laymen had long regarded him with an envious eye, and continually urged the monarch to repress his pride, and that of his nephews. But Stephen only answered, that the time was not ripe, "assuaging the bitterness of delay either by his respect for the piety of the bishops, or, as I rather think, from apprehensions of the odium he might incur, by seizing their castles." Roger was most likely fully aware that the king was only watching for an opportunity to effect his ruin. He seems to have gone to the council at Oxford with great reluctance. "I heard him," says Malmesbury, "speaking to the following purport: 'By my Lady St. Mary, I know not why, but my heart revolts at this journey: this I am sure of, that I shall be of much the same service at court as a foal is in battle.'" His foreboding was verified. A dispute arose between his followers and those of the Earl of Brittany, a nobleman who was then on a visit to the king. In the tumult several of the earl's men were wounded, and his nephew was nearly killed. The bishop's servants were the victors, but their victory was not gained without bloodshed: many of them were wounded, and a knight was slain. The affair is by some suspected to have been contrived by Stephen, as a pretext for obtaining possession of the bishops, and seizing on their estates. Be that as it may, he availed himself of it for casting off the appearance of friendship, and at once ordered the arrest of Bishop Roger and his nephews. Ely escaped, but the others were seized and treated with extreme harshness—from the effects of which Roger soon after died. The king speedily became convinced that, in the language of modern politicians, he had committed something worse than a crime—a blunder. The whole body of the prelates and clergy, with his brother, the

Bishop of Winchester, at their head, at once declared against him; and it is not difficult to trace much of his future ill-fortune to his conduct on this occasion. In the war between Stephen and Matilda, Oxford Castle was garrisoned for the empress-queen; and hither it was that she fled when driven out of London by the citizens. Somewhat later it was the scene of one of her most romantic adventures. Towards the end of 1142 she kept her court at Oxford. She had long baffled all Stephen's attempts to get her into his power; and he now marched against the city in which she was, with the avowed determination not to quit the siege till she was his prisoner. The city he soon stormed and burnt; but the queen retreated into the castle, which refused to listen to any terms. The winter set in with unusual severity, but the king prosecuted the siege with unabated vigour. For nearly three months he had been before the castle, and every effort that had been made to convey provisions to the besieged had been defeated. He knew that famine must soon open an entrance to him. He felt assured that at last the bird was in the toils, and every avenue of escape diligently guarded. The brave garrison, however, knew their duty. They might die, but they would not yield their queen a prisoner. It was not till she, as well as themselves, was nearly starved to death, that submission was spoken of. The surrender was fixed for the 21st of December; but on the night before it took place, the queen resolved to attempt an escape by one of those bold stratagems she knew so well how to contrive and execute, and which had been suggested to her by the rigour of the season. Snow covered the fields; the many arms into which the river here separates were frozen over. Here was her hope. Clothed in white, and accompanied by three trusty knights similarly clothed, about midnight she stole quietly out of a postern, and gliding, like a ghost, over the frozen river and snow-clad fields, passed unquestioned by the besiegers. If they saw her, they dared not stay one in such a shape. The party walked to Abingdon, where they procured horses, and on them arrived quickly and safely at Wallingford Castle, which had been held for her during the whole struggle by its redoubtable owner, Brien Fitz Count.

From the time of Henry II., the city is chiefly spoken of in connection with the University, upon whose prosperity it became, to a considerable extent, dependent. Not seldom is the record made on account of some dispute, or even battle, between the townsmen and scholars. One of the most serious of these tumults occurred in February 1345, when several, both of the scholars and townsmen, were killed. The townsmen were visited with a sufficiently heavy punishment, being placed under interdict by Grostête, bishop of Lincoln, to whose diocese the University then appertained. From this sentence they were not relieved till 1357, and then not till the mayor and sixty of the burgesses had bound themselves by oath, and under a penalty of a fine of one hundred marks for every omission, to attend at St. Mary's church on each anniversary of the day of St. Scholastica, and, after the performance of masses for the souls of the clerks and students slain in the tumult, offer each a penny at the high altar; and also to pay a fine of 100 marks yearly to the University. In after generations the duty became especially distasteful to the citizens, and in the changes consequent on the Reformation it for a while fell into abeyance. The University, however, in the fifteenth year of the reign of Elizabeth, cited the townsmen before the queen's council, claiming the sum of fifteen hundred marks for arrears. After a tedious suit, the council remitted the fines, but directed the future observance of the penance, though, of course, without the masses; and in a still more modified form the ceremony continued to be annually repeated till 1825, when it was abrogated by the Convocation.

We must pass more hastily over the remaining portion of the history of the city. That it often suffered by pestilence and was sometimes almost depopulated; that the civil wars, and religious changes wrought it grievous loss, will be readily supposed, and need hardly be related. Some amends were made to the town, however, by the erection of it into a bishopric, which was in a good measure endowed out of the spoils of Oseney Abbey. The next public event which we need stay to mention, is that of the mock trial and atrocious burning of the martyrs Latimer, Ridley, and Cranmer. The climax of the troubles of both city and University happened when they fell into the hands of the Puritans. As long as the cause of Charles was tenable Oxford held out, and when it was seized by his enemies it suffered for its loyalty. The townsmen were, perhaps, hardly so ill-treated as the members of the University, but all public buildings suffered alike. Not only were all "monuments of superstition" destroyed by the fanatics, but all "tokens of monarchy" were defaced with equal zeal, whether merely signs on door-posts or house-fronts, or noble specimens of art on college or chapel walls and windows. To the injury inflicted on the various buildings every public edifice in Oxford still bears testimony. In later times, the only thing worth mentioning in the history of the town is that the supposed right-divine principles of the University had wrought so strongly on the nerves of the rulers of England, that they thought it necessary, when the Pretender made his wild advance into England in 1715, to quarter troops in Oxford, to keep the warlike heads of houses in awe, and prevent any incipient rising among the juniors, by confining the students to their several colleges.

But it is time we turned to the University. To relate the history of Oxford University properly would be to relate the history of learning in England: we can do no more than mention a few of the more prominent circumstances connected with the establishment of a university here, and that must illustrate its course. Like Cambridge its origin is involved in fable. As was said in our account of Cambridge, the two Universities for a long period keenly disputed their seniority.

Cambridge traced its pedigree up to a very remote period; but Oxford went beyond it. When the Trojan prince Brute, it was said, came to Britain, some twelve hundred years before the Christian era, he brought with him a number of philosophers. Of these he established one moiety, famous for their Greek learning, in a pleasant locality on the upper part of the Thames; while to the others, whose chief skill was in the Latin tongue, he gave for a habitation, a village a few miles lower down the same river. The memory of their abode in those places, it was fancied, was retained in the names they yet bore—Crick-lade being a manifest corruption of the Greek, as Lech-lade was of the Latin town. In course of time the philosophers got tired of the dulness of their dwelling-places or their solitude, and agreed to remove together to a spot some twenty miles lower down the river, which till then was famed only as a ford for oxen. Thus arose the University of Oxenford. Old Antony-à-Wood having, in his History of the University, collected all the learning on the subject, takes great pains to prove the connection of Greeklade with Bellosite, which was the name the philosophers gave to their new town. Antony will not bate one jot from its antiquity. Some Oxonians, in the contest with the Cantabs, had been so faint-hearted as to be content to acknowledge Alfred as the founder of their University, in accordance with the notions of two or three monkish writers, who had also declared that Saints Neot and Grimbald were the first professors in it.[*] But Wood strenuously insists that there can be no doubt "there was at Oxford a school or academy of literature *before* the time of King Alfred; . . . . and that monarch, by his policy in the contrivance, and his endeavours used," only restored it from the obscurity into which it had declined. For further evidence of its antiquity the reader may refer to Antony's chapter "Against the impugners of, and entrenchers on the Antiquity of the University of Oxford." But we are constrained to admit that "honest Antony" is hardly a safe guide in this matter: —as may be gathered from his *naïve* commendation (in another work) of a brother antiquary's book on the same subject[†]—" In this are many pretty fancies, which may be of some use, as occasion shall serve, by way of reply for Oxon, against the far-fetched antiquities of Cambridge!" Antony loved truth well, but, like a duteous son, he loved Alma Mater better.

In truth, it is now generally admitted that all these stories about the antiquity of Oxford are—like those of Cambridge—at best only "pretty fancies." There may have been schools of learning at Oxford before

* In Asser's Life of Alfred there is a very specific account of Oxford as a seat of learning, and of the measures adopted by that monarch in order to put an end to the discord which sprung up between Grimbald and his foreign companions, and the scholars who were previously settled there; but the passage is generally regarded as an interpolation.

† Henry Lyte's Conjectural Notes on the Original of the University of Oxford.

the Conquest, though there is no mention of them in the Domesday survey. There can be no doubt that such schools did exist there at a very early period. The first authentic mention, however, of a university at Oxford occurs in the reign of Henry II.; but as early as 1149 Vacarius, an eminent civilian, taught the Roman law there, and his lectures were attended by a large number of students—a circumstance that denotes an approach to the character of a University. The first college—at least, according to authentic documents—was established in 1264.

Oxford University received its first charter from Henry III. The learning most esteemed in the thirteenth century was that scholastic theology and metaphysics of which Duns Scotus, an Oxford man, was the great master. In this learning Oxford became especially famous; so that before the reign of Edward III. it was reckoned only second to the University of Paris: indeed, it is affirmed that it possessed a more famous band of "subtle and invincible doctors" than any foreign university. Wood dwells with fond enthusiasm on this its time of glory :—"What university, I pray, can produce an invincible Hales, an admirable Bacon, an excellent well-grounded Middleton, a subtle Scotus, an approved Burley, a resolute Baconsthorpe, a singular Ockham, a solid and industrious Holcot, and a profound Bradwardine? all which persons flourished within the compass of one century. I doubt that neither Paris, Bologna, or Rome, that grand mistress of the Christian world, or any place else, can do what the renowned Bellosite hath done." Its fame spread far abroad. Scholars flocked to it from all parts of Europe. Wood says there were at this time three hundred halls and thirty thousand scholars in Oxford. This is undoubtedly rather beyond probability, but it is certain that a very large number of students did assemble there, and that they were of many nations; while the names are still preserved of many halls that have long ceased to exist. The vast number of ecclesiastics required at a time when, as it has been expressed, "the land swarmed with them," and when among them all the learned were ranked, would account for a very large number of scholars being collected in the most celebrated school of theology; and the very extravagance of the numbers handed down by tradition, testifies to the flourishing condition of the University.

From this its palmy state, however, it soon declined. The unsettled condition of the country, the difficulty, perhaps, of keeping up a succession of subtle and irrefragable professors, and, not least, the quarrelsome habits of the students, caused it to undergo many fluctuations. The pugnacious tastes of the students were indeed very marked; for logical disputations they were always famous, but, unhappily, they could not refrain from dealing with more material weapons than the quodlibets of the schools. The *argumentum ad baculum* was not the least favourite or frequently used of their *argumenta*; and the streets often witnessed its application. Englishmen fought against Scotchmen, and Irish against Welsh; while foreigners sided with one or the other of the bands, or occasionally got up an independent battle of their own: but all were ready to join their forces for a match with the townsmen, for whom, of course, they entertained a very proper academic contempt. These quarrels of the scholars among themselves, and with the citizens, produced, indeed, a very serious influence upon the University. More than once, owing to them, the scholars migrated in a body from Oxford, and it was not without much trouble that they were lured back again. In the foundation statutes of several of the oldest colleges, provision is made that "Northmen shall not abuse Southmen, nor Southmen Northmen." Their quarrels were not always, however, confined to themselves or the city: they are charged with having on one occasion assisted the "common rabble" of Abingdon in despoiling the monastery in that town, in revenge for some affront they had received from the Abbot. One of their most serious disputes, and that they came out of with the least success, occurred in 1238. Fuller tells the story in a very lively manner :—"Otho, cardinal, deacon of St. Nicholas, was sent the pope's legate into England; and going to Oxford, took up his lodgings in the abbey of Oseney. To him the scholars of Oxford sent a present of victuals before dinner; and after dinner, came to tender their attendance upon him. The porter, being an Italian, demanded their business; who answered him, that they came to wait on the lord legate; promising themselves a courteous reception, having read in the scripture 'A man's gift maketh room for him' (Prov. xviii. 16); though here, contrary to expectation, they were not received . . . . But whilst the porter held the door in a dubious posture, betwixt open and shut, the scholars forced their entrance. In this juncture of time, it unluckily happened that a poor Irish priest begged an alms, in whose face the clerk of the kitchen cast scalding water taken out of the cauldron. A Welsh clerk beholding this, bent his bow (by this time the scholars had got weapons) and shot the clerk of the kitchen stark dead on the place.

"This man thus killed, was much more than his plain place promised him to be, as no meaner than the brother of the legate himself; who, being suspicious that he might find Italy in England, and fearing to be poisoned, appointed his brother to oversee all food for his own eating. And now the three nations of Irish, Welsh, and English, fell downright on the Italians. The legate, fearing (as they came from the same womb) to be sent to the same grave with his brother, secured himself fast locked up in the tower of Oseney church, and there sat still and quiet, all attired in his canonical cope. But he, it seems, trusted not so much to his canonical cope, as the sable mantle of night, under the protection whereof he got out, without a guide, to make his escape; not without danger of drowning in the dark, being five times to cross the river, then swelling with late rain as much as the scholars with anger. He made fords where he found none, all known passages being waylaid; and heard the scholars following after, railing on, and calling him usurer, simoniac, deceiver of the prince, oppressor of the people, &c.; whilst the legate wisely turned his tongue into heels, spurring with might and main to Abingdon, where the Court lay." (Church Hist. b. iii.) We must tell the rest more briefly. The king not only " did most affectionately compassionate" the legate, but sent the Earl Warren next day with a body of soldiers " to deliver the remainder of the Italians, and to seize on the scholars." The earl arrested thirty of the scholars, and sent them bound to Wallingford gaol; while the legate adopted the more efficient revenge of placing under interdict all who had taken part in the fray, which seems to have been tantamount to placing the University itself under ban of the Church. It was only on the intercession of the bishops that the legate would remove the interdict; and then the Oxford clerks were compelled to do penance, and the bishops along with them, by walking from " St. Paul's in London to Durham House in the Strand,—no short Italian (but an English long) mile, all on foot," the scholars being obliged to go shoeless, and without cloaks or capes.

Towards the close of the reign of Edward III., and during the better part of his successor's, Wiclif was professor of theology at Oxford, and his zealous preaching of his new doctrines caused a great commotion in the University. Around him rallied not only the more earnest of the students, but he also gained over the more thoughtful of the clerks; while his devoted regard for the rights of the clergy, in opposition to the encroachments of the mendicant friars, secured for him the good-will of the University. Such was the influence he had won, that when his teaching was pronounced heretical, it went far towards breaking-up the schools of Oxford. Before the University could again grow prosperous, came the long wars between the houses of York and Lancaster, in the train of which followed pestilence; so that at the accession of Henry VII. it was greatly depressed. With the establishment of peace it again flourished. In what is termed the "revival of learning" in England the University took a very active share; and the study of the classics was diligently pursued, though many of the older members sturdily resisted the introduction of the heathen writers; for awhile, as Warton observes (Hist. of Poetry, ii. 4), "the University was rent into factions on account of these bold attempts; and the advocates of the recent improvements, when the gentler weapons of persuasion could not prevail, often proceeded to blows with the rigid champions of the schools." The University continued to prosper till the spoliation of religious houses, and afterwards the Reformation, for awhile, checked its progress. The immediate result of the suppression of monasteries was very disastrous to Oxford. It was, as Ant.-à-Wood says, the monasteries "from whence exhibitions for poor scholars principally proceeded . . . . and upon their suppression, many of those students that had not wherewith

to subsist in the University, were forced to leave it, and betake themselves to another course of life." And under the following year (1538) he states that "most of the halls or hostels were left empty, and threatened a decay; arts declined, and ignorance began to take place again. The canon law was much neglected, and few or none now took degrees in that faculty. Some of the religious houses in the University that were wont to educate many men eminent in their generations, were now dissolved, and their inhabitants, for the most part, turned out into the wide world. The rest expected daily their last doom, and were ready with the poor scholars to trudge a-begging, with bags by their sides, or wallets on their shoulders. Such strange and prodigious things were now performed, both here and throughout England, that the like was never before seen or heard." (Hist. of Univ. of Ox., ii. 67.) And nine years later, he informs us that, "Of hundreds of halls that tradition and record tell us have been in this University, but eight now remain. . . . . The dissolution of religious houses did so much discourage scholars, that they, fearing the utter ruin of learning, betook themselves to other employments."

But it was not alone by the loss of its scholars that the University suffered. Thomas Cromwell sent his commissioners as well to Oxford as to other places, and with a like result. That coarse ribald, Dr. Layton, was chosen to examine the University. His letter to Secretary Cromwell sufficiently illustrates his proceedings. We may quote a passage from it; propriety will not permit us to give it entire. He says, " We have set Dunce in Boccardo,* and utterly banished him Oxford for ever. . . . . The second time we came to New College, we found all the great quadrant-court full of leaves of Dunce, the winds blowing them into every corner, and there we found one Mr. Greenfield, of Buckinghamshire, gathering part of the said book-leaves (as he said) therewith to make him scuels, or blaunsheers, to keep the deer within the wood, thereby to have the better cry with his hounds." The mischief done on this occasion to what Wood well calls the University's "chief support, the libraries," appears to have been mainly confined to the volumes of scholastic theology. But on future occasions the destruction of MSS. was wider and irreparable — and these are the things we ought to bear in mind, when reading of the paucity of MSS. that have come down to us from what are called "the Dark Ages," and not at once conclude, as many historians have done, that because there are now few such MSS., there never were many. We should remember that all religious establishments in this country underwent a similar purgation.

In the 4th of Edward VI. (1550) commissioners, with Dr. Cox at their head, were sent to Oxford, to

---

* Dunce was Duns Scotus, the text-book of that scholastic learning for which Oxford was so famous; Boccardo was the common prison! but, as he goes on to boast, he had set him in a far viler place.

make search after popish books and superstitious relics. Wood tells the result:

"The ancient libraries, a glory to the University, as containing among them many rarities, the works of our own countrymen, besides many matters obtained from remote places, were by them, or their appointment, rifled. Many MSS., guilty of no other superstition than red letters in their fronts or titles, were either condemned to the fire or worse. Others also, that treated of controversial or scholastical divinity, were let loose from their chains, were given away, or sold to mechanics for servile uses. Such books wherein appeared angles, or mathematical diagrams, were thought sufficient to be destroyed, because accounted popish, or diabolical, or both. . . . As for the libraries belonging to colleges, they suffered the same fate almost as the public library, though not in so gross a manner. From Merton Coll. library a cart-load of MSS. and above were taken away, such that contained the lucubrations, chiefly of controversial divinity, astronomy and mathematics, of divers of the learned fellows thereof, in which studies they in the last two centuries obtained great renown." Other colleges were similarly rifled, "and the commissioners brought it so to pass, that certain rude young men should carry this great spoil of books about the city on biers; which being so done, to set them down in the common market-place, and there burn them. . . . This was by them styled the funeral of Scotus and Scotists." Wood sorrowfully adds: "Such a general destruction was now and some years before, as well in both the Universities as religious places, that many precious monuments, and thereby the most substantial parts of antiquity and history, were, to the great prejudice of mankind, irrecoverably lost." This reckless destruction was equally lamented by learned and moderate men of both parties, and some books and MSS. were saved by the zeal of private individuals; but such was the amount of spoil, that "books became mere dog-cheap, and whole libraries could be bought for an inconsiderable nothing." Bale, a contemporary, tells us that books were exported by the ship-load, and whole libraries appropriated to the commonest purposes. "I know," he says, "a merchantman, which shall at this time be nameless, that bought the contents of two noble libraries for forty shillings' price, a shame it is to be spoken. This stuff hath he occupied in the stead of gray paper by the space of more than these ten years, and yet he hath store enough for as many years to come."

Although Mary regarded the University with no ill-will, but was rather desirous of raising it in character and fortune, her bitter bigotry effectually frustrated any benefit that might else have resulted from her good intentions. She did some things that were calculated to be beneficial, but they were accompanied by others that more than counterbalanced the advantages they possessed. Commissioners were now sent to Oxford to search for and destroy all Protestant books, and English bibles; and all freedom of opinion was placed under ban. As a warning to the University, Oxford was chosen as the place where the Protestant leaders, Cranmer, Ridley, and Latimer, should be burnt.

With Elizabeth came brighter and happier days. Learning revived, and learned men were sought out and amply encouraged. Under her fostering care, our University quickly rose to an eminently flourishing condition; and, to borrow the words of Hallam, (Hist. of Lit. ii. 258,) "continued through her reign the seat of a progressive education." Her successor was equally anxious for its welfare. It was in his reign that it received the privilege of sending two representatives to the House of Commons. So long as Charles I. retained power, he manifested a warm regard for its interest, and, at the instigation of Laud, conferred many benefits upon it. But the disputes between Charles and the Parliament from their commencement involved Oxford in turmoil. The University was earnest in support of the king, while a great number of the younger students had adopted the principles of the puritans. When the civil war broke out, the University money, and a good deal of the plate, was sent to the king. Charles, as is well known, made Oxford for some time his head quarters, and assembled *his* parliament there. Teaching was of course neglected: the halls were most of them turned into barracks: both students and doctors very generally exchanged the cap for the helmet. At the termination of the war the University, as might be expected, was rather roughly treated. The heads of houses were for the most part ejected, and their places supplied by men whose religious principles were more accordant to the notions of the successful party. What had been left undone by previous commissioners in the "rooting out of popish books and pictures," was now completed by their more zealous successors. They did not their work negligently. "Pictures of prophets, apostles, and saints, painted in college chapels both in stalls and windows: the picture of Christ in our Lady's arms, or in other postures, whether cut in stone, wood, or painted: as also history in glass, crosses, &c. . . . as well as all other monuments of superstition, as they were pleased to style them," they utterly defaced: to say nothing of "popish books," which they did their best entirely to root out. The clearance was thorough.

But the University, though depressed, was not destroyed. Cromwell was elected its Chancellor; and he procured John Owen, the celebrated Independent minister, to be appointed Vice-chancellor, in whose hands the government of the University was, of course, in a good measure vested. Owen was a rigid puritan, and, as may be supposed, he made it one of his chief endeavours to eradicate every vestige of those ceremonies and practices against which his party had so loudly and zealously declaimed. The whole habits of the place underwent a change. A stern system of theology was taught, and the slightest departure from its requirements severely condemned. Among the novel apparatus set in motion by the puritan Vice, was the opening of an office for the satisfying of religious doubts and difficulties; or, as the students, to whom it offered an irresistible subject for the employment of their wit, termed it, a "scruple shop." But with all his "strictness" Owen was moderate and forbearing in conduct, and he did much to temper the violence of his party. He was, too, a man of real learning; and during his chancellorship the University was never deficient in teachers of solid erudition and ability, or scholars who profited by their instruction. Clarendon honestly owns that, during the Commonwealth period, "the University yielded a harvest of extraordinary, good, and sound knowledge in all parts of learning."

At the Restoration the puritan heads of houses, professors, and college-fellows, were in their turn ejected; and the old masters and fellows were reinstated, or their places filled, by others not suspected of puritanism. The University was restored to all its privileges, and soon regained its former splendour and prosperity. Its steady resistance to the encroachments of James II. will be remembered. Its subsequent history it is unnecessary to repeat here. No important or extraordinary circumstance has occurred to the University itself,—at least, none of a nature belonging to its outward history. The temporary fluctuations it has undergone have been such as were dependent mainly on the changing tone of public feeling. It falls not within our province to speak of the "church principles," whether "high" or "low," that at different times have prevailed, or been supposed to prevail, in it. For the same reason we shall only refer—as having a notable influence on the fortunes and character of the University—to the great religious movements which in the last and present centuries originated in Oxford.

It would be idle, in such a sketch of the University as we can offer, to enter into the question of its merits as a place of education, or to speak of the eminent men who have distinguished its several eras. That it has at different times fallen below the rank it ought to have held, none will dispute; but, on the other hand, it may fairly claim to have maintained a position at least equal to what the general character of the age would warrant an unprejudiced person in requiring from it, on a fair estimate of the inner history of the country at that period. And it is not too much to say, that there has never been a time when it has not sent forth some sons who would have done honour to any age.

The constitution of the University is nearly the same as that of Cambridge, which has been already described (vol. i. p. 117); but it will, perhaps, be as well to give a cursory account of it. The University is a corporate body, "styled and to be styled by none other name than the Chancellor, Masters, and Scholars of the University of Oxford." It is not, as is often supposed, a mere collection of colleges, nor do the colleges form part of the corporation, though its existence may be said to depend on a union of them. The business of the University is carried on in the two houses of Congregation and Convocation, which are made up of members of the University who have obtained the degree of M.A. The duty of the upper house, or Congregation, is principally to pass graces and dispensations, and grant degrees. The power of Convocation reaches to all the affairs of the University, though it can only entertain questions sent to it from the Hebdomadal Board, or heads of houses, who are so named from their meetings being held weekly; and its power is limited with regard to matters affecting the statutes of the University. Yet, while these houses are entrusted with such authority, their measures are subject to an absolute veto by the chancellor or vice-chancellor singly, and by the two proctors jointly. The chief officer of the University is the chancellor, who is elected for life, and holds, nominally at least, high powers; but, actually, these are delegated to the vice-chancellor. According to Oxford etiquette, the chancellor, after his installation, never enters the University, except when he is called upon to receive or accompany any royal visitants. The office is now an honorary one, and is always conferred upon some eminent nobleman who is already a member of the University. The resident head of the University is the vice-chancellor, who is chosen in rotation from the heads of houses, and holds his appointment for four consecutive years. He is the chief executive officer of the University, and his position is one of much dignity as well as importance. It is the vice-chancellor who is occasionally seen walking, in extraordinary state, in the streets of Oxford, being preceded by a number of esquires and yeoman bedels with wands, or, as they are styled by the profane, *pokers*. The vice-chancellor is also, by virtue of his office, a magistrate of the city and county of Oxford, and of the county of Berks. His immediate deputies are the two proctors, also officers of importance. The other University officers are the professors, and such as are required for carrying out its educational purposes, with those necessary for the enforcement of discipline, and the management of its pecuniary concerns. To enter into further particulars would be both tedious and useless, as their employments could not be understood by readers unacquainted with University customs, without such details as neither our plan nor space permits us to give.

The chief distinction in the members of the University is into those "on the foundation," and those "not on the foundation:" the former consisting of the heads of houses, or persons holding college fellowships or scholarships, and receiving from them a certain income; those not on the foundation being, on the other hand, such as maintain themselves, while at the University, wholly at their own expense. The distinction is pointed out in the term applied officially to the two classes, the one being styled "dependent," the other "independent" members. There is no difference in their privileges. All students who matriculate at the University are required to belong to some college.

There are nineteen colleges and five halls in Oxford. The colleges are incorporated bodies, each being governed by its fellows in accordance with the statutes provided by its founder, or at a subsequent period. The halls differ principally from the colleges in not being incorporated; their privileges are nearly the same. One rather striking difference, however, exists: the colleges, with one exception—that of Worcester, by much the most recent foundation—elect their own masters or principals, while the masters of the halls are appointed by the Crown, except St. Edmund's Hall, the master of which is appointed by Queen's College. The colleges owe their foundation to the piety of individuals who, at various periods, have aimed to serve the Church by the establishment of places for the education of youth, and the residence and support of men who should devote themselves to meditation and study in connection with the established religion. And in every foundation further rewards are held out to meritorious students, in the shape of comfortable advowsons, and the like. Indeed, as old Fuller somewhat quaintly observes, "it is not the least part of Oxford's happiness, that a moiety of her founders were prelates, who had an experimental knowledge of what belonged to the necessities and conveniences of scholars, and therefore have accommodated them accordingly; principally in providing them the patronage of many good benefices, whereby the fellows of those colleges are plentifully maintained after their leaving of the University." In truth, the student finds at Oxford all those external stimulants that have ever been considered, both by imaginative and practical men, of the highest value in the scholastic career,—namely, a proud train of historic recollections; the names of a long line of glorious ancestry, of whom the venerable buildings by which he is surrounded at every step recals the memory; the habits and traditions that impart what has been well termed "an atmosphere of learning" to the place; the spur of a generous and noble rivalry working along with the hope of honour; and the prospect of early and not scanty reward as the prize of academic success.

And now let us look round the city, and note a few of the more noticeable features. Even these, however, are too numerous to stay long in examining. So large is the number of collegiate buildings, and specimens of ecclesiastical architecture, and so interesting often are their contents, that weeks might be spent in their examination, and volumes would be required to convey a satisfactory notion of them. Wordsworth, on looking over the city, exclaims—

> "Ye spires of Oxford! domes and towers!
> Gardens and groves! Your presence overpowers
> The soberness of reason."

And an observer, no less skilful than Sir Walter Scott, wrote to a friend after his first visit: "The time has been much too short to convey to me separate and distinct ideas of all the variety of wonders which I saw. My memory only at present furnishes a grand but indistinct picture of towers, and chapels, and oriels, and vaulted halls, and libraries, and paintings:"

and yet he had spent a week there, diligently occupied in its exploration, and had been fortunate, as he said, in having Heber for his guide, "who was intimately acquainted with all, both animate and inanimate, that is worth knowing." Our rough general survey will then, we hope, hardly be complained of on account of incompleteness, or of some indistinctness of detail.

We must first visit the famous High Street—Oxford's pride—a place which never fails to surprise the stranger with its beauty, and one which no amount of intimacy with ever lessens in our estimation. Had it been designed merely with a view to the general effect, the result could not have been better. The great and rich variety of buildings—colleges and churches mingling with modern shops and old-fashioned dwellings,—and the diversity of the styles in which they are constructed—are brought, by the gentle curvature of the street, into combination and contrast in the most pleasing manner. Nothing can well surpass the way in which the splendid architectural array opens gradually upon the passenger who descends it from Magdalen Bridge. Well may the poet celebrate

> "The stream-like windings of that glorious street."

There is none other like it in England. Even Scott, in describing his "own romantic town" in the 'Provincial Antiquities,' when declaring that "it cannot be denied that the High Street of Edinburgh is the most magnificent in Great Britain,"—even he is forced to "except, perhaps, the High Street of Oxford;" while Dr. Waagen ('Art and Artists in England'), without any hesitation, asserts that "the High Street of Oxford has not its equal in the whole world." Be that as it may, it is a most noble street; and its general proportions are such as most favourably exhibit the magnificence of its edifices. It is of sufficient breadth * to preserve an air of dignity, without being so wide as to cause the stately structures on either side to appear dwarfed; while the easy curvature brings the varied architectural forms and styles into opposition, and prevents anything like formality. Our sketch (Cut, No. 2) is taken from near Queen's College, part of which is seen at the right-hand corner. The college beyond is that of All Souls. University College is at the left-hand corner. The highly-wrought spire seen above All Souls' College is that of the University Church; the church lower down the street is that of All Saints Generally the quiet of the street well accords with its academic appearance; the stillness being only broken by a few gownsmen, and two or three straggling passengers stepping leisurely along. Its scrupulously clean look, too, is generally noticed by the visitor. Yet a century back it must have been rather remarkable for the want of both these qualities. In the "Gentleman and Lady's Pocket Companion for Oxford, 1747," it is said that the butcher-market is held in the High Street. and "greatly diminishes the beauty of it;" and it also states, that "another great nuisance is the dirt which

* High Street is 2,038 feet long and 85 feet broad.

people bring out of their houses, and lay in the middle of the street in heaps every morning."

The High Street is the eastern and principal entrance to the city. The northern entrance is also very fine; the part called St. Giles's being a sort of " *place*" some two hundred and fifty feet broad and two thousand feet long, planted with noble trees, and having on one side the extensive buildings of St. John's College, and the University Galleries on the other, while Magdalen Church and the Martyrs' Memorial are directly in front. The southern entrance—that by which railway passengers enter the city over Folly Bridge—is the least imposing. The most noticeable thing here was an ancient sort of gatehouse, known as Friar Bacon's Study, which used to stand on the old bridge. To the tradition which identified it as the study of the re-doubted friar, was appended a prediction that it would fall whenever a man more learned than Roger passed under it. It remained, nevertheless, quite unshaken till near the close of the last century—a period when Oxford was in a wonderfully enlightened condition. Then, as is reported, certain senior fellows began to quake; and it being found very inconvenient to make the long, roundabout passage that had become neces-sary whenever they had occasion to go beyond the city in that direction,—it being feared, too, that in some fit of cogitation of more than ordinary depth, some one of them might even pass under it,—it was thought advis-able to remove the dangerous structure. Some thirty years later the bridge itself was pulled down, and the present one built in its place. The western entrance to the town has rather a singular appearance, from the road being carried across the meadows on a raised causeway. This road is known as the Seven Bridges, from its passing over the seven streams into which the Thames here separates. The immediate approach to the town in this direction is very mean.

It may be as well, in looking a little more particu-larly at the principal buildings, to commence with those belonging to the University. Of these the largest and most important is that called the Schools, which was so named from its being originally intended as the place in which the University lectures in the various faculties should be given. The names of these still remain in gold letters over the several doorways; but the building itself has long been applied to other purposes, only natural philosophy and medicine being now taught in it. The chief part of the upper story is appropriated to the Bodleian Library and Picture Gallery: the lower part is used for the exhibition of the Arundel Marbles, the preservation of University records, and for examination for degrees, and the trans-action of University business. The building consists of a very large quadrangle, the external front of which is 175 feet in length. The first stone was laid in 1613; and the style is rather fanciful than elegant, as will be supposed when it is mentioned that a chief beauty (and one which the cicerone never fails to point out) is that the tower " consists of the five orders of architecture." If, however, the visitor should

feel little inclined to linger over the exterior of the building, he will find treasures inside enough to occupy the longest time he can devote to them. A doorway at the left corner of the quadrangle is the entrance to the Bodleian Library. This noble library owes its foundation to the munificence and the zeal of Sir Thomas Bodley. When he retired from the public service in 1573, and took up his abode in Oxford, he discovered that of the public library which Humphrey, surnamed the good Duke of Gloucester, had founded in the fifteenth century, not above three or four volumes were left. To the task of refounding the library, Bodley devoted the remainder of his life. His own library, which he had accumulated on the Conti-nent at an expense of £10,000—a sum very much larger in those days than at present—served as the nucleus of the collection; and to its increase he zea-lously urged the noble and wealthy to contribute. His efforts were abundantly successful; and though he did not live to see the building completed which he began as soon as he found the number of books would re-quire a new house to contain them, he yet lived long enough to behold a library collected such as took rank among the very first in the kingdom, and a building rising worthy to contain it. In subsequent times additions have been made by various benefactors, on a scale worthy of the prince-like founder. Whole col-lections, often of a most costly character, have been presented; and endless have been the gifts of a lesser grade, both in printed books and manuscripts. The University too, has, for the last sixty-seven years, annually set aside a considerable sum for the purchase of books; while, by Act of Parliament, a copy of every new work has to be forwarded to the library by the publisher. By all these means the Bodleian Library has grown to be one of the finest public libra-ries in existence; and in some departments—that of Oriental Literature, for example—it is probably unri-valled. The management of the library is creditable to the liberality of the University. Literary men, whether belonging to the University or not, are freely admitted to the use of the books, upon proper intro-duction; while the rooms are open to the public three days in each week. Some of the most curious articles are exposed to general view in glass cases, and will be found interesting, else, perhaps, the mere outsides of books are not commonly very attractive. Still, even in the rooms appropriated to books, there will be found much that will repay the visit; to say nothing of the portraits of eminent literary men that hang upon the walls, or the curious ceilings of the rooms, or the arrangement of the presses which contain the books, and which, to those not accustomed to college libraries, have an air of novelty. From the Library we ascend the stairs to the Picture Gallery, which occupies the three upper stories of the quadrangle. The pictures consist for the most part of portraits, the chief interest of which arises from their representing men of literary eminence, or benefactors to the University. Some of them, however, are valuable as works of art. Several are by Holbein; one or two are attributed to Jansen; Vandyke, Lily, Kneller, Reynolds, Phillips, and Wilkie are the painters of others. Among those by Holbein, the portraits of Henry VIII., as well of his noble victims, the Earl of Surrey and Sir Thomas More, will attract attention; as will also those of Luther and Erasmus, of Wolsey and Thomas Cromwell, though a connoisseur would, perhaps, hesitate before he acquiesced in every instance either in the authenticity of the portrait or the genuineness of the master. Among the more interesting of those which bear the name of Vandyke are those of Charles and his queen, of Laud, and of the earls of Strafford, Falkland, and Pembroke. Ben Jonson, Dryden, Cowley, Addison, Swift, Prior, and Locke, may be taken as samples of the literary men whose likenesses adorn the walls. The portrait of Handel is said to be the only one for which he sat. 'Paine, the Architect, instructing his Son,' is a very pleasing example of the genius of Sir Joshua Reynolds. The two full-length portraits of William IV. and Queen Adelaide, by Wilkie, are by no means favourable specimens of his powers. One of the latest additions to the gallery is the large portrait, by Lucas, of the Duke of Wellington, in his robes, as Chancellor of the University. In the centre room are a few casts from Grecian statues, and also some original busts. One of the best of these is Chantrey's bust of the Duke of Wellington: there is another, by the same artist, of the late Dean of Westminster, Dr. Ireland. Those of Newton and Sir Christopher Wren are by Wilton and Bacon. One of the most striking objects in this room is a brass statue of the Earl of Pembroke, Chancellor of the University from 1616 to 1630. It is the work of Le Soeur, but is traditionally said to have been designed by Rubens. Along the centre of the rooms are numerous models of the ancient temples of Greece and Italy; a very curious one of a subterraneous palace in Guzerat; an elaborate model of the Cathedral of Calcutta; and two, of extremely beautiful execution, of the Eleanor Cross at Waltham, and the Martyrs' Memorial at Oxford. Among the "rarities" in the room are a chair made out of the ship in which Drake sailed round the world, and the veritable lantern of Guido Fawkes!

In a room on the basement story are the celebrated Arundel Marbles. They consist of inscribed stones, brought mostly from Smyrna, and were part of the collection made by the Earl of Arundel in the seventeenth century. Their chief value is, of course, for students of classic antiquities, but they are otherwise interesting, as being a part of the earliest collection of ancient sculpture brought to this country, and as having done much to excite the study of antiquity in England. Selden wrote a description of the Earl's collection; his own stores are now deposited along with them.

Close by the Picture Gallery is the Divinity School, wherein the exercises for degrees in divinity are performed. It is a large and noble room, and in its original state, before the elaborate carvings were defaced or the painted windows broken, must have had a splendid appearance. It was built in 1480, and was one of the richest specimens of the architecture of that age. During the religious troubles, however, it was greatly injured, so that in the reign of Edward VI. it was in a state of dilapidation; the lead was stript from the roof, the fittings were stolen from the interior, and nettles and brambles grew about it. During the civil wars it was used as a storehouse for corn. It was not till the beginning of the eighteenth century that it was restored to its present condition. The upper room, which was used for Duke Humphrey's library, now contains a portion of the Bodleian. From the Divinity School a door leads into the Convocation House, where the members of convocation meet for the transaction of the University business, and the conferring of degrees. The building itself has nothing remarkable about it—only at a convocation would it be worth seeing.

The buildings we have been noticing are all united with each other, and most of the other University buildings are close at hand. The Theatre will of course be visited. It is a large semi-classic structure, of the style that Jones and Wren made so popular in England. It was erected under the superintendence of Sir Christopher Wren, who is said to have taken the ground plan from the theatre of Marcellus at Rome. The interior area is 80 feet by 70; and the roof which spans it, unsupported by a single pillar, is one of the largest roofs in existence which is borne merely by the walls. There is a tradition at King's College, Cambridge, that Sir Christopher used annually to visit their famous chapel in order to study the manner in which its ponderous roof is hung aloft; but if so, he did not succeed in discovering the secret of its stability: this roof at Oxford, when it had stood little more than a century, seemed "nodding to its fall," and it had to be rebuilt in 1802, while that at King's is still as firm as though it were but of yesterday's erection. The Theatre is sometimes called Sheldon's Theatre, from having been built at the expense of that prelate, who paid £15,000 for its construction, and gave a further sum of £2,000 to be laid out in estates, the rents of which are appropriated to its repair. It is used for the public ceremonials of the University, for which it is admirably adapted. It will contain above three thousand persons, and the vast space being entirely unobstructed, permits all the proceedings to be freely seen. The room, too, is a very splendid one, and richly painted and gilt. The ceiling is intended to represent painted canvass strained over gilt cordage, after the fashion of a Roman amphitheatre. On great occasions the area is occupied by masters of arts and strangers, the latter, perhaps, in brilliant uniforms; on the semicircle at the northern end sit the University magnates and noblemen in their robes of scarlet or purple, and gold; the lower galleries are filled with ladies, in all the glory of beauty—and full dress; while the upper galleries are crowded by undergraduates:—as will be conceived, a brave sight.

Some senior fellows love yet to talk of its appearance when the allied monarchs were entertained in it in 1814. The most memorable of its latest gala days is the visit of the Queen and Prince Albert in 1841 ; to which may perhaps be added the entertainment of the *savans* in 1847, on occasion of the meeting of the British Association at Oxford. For many years after the erection of the Theatre the University press was worked in the roof, and long after the printing was done in the building called the Clarendon, all books printed by the University bore the words "E Theatro Sheldoniano." The Clarendon Press stands just by the Theatre : it is a neat building, which was erected out of the profits of the University edition of Clarendon's History, whence its name ; Vanbrugh was the architect. It was used as the University printing office for above a century, but when, in consequence of the great increase in the printing business, the present large building was erected, the old Clarendon was of course applied to other uses. The Museums of Geology and Mineralogy, collected by Doctors Buckland and Simmons, are now deposited in it : they are open to the public. At a little distance from the Clarendon is the Ashmoleian Museum, so called after that odd compound of learning and quackery, Elias Ashmole, who presented his museum to the University. In its former state it was a choice collection of 'rarities;' including all kinds of marvellous relics, from the head of the Dodo down to 'a very curious shoe made of more than a thousand pieces of leather.' Ashmole's collection was the Tradescant Museum so famous in its day, swelled by the addition of coins, manuscripts, and all sorts of oddities accumulated by himself. The library of Lilly, the notorious astrologer, is among its treasures. Within these few years it has undergone a careful rearrangement ; the worthless rarities are dismissed or removed out of sight ; judicious selections have been made of new objects of natural history, and without becoming a mere dry and formally-arranged collection of scientific display, it is now rendered instructive to the naturalist and antiquary, and interesting to the general visitor.

In the centre of the square of which the Schools form one side, stands the Radcliffe Library, a building which presents a curious contrast to the surrounding edifices. The building itself is supported upon arches and surmounted by a dome. The basement consists of a double octagon ; the upper part is round, and has attached Corinthian columns. Not much can be said either for its grandeur or beauty when seen close at hand, but the lofty dome is a striking object from a distance, and adds a pleasing variety to the general view of the "city of spires and pinnacles." Gibbs was the architect ; and the building occupied from 1737 to 1749. Whatever others may think of the pile, the architect himself was very well satisfied with his work ; of which he published an elaborate series of elevations and working plates, under the title of 'Bibliotheca Radclivinia,' fol., 1747. The building was founded by the eccentric but eminent physician,

Dr. Radcliffe, who bequeathed the sum of £40,000 for the purpose ; to which he added an endowment of £350 a year for the purchase of books, the salary of a librarian, and the repairs of the building. The library and collections are to be especially connected with the study of natural philosophy, whence it used to be sometimes called the Physic Library. On no account should the stranger omit to visit the Radcliffe. By the door is a bust of the founder, by Rysbrach. Another, with the comical physiognomy of the architect (which looks as if Hogarth might have moulded it), stands at the top of the staircase. The interior of the library is light and graceful, though perhaps not very appropriate. A gallery, supported by Ionic pilasters, is carried round the room. The dome, which is forty-six feet in height from the floor, is divided into compartments, and, like the walls, elaborately ornamented in stucco. The contents of the room deserve a leisurely examination. Among the works of art are casts of some of the most celebrated antique statues, which are so arranged as very considerably to heighten the general effect of the room ; but of more value to the visitor are the few original antiquities, such as the marble candelabra found in the ruins of the Emperor Adrian's villa. There are also some busts of eminent naturalists, the first place among which is due, perhaps, to that of Cuvier, by the younger David. Among the more generally interesting of the objects connected with the particular purpose of the library, are the large and choice collections of Italian and other marbles, which display a variety that not a little surprises a novice ; and some excellent models, illustrative of geology and physical geography. From the interior you pass to the balustrade which surrounds the dome on the exterior, from whence you may obtain an excellent view of the city. It was for this, as much as for the library itself, that we counselled the stranger not to omit visiting the Radcliffe. The building stands nearly in the centre of the city, and from it you have a panoramic view of Oxford, such as should not be missed. The marvellous assemblage of academic architecture can here be fairly understood ; the extent and variety are perceived, and their positions and connection become clear ; while the height, although quite sufficient to let the whole of the city, and a good portion of the suburbs, be seen, is yet not so great as to produce that very unsatisfactory appearance common in what are called bird's-eye views.

The buildings we have been noticing are placed close together : the other University buildings are situate at some distance from them. The Radcliffe Observatory stands a short distance north of the city : the University Press is only just within the limits. Neither of these shall we visit. The former has nothing in its exterior to attract the stranger, who is, of course, not admitted inside. The University Printing-office is a very large building, having a frontage of 250 feet, and projecting wings 288 feet long ; and it has some architectural pretensions. The erection of it was commenced in 1826. A press-room in the south wing is

2.—HIGH STREET.

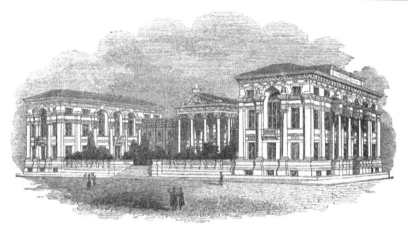

3.—TAYLOR INSTITUTE.

288 feet long, and 33 feet wide, being, it is said, the largest in the kingdom. One other building belonging to the University remains, which must not be passed unnoticed,—the University Galleries. This is the last building of importance that has been erected in Oxford, and the most important that has been erected there for many years. Sir Robert Taylor and Dr. Randolph bequeathed sums of money, the one "for erecting a proper edifice, and for establishing a foundation for the teaching and improving the European languages" —the other for erecting galleries for the reception of the Pomfret Statues belonging to the University, "and for paintings, engravings, and other curiosities, which may occasionally be left to that learned body." It being found difficult to procure ground suitable for these two buildings, the authorities determined to unite them in one; and C. R. Cockerell, Esq., R.A., was the architect appointed to carry out the intentions of the founders. The result is certainly a very magnificent edifice—vast in size, substantial in character, ornate in the details; but though very picturesque in effect, perhaps wanting something in impressiveness as a whole. To us, at least, the parts have an unconnected appearance. The fault, if it exist, may arise from the difficulty of uniting in one design objects so different as galleries of art and lecture-rooms for modern languages, and moulding it so as that while the parts are appropriate, the whole shall preserve unity and dignity of character. The central building is about 150 feet long, and has a tetrastyle Corinthian portico rising above the building itself to a level with the wings. The wings, which project about 70 feet beyond the centre, have Ionic columns, and very large arched windows, which cut through the entablature— a feature not unusual in Mr. Cockerell's works. The east wing is the Taylor building; the west, the Ran-

dolph building. The front of the Taylor building in St. Giles's-street, has an unusual richness and piquancy of character from the capitals of the four columns being surmounted by statues of France, Germany, Italy, and Spain—the nations whose languages are taught in the institution. (Cut, No. 3.) Internally, the rooms seem well adapted for their several purposes. Visitors will, of course, only be attracted by the Galleries. They consist of galleries for ancient and modern sculpture; and for paintings, drawings, and engravings. Already they contain many noble specimens of art. In ancient sculpture, there is the Pomfret collection, which, though of but meagre interest compared with those in the British Museum, is yet of considerable value. It is, however, to be regretted that many of the statues were grievously injured by one Guelfi, an Italian, who was employed by the father of Earl Pomfret, when they came into his possession, to restore them. Guelfi mistook the original intent of every statue he operated on, and spoiled nearly all. The modern sculpture includes the "munificent gift," as the University well termed it, of the original models of the entire series of Sir Francis Chantrey's busts, the greater part of his monumental figures, and also his studies from the antique, which his widow presented to the University, "on condition that a permanent place be assigned to them in the Western Sculpture Gallery . . . it being understood that, if removed, the whole collection, under the name of the Chantrey Collection, shall always be kept together.' It is not easy to overrate the value of this collection. Probably no sculptor ever equalled Chantrey in the execution of a bust. Almost invariably he seized the most characteristic expression, and he always represented the features with fidelity, and in a masterly breadth of style. His chisel perpetuated, as is well known, a large proportion of the most eminent of his contemporaries; and these invaluable records, in all their original freshness of conception, are here brought together in one gallery. And interesting as they are now, their interest will be continually increasing as, one after another, the men become mere historic names. Nor should the value of such an opportunity to the student of art, of studying the entire works of so eminent an artist, be overlooked: it is to him what the original records of an age are to the historian. But valuable as is this collection, it is far surpassed by the drawings of Michael Angelo and Raffaelle, which are in the rooms above. These formed a part of the matchless collection of drawings which belonged to Sir Thomas Lawrence. After his decease, the entire collection, upon the Government declining to purchase it, passed into the hands of the Messrs. Woodburn, the picture-dealers. Eventually, the drawings of Michael Angelo and Raffaelle were purchased by the University for the sum of £7,000; towards which the Earl of Eldon subscribed no less than £4,150. We remember the drawings when they were at Woodburn's, and miss some of them here, which were among the best, and which, as we are informed, were selected by foreign purchasers. There are here fifty-three drawings by Angelo, and one hundred and thirty-seven by Raffaelle. Some of them are questionable, but the greater part are undoubted originals. They are framed, and shown in the new gallery to considerable advantage. They are chiefly executed with the pen in bistre, or with the metal point, and the lights heightened with white; and they range from the rudest sketch to the most carefully-finished study, from which the picture has been pricked off upon the pannel. Michael Angelo's drawings, are marked with all the grandeur and force of conception and daring execution that distinguish his completed works; often they show, what might less be looked for, a delicacy and gracefulness not to be surpassed even by Raffaelle. The drawings of Raffaelle have all the characteristics of his genius. Some of them are exquisitely beautiful: and in his drawings, as in those of his great rival, it is very instructive to observe the scrupulous pains taken to arrive at correctness, and the earnestness with which even the most trifling of the accessories are studied. The lesson may be profitably considered by other students besides those of Art.

The picture-gallery is a handsome room, 96 feet long by 28 wide. Its contents are not very valuable. Oxford is not very rich in paintings. The most noticeable feature, perhaps, here, is the series of copies, in oil, of Raffaelle's Cartoons, made by Henry Cooke, who was employed by William III. to repair the originals. They are not without their value, but are by no means of a high standard of excellence. A very superior work is the copy of Raffaelle's 'School of Athens,' which has been attributed, apparently without sufficient reason, to Julio Romano. Among the original pictures may be mentioned half-a-dozen portraits of painters, of their own painting: the rest are nought.

We may commence our visits to the colleges with the chief of them — Christ Church; a magnificent institution, for which Oxford is indebted to the 'king-cardinal,' and for which our great poet has predicted, that

" Christendom shall ever speak his virtue."

Had Wolsey been able to accomplish his plan, he would have made this college the most splendid in Europe. Having matured his design, and obtained the consent of the king, he procured, in 1524 and 1525, two bulls from Pope Clement VII., empowering him to suppress twenty-two of the minor monasteries, and endow with their revenues a school at Ipswich, and a college at Oxford. The latter, he proposed, should consist of a dean, sub-dean, one hundred canons, ten public readers, thirteen chaplains, an organist, twelve clerks, and thirteen choristers; for whose support he provided with princely liberality. He proposed to invite the most learned men from all parts of Europe to enter the foundation, and to procure transcripts of all the curious literary treasures of the Vatican. A convenient site was found for the building in the ground on which the Priory of St. Frideswide, one of the suppressed monasteries, had stood; and he at once set about the erection of CARDINAL COLLEGE, as it was proudly named. Before it had advanced far, however, the cardinal had fallen from his high estate, and the first care of his pious master was, of course, to appropriate the revenues to his own use. But Wolsey did not forget, in his adversity, the college that he had in his prosperity originated. One of his latest acts was to implore the king " that his college at Oxford might go on." Some years afterwards Henry did cause the works to proceed, though upon a lessened scale; and taking care, at the same time, to transfer the credit of the foundation from the cardinal to himself, by directing that it should be styled the " College of King Henry the Eighth." Yet this arrangement was only temporary. On the general suppression of monasteries, Henry erected Oxford into a bishopric, making Oseney Abbey to be the seat of the diocese; but he afterwards dismantled the abbey, and transferred the see to St. Frideswide's, connecting it with his newly-endowed college, and making the foundation partly ecclesiastical and partly academical. From this time the college was known as Christ Church. The foundation of Christ Church College now consists of a dean, eight canons, eight chaplains, a school-master, an organist, eight clerks, eight choristers, and 101 students. Besides these, there are generally between 900 and 1,000 independent members, consisting of noblemen, gentlemen-commoners, and commoners. Christ Church has produced a number of eminent sons fully proportioned to the large numbers who have been educated in it. Of prelates and divines it boasts a long and bright list; among statesmen it claims Sir Dudley Carleton, Godolphin, Bolingbroke, Wyndham, Mansfield, Canning, and Sir Robert Peel: Sir Philip Sydney and Ben Jonson may represent its poets;

Locke, Penn, South, and Camden, its philosophers, philanthropists, wits, and scholars.

The front of the college in St. Aldate's has a striking effect, both from its architectural excellences and its great extent—its length being about 400 feet. In the centre is a lofty entrance-tower, the famous Tom Gateway; which, though begun at the foundation of the college, was only completed in 1682, under the direction of Sir Christopher Wren—to whom other parts of the college also owe some ornaments of a kind not very consistent with the original buildings. The gateway is named the Tom from the cupola containing the great bell of that name, whose sonorous voice is so well known to all Oxonians. It was brought from Oseney Abbey, and weighs some 17,000 pounds. Every night, at ten minutes past nine, Tom tolls 101 times, that being the number of students on the foundation; and at the sound the gates of most of the colleges are closed. Christ Church men have been used to regard their Tom as the very prince of bells; but we perceive in Parker's New Hand-Book its fame is assailed; it does not ring, so it is said, a perfect B flat, as it ought; but as our ears are not sufficiently sharp to note the dissonance, we must be content to leave the matter to the visitor's own judgment. The quadrangle into which the gateway leads is the largest in Oxford, being 264 feet by 261; and though not quite so large as that of Trinity at Cambridge, nor perhaps quite so magnificent in its appearance, is yet a most noble one. This 'quad.' (as Oxford men familiarly term their quadrangles) was a part of the original design of Wolsey, and may serve to show the scale on which he proposed to work. In its present state it dates only from about 1668, the original quadrangle having been in a good measure destroyed during the Commonwealth period by the Puritan dean and chapter, who were accustomed to tear down the woodwork of the old house for fuel! On the south side of the quadrangle is the Hall; the entrance to which is of remarkable beauty. The visitor will not fail to notice the very characteristic statue of the cardinal over the door; nor, as he enters the passage, the handsome groined roof, with its single supporting pillar. The Hall itself is the noblest in Oxford, and one of the finest refectories in England. Its proportions are ample, and the fittings commensurate with its size and the wealth of the institution. It is 115 feet long, 40 wide, and 50 high. The open roof is of carved oak, profusely decorated with the arms of Henry and Wolsey, and has richly-carved pendants. The large fireplaces have also elaborate carvings, and the noble bay-window at the south end has a carved canopy. The sides of the room are hung with a splendid series of portraits, one hundred and twenty in number, mostly the work of eminent artists, and representing the most distinguished men who have been on the college foundation. Even on ordinary occasions, the noble Hall, at the dinner-hour, filled with the robed host of doctors and students—the arrangements so redolent of the old feudal times—

magnates sitting in state on the dais, masters and bachelors at the side-tables, and under-graduates occupying all the lower end—is a sight worth seeing. But Christ Church being the official residence of the sovereign when at Oxford, this Hall has at times displayed a far more splendid appearance. At such times a similar system of arranging the tables is adopted, with, of course, a suitable attention to the different ranks of the parties; and those who have witnessed the spectacle describe it as no less impressive than singular.

When it was the custom to exhibit plays before the sovereign, on visiting the universities, this was the place Oxford selected for their performances; and some of the exhibitions must have been not a little curious. Elizabeth was entertained here in 1566, with a Latin comedy of Marcus Geminus, a Latin tragedy of Progne, and an English comedy founded on Chaucer's 'Palamon and Arcite.' Progne did not please her majesty. The scaffold on which Palamon and Arcite was to be acted, unfortunately gave way, whereby three persons were killed: a second part, however, was afterwards acted, to the great contentment of the queen, who edified her courtiers after the performance by a critical disquisition on the play and the players, who were all students of the University. The boy who represented Emilia, the only female character in the piece, she especially praised, for so handsomely showing her as "a virgin of uncorrupted purity and unblemished simplicity," and presented him with a gift of eight guineas. It is recorded, too, that "a cry of hounds belonging to Theseus" having been counterfeited in the quadrangle during the performance, the students were seized with a sudden transport; whereat her majesty cried out, "O excellent! these boys, in very troth, are ready to leap out of the windows to follow the hounds." At another visit which she made twenty years later, she was hardly so well pleased either with the performances in this Hall, or her general entertainment in the University.

When James I., with his queen, visited Oxford in 1605, he was entertained with plays in plenty; but they were little to his taste in comparison with the scholastic disputations, which afforded him vast delight. The college stage-managers were, indeed, not at all successful on the occasion, though they now, for the first time, exhibited scenery, and, moreover, called in the aid of Inigo Jones, in the contrivance of the devices. The first play was a pastoral, called 'Alba;' and in it five rustics appeared, who were so scantily dressed as to shock the delicacy of the queen and her maids of honour; and even the king was moved to wrath by the exhibition. At the next play, which was in Latin, and called 'Vertumnia,' his majesty went fast asleep. The third play was the 'Ajax' of Sophocles; and this time "the king was very weary before he came thither, but much more wearied by it, and spoke many words of dislike." Charles I. also witnessed some plays in this Hall. At a play which was exhibited here for the entertainment of Prince Alasco, in 1583, the learned men brewed a storm, that, as old Wood says, "was very strange to the beholders." The piece was the tragedy of 'Dido;' and in the tempest which drove Æneas and Dido into the cave, "it rained small comfits, and rose-water, and snew artificial snow (of sugar)!"

Before leaving the Hall, the visitor must carefully look along the portraits. They are the productions of nearly all the leading portrait-painters who have practised in England from Holbein to Sir Martin Archer Shee. Holbein has the Cardinal and Henry VIII. Vandyke has Bishop Corbet, and a couple more. Lely has several. There is a fine portrait of John Locke, by Kneller. Hogarth has one of Bishop Hooper. Several are by Sir Joshua Reynolds: one of them, that of Archbishop Markham, being reckoned among his best works. Lawrence has a good portrait of Canning; and many others, by old and new masters, may well claim attention as works of art; while there are few out of the whole number that do not possess interest on account of the men they represent.

From the Hall visitors are led by a natural transition to the Kitchen, which it may not be amiss perhaps just to look into, as a specimen of a genuine old English kitchen; and also to catch an idea of the economy of a college *cuisine*. This is the oldest part of the building, Wolsey having commenced the erection of his college by first constructing the kitchen—a circumstance which gave some exercise to the wits of that day. Strangers look with admiration on a huge gridiron that is moved upon wheels, and that was used for cooking large joints or whole animals upon before jacks and ranges were invented, or meat was cut up into the little snips it is now-a-days. Upon it a whole bullock might have been broiled, over a primitive hearth, as easily as a steak at one of the kitchen-ranges of these degenerate times.

On leaving the kitchen you need not turn aside to the Chaplain's Quadrangle, but proceed across the Large Quadrangle to Peckwater Quadrangle, the south side of which is the Library, one of the finest in the University. Originally this building was intended to stand upon high columns; but before its completion it was found that the space below could not be spared, and it was accordingly finished as it now appears. The ground-floor is chiefly occupied by the Guise collection of pictures: a collection of considerable value, as containing a good many specimens of the very early masters, whose works are rather scarce in this country. There are also some examples of the later and more famous Italian masters. Many of the pictures are, indeed, of more than doubtful genuineness; but the collection, if it were arranged in a place where the pictures could be better seen, would attract much more attention than it now obtains. There are also in this room several capital busts, by Rysbrach, Roubiliac, Bacon, and Chantrey. On the staircase leading to the library is a statue of Locke, by Roubiliac. The upper room, the Library, is a noble room, 140 feet long, 30 wide, and 37 high; the wainscot, pillars, and presses are of oak; the ceiling is richly ornamented

in stucco; about the room a number of antique statues and busts are arranged so as to increase the general effect; and the whole has a very appropriate scholastic air. The Peckwater Quadrangle is a specimen of the skill of an amateur architect, Dean Aldrich, of whose practical ability several other proofs may be seen in Oxford. Canterbury Quadrangle, which adjoins the Peckwater on the east, was erected in 1775 and following years, under the superintendence of Wyatt. It is Doric in style, and has a substantial look, but suffers by comparison with the more picturesque Gothic which abounds in this city. It received its name from being built on the site of Canterbury Hall; a lapsed foundation of which Wiclif was at one time warden, and Sir Thomas More a student. The court in which are the Grammar-school and the Anatomical Theatre, Fell's Buildings, the Cloisters, and other buildings belonging to this magnificent institution, we may pass by, and proceed to its Chapel — the Cathedral of Oxford

As a cathedral, Oxford is inferior to most, both in size and splendour. It is cruciform, and has a spire springing from the intersection of the arms of the cross. The extreme length is 154 feet; the breadth is 102 feet. It is of different ages, and consequently exhibits considerable diversity of style. The oldest parts are Norman, and belonged to the church of St. Frideswide's Priory, which, according to Dr. Ingram, was consecrated in 1180. Wolsey pulled down 50 feet of the nave, and otherwise altered and adapted it to the use of his college. The additions and alterations that have been made to the original church at different periods, although destructive of all uniformity, have perhaps tended to increase the picturesqueness of parts, and afford curious examples of the progressive changes in taste in English ecclesiastical architecture. The Norman choir is especially deserving of notice from the peculiar double arches; and the singular effect produced by the elaborate groined roof with its carved pendants, the additions of Wolsey, which contrast strangely with the massive simplicity of the Norman work below. The body of the choir is sadly lumbered up with the seats and stalls necessary for the large body of collegians, and the windows lack the storied glass that should shed a dim religious light; but the appearance during the performance of divine service is both impressive and remarkable from the numerous band of robed students who crowd the entire area. It is only equalled by the chapel of Trinity at Cambridge. We have hinted that there are no old stained-glass windows: only a few fragments, in fact, remain to attest the ancient opulence. Christ Church was an especial sufferer from the ruthless zeal of the Puritans. And this, too, as Wood records, through the violence of one of its own canons, Henry Wilkinson, who was the Parliamentary visitor, and who, when the statues, pictures, crosses, and painted windows "were taken down, was so far from having them laid up and preserved, that he furiously stamped upon many parts of, and utterly defaced them." The few painted windows that are now in the church are mostly of recent date and little worth. In walking round the church the visitor should not overlook the very beautiful Chantry chapel, now called the Latin chapel, from service being performed in it in Latin, which is said to have been built by Lady Montacute in the fourteenth century : in its windows are choice examples of that beautiful tracery which distinguishes what is called the decorated style. We may also point attention to a singular decorated window which has been inserted into the south transept, and which bears considerable resemblance to some of those in the Flamboyant style, so frequently met with in continental churches. In the various parts of the church are a great many monuments both ancient and modern of considerable interest. That called the Shrine of St. Frideswide is the most striking: it is a lofty and richly-sculptured shrine, three stories high, of perpendicular work, and is supposed to have been erected about 1480, over the bones of the saint. The monument to the memory of Lady Montacute, who died 1355, has on it some graceful sculpture. Many other ancient monuments are exceedingly curious. Among the more modern the best known is the rather singular one to the memory of the author of the ' Anatomy of Melancholy.' Of those erected in our own day the noble statue of Dean Jackson, by Chantrey, is sure to command notice. If the tourist is desirous to test his archæological skill, he may do so upon a curious piece of sculpture which he will find in the verger's garden, built into the wall by one of the buttresses at the south end of the chapel. On the three sides which are visible are carved the Fall of Man, the Sacrifice of Isaac, and another subject, the meaning of which is not clear: the point which the learned cannot decide is what was its original use; opinion being divided whether it was "the ancient font of the church," or the "altar or reliquary of St. Frideswade, in which her bones were enshrined." We ought to have mentioned before that this cathedral, as well as most of the original part of the college, is undergoing repair and restoration—and there is little doubt that the whole will ultimately be rendered worthy of this magnificent foundation. The Christ Church Meadows we will visit after we have looked through a few more of the colleges.

We may quit Christ Church by the Canterbury Gate, and proceed up Merton Lane, from the largest of the colleges to the oldest. On our way thither, however, we must pass between two other colleges, standing directly opposite each other, that deserve a passing recognition, though it were only on account of the men who had been nurtured in them. That on the right is Corpus Christi, which was founded by the liberal Bishop Fox, early in the reign of Henry VIII. The buildings are partly of the date of the foundation ; others are more recent : neither require particular mention. The more ancient have suffered from many alterations ; but, as recently restored, the Chapel and Hall will repay a visit : the modern buildings are but commonplace. But it has large claims on the respect of every true churchman. The two most famous champions of the Church of England—Bishop Jewel and the judicious Hooker—are both of Corpus Christi ; nor are the names of many honourable successors of those giants of old wanting in the list of the college worthies.

Opposite Corpus stands Oriel College, a much older establishment ; it having been founded in 1326, by Edward II., at the instigation of Adam de Brom, his almoner. The oldest of the present buildings, however, is not of earlier date than about 1620. These parts are not remarkable either for beauty or grandeur ; but they are pleasing and picturesque. The library was erected, in 1788, from a design by Wyatt. It bears no resemblance to any of the earlier buildings, but is a substantial and stately pile ; and it contains a choice store of books. Among the " men of fame who have renowned this *college*," Sir Walter Raleigh and Bishop Butler stand pre-eminent. William Prynne, the celebrated Parliament scribe, was also one of its members ; and he bequeathed his valuable library to it. Of the notable men of the present day, it claims a goodly share : of these the names of Archbishop Whately, Bishops Coplestone and Wilberforce, and Dr. Arnold, may suffice.

Come we now to Merton College,—the most ancient foundation in Oxford, and one that is the more interesting to the visitor, inasmuch as, though scarcely any portion of the original structure is left, it possesses buildings of an earlier date than any other college. The founder was Walter de Merton, a man who in his day held many civil as well as ecclesiastical offices, and was Chancellor of England and Bishop of Rochester at his death in 1277. The foundation charter bears date January 7, 1264 ; and the statutes laid down in it for the government of Merton have served as the model for those of all, or nearly all, the later establishments. Before the foundation of colleges, the students at Oxford (of course with the exception of those attached to St. Frideswide's Priory, and other religious houses in the city or its vicinity) lodged, like those of Cambridge (vol. i., p. 116), in halls, inns, or hostels, as they were variously called, under the governance of a principal, but at their own expense. On the first establishment of colleges, it is probable that only those students were educated in them who were on the foundation ; but, as the rule was relaxed, the superior advantages connected with the incorporated institutions would naturally attract independent scholars to them, the old hostels gradually disappeared, or were endowed by benevolent individuals, and the collegiate system became the exclusive one. The original foundation of Merton was for a warden, certain priests, and twenty scholars ; but the numbers were to be regulated by the state of the funds. As we do not intend to trace the history of the colleges, or to enter into particulars that belong especially to the Calender or the Guide-book, we shall merely state that the foundation now consists of a warden, twenty-four fellows, fourteen postmasters (or exhibitioners—the term is peculiar to Merton), four scholars, two chaplains, and two clerks. Including those not on the foundation, there are now about one hundred and sixty members on the college books. As has been said already, Merton was, in its early days, famous for its professors in scholastic theology. The " profound Bradwardine," " subtle Scotus," and " invincible Occam," were all members of it. Wiclif was also a scholar of Merton. Nor ought the untiring antiquary Antony-à-Wood to pass unnamed; for if neither his logical or rhetorical skill will add much credit to his college, his devotion to it, which led him to the most laborious and ungrudging researches into its history, and the preservation of much that is valuable as well as curious respecting it, should gain for him honourable mention from all who treat of his college.

The buildings of Merton consist of three courts: the tourist should stroll through them. Before entering he must not omit to notice the singular sculpture over the gateway, or the statues of Henry III. and the founder that stand on either side of it; nor, as he enters, the bold groins and bosses of the gateway roof. The largest quadrangle is only of the time of James I., and has been not inaptly termed " the schools in miniature :" it is in the smaller courts that the older parts are to be found. Of these the noblest by far is the chapel, the choir of which may be of the age of the founder, and is certainly not later than the commencement of the fourteenth century. Originally the chapel was intended to be of the form of a cross; but this design was never carried out. When only the choir and the arches were erected, the works were suspended; and the chapel remained in this state for above a century. In 1417 the works were recommenced, and they were brought to a close by 1424, when the chapel was re-dedicated with much solemnity. The chapel now consists of a choir, tower, and transepts, neither nave nor side-aisles having ever been built. As it stands, it is, however, a very fine edifice, and commands the admiration of all whose judgment is worth regarding. Internally it has suffered from the zeal of both church-destroyers and church-beautifiers; but the society, who are fully alive to the value of their charge, have done something towards its entire restoration, and will soon, we hope, do more. When the vile modern ceiling and stalls shall be removed, and their place supplied by others accordant with the style of the building, the splendid choir, one of the longest and handsomest in Oxford, will be fairly seen, and its beauty properly appreciated. As it is, however, the effect of its graceful proportions, and the long series of elaborately decorated windows on the sides, with the noble one at the end, is very striking. The windows about the chapel are, many of them, uncommonly beautiful. Those old masons of the dark ages seem to have moulded their stone tracery as though they were working in some plastic material; and here may be seen samples of their cunning, of dates from the thirteenth century, when their art was at its highest, down to the sixteenth, when it was

about to perish. The visitor will hardly need to have his attention directed to the elegant tracery in the side windows (there are fourteen of them); and he cannot help being struck by the marvellous beauty of the great east, or, as it is often called, the Catherine-wheel, window. A good deal of the original stained glass remains in the side windows, and adds much to their value. There are, too, in the chapel some monuments that should not be overlooked. Two brasses, of the fourteenth and fifteenth centuries, are good examples of the incised work of their respective times. One of the monuments is to the memory of Sir Thomas Bodley, the munificent founder of the Bodleian Library; another, to the memory of Sir Henry Saville, exhibits a representation of the colleges of Eton and Merton as they appeared in 1621. The tourist may here see a curious instance of the strange taste that at one time possessed the conservators of our ecclesiastical edifices, and what unsuspected beauty may lie hidden under the lath and plaster of the eighteenth-century Vandals. On entering the chapel he must have been struck with the beauty of the shafts that support the arches of the tower, and the quaint gracefulness of the carved oak lantern under the belfry, with the open gallery for the ringers; yet a few years ago none of these things were visible, and their existence was unknown. The handsome columns and arches were concealed behind wainscotting and other trumpery, upon removing part of which, about five-and-twenty years ago, they were discovered. The paltry plaster ceiling which hid the belfry lantern has only been got rid of quite recently. Externally the tower of Merton Chapel is very fine from Merton field and the adjacent meadows its appearance is most majestic, and it tells well in every general view of the city.

In the first court stands the Hall, once a handsome building; but having lost some of its freshness from age, it was placed under the care of Mr. Wyatt to renovate and beautify,—a task he performed so effectually, that, in the language of advertisements, its charms must now " be seen to be appreciated; they defy description." The third court, or Mob Quad., is the smallest of the three courts; but it is the oldest, and is, indeed, one of the most perfect examples left of an ancient college quadrangle. The larger part of the south and west sides of it are taken up by the library, which is known, by the college records, to have been erected in 1377, and is generally regarded as one of the most ancient libraries in the kingdom; Chalmers (' Hist. of the Colleges, &c., of Oxford,' vol. i., p. 10), thus describes it :—" It is lighted by two series of windows, the upper, of the bay kind, projecting from the outer roof in three compartments; the lower series are oblong and very narrow, and in both are painted arms of the benefactors, &c. . . . Whatever may be thought of this library as a work of art, it cannot fail to be contemplated with peculiar veneration by the antiquary, as the most ancient library in the kingdom. Before the establishment of colleges, there was no distinct building under the name of a library. In monasteries and other religious houses, which were the only repositories of learning, books were kept in chests, where most convenient. Merton, therefore, which exhibited the first regular college, gave also the first exemplar of a library." Whether this be the most ancient library in existence or not, it unquestionably is one of the most ancient in this kingdom, and it retains its early character more perfectly than any other. That its contents have not been so faithfully preserved, we have already read. By the entrance to the Mob Quad. is seen the treasury, or record-room, a curious-looking, high-roofed, fire-proof building, supposed to be that erected at the foundation of the college. It is scarcely worth while to add, that the gardens of Merton are much admired, and that there are some pleasant prospects from the terraces, since strangers are not permitted to see them.

Merton is the oldest college that can produce title-deeds in support of its antiquity; but University College asserts its precedence, carrying back its origin to the ninth century, and claiming the great Alfred for its founder. On this claim we shall not venture a remark: for though its historical supports seem sufficiently slight, and, as we said, it has no lawful parchment deeds, yet it has legal authority sufficient to silence one not disposed to unnecessary dispute. The sovereign is the visitor of this college; and when an attempt was made about a century back, to show that no such right was vested in the crown, it was decided, after all due and sufficient argumentation, in the Court of King's Bench, that University College *is* a foundation of King Alfred's, and that *therefore* the sovereign is the rightful visitor. But whatever be the fact (not the legal fact—for that is clear—but the historical) about Alfred, it is admitted by all, that University College is one of the oldest of the colleges; and as it lies at no great distance from Merton, we will now visit it. This is the college whose long, black, weatherbeaten front forms so noticeable a feature in the High-street. A portion of it is seen in the left-hand corner of the engraving (Cut, No. 2). This frontage, which is above 260 feet long, would be imposing, if only from its extent; but it has a good deal of architectural merit, though wanting in the richness of the olden Gothic. None of the buildings of this college are earlier than the reign of Charles I. The principal front is a regular and substantial structure, rather plain, though stately; but the general elevation is relieved by two lofty gateway towers, which stand at equal distances from the extremities, and have bay windows with canopied statues, and somewhat more of ornament than the remainder of the frontage. These gateways lead into the two quadrangles which contain the college buildings. The western and principal quadrangle is about 100 feet square. Its construction was begun in 1634, but it was not completed till 1674. The statue over the gateway leading to this quadrangle is that of Queen Anne; on the inner side is a corresponding statue of James II., which was presented to the college in the mastership of Obadiah Walker, who, it

will be remembered, joined the Romish Church on the accession of James, and lost his post at the Revolution. This is said to be the only statue remaining of James II., besides that at Whitehall. The other gateway leads to the eastern quadrangle, which is about 80 feet square. Only three of the sides have buildings. The north and east sides were built at the cost of Dr. Radcliffe. The statue placed over the front of the gateway which leads to this quadrangle is that of Queen Mary, wife of William III.; the corresponding statue on the inner side is one of Dr. Radcliffe—a much more appropriate choice than that of the king, who overlooks the other quadrangle. The hall and library, with many blemishes and incongruities, have not a few redeeming qualities, but they need not detain us while so many fine buildings remain to be visited. The chapel may be just glanced at. It is in no acknowledged style of architecture, Gothic and classic being freely intermingled, but it has considerable elegance of appearance. It was begun in 1635, but it remained unfinished till 1665. Much of the carving is by Grinling Gibbons, and exhibits all his usual delicacy of execution. There are some painted windows, but they are in a barbarous taste. There is also an altar-piece of that abominable kind of *art*, called "poker-painting," which the refinement of the last century introduced. A work more worthy of the place, and for which alone the chapel should be visited, is Flaxman's celebrated relievo in memory of Sir William Jones, who was a fellow of this College. Within the last three or four years an additional building has been erected from the design of Barry, the architect of the 'Palace at Westminster,' and it will be admitted to be a most graceful addition to the architecture of the High-street of Oxford. Before leaving University College, we ought to mention a singular custom that is regularly kept up in it, but the origin of which is unknown, and does not seem easy to explain: it is called "Chopping at the Tree," and is thus performed:—On Easter-Sunday a bough is dressed up with flowers and evergreens, and laid on a turf by the buttery. After dinner each member, as he leaves the hall, takes up a cleaver and chops at the tree; and then hands over "largess" to the cook, who stands by with a plate. The contribution is, for the master, half-a-guinea; the fellows, five shillings; and other members half-a-crown each.

We have said that the front of University College is black and weatherbeaten; many would therefore like to see it "restored," and now that restoring is so much the fashion in Oxford, it is not very unlikely to be done. We hope it will escape, however, yet awhile. Up to a certain stage—so long, in fact, as the idea of instability is not suggested—the corrosion of the surface of almost every building, while it invariably increases the picturesqueness, often adds something of venerableness to its aspect, that more than atones for the loss of the sharpness and freshness of the details. Not a little is the impressiveness of many an old cathedral heightened by this effect. But Gothic architecture has so rich a surface from the multitudinous ornament which adorns it, that when all is new and sharp it is still pleasing. True Grecian structures, also, from their majestic simplicity and grandeur of outline, depend comparatively little on either newness or antiquity for their influence. With that spurious class of "classic" edifices, of which our cities have so many examples, however, it is otherwise. To an educated eye their pretension and poverty are exceedingly disagreeable, if seen in all their nakedness: yet, even on them, Time works often surprising changes. What was harsh, formal and pedantic when new, becomes at least respectable when age has softened or worn off its peculiarities. The college immediately opposite to University is a most striking example of this. A few years ago, its mouldering front not only helped largely, by its peculiar style, to add variety to the general appearance of the High-street, but it was pleasing, and eminently picturesque in itself. Now that the marks of the "gnawing tooth of Time" are removed, it looks cold, feeble, and common-place; the only attraction about it consisting in its oddity. So at least it seems to us, but there are many who regard the front of Queen's College as a triumph of architectural skill.

After this escapade we will not linger over the buildings of Queen's, but it is needful so far to make amends, as to except in some degree the chapel and hall from the censure. The library, too, is a very handsome room inside; so is the basement floor, which a few years ago was fitted up by Mr. Cockerell as an addition to the old room—a measure which was rendered necessary by the munificent gift of Dr. Mason, who, besides his own books and antiquities, left the sum of £30,000 to his old college for the purchase of books. Queen's College received its name from Queen Philippa, wife of Edward III., who was its patroness; and it has ever since been regarded as especially under the patronage of the queens of England, who have often been considerable benefactors to it. The founder of it was Robert de Eglesfeld, chaplain to Queen Philippa. The institution is a highly prosperous one, and has had a good share of famous and (as we have seen in one instance) grateful sons. There are commonly about 300 members on the books. This college still retains some curious old customs. It was directed in the statutes of the founder that there should be twelve fellows and seventy poor scholars, (the numbers being allusive to the twelve apostles and seventy disciples of our Lord.) They were to be

4.—MAGDALEN GATEWAY.

3.—GARDEN-FRONT OF WADHAM COLLEGE.

summoned to dinner by the sound of a trumpet; and then the fellows, in scarlet robes, were to sit on one side of the table, while the poor scholars were to be ranged on the other, kneeling, in token of humility, and dispute in philosophy,—we hope not till they had satisfied the "sacred rage of hunger." This latter direction, however, does not seem to have been ever carried out, but the members are still summoned to dinner by sound of trumpet. On New Year's Day, the burser (*i. e.*, treasurer) presents to every member a needle and thread, with the words (very apt advice for Oxonians) — "Take this and be thrifty." The needle and thread—*aiguille et fils*—is supposed to be a rebus on the name of the founder, Eglesfeld. One other old custom is that of having a boar's head brought into the hall in procession on Christmas-day, while the old carol is sung—

> " The Boar's head in hand bear I
> Bedeck'd with bays and rosemary ;
> And I pray you, my masters, be merry,
> Qui estis in convivio,
> Caput Apri defero,
> Reddens laudes Domino."

A little lower down the High-street is the very handsome front of All Souls' College; and the restorations here have undoubtedly been most beneficial. The buildings of All Souls' are extensive and varied. The Old Quadrangle is a quiet, characteristic example of collegiate architecture. The New Quadrangle, or Grand Court, 172 feet by 155, remarkable for its differing so widely from the rest of the buildings, owes its peculiar appearance to the inventive powers of Hawksmoor,

who was the architect employed to construct it. He designed the several buildings with a view to their picturesque effect in combination with each other, and with the surrounding edifices ; and he succeeded in producing a striking result. In this quadrangle the chapel and hall occupy the south, the cloisters and gateway the west, and the common rooms, with the two towers, the east sides. They are in what has been called by Hawksmoor's admirers the mixed Gothic style ; and though, considered apart, much may be objected to in them, they certainly display a good deal of originality of conception, and, as we have said, their general effect is very striking. The two towers above-mentioned, are a leading feature in every distant view of the city. The chapel has been among the most admired buildings in Oxford, but it does not deserve a moment's comparison with the chapels of New, Magdalen, or Merton Colleges, and is greatly inferior to several others. Having mentioned the customs of other colleges, we must not leave unnoticed a famous one of All Souls'. Thus it arose :—In digging for the foundations of the college a mallard of superb size was discovered, domiciled in an old drain. He was caught, cooked, and found most sapid. Such a mallard as he, it was felt, ought not to be forgotten. He is therefore duly commemorated on the day of his capture. The 14th of January, being the foundation day, is, of course, a College "gaudy," and then, when the best mallard that can be found is introduced, all Mallardians present join " a hundred men singing like one," in chanting forth, *ore rotundo*,

> " O the swapping, swapping mallard," &c.

On quitting All Souls', the tourist had better pass by Magdalen Hall (just glancing at it in passing as a sample of modern Gothic, which may help him the better to estimate the older specimen he is going to visit) and proceed to New College, one of the proudest ornaments of Oxford. The founder of New College was one of those giants of the olden days, that modern times can only marvel at, and admire, without hoping to emulate. He at the same time filled the most important offices both in church and state; and, what sounds strange to readers unacquainted with the studies of ecclesiastics in the middle ages, he was the royal architect. That the multiplicity and diversity of his offices did not cause him to neglect the duties of either of them, we have sufficient evidence. With his civil services, Edward III.—no mean judge—was so well satisfied that, as Froissart tells us, "Wykeham was so much in favour with the king of England, that everything was done by him, and nothing was done without him." And as a proof of his favour, he raised him to be Chancellor of England and Bishop of Winchester. As a priest and a prelate his contemporaries describe him as pious, diligent, and boundlessly munificent. Testimony to his architectural genius will not be wanting, while Windsor Castle, Winchester Cathedral, and New College are standing to vouch for it.

But our business is with the College, not the man. Impressed with the insufficiency of the schools provided for the education of the clergy, he long revolved in his mind the best means of remedying the evil, and finally matured a plan, which the vast wealth he had acquired in the course of his active and prosperous life happily enabled him to accomplish—namely, to found a college at Oxford which should furnish the most liberal education in philosophy and theology; and another at Winchester, which should serve as a nursery for it. His own disgrace towards the close of the reign of Edward, and in the early part of that of his successor, and the various obstructions he met with, for a long while hindered the execution of his grand design, but nothing could induce him to lay it aside. At length, on the 5th of March, 1380, Wykeham laid the first stone of his New College; and 'being finished, the first warden and fellows took possession of it April 14, 1386, at three of the clock in the morning:" the following year the Bishop commenced the erection of his college at Winchester; and he lived after that was finished to rebuild the best part of his cathedral.

As the buildings of New College were left by their munificent founder, so to a great degree they remain. They are the most complete examples of a college erected by the ablest architect in the best age of Gothic architecture. The original buildings consisted of the principal quadrangle, in which are the chapel, hall, and library; the cloisters, and the tower. The additions have been a third story to the Quadrangle, which originally consisted only of two stories, and the garden-court, designed, it is said, by Sir Christopher Wren, from the Palace of Versailles. You enter the college by a gate-house of rather plain but pleasing design, having on the front three statues—of the Virgin, of the founder kneeling, and another. The Great Quadrangle, into which this leads, is 168 feet by 129 feet; and is at once dignified yet chaste in character; though suffering somewhat from the additional story. From this a short cloister leads to the chapel—by common consent the noblest in Oxford. After the lavish praises he has heard bestowed on this chapel, many a visitor feels somewhat disappointed to find it less splendid in its appearance—less overspread with sculptured forms and tracery than many another he has seen. But it deserves its reputation. The grand merit it now possesses consists in the elegance of its proportions, and the propriety of the ornament which really adorns it. In its original condition there was no want of splendour, and its appearance then must have been of surpassing grandeur. The niches by the east window are said to have been filled with statues of gold and silver; but these, the statues of stone, and much of the sculpture on the walls, and the paintings in the windows, were removed or destroyed by those who regarded such things as profane, and the gold and colours that were employed with no sparing hand on the carvings were hidden under white-wash. About sixty years ago the chapel was restored under the direction of Mr. Wyatt, and more successfully than could be expected from his taste in Gothic architecture and the taste of the age: but the restoration left the building much balder than would now be permitted. Painted windows were inserted, from designs made for the purpose by Sir Joshua Reynolds. They were admired at the time, and they are admired still. But whatever may be their value as pictures, it is not too much to say that, as windows—which are not meant to exclude the light—they are a failure. In the beautiful ante-chapel some of the original stained glass may be seen; and it will prove that the old workmen understood the purpose of their material. The choir is 100 feet long; the nave, or ante-chapel, 80 feet; it is 65 feet high, and 35 feet broad. The style is what is called the early perpendicular; retaining much of the simplicity of the decorated, but yet displaying the decided peculiarities of the later style. We should mention that the organ is considered to be one of the finest in England; and we need hardly add, that in the choral service its capabilities are gloriously exhibited. Before he leaves the chapel, the stranger will be shown the silver-gilt crosier of the founder—a relique of rare worth and beauty, and greatly prized. We may here observe, that notwithstanding commissioners of all kinds have destroyed, or carried off, an enormous quantity of the plate and church-furniture belonging to the several colleges, and the fellows themselves "lent" a good deal more to Charles I. in his exigencies, there yet remains a great deal distributed throughout them, and almost every old college has some choice sample; as the reader who is curious in such matters may see on consulting Shaw's valuable essay on the 'Ancient Plate and Furniture in Oxford.

The hall has suffered too much by the substitution of a vulgar modern ceiling, wainscoting, and other barbarisms, to allow its original beauty to be judged of. It contains a good many interesting portraits; in the windows are various coats of arms. The library has been remodelled and refitted by Mr. Wyatt. The tower will be admired for its fine proportions; internally it has little or nothing to attract the general visitor. All these three buildings, perhaps, will be seen sufficiently, and certainly to most advantage, only on the outside. The cloisters, which enclose an area of 130 feet by 85 feet, were with the area consecrated in 1400, as a cemetery for the collegians. In design they are marked by an appropriate sobriety of character. The ribbed roof which covers them is very curious, bearing a marked resemblance to the rib-work of a ship's hull.

The visitor must not leave the college without seeing the garden, which he may freely enter; it is not only worth seeing for its own sake—and it is one of the pleasantest, where there are so many pleasant ones—but parts of the college buildings show most picturesquely from it; and it has a unique bit of the old city wall, kept in as good repair as though it might still repel a foe. It was part of the contract Wykeham entered into with the city when he purchased the land, that the college should maintain for ever that part of the wall which bounded the college property; and the agreement is still faithfully adhered to.

But beautiful as is New College, were we to be asked to conduct a stranger to the most perfect example of an Oxford college, we should point to Magdalen. We refer, of course, to its substantial temporalities—to those "good things" that cause Oxford to be so much envied, and so well grumbled at—not to the intellectual parts; for with them we have here no concern. Magdalen is, indeed, a glorious place. Buildings it has that gladden the heart and delight the imagination—from the

"High embowed roof,
With antique pillars massy proof,"

down to "studious cloisters:" trim gardens, too, are there; smooth-shaven lawns, and "arched walks of twilight groves;" ample endowments also, that provide abundance for the passing day, and promise a tolerable *living* for a future; choice books, (no doubt old wines,) good society, with gentlemanly leisure to enjoy them all, or just enough employment to give wings to the hours that would else linger, and convert these academic courts and groves into courts and gardens, like those fabled ones,

"Where, sooth to say,
Ne living wight might work ne cared e'en for play."

As it is, these are almost a realization of the scenes that haunted the mind of the young author of 'Il Penseroso.' "Surely," as Wordsworth somewhere says,

"Those *fellows* needs must live
A comfortable life who sojourn here!"

One wonders how they can ever give up such good "lodgings" to commence housekeeping on their own account. But they do. And unusually threatening as the prospect of a change of life must seem to them, yet, strange as it may appear, we never heard that the fellows of Magdalen were more backward than those of any less-favoured college, to leave it for a living and a wife when they had the chance.

But we must look at this pleasant house and gardens a little more closely. The buildings, which are comprised in three quadrangles, cover an area of above eleven acres; the grounds occupy more than a hundred acres. The founder of Magdalen College was William Waynflete, bishop of Winchester and Lord Chancellor of England in the reign of Henry VI., who was, we may hope, moved to this good work by the example of his great predecessor in those offices. Waynflete laid the first stone of the Great Quadrangle in 1473, and employed William Orchard as master-mason, to construct it; but whether Orchard is to be considered as architect, or merely builder, is not clear—some have attributed the designs to Waynflete himself. The entrance to the college is by the New Gateway at the top of High-street (Cut, No. 4), which was erected in 1844 by Mr. Pugin. It is a very pretty thing of its kind, and exhibits an uncompromising return to the old manner. On the outside are canopied statues of Mary Magdalen, St. John Baptist, and the founder; a statue of the Virgin and Child is on the inside. Shields of arms, the lily and other emblems, and inscriptions in illuminated Gothic characters are plentifully distributed about. The appearance of the buildings on passing through the gateway is very fine. Immediately in front is the western end of the chapel, displaying a splendid window, and beneath it an elaborately-ornamented doorway, with a shallow porch richly sculptured, and surmounted by five statues in canopied niches—forming altogether an uncommonly handsome elevation; with which the summit of the lofty tower that is seen rising above, though a detached building, very well composes, as a painter would say. On the left hand, in front of the President's lodgings, is seen a noble gateway-tower, the original entrance into the Great Quadrangle. The gateway is adorned, like the chapel porch, with canopied statues; these being of St. John, St. Mary, Henry III., and the founder. The elegant groined roof of the gateway should also be noticed. The room over the gateway is called the Founder's Chamber.

In the right hand corner of this court is a curious stone pulpit, from which a sermon used to be annually preached to the members of the University on St. John the Baptist's day, the members standing during it in the open quad., which on the occasion was dressed with boughs and strewed with rushes. The custom has long been discontinued, but it was observed less than a century ago; for the Rev. W. Jones (of Nayland) in his 'Life of Bishop Horne,' when mentioning that the bishop was appointed to preach this sermon in 1755, says, "so long as the stone pulpit was in use (of which I have been a witness) the quadrangle was furnished round the sides with a large fence of green boughs, that the preaching might more nearly resemble that of John the Baptist in the wilderness; and a pleasant sight it was."

The chapel is one of the finest buildings in Oxford. It was completed by the founder, and is a choice specimen of the perpendicular style. Since its erection it has undergone many mutations. At the Reformation it was despoiled of much of its sculpture and furniture; and the Commonwealth soldiers treated it much worse. Then after the Restoration it was repaired, but only in an indifferent manner. In 1740 it endured a beautifying, and the glorious Gothic pile was made as fine as "Grecian" screens and panelling, nondescript stalls, and plaster ceiling could make it. Happily it is once more restored (as far as could be desired) to nearly its primal glory—only the roof remains to be renewed. In 1833, it underwent a thorough and most costly restoration under the direction of the late Mr. Cottingham, who carried through his undertaking with great skill and the most painstaking diligence. The carvings, whether in stone on the walls or in the oak stalls, are all executed with a care and felicity that the old monkish architects would have admired. The stone organ-screen is well worthy of scrutiny. The organ itself has a curious history. It was cast down as superstitious at the Puritan clearance; but Cromwell had heard it and liked its tone, and he accordingly had it removed to Hampton Court, and set up there for his own particular delectation. There it remained till the return of Charles, when it was replaced in Magdalen College chapel. All the recent improvements have been added to it, and it is now much admired by the lovers of church music. The visitor should attend a choral service at Magdalen chapel and hear

"The pealing organ blow
To the full voiced-choir below."

It is solemn and impressive in no ordinary degree.

The Hall is a fine room, and contains many good portraits of eminent members, but we cannot stay to describe it; nor to speak of the royal and distinguished visitors it has entertained. We must also pass by the Library, merely mentioning that it is equal to most, that it contains a capital collection of books, and a few good busts. The large cloistered quadrangle should be seen. It was begun by the founder in 1473, but the south cloister was not erected till 1490. Its appearance is at once grand and singular. It contains the chapel, hall, library, and president's lodgings, with the cloisters, as we said, running all round. Along the inside of the quad. is a series of strange grotesque figures, the purpose of which appears inexplicable. A clever explanation of them was drawn up by one of the fellows in the last century, which regards them as symbolical, and attributes to them certain moral significations. Their appearance is not a little ludicrous —we confess to not regarding them as any ornament to the place. They do not form part of the original design, having been added in 1509; when first set

up they are said to have been coloured. The New Buildings, erected about a century back, we do not advise the stranger to visit: they are three hundred feet long, three stories high, and the apartments into which they are divided are lofty and convenient. All their excellences are told: the external design is about on a level with that of Pickford's warehouses. It was seriously proposed, in that most tasteful eighteenth century, to take down all the old buildings and erect a new college altogether in some such style as this new building! One other structure remains to be noticed— the splendid Magdalen Tower—one of the chief ornaments of Oxford, and perhaps the most noticeable feature from all parts of the city and the suburbs. Close at hand it is perhaps best seen from the little court called the Chaplain's Quad. This tower is a lofty detached pile a hundred and fifty feet high; of the most entire simplicity of form, and graceful proportions—perhaps the most beautiful structure in England of its kind and style. It was begun in 1492 and finished in 1498; Cardinal Wolsey was then Burser of the college, and some writers have attributed a share of the design to him, while others insinuate that though he assisted in its erection it was chiefly by an undue appropriation of the college money to the purpose. Before the Reformation, a mass used to be said on the top of this tower every May-morning. And still, though the mass is discontinued, some choral melody is regularly sung there at five o'clock on that morning. We must let the grounds be unpraised, though the theme be so tempting. How soft and pleasant are the lawns, how cool and shady the avenues, how delightful the water-walk alongside the cheerful Cherwell, with the peep at that antique-looking water-mill! And then that dainty relic of monastic days, the little Deer Park, how old-world like it seems to step out of the High-street of a great city upon a quiet secluded nook like this, where deer are browsing quite unconcernedly among huge old elms! Cambridge gardens, beautiful as they are, have nought like this.

Well, we must away: and now let us stroll together to another college, not so magnificent as this, but as quiet and pleasant a place for education, and as agreeable and gentlemanly a retreat after education be completed, as by a contemplative scholar could well be desired. Wadham College is of more recent date than any we have yet visited, having been founded by Nicholas Wadham, and built, after his death, by his widow, between the years 1610 and 1613. Perhaps this college affords the most favourable example of Gothic architecture of so late a date. Though debased, there is yet much of the genuine old spirit about these buildings; they have an air of neatness and compactness, and the general effect is remarkably good. The front is very effective; and the entrance gate-tower is excellent. On passing through this, you find yourself in a quadrangle 130 feet square, having directly in front a well-proportioned hall and chapel; and on either side buildings of a regular and handsome elevation,—in fact, "one of the prettiest quads. in Oxford," as a senior-fellow remarked to us the other day. The hall is a remarkably fine room, 82 feet long, 35 feet wide, and 37 feet high, with an open timber roof of high pitch, and a handsome oak screen. The great window and the oriel in this hall are much admired. Round the walls hang some capital portraits, by Reynolds and others, of the more eminent members of the college. The chapel is, perhaps, still finer than the hall: it has recently been admirably repaired and altered by Mr. Blore, and perhaps is now even more effective than when first built. This chapel, by the way, is a proof of the care that is needful in deciding on the age of a building merely by certain peculiarities in the architectural details. Many experienced archæologists have pronounced this to be genuine perpendicular; and, in support of their fancy, supposed that it had been part of the Austin Priory, on whose site the college was built; but the college records prove incontestibly that it was erected at the same time as the other collegiate buildings. Being privileged folk, we may take the liberty to walk into the garden, though it be not open to the public. And we confess that it was as much to show him a good specimen of a private college-garden, as a good specimen of one of the later colleges, that we brought the visitor here. Those who merely think of a garden as a piece of pleasure-ground attached to an ordinary house, can hardly imagine how different, how much more beautiful, it is when attached to these glorious Gothic buildings, which at every turn yield some fresh feature of picturesque beauty. This garden of Wadham is not better, perhaps, than a great many of the other small *pleasaunces* attached to Oxford colleges; but it is so beautiful that we thought we might select it as a good example of one. Like most of them, too, it is always perfectly "trim," as such gardens should be. We have given (Cut, No. 5,) a sketch of the Chapel and part of the Fellows' Apartments, as seen in connection with a portion of this garden: there are a score other such picturesque "bits" to be seen in different parts of it.

The colleges we have inspected may be taken as samples of the Oxford colleges: we can only glance at one or two more in a cursory way, and leave the rest unnoticed: we shall, however, have seen the more characteristic. Balliol College need not stay the stranger's feet: Trinity, which lies behind it, is generally pointed out as worth visiting; and it doubtless is, by those who have plenty of time: we have not, and, moreover, are just going to run hurriedly over St. John's. The buildings of St. John's are chiefly comprised in two large quadrangles. The first, or Old Quadrangle, has an air of simple grandeur; the second, built by Inigo Jones, with the exception of the library on the south side, at the expense of Archbishop Laud, has more pretension, but, to our thinking, much less propriety of character. The east and west sides are built upon an Ionic colonnade, above which are statues of Charles I. and his queen. The chapel is the most interesting building at St. John's; and, since its

restoration, it is one of the best of the second rank in Oxford. Before its alteration it was defaced by all sorts of eye-sores: under the care of Mr. Blore it has been brought to a uniformity and propriety of character that is quite refreshing to contemplate. The effect of the organ being removed into the mortuary chapel is as pleasing as novel. At the east end of the chapel are deposited the remains of Archbishops Laud and Juxon, who were both members of this college; and close by are those of Sir Thomas White, the founder. The gardens of St. John's are generally regarded as among the finest in Oxford; they occupy a space of three acres, and are laid out with much taste. They are, like the other large gardens, freely open to the public.

We have now looked, with more or less care, at about half the colleges in Oxford; the remainder of them, and all the halls, we shall leave unvisited, feeling that we have shown enough to give a rude notion of the amazing riches of this city, yet fearful that our companions will have already become weary of so long a tarriance over one class of objects. And yet we cannot help reminding the tourist that he ought to visit Pembroke College for the sake of Samuel Johnson, whose connection with any place so invariably makes his name recur to the memory of every one who looks upon it. Pembroke College is entered from the square directly opposite the Tom gate of Christ Church. Johnson's room is on the second floor over the entrance gateway; and from that window it was that the "heroic student" pitched, in furious ire, the pair of new shoes that some well-meaning neighbour had placed against his door, on seeing that his feet were peering out of his old ones. Johnson, as is well known, left Oxford long before the usual time, and, beyond doubt, from poverty: but he read, as he said, "solidly" while there; and he always regarded the University, and his college in particular, with veneration; and, in return, his memory is cherished here as it ought to be. Pembroke is one of the colleges that has undergone restoration, and the tower has now a smarter appearance than when Johnson lodged in it.

———

Having surveyed, as far as appears needful, what belongs to the University, we may now turn to the city. In population it exceeds Cambridge by a few hundreds only, being 23,656 at the census of 1841; the number of residents in the University was, at the same time, somewhat under 2,000. Oxford is a corporate city, governed by a mayor, aldermen, and town-councillors, and it sends two members to Parliament. It has the usual corporate buildings; but there is nothing in them to call for description here. Of the general appearance of the town we have spoken. The streets have some shops and private houses about them that are noticeable on account of their antiquity; and there is scarcely a street in any part of the city that does not, from some point, show one or more of the academic buildings combining with the neighbouring houses into a picturesque group. The modern shops are, many of them, of the most approved and newest style, and, both in that respect and in the display of goods, would do credit to the metropolis. In our account of Cambridge we spoke of the very characteristic quiet of the streets : this is observable also at Oxford, but not, perhaps, to the same degree. The difference may arise from its being nearer London, and in a more frequented line of road ; but we doubt if it does entirely. Oxford has altogether a more " stylish" air,—perhaps from the students being, on the whole, of a more aristocratic class,—and also has the appearance of not being so fully given up to educational observances. All who know Oxford know that it has a goodly band of earnest and laborious and most devoted students ; but perhaps it has also a larger proportion of idlers, and their doings are such as most catch the attention of a looker-on.

We have mentioned the walls of Oxford, and that a piece is to be seen, in a perfect state, in the garden of New College. Other fragments may be seen by Merton College, in George-lane, and elsewhere ; but as they are not in nearly so perfect a condition, it is not worth while to refer to them more particularly. A tower of the old castle is still standing. The site of the other parts of it is now occupied by the County Hall, a prodigious structure, built some seven or eight years ago, in the modern castellated style. The old tower, which can be pretty well seen from the Mill-stream, is called St. George's Tower. A small crypt and some other slight vestiges of the castle also remain, but they are only of interest to the professed antiquary. Some mounds, that are supposed to have been thrown up at the famous siege, may be seen close to the remains of the castle. These are all the remains that are left, of a warlike nature, connected with the old city.

Two or three churches must be briefly noticed. Oxford has a good many that would be considered of uncommon value elsewhere, but here may be safely left unnamed. All that it has are now well cared for ; several have been restored with great taste ; and probably in no other place where there are so many churches (there are here fourteen or fifteen parish churches), are they in such beautiful condition. The oldest church in Oxford is St. Peter's-in-the-East, which stands just by Queen's College, and adjoining to St. Edmund's Hall. A more interesting church than this, of its size, it would be difficult to find. It has a crypt of very ancient date—it is generally said, of the ninth century, but probably Norman,—which is almost a repetition, in little, of the crypt of Winchester Cathedral. The chancel of the church is Norman, and has a groined roof ; the nave is also partly Norman, but it has windows of later date ; and the south aisle is altogether of the decorated order. The whole has been restored with the greatest care ; and its appearance inside is exquisite, almost the ideal of an English Protestant church. The exterior is no less striking than the

inside : the Norman parts show traces of the ancient carvings, but they are mostly destroyed. The porch is a fine one of the time of Henry VI., and above it is a room for a priest. Altogether the parts, though of such various times and differences in style, appear by no means discordant, but group together most artistically. A Guide-book, of a century back, thus records the glory of the parish of which this is the parish church :—" This has more to boast of than any other parish in Europe, or even in the world, as containing within itself, besides the grand colleges (not to say palaces) of Magdalen, New, Queen's, and, in part, University ; also Hertford ; the Halls of St. Edmund, Magdalen, and part of St. Alban's ; and as having two peals of ten bells, one of six, and three organs, two of which are used, twice a day, in choral service."

But the most magnificent church in Oxford is St. Mary's, the University Church, so called from the University sermons being preached in it. No one who has been at Oxford can forget this church, from the grand feature its spire forms in every view of the High-street, and, indeed, from all the most visited parts of the city. The church itself is large, and of noble appearance. The various parts, as is so frequently the case in ancient churches, have been built at very different periods ; but, internally at least, they harmonise admirably since the late very judicious alterations and repairs. The arrangements of the Vice-chancellor's throne and the stalls of the University dignitaries, and, indeed, the whole of the fittings, contribute not a little to the general good effect. When, on some " gaudy," all the great men and doctors are assembled in their robes of scarlet and gold, with the rest of the members in full state, the church affords a rare sight to a stranger ; but at all times it is an interesting and characteristic one, and should be seen. After all it is the outside that dwells most on the memory ; and of this the " chief, probably, in point of interest to every visitor of the University, is the exquisitely beautiful tower and spire." We quote from Parker's ' Handbook to Oxford,' an admirable guide to the architecture of the good city ; the account of the spire is thus continued :—" The panels and gables of the pinnacles testify to its date, being lined with a profusion of pomegranates in honour of Eleanor of Castile, the mother of Edward II., in whose reign it appears probable the work was completed. The superintendent of the work was Eleanor's almoner, Adam de Brom, whose chapel beneath, on the western side of the tower-base, was founded at this time, but rebuilt in the fifteenth century, at the same time with the nave." This spire is shown prominently in the engraving of the High-street ; but its marvellous beauty can there only be faintly pourtrayed. The carving that covers, without crowding, the buttresses and finials, has a richness and intricacy that it would require a Prout or Roberts to give effect to. From the nature of the stone, of which this and a large part of the other buildings of Oxford are constructed, the surface undergoes constant disintegration, and produces on the old Gothic work the peculiar richness, to which we before alluded. The effect on this spire has gone as far as it can with safety be permitted. When examined from the outside of the Radcliffe dome, which brings you about on a level with the base of the spire, the eroded appearance is quite startling: much that from below you thought to be the effect of elaborate workmanship is here seen to be the result of decay; and a large portion has become wholly indistinct. We suppose the tourist does not need to be told that he will only half see the city, unless he sees it by "the pale moonlight." The effect of the moonlight on this church and spire is delicious: it brightens in that mystic manner poets often attempt to describe, but no words can adequately convey a notion of. But all Oxford is glorious by moonlight. The High-street puts on quite a new splendour.

Before we leave the church we may notice the singular porch opposite Oriel-street, whose twisted columns and entirely unusual style is sure to attract attention. A piece of history is attached to it:—"It was erected in 1637, by Dr. Morgan Owens, chaplain to Archbishop Laud, at an expense of £230. Over it is a statue of the Virgin with the Child in her arms, holding a small crucifix, which at the time of its erection gave such offence to the puritans, that it was included in the articles of impeachment against the archbishop," (Parker.)

The spire seen beyond that of St. Mary's, in the engraving of the High-street, belongs to All Saints' church, a curious structure, erected, at the beginning of the eighteenth century, by Dean Aldrich, D.D., the author of 'Elements of Civil Architecture,' who has here attempted the impracticable task of uniting the characteristics of Grecian and Gothic architecture.

Leaving all the rest of the churches, we shall visit one more edifice, one of the latest and most graceful of the recent architectural additions to Oxford—the Martyrs' Memorial (Cut, No. 6). It stands at the northern entrance to the town, just by Mary Magdalen church, being the nearest suitable spot to the scene where the martyrs Cranmer, Ridley, and Latimer met their doom. The history of that event is too familiar to need repeating here. The imprisonment, the mock disputations and trial, the momentary retraction of Cranmer—are all a household tale. The exact spot where the stakes were fixed is not quite certain; but it is believed to have been in the city ditch, opposite Balliol College, where now stands the row of houses in Broad-street. Previous to their execution the prelates were confined in a prison called Boccardo, a gate-house which stood across Cornmarket-street, by St. Michael's Church; it was removed in 1778. From the top of this prison Cranmer is said to have beheld the execution of his old associates. The memorial of their martyrdom was at first intended to be a church; but, for various reasons, it was finally deemed advisable to erect a cross, and, with the surplus funds, to add an additional aisle to the neighbouring church of St. Mary Magdalene, which should be called the Martyrs' Aisle. The first stone of the Memorial was .aid on the 19th of May, 1841, exactly three centuries after Cranmer's English Bill was finished and "authorised by royal authority" to be read. Messrs. Scott and Moffatt were the architects whose design was selected for execution; and, as it now stands completed, a very beautiful one it is. These gentlemen took for their model the Eleanor Cross at Waltham; but, instead of a mere copy, they produced a work that, in many respects, certainly surpasses their original. It is an hexagonal structure of three stories, mounted on a platform of steps. The total height is 73 feet, and the gradations are so easy that the whole is at once airy and substantial. The style is the decorated, and every part is enriched with most elaborate carvings. The lower story has the inscription. In the second story, under canopies of exceeding richness, are the statues of the three martyrs, admirably sculptured by Mr. Weekes. The whole is surmounted by a very elegant cross. The position of the Memorial is a very happy one, and it is no small ornament to the northern approach to the city: altogether it would be difficult to find a public memorial that exhibits more of beauty and propriety. The adjacent aisle of the church is in the same style of architecture, and is made to be, in its ornamentation, allusive to the martyrs.

Before he quits Oxford for good the visitor should stroll at leisure over the Christ Church Meadow, and peep again into the groves of Magdalen. The Meadow belongs to Christ Church College, and is kept in order at the cost of the college, but it is open to the public without any reserve. The Isis and Cherwell bound three sides of it, on the fourth are the college buildings and Merton field. It is a mile and a quarter round; the Wide Walk, a fine avenue of elms—now beginning to decay—is a quarter of a mile long. In thinking of these meadows, it is hardly possible not to contrast them with the Walks of Cambridge, yet there are few points of comparison between them; the walks of Cambridge are beautiful in themselves, but they derive their chief beauty from the backs of so many of the principal colleges opening upon them. It is not so here. These meadows are so situated, that only occasional and partial glimpses are caught of the buildings; when such are caught, they are very lovely, but they are few and far between; in Cambridge they are continuous. Yet there is a great charm about these meadows. The long winding shady walks by the Cherwell, a succession of close shut-in reaches, yet constantly changing; and though you know that you are far from alone, so seemingly secluded: then that, again, by the Isis (as the Thames is called here), always so lively and gay; and the many other walks that need not be mentioned; it is impossible not to have a kind of liking for them that is not felt for those of the sister University. And you can get, too, so readily over to those more retired ones of Magdalen, the perfection of Academic groves! We give a representation of a favourite peep from Christ

Church Meadows, over Merton field, where the spire
of the Cathedral, the Tom gateway, and parts of the
buildings of Christ Church and Merton Colleges,
form a very pretty architectural back-ground. (Cut,
No. 7.)

And now we must bid Oxford farewell! Gentle
reader, if you have not been there, take our advice
and go as soon as you can. It is a pleasant place to
visit. We have told you what is to be seen in it, and
you will find the readiest and most courteous access
to whatever is worth seeing. The University build-
ngs are generally open. Into and about the college
quadrangles you may stroll at pleasure, and about the
gardens, too, in most instances. If you wish to look
over a college hall or chapel, the porter (whose den
is generally in the entrance gateway) will readily open
it to you. Then there are several very good Guide-
books, with maps attached, that will direct you to
every locality : or you may carry in your hand one of
Spiers's pretty cards, which will still more readily
indicate the whereabouts of each object. If, however,
you prefer a living 'Guide,' you may be suited : the
profession is rather numerous in Oxford. There are
always some hanging on at the inns, and hotels, and
about the chief buildings. You may trust to their
guidance. They know every crook and corner, and
are quite expert in leading most readily to every object.
They are rather proud of their dexterity that way.
We knew one who boasted that he could save a party
three hours in "going the round," though they had a
proctor to lead them. Generally, every real guide (for
alas ! there are charlatans, even at Oxford,) has a
regular routine ; and if you catch one of the old hands,
it may be rather amusing to watch him. They are a
somewhat characteristic class. They have commonly
a sort of decayed look, are grave in the face, short and
reserved in speech, and are clad in a suit that looks
like the exuvia of some reverend demy, or Merton
post-master — though sometimes they sport a seedy
green shooting-jacket, the vestige of some studious
junior soph. They always carry a short stick, in
unconscious imitation, we imagine, of the vice's
pokers, for their respect for all University customs
is profound—nay, awful. They move along in front
of their party with a short, springy, but serious
step, never stopping,—except at some "station," to
tell you that "here you have a fine view of the
towers of All Souls, which are thought so much of,
and the Dome of Radcliffe ;" or that "this is the
place where the 'drawing gents' stand to take off the
High-street," or some such thing,—till they bring you
to the door of the show place, when, with a respectful
bow, they step aside, and wait till you come out again,
for they seldom enter a building. Wonderful is their
knowledge, too, of all sorts of men in authority, and
perfect their information respecting University costume.

6.—THE MARTYR'S MEMORIAL.

7.—VIEW FROM CHRIST-CHURCH MEADOWS.

They know the exact obeisance that is due to every one, from the Vice-Chancellor down to the scout ; and are great upon the theme of sleeves and leading-strings. But as we said, withal they are bashful. They have a growing, uncomfortable, depressing suspicion that their day is almost over—that they are behind the age! They see with dismay the increasing habit people have of referring to books, instead of to them, for information. And they resent it "in sullen silence." Seldom, now, do they volunteer an explanation. It is only when they have to guide a rustic party—fortunately for them a very common case—that they in these days come out in force. At such times they are sure they will be credited, that those who seem to listen are not doing so in mere scorn, and they pour out a whole flood of traditive lore.

But let us warn the visitor not to suffer either guide-book or guide to persuade him that after a hasty scamper through the city, and a hurried peep into a few of the buildings, he knows " all about Oxford." As we said before, if you were a Scott, and had spent a week in its exploration, with a Heber to guide you, you would find at the end of it that "the time had been too short to convey" more than " a grand but indistinct picture of towers and chapels, and oriels, and vaulted halls, and libraries, and paintings." But as he hoped, so you will find, that "in a little time your ideas will develop themselves more distinctly ;" and you will recollect your visit with a pleasure such as no other city will yield. This is essentially one of those places, in looking on which, you are impressed

" Not only with the sense
Of present pleasure, but with pleasing thought
That in this moment there is life and food
For future years."

A visit to Oxford, whether in fact or in description, would be thought very imperfect if some of the celebrated places in its vicinity were not visited also. To have been at Oxford, and not to have visited Blenheim, would be regarded as an evidence of strange insensibility, or profound want of taste. Howard's being at Rome, without entering the Vatican, would hardly be thought more unaccountable. It would be a thing, in short, that a man who should confess to, had need have a very superior character for wit, or wisdom, or wealth, to save him from being pitied for want of capacity, or laughed at for an ignoramus. We cannot afford to leave Blenheim unvisited.

Blenheim is about eight miles from Oxford; you had better get there as speedily as you can by the morning coach : the house can only be seen between eleven o'clock and one, and there is nothing to look at on the road. Woodstock you may see, after your return from the Park. You enter the grounds of Blenheim by the ' grand triumphal arch,' built in honour of the famous Duke of Marlborough by his

scarcely less famous duchess. Nothing whatever is seen either of the house or grounds till you pass through this gate, and the effect is certainly magnificent, as they burst at once upon you. Dr. Waagen says of Blenheim, " If nothing were to be seen in England but this seat and its treasures of art, there would be no reason to complain of going to this country. The whole is on so grand a scale, that no prince in the world need to be ashamed of it for his summer residence ; and at the same time it is a noble monument of the gratitude of the English nation to the great Duke of Marlborough." (' Art and Artists in England,' v. ii. p. 27.) What the learned German says is very true, the only drawback being the recollection of the pitiful manner in which the nation carried out the expression of its gratitude. The history of the erection of Blenheim is quite a dramatic chapter (serio-comic) in the history of English architecture. The parliament voted the building of the palace, but neglected to provide funds for the purpose—leaving that part for Queen Anne to see to ; and while the queen lived the works went on pretty regularly. After her death, however, the Court would no longer issue treasury orders ; and the duke very naturally objected to pay money for a house that the country had by its legislature resolved should be built for and not by him. Somehow the works went on, though very slowly ; while the accounts and responsibilities became continually more involved, till the climax was reached by getting into Chancery. The duke seems to have in part paid the workmen (who were never wholly paid), and after his death the building was completed by his duchess. But never was poor architect worse used than the designer of Blenheim. Vanbrugh was appointed to realize in stone and mortar the gratitude of the country. From the death of the queen, the building that was to immortalize his name was a constant source of vexation to him. He could not only get no money for his own labours, but, for a time, there seemed a chance of his having to pay the workmen out of his own pocket—at least the duchess's lawyers endeavoured to show that he was the party liable. Vanbrugh had provoked that celebrated virago, by the rather free exercise of both tongue and pen at her expense, and she had too much wit herself not to feel the keenness of his wit, and too fiery a temper to sit quietly under an affront. The duke, in his will, left her £10,000 a-year, as Vanbrugh wrote, " to spoil Blenheim her own way." Her first step was to dismiss Vanbrugh ; and though she had wit enough to cause his designs to be adhered to, she would not permit him so much as to see his own building. She even carried her haughtiness further ; for when, on one occasion, he accompanied the noble family of the Howards, who wished to see Blenheim, the duchess, not content with the standing order she had given against his admission, having (as Vanbrugh tells the story) "somehow learned that his wife was one of the company, sent an express the night before we came there, with orders that, if she came with the

Castle-Howard ladies, the servants should not suffer her to see either house, garden, or even to enter the park : so she was forced to sit all day long, and keep me company at the inn."* But Vanbrugh's vexations did not cease with the building. Its completion was the signal for a general and unanimous attack from the wits and satirists of the day, who could not understand how a clever playwright should also be a clever architect. If ridicule, in every variety of wit and banter, could prove a work of art to be a failure, Blenheim would only exist to be laughed at. For awhile the ridicule was successful, and no one was found bold enough to admire, or even to defend, the " hollowed quarry," till Sir Joshua Reynolds went a little out of his way in one of his Presidential Discourses (the thirteenth), to point out " the greater display of imagination than is to be found, perhaps, in any other," the poetic feeling, the grandeur, and the painter-like effects of light and shadow ; then, indeed, it found admirers enough, and the praise became as excessive as the censure had hitherto been. Now that it is looked at impartially, professional men seem pretty well agreed that it is a work of uncommon excellence and of undeniable defects ; while the ordinary observer, who cares little whether it is built in exact accordance with every classic rule, or in entire defiance of all of them, sees in it a work of manifest splendour, united with a solidity that appears to defy the assaults of time ; and if he be offended with a multiplicity of parts that seem to overload and destroy the simplicity and unity of the general design, he also recognises a variety and play of outline combining with the massiveness that is so striking, and together forming a whole that is as pleasing as it is uncommon. (Cut, No. 8.)

However much he may have admired the exterior, the visitor will hardly have been prepared for the splendid effect of the Hall, in which surely Vanbrugh has shown no small share of poetic genius. It is perhaps the most striking entrance hall in the kingdom. The impression of magnificence produced on entering the building is fully retained throughout it. The rooms are nobly proportioned, and admirably calculated for the display of princely pomp. The architectural grandeur of the various apartments is abundantly supported by the richness of the furniture and fittings, and the value and beauty of the works of art and vertû that adorn them. It is well known that the paintings at Blenheim are among the finest in England. For obtaining masterpieces of art, the great duke possessed unusual opportunities from the state of the continent at that time, his own connections there, and his great wealth ; of all which he fully availed himself. The number of paintings is very large, and their rank is of the highest. Among them are works of most of the great masters, and

* The reader will find the particulars of the building of Blenheim, and of the architect's vexations, very pleasantly related in Disraeli's ' Curiosities of Literature.'

generally they are valuable specimens of their abilities. Of Raffaelle there is one remarkably fine picture : it is a large altar-piece having the Virgin and Child in the centre ; the date on it is 1505, and it is generally referred to by judges as a characteristic and valuable example of the great painter's early manner. Nothing hardly can surpass its simplicity, purity, and beauty, or the quiet religious character it possesses. There are also several very good Titians ; but the grand feature of the collection is the Rubenses. Dr. Waagen, who was already familiar with every leading gallery of pictures in Europe, calls this " the most considerable collection of paintings by Rubens in the possession of any private person ; and with which not even any royal galleries can be compared, except those of Munich, Vienna, Madrid and Paris." " It is especially important," he continues, " and his opinion is the more noteworthy because he is throughly conversant with all that is technical and mechanical in pictures, and is consequently a thoroughly competent judge in that respect,—" it is especially important, because the pictures are almost throughout by the hand of Rubens alone, and are chiefly of his earlier and middle periods." The Rubenses are indeed a rich treat. Waagen said it was worth travelling from Germany only to see Blenheim ; we may more soberly affirm that the examination of these Rubenses would amply repay a journey from any part of England. Wonderful as many of the paintings of Rubens seem when viewed apart, it is only when you can examine such a collection of them as is here assembled, that the amazing luxuriance of his pencil can be appreciated. You then begin to understand the enthusiasm with which painters are accustomed to talk of Rubens. And to see many is needful, for at first view there appears to be something contradictory in what is said of the fascination of his style. Here, for example, is the widest range of subjects, from the gravest in the Christian history to the most sensual in the heathen mythology ; and neither in the one class is their aught of religious severity or even sobriety, nor in the other of classic beauty or grace, and yet though wanting what should seem these first requisites, every competent judge acknowleges his productions to be most admirable as works of art. We know what is always said about the overpowering splendour and vivid harmony of his colouring, and the facility of his execution ; but these alone would not be sufficient. The real charm that goes along with that of his colour and executive power, and indeed is the cause of them, is here seen ; it is the painter's own intense enjoyment of his work. You can no more doubt that Rubens' heart was in his employment when using his brush, than you can that Burns had his engaged when writing his vivid poems. The bold disregard of all those minor beauties and blemishes which so perplex and cramp ordinary men, marks alike the man of genius and the enjoyment of genius in its work. And hence that thorough abandonment of himself to his theme, and the consequent genuineness and originality. But we must pass on :

we should like to gossip over some of these pictures, but we may not,—

> " Our time
> Asks thriftier using."

Hardly less choice in their way are the Vandykes. The picture of Charles I. on the dun horse, and several others, are universally famed. Nor do the Reynoldses suffer very much alongside of the Vandykes. Had Reynolds but had a safer palette, we should have still more reason to point with pride to the portraits of our great countryman. Of the rooms we cannot of course speak particularly, but two seem to require separate mention—the chapel and the library. The former contains an immense piece of sculpture, the monument to the Duke and Duchess of Marlborough, by Rysbrach—which is admitted by all connoisseurs to be the greatest work of that artist, though the word is used by them in different senses. The library is a remarkably fine room—too fine, indeed, for a library. In it is a most elaborate statue of Queen Anne, also by Rysbrach. We need hardly say that there is no deficiency in busts and portraits of the great duke, in whose honour this splendid palace was raised. On leaving the house the porter will show any gentleman, who may desire it, the Titian-room, as it is called. It contains a number of paintings which were discovered by Sir Joshua Reynolds, packed up in some obscure place about the mansion, and at his instance they were hung in a room fitted up for their reception. They are called 'The Loves of the Gods,' and a good deal of mystery used to be attached to them. But they are really very frigid affairs, and might even hang in a Quaker's private study without much danger. They are painted on leather, and have a dull trellised back-ground. To call them Titian's is a pure absurdity. That fiery old Venetian would indeed have made something of such a series: so would Rubens or Etty. These are the works of a more mechanic mythology-monger, and are as cold as though wrought by a scholiast on Ovid. As paintings, they are of but very moderate power.

But we must on. The private gardens are of much celebrity : the public are not admitted, without a special order, to view them. The park may be freely seen ; and it is worth rambling over. It is a delightful thing,

8.—BLENHEIM.

on a fine summer's day, to stroll about its glades, or rest under the shadow of the mighty trees, after an hour or two spent in conning the treasures of the palace. The park contains a very prominent memorial to Marlborough, in the shape of a lofty column, which is surmounted by the statue of the hero ; while on the base is an inscription, of wonderful length, recording his deeds, &c. The column was erected by the duchess : the inscription is said to have been written by Bolingbroke. The visitor may read it, and judge for himself whether it be laid at the right door. We have read a good many of Bolingbroke's writings, but as we never succeeded in getting any way near the end of this inscription, we cannot pretend to be competent to speak from the resemblance of style. As he returns towards the bridge, the visitor should take notice of the house, as seen with the broad sheet of water in front ; and also as seen (and Vanbrugh evidently meant it to be so seen) in combination with the piquant bridge. If we mistake not, the excellence Reynolds pointed out will be recognized—the union of the building with the surrounding locality, and the great care which " the architect took that his work should not appear crude and hard : that is, that it did not abruptly start out of the ground without expectation or preparation."

Woodstock will, of course, be looked at on quitting Blenheim. But there is nothing in it worthy of note. It is a *most* dull town—the very realization of stagnation. You welcome the glove-shops (the only shops in the town !) as a relief—though there is nobody in them, or looking at them. Everybody stops in-doors at Woodstock. The very children stay at home. Even curiosity seems dead. We never once, at any time, saw a female of any age or grade come to a door or window to look after a stranger—a circumstance we never observed in any other town or village in Great Britain. The dulness is perfect, and infects our pen— we shall leave off talking about it.

In olden times we fancy there was not much more to see in Woodstock ; for old Camden observes, with very unusual gruffness, that Woodstock having nothing of its own to show, boasts of having given birth to Chaucer. Alas ! the boast is a vain one. But there does seem reason to believe that he did not only dwell but also write some of his poems (if not the ' Canterbury Tales') there,

" Within a lodge out of the way,
Beside a well in a forest."

And our " Bonny Queen Bess " was imprisoned for a while at Woodstock Palace ; and there, as Holinshed tells us, " she hearing upon a time out of her garden a certain milkmaid singing pleasantly, wished herself to be a milkmaid as she was, saying that her case was better, and her life merrier."

Perhaps the reader has recollected that the Fair Rosamond dwelt at Woodstock, and wondered why we have not mentioned her. The omission was intentional, or rather the notice was intentionally deferred, that we might say all that concerned her at once—for Woodstock is not the only place in the neighbourhood of Oxford that claims a share in that fair dame. We need not now say that the labyrinth at Woodstock is an invention. If the visitor is anxious to see what relic there is here of her, he will find her " spring " or " bath " in Blenheim Park, close by the north side of the bridge. If he can credit the tradition that asserts it to have been hers, well ; if not, the spot is at any rate a quiet, cool spot, and he will not repent having sought it out. But if nothing marks the residence of Rosamond at Woodstock, he may find, about a couple of miles up the Thames from Oxford, on the Berkshire side of the river, the remains of a little priory chapel, wherein she was undoubtedly buried. The last years of her life were spent in the nunnery at Godstow, to which she was a considerable benefactress ; and there her bones were laid. A certain bishop some years afterwards had them cast out from the sacred edifice ; but the more generous nuns collected them as soon as they dared, and reinterred them by the altar ; and there they remained till Thomas Cromwell's commissioners broke open her tomb. The ruins of Godstow Nunnery lie in a pleasant spot by the " silver Thames," to which there is a very pleasant river-side stroll from the learned city.

About three miles west of Oxford is a place that the pen of the Northern Magician has made famous. The enthusiastic romancist who visits it, however, will, we fear, be disappointed. Mickle tells us that

" Full many a traveller oft hath sigh'd,
And pensive wept the countess' fall,
As wand'ring onwards they've espied
The haunted towers of Cumnor Hall."

Much more then might the pensive traveller, who carries ' Kenilworth ' in his memory, expect to weep now. But, alas ! there is now nothing to weep over, unless (as has been recommended) he carry ' Kenilworth ' in his pocket. The haunted towers are no longer to be espied : indeed, it will need some skill to trace even the foundations of Cumnor Hall. There remains, however, an inn, and swinging in front of it is " the sign of the bonny Black Bear," with " Giles Gosling " written under it, as of old, and the stranger may, if he pleases, believe it *the* inn, and " avouch himself *not* utterly indifferent to reputation as a traveller, by wetting a cup at it." The church may help him a little, for there he will see a showy tomb to the memory of the veritable Antony Foster ; though he will perhaps be provoked by the encomiastic inscription upon it. There is also an old building now used for an almshouse, or something of the sort ; but we do not recollect whether there be any history attached to it.

If possible, the visitor should not depart from Oxford without indulging in a *row* down the river to Nuneham Courtney. Nuneham is one of the chief lions of the neighbourhood, though it is, perhaps, hardly in such repute as a few years back; but it is a very beautiful place, and the row to it will afford some very lovely glimpses of Thames scenery—and also, in all probability, some glimpses of Oxford boating. Nuneham was the creation of a somewhat eccentric nobleman, the Earl of Harcourt, who sought to cultivate here all the arts and some of the moralities. He built (or altered) the mansion, built the church, pulled down the old village, and built a new one at some distance further from the house; kept a small college of poets, who spun a large quantity of verse; collected pictures and statues, or had them made after patterns designed on the establishment; had his park carved out and planted in the most scientific style of landscape-gardening; and then, in the way of the morals, gave prizes for a good many of them to the villagers, with stars, and ribbons, and inscriptions on the outside of their houses! Withal he made Nuneham a remarkable place. The house, partly from his own design, is not very handsome; but it was admired at the time for " simple dignity." (Cut, No. 9.) The church is the oddest in the county—the chief feature of it being " six Ionic columns, that support a pediment, above which a dome rises in the centre :" it was designed by Earl Harcourt, with some aid from Athenian Stuart. Near the house is a flower-garden, formed by the taste of Mason, the chief of his lordship's band of poets, and largely decorated with columns and urns and tablets, on which are poetic inscriptions selected from the Idyllic poets of ancient Rome and modern Italy, and our own older bards; or composed for the purpose by Mason or Whitehead. The gardens may be seen on Wednesday or Friday, and are worth seeing, as one of the most elaborate specimens of the horticultural taste of the last century, as propounded by the author of the ' English Garden.' The house used to contain some very curious tapestry, a collection of pictures, and various works of art or rarity, that were rather celebrated; but they have been to a considerable extent removed; and as the apartments are not now open to the public, it hardly seems worth while to inquire particularly what remain. But if nothing be seen but the park, the journey will not be in vain. It is of considerable extent, covering some twelve hundred acres, and is well stored with timber; and the surface is broken into gentle elevations, woody banks and glens, and broad verdant glades. ' Capability Brown' brought the domain into its present form, and it was considered as a grand triumph of his skill. Walpole, in his *dilettanti* style, declared it to contain " scenes worthy of the bold pencil of Rubens, and subjects for the tranquil sunshine of Claude de Lorraine." Happily, Nature has broken away from the confines in which Brown had bound her, and the stiffness and pedantry have given place to ease and freedom, though somewhat too many traces of the old boarding-school training are yet visible about her. The views from the park are of exceeding beauty. The "shining spires and pinnacles" of Oxford in the far distance have a singular charm; and the windings of the Thames lead the delighted eye along luxuriant meads, and banks crowded with lofty trees, into a wide and varied range of gently undulating distance. In every direction the prospect is different, and in all beautiful. It is hardly worth while to add, that in the park are several objects that visitors will do well to notice. The most attractive, from its size and singularity, is the large square conduit called Carfax, that formerly stood at the meeting of the four principal streets in Oxford (whence its name, corrupted from *quatrefois* or *voies*). Another is a tree which stands by the terrace, known as ' Bab's Tree ;' its history is commemorated in some verses by Whitehead, which are placed by it, and may be found told in his usual pleasant prose, by Southey, in the recently published volume of ' The Doctor.' We must not forget also to state that the grounds are, and have been for a long time, liberally and freely thrown open to the public. The late Earl caused a picturesque cottage to be erected for the accommodation of the holiday visitors, which stands on the bank of a branch of the Thames, across which is thrown a rustic bridge.

———

On his way to or from Nuneham, the visitor should on no account fail to turn aside to Iffley. The village is merely a rude, irregular gathering of houses along a hill-side; but the church is perhaps the finest example left of a Norman village church. It consists of a very heavy massive tower, of singularly sombre appearance from the river and adjacent country, a nave and chancel. "The tower is low, and divides the church into two nearly equal portions. On each side of it are two windows with circular arches supported by pillars. As in almost all these Norman edifices, the doorways are the most elaborately ornamented, and most striking features. That on the western side is the finest, and has long been known and admired by antiquaries. It is large, and has a bold circular arch with receding mouldings, carved in the richest manner, with the zigzag and other ornaments; the outer arch has a double row of grotesque heads, and one of animals above. These carvings have been supposed to have an allegoric signification ; they are rude in style, but they possess on the whole somewhat of grandeur of effect. The doorways on the northern and southern sides of the church are likewise considerably enriched. The southern is singular, but far less beautiful than the western doorway. On each side of it are two pillars, with the usual Norman ornaments, but all differing from each other ; they support a circular enriched arch. Over the western door there was originally a circular window ornamented with zigzag tracery, but a window with a pointed arch was inserted within it on occasion of some alterations being made in the church, it is supposed, from the form of the arch, in the fifteenth century. At the same time, several other windows in the sides of the building were altered in a similar manner. The original circle is still plainly visible, however, in each instance."—*Rambles by Rivers : The Thames.*

The whole has recently been restored in excellent taste, and is now such a village church as it is quite a pleasure to meet with ; to say nothing of its claim on account of its venerable antiquity. In the churchyard is a fragment of an ancient cross ; and close by it is a yew-tree of enormous girth. Down in a nook by the river, where the pedestrian may cross the Thames, is a very old and picturesque water-mill, that has found a place in the sketch-book of almost every artist who has seen it.

9.—NUNEHAM COURTNEY.

NORTHAMPTONSHIRE.

BLISWORTH is the central station of the county; from whence diverges the great line to Peterborough, with sixteen stations,—the route of which presents a constant succession of beautiful and truly English rural scenery, of rich lowland pastures, watered by the winding rivers, and bounded by hills, on which, like sentinels, stands a row of ancient church towers.

The first station is NORTHAMPTON, which stands on a hill on the banks of the river Nene. It is a remarkably pleasant town, with several fine old buildings, an ancient church, an open market square, neat clean streets, and suburbs of pretty villas, overlooking, from the hill top, fat green meadows, flooded in winter. Shoemaking, on a wholesale scale, is the principal occupation of the inhabitants. For strong shoes Northampton can compete in any foreign market; and a good many light articles, cut after French patterns, have been successfully made since the trade was thrown open by Peel's tariff. There are several factories, in which large numbers of young persons are employed; but the majority work by the piece at home for the master manufacturers. Northampton is also great in the fairs and markets of a rich agricultural district, and rejoices over races twice a-year, in which the facilities of the railroad have rendered some compensation to the innkeepers for the loss of the coaching trade. The church of All Saints, in the centre of the town, has an ancient embattled tower, which escaped the great fire of 1675; St. Peter's, near the West Bridge, a remarkably curious specimen of enriched Norman; St. Sepulchre's, a round church of the twelfth century, all deserve enumeration. There are also two hospitals, the only remains of many religious houses which existed before the Réformation. St. John's consists of a chapel and a large hall, with apartments for inferior poor persons; St. Thomas's is for twenty poor alms-women. No vestiges, beyond the earthworks, remain of the castle built by Simon de St. Liz, who was created Earl of Northampton by William the Conqueror. Northampton was a royal residence during the reigns of Richard I., John, and Henry III.; a battlefield during the wars of the Barons and the wars of the Roses; but the ancient character of the town was almost entirely destroyed by the great fire of 1675—not without benefit to the health, though at the expense of the picturesqueness of this ancient borough. Northampton is important as the capital town of one of our finest grazing and hunting counties, where soil and climate are both favourable to the farmer. Large numbers of the Scotch, Welch, and Herefords, sold in Smithfield, are fed in the yards and finished in the pastures of Northamptonshire.

WEEDON is the next station, after Blisworth. The church, a very ancient building, contains portions of Norman, and various styles of English architecture. The importance of Weedon rests in its being the site of a strongly-fortified central depot for artillery, small arms, and ammunition, with extensive barracks, well worth seeing, but not to be seen without an order from the Board of Ordnance. The Weedon system of fortification eschews lofty towers and threatening embattled walls, and all that constitutes the picturesque; so that Weedon Barracks look scarcely more warlike than a royal rope manufactory.

After leaving Weedon we pass through Kilsby Tunnel, which was once considered as one of the wonders of the world—being 2423 yards in length.

WARWICKSHIRE.

RUGBY, which is situated about eighty-eight miles from London, is the great central station of the county. Here commences one of several roads to the north, either by Leicester, Nottingham, and Lincoln, or by Derby and Sheffield; and hence we may either proceed to Stafford by the direct route of the Trent Valley—a line which is rendered classical by the memory of Sir Robert Peel, who turned its first sod with a silver spade—or we may select the old original line through Coventry, Birmingham, and Wolverhampton, passing through a network of little railways leading to Warwick and Leamington. A continuation of the Trent Valley line intersects the Pottery district, where the cheapest delft and the most exquisite specimens of china ware are produced with equal success.

Rugby owes its chief importance to its celebrated public school, which was founded in the time of Queen Elizabeth. It is built in the Tudor style, and consists mostly of a fine quadrangle, with cloisters, and an elegantly detached chapel.   It has about 300 scholars, 50 of whom are on the foundation, an endowment now producing about £5000 a-year, and 14 valuable exhibitions to the universities. In the year 1827 the head mastership of the School became vacant ; and the trustees—a body of twelve country gentlemen and noblemen—selected, to the dismay of all the orthodox, the Rev. Thomas Arnold, late fellow of Oriel College, Oxford. He raised and improved the standard of classical learning, in its widest sense, from which the scholars of Rugby gained a high standing at the universities.

From Rugby we proceed to the important city of COVENTRY, the great Warwickshire manufactory and mart of ribands and watches. First is seen the graceful spire of St. Michael's church ; then the green pastures of the Lammas, on which for centuries the freemen of Coventry have fed their cattle, appear in sight ; and we suddenly enter the venerable city and county of Coventry. A railroad here branches off to Nuneaton, distant ten miles, a sort of manufacturing dependancy of the great city ; and on the other, at the same distance, to Leamington, with a station at Kenilworth.

In addition to its manufacturing importance, Coventry affords rich food for the antiquarian, scenes of deep interest to the historical student, a legend for poets, a pageant for melodramatists, and a tableau for amateurs of *poses plastiques*.   Once upon a time kings held their courts and summoned parliaments at Coventry ; four hundred years ago the guilds of Coventry recruited, armed, clothed, and sent forth six hundred stout fellows to take part in the Wars of the Roses ; at Coventry the lists were pitched for Mary of Lancaster and Philip Mowbray, Duke of Norfolk, to decide in single combat their counter-charges before Richard II. At Coventry you will find the effigy of vile Peeping Tom, and can follow the course through which the fair Godiva rode naked, veiled by her modesty and flowing tresses, to save her townsmen from a grievous tax. To be sure, some English Niebuhrs have undertaken to prove the whole story a legend ; but mankind are still determined to believe in tradition and Alfred Tennyson's sonnet.

There are three ancient churches in Coventry—of which St. Michael's, built in the reign of Henry I., is the first ; the spire rising 303 feet from the ground, the lofty interior ornamented with a roof of oak, curiously carved, and several windows of stained glass.   St. Mary's Hall, a large building, now used for corporation council-meetings and festivities, erected in the reign of Henry VI., is one of the richest and most interesting vestiges of the ornamental architecture of England.   The principal room has a grotesquely-carved roof of oak, a gallery for minstrels, an armoury, a chair of state, and a great painted window, which need only the filling up of royal and noble personages, their attendants, and the rich burgesses of Coventry, to recall the time when Richard II. held his court in this ancient city, and, with "old John of Gaunt," settled the sentence on Harry of Hereford and Philip of Norfolk. In this chamber is to be seen a beautiful piece of tapestry, executed in 1450, measuring thirty feet by ten, and containing eighty figures.

In the free school, founded by John Moles in the reign of Henry VIII., Sir William Dugdale, the antiquarian and historian of Warwickshire, was educated.   The income is about £900 a-year, and the scholars have open to competition two fellowships of St. John's College, Oxon, one at Catherine's Hall, Cambridge, and six exhibitions at either university.   Previous to the investigations of the Charity Commissioners, the fine school-room was locked up, and the books of the library torn for waste paper to light fires. At present, under the reformed system, the school is attended by a large number of scholars.

There are more than a dozen educational and other charities for the benefit of the poor, enjoying a revenue of many thousands a-year.

OUR next station is the important one of BIRMINGHAM, the great focus of manufacturing industry, and the vast centre of railway reticulation. As a railway starting-point, Birmingham has become a wonderful place. In addition to those main lines and branches passed and noted on our journey down, it is also the centre at which meet the railroads to Derby and Sheffield ; to Worcester, Cheltenham, Gloucester, and Bristol ; to London through Oxford, by the Broad Gauge Great Western ; to Shrewsbury and Chester through Wolverhampton ; beside the little South Staffordshire lines, which form an omnibus route between Birmingham, Walsall, Dudley, and Lichfield, and other iron nets.

The old railway station of Birmingham stands at the foot of one of the hills on which the Hardware Village is built ; but the new station lands the passengers behind the Grammar School, in New Street,—the principal, and indeed the only handsome street of any length in Birmingham.

BIRMINGHAM.

A Bird's-Eye View.

There is a castle-keep, not far from the centre of the kingdom, from whence can be obtained one of the most remarkable views anywhere presented to the artist or the tourist. It is not a view of hill and dale, of mountain and water-fall, of craggy rock and dizzy precipice; it is not a sweep of country, spotted over with the ruins of cathedrals, abbeys, castles, baronial mansions, and other erections that tell of past days; it is not a commingling of lake scenery with land scenery, nor any of those picturesque groupings which distinguish a sea-coast.

Dudley Castle is the point of sight here selected; and the landscape viewed from it is the coal and iron district of South Staffordshire. On whichever side the view is taken, but especially towards the north and the east, the evidences of mining industry are truly remarkable. The grass of the fields shows no disinclination to grow, nor are there wanting many pleasant undulations of country; but the crust of the earth has been pierced in a hundred places; and wherever these perforations have occurred, there do we see red buildings and black smoke. These buildings and this smoke increase year after year—age after age; and if purchasers for the mining produce become as numerous as the sellers could wish, the buildings and the smoke will still further increase, and the green fields will be still further encroached upon

Although the name of South Staffordshire is here mentioned, a visitor to the district must be prepared to find himself repeatedly in the wrong as to the county in which he happens to be located at a particular moment. Geology has very little to do with counties. Geology makes the district what it is: counties are man's divisions. Taking Dudley Castle as a centre, we have to the north of us Tipton, Gornal, Sedgley, Bilston, Wolverhampton, Willenhall, and Wednesfield —all in Staffordshire, all within a distance of eight or nine miles, and all marked by the perforations into the "world underground," the red brick houses, and the black smoke. Taking next a more eastern direction, we find Great Bridge, Toll End, Darlaston, Wednesbury, Christchurch, West Bromwich, and Swan Village, all coming under the same description as the former group. But when the view bends round farther to the south, we find that the iron towns (for so they may well be termed) are fewer, and wider apart, and that they lie in four counties which are very much entangled together. For instance, Birmingham—the giant of the district—is in Warwickshire; Smethwick, Rowley Regis, Brierley Hill, Wordesley, and Kingswinford, are in Staffordshire; Oldbury and Halesowen are in Shropshire; while Dudley, Dudley Port, and Stourbridge, are in Worcestershire. So numerous are the outlying fragments of counties in this neighbourhood, that in going from Birmingham to Dudley Castle by way of

Oldbury, a distance by coach-road of about eight miles, we pass out of Warwickshire into Staffordshire, thence into Shropshire, thence again into Staffordshire, thence into Worcestershire, and a third time into Staffordshire; for although Dudley Town is in Worcestershire, Dudley Castle and grounds are in Staffordshire.

All the above towns, then, belong to the mining and manufacturing district, known by the general name of South Staffordshire. We shall have a little to say about most of them in a future page; but it will be well to take up the proposition just expressed, that "Geology makes the district what it is," and to show what is the nature of the mineral wealth that lies beneath the surface.

The district forms what is called by geologists a *coal-field*: it has layers of coal running, so far as is known, beneath the whole surface. This coal-field forms an irregular oblong, extending nearly from Rugeley in the north, to Halesowen in the south: but the northern half of this district is much less rich in coal and iron than the southern; insomuch that we may take Wednesfield and Halesowen as the north and south limits of the effective coal-field. The western limit approaches to Wolverhampton, and the eastern nearly to Birmingham. Taking the extreme limit up to Rugeley, the district measures about twenty miles long by six or seven broad. This coal-field is encircled on all sides by the new red sandstone formation. The transition from one to the other of these geological formations is very distinct, not only in the appearance of the surface, but in the existing state of vegetation, the extinct species of fossil animals and vegetables, the industrial employments, and even the moral and physical characteristics of the people. *Within* the district, almost every one is employed in raising coal, in raising iron ore, or in bringing that ore into the forms of smelted and manufactured iron; *beyond* the district the surface is wholly agricultural, and marked by the same natural and industrial features as agricultural regions generally; but at the *margin* of the district, where the change occurs, the soil is of a mixed character; and the population, lower in moral character than either of the others, are mostly employed in nail-making.

Wolverhampton is at the extreme north-west extremity of this coal-field, while Birmingham is at the extreme south-east: indeed the latter is, in strictness, wholly beyond the limits of the mining district, for there are no mines or collieries under Birmingham. How, then, it may be asked, has it arisen, that Birmingham, exterior to the coal and iron district, is a more important manufacturing town than any within the district? The following has been suggested as a mode of explaining this point. The *iron* of the district has been longer known and wrought than the *coal;* and, indeed, if this had not been the case, still it was formerly the practice to smelt all iron with wood-charcoal, rather than with coal: hence all iron-works used to be situated near

BIRMINGHAM, FROM THE SOUTH.

forests, in order that a supply of fuel might be obtained. Now it is known, from Domesday-book and other authorities, that the southern part of Staffordshire and the northern part of Warwickshire were in former days covered with forests. Scarcely a vestige of such forests now remain; and it is inferred that much of the timber has been used for charcoal for iron-smelting. The part of Warwickshire now under notice was formerly called *Arden,* from a British or Celtic word, implying woodland: there are still towns in it called Hampden-in-Arden, and Henley-in-Arden. It is supposed that, when the wood of Staffordshire had been largely consumed for smelting Staffordshire iron, the forests of Warwickshire were appealed to; and that Birmingham, being situated on the confines of the two counties, became a nucleus of manufacture and trade. It is always difficult to trace exactly the circumstances which led to the establishment of a particular manufacture in a particular town; but they are generally to be sought for in some natural features of the district.

Whether or not Birmingham owed its growth and importance to the vicinage of Staffordshire iron and Warwickshire wood, it is certain that the prosperity of South Staffordshire hinged upon the discovery of a mode of smelting iron by means of coal. During the sixteenth and seventeenth centuries the legislature gave many indications of alarm at the prospective destruction of timber, by lessening or prohibiting the use of charcoal fuel at iron-works; but as no other mode of smelting was then known, the existence of the iron-manufacture itself became much perilled. During the reigns of James I. and Charles I., many persons attempted to smelt iron by the aid of pit-coal, but without success. In the reign of Charles II., however, Dud Dudley, of Dudley Castle, after infinite trouble, difficulty, and expense, succeeded in showing that iron might be smelted by pit-coal; and from that period we may date the commencement of the present state of things in South Staffordshire, seeing that the operations for coal and for iron have ever since gone on *pari passu.*

The object of this paper will be best attained by postponing a rapid sketch of these mining towns, until we have made acquaintance with Birmingham and its singulrly remarkable development of industry.

BIRMINGHAM IN PAST DAYS.

William Hutton runs a tilt against the old chroniclers, because they do not mention Birmingham (or *Bermyngeham, Burmyngham, Bermyngham, Byrmyngham, Bromicham, Bromwycham, Brumwycheham*—for it has been spelled in all these different ways, and possibly many more). "It is matter of surprise," he says, "that none of those religious drones, the monks, who lived in the priory for fifteen or twenty generations, ever thought of indulging posterity with a history of Birmingham. They could not want opportunity, for they lived a life of indolence; nor materials, for they were nearer the infancy of time, and were possessed of historical facts now totally lost."—"None of the histories

which I have seen," he says in another paragraph, "bestow upon it more than a few lines, in which we are sure to be treated with the noise of hammers and anvils; as if the historian thought us a race of dealers in thunder, lightning, and wind; or infernals, puffing in blast and smoke."

Hutton supposes that two vestiges of Birmingham's infant state still survive, in Aston Forge and Wednesbury Old Field, which show indications of iron-works having been there in the time of the Romans, or perhaps of the Britons. Birmingham is now known as the seat of manufacture in various metals; but from its earliest state till the time of Charles II., its manufactures were almost exclusively in iron. Instruments of husbandry, tools for carpenters and other artificers, kitchen furniture — these were the main articles of produce; and until the middle of the last century, the forges at which these articles were made occupied the shops fronting the street: the old street called Digbeth had a dozen such forge-shops in front of the street in Hutton's time. Hutton describes the roads which led out of Birmingham, in the olden times, as having been sunk far beneath the surface of the adjoining country. Holloway Head, Dale End, Summer Hill, a road from Gosta Green to Aston Brook, Coleshill Street, and a road between Deritend and Camp Hill—all well-known localities in Birmingham—were formerly sunk below the level of the surrounding country to a depth varying from six to fifty feet; so that "the traveller of old, who came to purchase the produce of Birmingham, or to sell his own, seemed to approach her by sap." The old topographer views these hollow ways as indications of the antiquity and commercial influence of Birmingham. He says that they coincided with hilly parts of the town; that some of them, no doubt, were formed by the spade, to soften the fatigue of climbing the hill; that most of them, however, were owing to the effects of time, rain, and horse-traffic; and that, as rain must have been the most effective of these three agents, the formation of such deep gullies must have proved the great antiquity of Birmingham. This theory is ingenious, but not wholly satisfactory.

Leland, in the time of Henry VIII., gave the following picture of Birmingham, as it appeared to him on a hasty visit, in the early part of the sixteenth century: "I came through a pretty street as ever I entered, into Birmingham town: this street, as I remember, is called 'Dirtey' (Deritend). In it dwell smiths and cutlers; and there is a brook that divides this street from Birmingham, an hamlet or member, belonging to the parish therebye. There is at the end of Dirtey a proper chappel, and mansion-house of tymber (the Moat), hard on the ripe (bank), as the brook runneth down; and as I went through the ford, by the bridge, the water came down on the right hand, and a few miles below goeth into Tame. This brook, above Dirtey, breaketh in two arms, that a little beneath the bridge close again. This brook riseth, as some say, four or five miles above Birmingham, towards Black-hills. The beauty of Birmingham, a good market-town in the extreme parts of

L.—THE BULL RING.

Warwickshire, is one street going up along, almost from the left ripe of the brook, up a mean hill, by the length of a quarter of a mile. I saw but one parish church in the town. There be many smiths in the town that use to make knives and all manner of cutting tools ; and many lorimers that make bitts, and a great many nailors ; so that a great part of the town is maintained by smithes, who have their iron and sea-coal out of Staffordshire." Hutton dismisses this description, by saying, " Here we find some intelligence, and more mistake." The great family which formerly gave the tone to Birmingham, and received a title from it, were the Lords de Birmingham, of whom frequent mention was made in the times of the Edwards and Henrys.

Hutton draws a picture—in part probably an imaginary one, of Birmingham in the twelfth century. The houses, he says, were of timber, mean and low, and lining both sides of dirty and narrow streets ; her public buildings consisted of but one—the Church of St. Martin in the Bull Ring. Two centuries later, the town exhibited a greater number but scarcely a better kind of houses ; her narrow streets had become narrower by encroachments from either side ; her public buildings had been increased by three additional structures ; viz., a Priory, a Guildhall, and a Chapel at Deritend. The description by Leland, so far as it gives intelligible or trustworthy details, may serve to represent Birmingham in the fifteenth and sixteenth centuries. In the seventeenth century, the Birmingham men took part with the Parliamentarians against Charles I.

It was about the reign of Charles II. that the modern era of Birmingham may be said to have commenced. We have mentioned the introduction of smelting iron with coal, as having placed South Staffordshire in an improved position. Birmingham shared in that improvement ; and about the same time building-leases became prevalent ; and many new branches of ornamental manufacture began to spring up. Hutton, who delighted to put his description into quaint language, thus speaks of the change in Birmingham at the period now under notice :—" Though we have attended her through so immense a space, we have only seen her in infancy. Comparatively small in her size, homely in her person, and coarse in her dress. Her ornaments wholly of iron, from her own forge. But now her growth will be amazing, her expansion rapid, perhaps not to be paralleled in history. We shall see her rise in all the beauty of youth, of grace, of elegance, and attract the notice of the commercial world. She will also add to her iron ornaments the lustre of every metal that the whole earth can produce, with all their illustrious race of compounds heightened by fancy and garnished with jewels. She will draw from the fossil and the vegetable kingdoms ; press the ocean for shell, skin, and coral. She will also tax the animal for horn, bone, and ivory, and she will decorate the whole with the touches of her pencil."

The old bibliopole was right. Birmingham has done all that he predicted. It is rather over a century ago that that singular writer first set foot in Birmingham ; and ever since that period a steady process of advancement has been going on. New branches of manufacture have sprung up year after year ; and the consumption of raw materials has become immense.

BIRMINGHAM IN THE PRESENT DAY.

Birmingham, we have before stated, lies in Warwickshire. It is very near the north-western extremity of that county. On approaching it from any side, the traveller should hesitate to pass judgment on it till he has taken the state of the weather into consideration. If it be fine, he may enter Birmingham in cheerfulness in spite of its smoke ; if it be wet or foggy, he must buckle up his courage and draw upon his philosophy, or he will very likely think Birmingham a dismal place. It is rather unlucky, for a tourist who may be sensitive in these matters, that the railway stations are in such a poor-looking locality. The Grand Junction, the London and Birmingham, and Birmingham and Derby Companies, all fixed upon one district at the eastern margin of the town for their stations ; and to get from thence to the busy heart of the place, we must traverse several queer and unattractive streets. When the present stupendous works are completed, (of which more anon,) this disadvantage will be obviated ; but at present the entrance to Birmingham from the railways is anything but a pictorial one.

Perhaps the best mode of entering Birmingham, to see what it has been in past times, is by the London Road, through Bordesley and Digbeth, toward the Bull Ring and High Street. Here we come to the centre of old Birmingham. Here we see how prone our ancestors were to form streets, in every imaginable direction, in perfect contempt of all Euclid's propositions about right angles. Take the line from Bordesley to High Street : as tortuous a serpentine as we should wish to meet with. Turn up Moor Street, or Dale-End, or Bull Street, or New Street, or Edgbaston Street, or Worcester Street, or Spiceal Street—nothing is at right angles or parallel with anything else : each street pursues its own way, and a very crooked way it often is. Yet it is pleasant to see this odd-shaped spot ; for it was the nucleus of all that Birmingham has since become. The approach from the east is not favourable ; there is a long range of poor, dull, uninteresting streets to traverse before reaching the heart of the town. The northern inlets are better. Whether we come along Lichfield Road, through Aston, or along the Wolverhampton Road, the approaches are more frequently speckled over with villas and neat residences. But the approaches from Halesowen and Harbourne, on the west, are the best of all ; for they form, in fact, the " west end," in more senses than one. As seen from the open fields southward of the town, Birmingham presents a very busy aspect. (See Plate.)

From whichever way entered, Birmingham presents rather a flat appearance. It has no hilly spot ; its spires are not conspicuous for loftiness ; its only visible giants are its chimneys. Yet is Birmingham anything but a dead-level town. Fortunately for its inhabitants, the town is built on a succession of elevations and depressions. The elevations are not high enough to deserve the name of hills, yet sufficiently so to give a capital drainage to the streets; whereby Birmingham occupies a place, in 'Health of Towns' reports, not quite so dismal as most other manufacturing towns. A Londoner is, however, very likely to pray for the abolition of pebbles, and to vote for flag pavements. Many of the second-rate streets of Birmingham have not yet advanced to the honours of smooth foot-pavements : they have the little round thickly-set pebbles which are so often seen in country towns, but which have so nearly disappeared from the metropolis.

If it were any use to regret such matters, we would regret that Birmingham has no river. The River Rea, which crosses the London Road at Digbeth, and traverses an extreme nook of the town, scarcely deserves the name of a river; it is a mere rivulet, dribbling down its small supply to the Tame. All the life, and bustle, and breeze, and heathful cheerfulness which accompany a good-sized river are here wanting. All the bathing and the boating; all the steam-boat excursions—are things to be talked about, not met with. There are probably many persons in Birmingham who have never yet seen a steam-boat. There is also another want which occurs to the mind of those who have seen Birkenhead, Manchester, or Derby—there are no public parks, walks, greens, or open spots for exercise : there are very few of those 'squares' which serve as breathing spots in London. The consequence is, that the whole town is one mass of brick and mortar; and the inhabitants have to go far and wide before they can meet with a bit of green fields; and even then it is a sort of trespass to go into them, for they belong to private individuals and not to the town as a whole. Could not Birmingham club its resources together, and make a park for the people ? It would be worth the cost. The people would be all the better citizens for it.

As a consequence of the irregularity lately alluded to, the streets of Birmingham do not traverse the town in a direct manner. In some respects, however, this irregularity is advantageous, for it gives nooks and corners which, well managed, form excellent sites for public buildings. The angular approach to the Town Hall up New Street, is an example of this kind. The site of Christ Church, near the Town Hall, is so fine, that it were to be wished the building itself was better. St. Martin's Church, in the Bull Ring, has a similarly fine site. The corner of Dale-End and Bull Street, and the corner of High Street and New Street, are in like manner salient angles, which would afford scope for fine buildings. As for the streets themselves, the better among them are lively and bustling, full of good shops, and crowded with people. New Street is the best—it is the Bond Street of Birmingham : what with its glittering array of shops, its inns, its fine Elizabethan School, its School of Arts,

its Theatre, its Post-office, it gives the ton to that part of the town. High Street and Bull Street are localities of good shops, and apparently good trade. North-west of these is a large region of semi-private streets, having very few shops in them, but almost entirely occupied by warehouses and workshops of the numerous varieties of Birmingham manufacturers. Broad Street and Islington, at the western extremity of the town, are among the widest and best-built of the streets.

THE PUBLIC BUILDINGS.

The public buildings of Birmingham are scarcely so numerous as we should expect to meet with in a town of 200,000 inhabitants; and only few of them are striking as works of art.

Of the churches, the venerable St. Martin's must take the lead. Hutton gives such a high antiquity to this church, that we can scarcely venture to follow him. But there is sufficient evidence that a church at this spot must have been one of the earliest erections in the town. The present structure is supposed to have been built in the early part of the thirteenth century. There is a triangular space of ground, in the centre of what we have called old Birmingham, designated the Bull Ring, (Cut, No. 1 ;) and at the southern side of this Bull Ring is the church. Many are the alterations which it must have undergone since its erection ; for its general appearance is not so old as the date above assigned. It consists of a nave and clerestory, a chancel, a south aisle with a vestry attached, and a north aisle, at the west end of which stands the tower, surmounted by a spire. The early decorated style of architecture has been met with in several parts of the church, belonging to the period of the thirteenth century ; but almost all of these have been obliterated. The church and tower were cased with brick, about a century and a half ago ; and the spire has been several times altered and partially rebuilt. The exterior has suffered so many changes that it reveals less of former times than the interior. In 1846 the restoration of the monuments of the Lords of Birmingham, the most curious relics in the church, took place.

There is no other church in Birmingham which attracts notice by its association with the times of the Edwards and the Henrys. St. Philip's (Cut, No. 2) is admirably placed in the midst of an open space in the middle of the town, bounded by Colmore Row and Temple Row. The greater part of this space is occupied as a churchyard ; but as this churchyard is railed off into compartments, and is intersected by well-paved avenues crossing in various directions, it forms the largest and most pleasant open space in Birmingham. The church itself is of the time of Queen Anne, and is a kind of miniature St. Paul's—not very pure, perhaps, in its architecture, but a handsome and good-looking structure. Its nearest neighbour, Christchurch, near the Town Hall, is far inferior to it: it is a century younger than St. Philip's, but is a bald and tame production. St. Bartholomew's, near the railway-station,

2.—ST. PHILIP'S CHURCH.

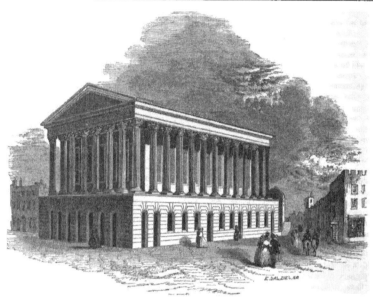

3.—THE TOWN HALL

is a brick building, about a century old. St. Peter's, in Dale-End, was built by the New Churches' Commissioners, about twenty years ago : it has a tetrastyle Doric portico in front, and an octagonal turret over the roof. St. Mary's stands in a tolerably large open space, in the midst of a poor neighbourhood : it is an octagonal brick structure, and was built about seventy or eighty years ago. St. George's, near the road to Wolverhampton, is one of Rickman's careful imitations of the pointed style, and is an attractive building. St. Paul's, a little way south-west of St. George's, is chiefly note-worthy for its spire. St. Thomas's, near the western end of the town, has an Ionic hexastyle west front. There are several other churches within the limits of the town ; and in nearly all cases the land on which the churches were built was presented by inhabitants of Birmingham.

The chapels belonging to the various Christian denominations are numerous, but for the most part plain and simple. The new Catholic cathedral, built within the last few years, at the junction of Bath Street with Shadwell Street, near the northern part of the town, is a more ambitious structure. It is one of Pugin's mediæval creations ; and with some points of beauty about it, is on the whole a heavy and tasteless work. It is built mostly of the same red brick which is visible in all the houses of Birmingham. From the confined situation in which it is placed, the length is small compared with the width. The nave is separated, by six pillars on each side, from the aisles ; and from these pillars spring arches which reach up to the roof without the intervention either of triforium or clerestory. This arrangement gives to the nave-arches an unusual elevation. A rich screen separates the choir from the nave, and another screen separates the Lady Chapel from the north aisle. There is a good deal of stained glass in the cathedral ; and also some elaborate carvings belonging to the fifteenth and sixteenth centuries. The Bishop's Palace, near the cathedral, is, like it, a red brick structure, and as unlike anything modern as could possibly be : it is a purposed reproduction of all the ancient features of catholic times ; and contains a cloister, almonry, library, chapel, and refectory, in addition to suites of private apartments. There is a nunnery, or convent, of the Sisters of Mercy, at Birmingham. It is situated at a considerable distance from the cathedral and Bishop's Palace, but is like them in general architectural character. It contains, besides the living-rooms, a chapel, cloisters, oratory, cemetery, refectory, and cells. The inmates of this building, whether we join them in religious belief or not, must command respect for the deeds of goodness and kindness which it is the business of their lives to perform. There is a separate building attached to their convent, called the House of Mercy, which is said to have been built at the expense of the sisterhood themselves. In this house, poor destitute young women are boarded, clothed, and provided with work, until situations can be provided for them as domestic servants : they are taught all sorts of industrial duties likely to be useful to them in after life; and they help to support themselves by their talents while in the house. The Sisters of Mercy are the teachers, the matrons, the friends of these poor females.

Of the remaining public buildings in Birmingham, the Town Hall (Cut, No. 3,) is the most conspicuous and attractive. It is a remarkable attempt to apply to modern purposes a style of structure which belonged essentially to the Greek temples. Architectural criticism on it has been most minute and diverse; and the sticklers for rigorous ' classicality' have not failed to find defects in it : but popular opinion has decided that the Town Hall is an honour to Birmingham, and this popular opinion is right. The Hall is a peristylar composition : that is, it presents ranges of columns along the sides and fronts. There is in the first place a rusticated basement, rising to the height of about 20 feet, and pierced with doorways and windows for the accommodation of the interior. Upon and above this basement the body of the building is placed; in front of which, on three sides and the structure, are placed ranges of noble Corinthian columns, supporting entablatures above. There are thirteen of these columns along each side, and eight in the principal front. A lofty pediment surmounts the columns of the chief front. Behind the columns, in the body of the building, are ranges of windows, one to each intercolumniation. The columns are about 40 feet high ; and being elevated to so great a height above the ground, they form a very noble and majestic object, as seen from various parts of Birmingham. As the building was constructed for the holding of large meetings and assemblies, there is one large hall, which occupies the main part of the interior area. This hall is 145 feet long, 65 wide, and 65 high : it is somewhat smaller than Exeter Hall, but is unquestionably a noble room. At one end is a fine organ, which was constructed at a cost of £3,000 or £4,000 : it is one of Hill's best productions. The outer case is 40 feet wide, 45 feet high, and 17 feet deep; there are 78 drawstops, four sets of keys, and above 4,000 pipes ; the largest wooden pipe has an interior capacity of 224 cubic feet.

This capacious hall is a most useful adjunct to the other buildings of Birmingham. Before its erection there was no fitting structure for the holding of large meetings ; but the hall is now the place of assembly for politicians, for musical folks, and for all who wish to meet in large numbers. The admirable ' Musical Festivals' are closely associated with the history of this building. Before the erection of this Town Hall, in 1834, triennial musical festivals were held in St. Philip's Church, for the benefit of the General Hospital of the town ; but the larger and more appropriate Hall is now applied to that purpose. Concerts of a less ambitious character are often held there ; and the most interesting, perhaps, of these, is a kind of humble man's concert, held every Monday evening. The hall belongs to the corporation ; the organ belongs to the General Hospital ; and both parties lend their aid towards the establishment of a regular weekly concert, at such terms as shall induce the working classes to indulge occasionally in this very rational and acceptable amusement The admission charge is as low as *threepence*, for which two or three hours of excellent music is given. The organ is the only musical instrument : there are a few singers engaged ; and the selection always includes many sacred pieces. Let us take one evening's programme, as an example of the kind of musical fare offered to the visitors : The organist displayed the powers of the noble organ in the performance of one of Wesley's Organ Fugues ; the andante from Haydn's ' Third Symphony ;' Handel's ' Dead March in Saul ;' Haydn's ' Heavens are Telling ;' an ' Introduction and Fugue,' by Hesse; Mendelssohn's anthem, ' Oh, rest in the Lord ;' and Haydn's fine Austrian national hymn, ' God preserve the Emperor ;' while the harmonized vocal pieces were, Callcott's glee, ' Are the white hours for ever fled ?' Knyvett's quartette, ' Beyond yon hills, where Lugar flows ;' Spofforth's glee, ' Hail ! smiling Morn ;' Horsley's trio, ' When shall we three meet again ;' and Ford's madrigal, ' Since first I saw.' Now, if the reader has any ' music in his soul,' he will at once agree that such a concert is well worth threepence ; if he has *not*, he must take our word for it. It is impossible that such weekly meetings can be without good effect in a large and busy town : a purifying influence, though silent and almost imperceptible, must and does accompany them. The owners of the hall and of the organ are thankworthy for what they have done and are doing.

The only building in Birmingham which can vie with the Town Hall in architectural importance is the Grammar School, in New Street (Cut, No. 4.) While Messrs. Hansom and Welch took a Greek temple as the model for the one, Mr. Barry went to our own Elizabethan times for authorities for the other. This foundation is one of the many which date their commencement in the reign of Edward VI. The original building was replaced by a second, in 1707 ; and this becoming dilapidated a few years ago, the governors resolved to employ Mr. Barry to construct the present edifice. The choice was a felicitous one ; for the structure is a worthy ornament to the town. It belongs to the same general style which Mr. Barry has since employed in the new palace of the legislature ; and the elaborate carvings in Derbyshire stone impart to it a very enriched appearance. It presents a frontage of about 174 feet ; its depth is 127 feet, and height 60 feet. There are seven ranges of flattish windows in front, with the accompanying buttresses, pinnacles, crowns, crosses, &c.; while there are bolder bay-windows at each extremity. The interior is fitted up commodiously for the requirements of a large school. The entire building is said to have cost no less than £40,000.

There has recently been erected a Corn Exchange, in a part of the town singularly destitute of attractive buildings. It is an oblong structure, with entrances at both ends, and counters and desks arranged on either side for the accommodation of the dealers. The best feature in the building is the roof, which is wagon-vaulted, and remarkably light and elegant in its appearance. Another market-house—*the* market of Birmingham in respect to size and importance — is a large building lying on the western side of the Bull Ring, near St. Martin's church. It is, like the new markets of Liverpool, Birkenhead, and Newcastle, a quadrangular covered area, divided into avenues, and lighted by skylights or lanterns in an iron-framed roof over head. The market has a sort of Doric front, and on either side is a range of twenty-five windows; it is 360 feet long, 108 wide, and 60 high, and contains accommodation for 600 stalls. Immediately in front of this market-hall is Westmacott's statue of Nelson, which was put up about forty years ago : being placed in the open spot called the Bull Ring, its position is advantageous. A lover of the fine arts, or even a simple admirer of public decorations to a town, cannot fail to remark how little of *sculpture* is presented by Birmingham. When are its marble and bronze monuments to arrive ? Are not the Watts, the Boultons, the Murdochs, the Baskervilles, worthy of some such note ? and if not, are there no other public men whose statues we should like to gaze upon ? Mr. Kohl, in his ' England,' gives Birmingham a little castigation in relation to this matter.

The School of Arts, in New Street, is an important establishment for Birmingham, in so far as it fosters a taste for the arts of design, which are so important to her. Considered simply as a building, it consists mainly of a circular exhibition-room, about fifty feet in diameter, with a number of smaller rooms ; while the exterior presents a tetrastyle Corinthian portico, comparatively narrow in width. It was established in 1821, mainly through the exertions of Sir Robert Lawley, as a School of Arts or Society of Artists, and was supplied with a collection of casts and other works of art ; but when the Government established a School of Design in London, and it was thought proper to give Birmingham the advantage of a similar school, the building now under notice was found to be a fitting locality for it, and the necessary arrangements were made. A grant of money, casts, and furniture, was made by the Government in 1843 ; and so well has the management been conducted, that the Birmingham School of Design is now, we believe, regarded as the largest in the kingdom. So much do the reputation and the prosperity of Birmingham depend on the taste displayed in her manufactures, that the leading men of the town have abundant reason for fostering this taste among the designers and workmen. Ten or twelve years ago, when a Parliamentary Committee collected evidence relating to the application of the fine arts to manufactures, many witnesses from Birmingham stated how anxiously that town would welcome any more systematic mode of instructing designers in matters of taste and elegance. Since then an immense advance has been made. The manufactures in gold, silver, brass, bronze, steel, papier maché, and japan, now exhibit great beauty of design. The expositions of manufactures within the last few years, at Westminster Hall

and at the Society of Arts, show that Birmingham is very little, if at all, behind France in elegance of design. Much of this advancement is doubtless due to the School of Design, which has for five years been educating the designers and modellers in those inventive powers which shall enable them to give grace and symmetry to manufactured goods. The human figure, drapery, fruit, flowers, foliage, landscape, architecture, geometrical curves, ornament—all are studied in this school, and all are available to the future designer.

The banking-houses, the hotels and inns, the barracks, the hospitals, the school-houses, the theatre, the post-office, the subscription libraries, the news-rooms, the public offices, are for the most part such as do not make much pretension to architectural beauty ; while the interior arrangements are in the usual accordance with the purposes to which the respective buildings are appropriated. The General Hospital, situated near the northern extremity of the town, is a large brick building, erected about seventy years ago. It contains a couple of portraits by Reynolds and Phillips ; but it is more generally known from the triennial musical festivals, alluded to in a preceding paragraph. These festivals were established as a means of contributing to the funds of the hospital ; the whole profits accruing from them, amounting on an average to £4,000 or £5,000 from each festival, being handed over to the treasurer of the hospital. The festivals have taken place regularly, ever since 1778—first, in St. Philip's Church, then in the Town Hall ; they have always occupied a very high position in the musical circles ; and it is certainly a felicitous mode of providing a helping fund for the sick and wounded. The Queen's College, (Cut, No. 5,) situated near the Town Hall, was established in 1843. It is, externally, an imitation, on a humble scale, of the Grammar School ; but is far inferior to it. The institution is for giving a course of medical and surgical education ; and the lectures qualify for examination for the diplomas of the University of London, the Royal College of Surgeons, and the Society of Apothecaries.

THE RAILWAYS.

If railways and railway-stations are public buildings, then will Birmingham ere long possess some of the most astonishing public buildings in England. The works at present in progress, relating to these matters, are perfectly astounding. One would think that all the Birmingham men are perpetually travelling about, and could never rest for an hour in their own town, if we judge from the accommodation for locomotion afforded to them. Whole streets are being pulled down ; viaducts are being carried aloft over head ; tunnels are burrowing beneath the feet ; and two Companies seem to be trying which can expend the most money.

Let us see how these mighty works have grown up. Two of the earliest and most important railways were the London and Birmingham, and the Grand Junction, both meeting at the eastern side of Birmingham.

4.—KING EDWARD'S GRAMMAR-SCHOOL.

Before these were planned, the service of the roads was centred in some of those fine, dashing, well-appointed stage-coaches, such as our own country alone can present. Nearly a dozen excellent turnpike-roads radiate from Birmingham, placing that town in connection with all the great towns of the kingdom. In addition to the turnpike-roads, Birmingham is intersected with numerous canals, which have for many years formed media of conveyance to and from the manufacturing towns. But we live in such 'go-a-head' days, that both coaches and canals are well nigh held in contempt. Nothing will now suffice but the puffing, dashing, fly-away locomotive, which is accused of intolerable slowness if it does not master thirty or forty miles an hour. When the two railway Companies before-mentioned arranged to join their lines at Birmingham, they thought they were doing brave things to afford such handsome stations at the eastern margin of the town. And so indeed they were : the works were large, comprehensive, and commodious (Cut No. 6); although the competition of more recent years bids fair to render them nearly useless. That which is now the Queen's Hotel was once the offices of the Company ; but offices of a much larger character became speedily required. The booking-offices and passenger-sheds, at the rear or east of the hotel, cover an immense area. So long as the London and Birmingham, and the Grand Junction Companies remained separate, each one required a large station, both for passengers and goods, at Birmingham ; but when the two 'amalgamated' (how little do railway companies seem to remember that an *amalgam* is in

reality a union of quicksilver with some other metal !) both stations were thrown into one. The Birmingham and Gloucester, and the Birmingham and Derby lines also brought their termini pretty nearly to the same spot.

Why then should there be any vast additional railway works in the heart of Birmingham ? Let the ' Battle of the Gauges' answer this question : a battle which, though not bloody, has cost the commercial world millions of good money, much of which will never bring an adequate return. In 1845, the broad gauge was first permitted to trace its giant steps towards the north. The Oxford, Worcester, and Wolverhampton, and the Oxford and Rugby Railways received Parliamentary sanction in that year. Thus was the narrow gauge of Birmingham threatened both in the east and the west : the army of General Stephenson was attacked on both flanks by that of General Brunel. In the next following year the Oxford, Worcester, and Wolverhampton Company obtained increased powers to render the accommodation of their district more efficient ; while another Company obtained Legislative sanction for the Oxford and Birmingham Line— all these lines being closely associated with the Great Western Company. Here was a bold step. The invading army actually entered Birmingham ; nay, more, an additional sum of nearly half a million sterling was sanctioned for carrying the broad gauge right through the town itself. Even this was not all ; for a new Company, under the name of the Birmingham, Wolverhampton, and Dudley Railway Company, were

5.—QUEEN'S COLLEGE SCHOOL.

empowered to spend nearly a million sterling in making about fifteen miles of broad gauge between those three towns.

Was the narrow gauge to beat a retreat, or surrender at discretion, at such a time? Was General Stephenson to be vanquished in this way? The ulterior measures will show. The narrow gauge party obtained an Act by which they were authorized to spend more than one-third of a million sterling in carrying their old line into the heart of Birmingham; while they supported the Birmingham, Wolverhampton, and Stour Valley Company in obtaining an Act for a narrow gauge line from Birmingham to Wolverhampton, with a power of raising about a million and a half sterling. In 1847, further Acts were obtained by both the rival parties, to make additional bits of lines to complete their respective systems. Every scrap of these new lines which is to be on the narrow gauge, together with a very large portion of the canal navigation of the whole district, have become absorbed in the gigantic London and North Western Company; while the whole of the broad gauge portion will probably ultimately belong to the Great Western. The two have made desperate struggles to obtain possession, by purchase, of the Birmingham and Oxford line; which struggles have been marked by the most extraordinary features, perhaps, ever presented by a joint-stock undertaking. The battle is not yet ended; the two gauges regard each other as fiercely as ever, and the battle-field is even divided against itself,—shareholders against directors; and eighteen months of Parliamentary and legal proceedings

have succeeded in landing all parties in a 'fix,' from which they do not seem to know how to extricate themselves. Meanwhile money has been absorbed at a frightful rate; the whole of the capital for this much-coveted line has been called up, before the line itself even approaches to completion; and when the decision is finally made, and the oyster fairly divided, it appears very much as if there would be just a shell a piece for the combatants.

In sober truth, this railway campaigning at Birmingham is a very wild affair: it outruns all reasonable limits. The new works on both gauges, within fifteen miles of Birmingham, will probably not be brought into working order for less than four millions sterling— of which one million will be spent within Birmingham itself! Both lines run completely through Birmingham from one side to the other, and both lines run from Birmingham to Wolverhampton and Dudley, independently of the old Grand Junction Railway, which also runs from Birmingham very near to Wolverhampton. Parliament did not know which to sanction, so it sanctioned both; and neither Company will abandon or suspend its works, for fear of the rivalry of the other. It will not perhaps arrive at a 'Kilkenny cat' conclusion, but it will make a nearer approach thereto than is consistent with the interests of the respective Companies. The North Western Company, especially, will smart for it in future years.

But if the combatants will share between them the shells of the oyster, who will have the oyster itself? The town of Birmingham. Birmingham will have almost unprecedented advantages in respect to communications with other towns. Two stations in the very heart of the town, replete with all the conveniences for traffic that ingenuity can suggest, and connecting-links between these stations and all the great towns of England—these are the results which Birmingham will get out of the *mêlée*. The old or narrow gauge line will send off its branch or extension, a little eastward of the present station; and this branch will cross several streets and lanes, until it reaches Pinfold Street, southward of New Street. Here an immense group of houses, mostly of a humble character, are being levelled with the ground, to make room for a passenger-station of magnificent dimensions, from which station a new road of communication will be formed into New Street, the principal avenue in the town. From this station the line will take its start onward to Dudley and Wolverhampton. The other line, the broad gauge, will enter Birmingham at the south-east corner, pass a little to the west of the present narrow gauge station, and arrive near the heart of the town, at the junction of High Street, Bull Street, and Dale-End. A little north-west of this point an immense quadrangle of houses is to be cleared away, bounded by Monmouth, Livery, and Great Charles Streets, and Snow Hill; and here the broad gauge station is to be, not a whit less vast and costly, apparently, than its rival. From this station the line will pass out into the open country, on its way to Dudley and Wolverhampton. In carrying these two new lines through Birmingham, the works assume a very diversified character; for, owing to the many inequalities in the level of the streets, there are on each line combinations of viaduct, open cutting, and tunnelling, of a most costly nature. If the shareholders in all these lines gain as much advantage as Birmingham itself, it will be well: but we doubt.

BIRMINGHAM INDUSTRY.

What is this Birmingham, for which such a railway rout is made? What do the inhabitants do—how do they live—what has made them famous? The answers to these questions would carry us into such a maze of manufactures, that we must purposely glance only at the most broad and salient features.

Birmingham is, beyond all question, the most remarkable centre of manufactures in metal, in the world. There may perhaps be other towns where more iron is used; there are, as at Sheffield, places where more steel is wrought into manufactured forms; there is in London, a larger production of costly articles in gold and silver; there are other towns, where large and complicated engines and machines are made in greater number; but there is no place to equal Birmingham in respect to the diversity and subdivision of metal manufactures, or to the number of persons so employed. It was at one time called the "toy-shop of Europe;" but this, though a smart sort of cognomen, is not worth much. If the world wants metal toys,

Birmingham can make them; but if articles of utility are wanted, Birmingham is equally alive to the best mode of producing them. Whatever metal *can* do, Birmingham will make it do; from a pin's-head to a steam-engine; from a pewter pot to a copper boiler; from a gilt button to a brass bedstead. Every ounce of metal is made to do so much work in Birmingham, as to illustrate the economy of material more strikingly than in most other places. No place knows better than Birmingham how to make metallic articles thin, when the price will not pay for a greater thickness. No place can contrive better to give an ornamental exterior to that which, for economising material, is hollow within. And if many Birmingham goods are ' Brummagem' goods, whose fault is this? If people *will* have goods so cheap that a fair remunerating price can hardly be left to the manufacturer, is it matter for wonder that the latter taxes his ingenuity how to produce a showy affair for "next to nothing?" So long as Birmingham can show her ability to produce the highest class of manufactured articles in metal when properly paid for, no one has reason to blame her for trying to please the pence-gentry as well as the guinea-gentry. Nay, we may go further;—the cottages and humble dwellings of England are indebted to Birmingham and its neighbourhood, for a greater amount of neat interior fittings, useful utensils, and ingenious knick-knacks of all kinds, than fall to the lot, perhaps, of any other country in the world. Let the reader take his eyes off this sheet for a few minutes, and glance round the room in which he may be sitting—we care not whether it be in a house of £10 or £100 a year rental: let him look at the doors, the windows, the fire-place, the cupboards or closets, the furniture, the implements and vessels, the ornaments or decorations—wherever he may look, Birmingham is before him. There is scarcely a room in this country, except in the most poverty-stricken hovel, that does not contain some article of Birmingham manufacture. Let him then go from houses to persons: let him look at English dress, in all its endless variety, and then say whether there is one such dress that is not indebted to Birmingham for something or other in a metallic form. It may be trivial, it is true; but this very triviality only the better illustrates the minute applications which are now made of metal. Will not a beaver or silk hat escape this enumeration? Look at the little buckle that fastens the band. Are not our boots excepted? Look at the nails and 'tips' or at the tags of laces. Female attire? Let the buttons and buckles and clasps, the pins and hooks-and-eyes and lace-holes, the combs and bracelets and armlets, the rings and brooches and necklaces—let them all give evidence to the part which Birmingham and its vicinity have taken in decking out any and every Englishwoman. If you write a letter, look at your desk, your inkstand, your steel-pen, your pen-holder, your wafer-stamp, your seal, your candlestick or taper-stand, and think how far Birmingham has been concerned in them. If a lady, seated at her work, would gossip a little about her work-trinkets, the needles, pins, thimble, bodkin, piercer, crochet and knitting-needles—all would tell of Birmingham, or in some few instances of Sheffield or Redditch. If you walk abroad, and rain befall you, ask who made the metal work of your umbrella. If you ride on horseback, think where the bridle-bit, the stirrups, and the buckles came from. In short, do anything, go anywhere, buy, beg, borrow, make, alter, eat, drink, walk, ride, look, hear, touch—you cannot shake off Birmingham for many minutes together.

If, then, there be such a multiplicity of articles made of metal in Birmingham, the reader may reasonably expect that there must be vast factories in that town, replete with all the wonderful organization of labour that marks the Manchester cotton factories. This, however, is not exactly the case. Chimneys there are in plenty, smoke there is in more than plenty; but the chimneys and the smoke belong to *workshops* rather than to *factories*. So much of Birmingham work is effected by manipulative skill, that the steam-engine is less autocratic in that town than in Manchester or Leeds. It is true there are numerous steam-engines always employed, but the power afforded by these engines is applied principally to the rougher kinds of work. One ball of cotton is so like another, one yard of calico is so like another, that as soon as steam machinery has been enabled to spin the one or weave the other, millions of each kind are struck off in a very short time. But in Birmingham the different varieties and sizes and patterns of articles are so numerous, that the adjustment of the steam-engine to do the work of all would be almost impracticable, and unprofitable if practicable. The adjustments required by the ever-varying tastes and wants of the age can be effected only by men's fingers : the steam-engine being appealed to for that kind of service which may be common to all the works required.

It is the multiplicity and diversity of the manufactures of Birmingham that lead to the peculiar mode of managing the arrangements between master and workmen. There are some establishments which contain several hundred workmen under one roof ; but, in general, the numbers must be reckoned by dozens rather than by hundreds. The buildings are really workshops, and not huge factories with five or six long ranges of windows speckling the fronts. But we must come down even to less numbers than dozens, to catch the spirit of Birmingham manufactures in a proper manner. The division and subdivision of labour are carried in that town to a most extraordinary degree of minuteness ; insomuch that an article which might appear to us to emanate from one factory or workshop, has been really produced at a dozen—each manufacturer or workman fabricating only a portion of it. There is master under master, workman under workman ; and when the finished article is ready for sale, its price is made up of a number of fragments of wages, and fragments of profits, besides the cost of the original material.

THE IRON AND STEEL TRADES.

Let us glance a little at some of the more prominent departments of productive industry, and see how they bear on the social features of Birmingham life.

And first for *Iron*. There are no iron mines, and no coal mines under Birmingham itself. All the iron and all the coal are brought from the busy district north-west of the town. The iron-masters of Staffordshire usually come to Birmingham on Thursday in each week, to arrange all the matters incident to the sale of iron to the Birmingham manufacturers. They also meet once a quarter, to settle among themselves the price at which iron shall be sold ; for there is, in this respect, an arrangement something like that adopted by the coal-owners of Durham and Northumberland. The iron is sent to Birmingham, mostly by canal, in the form of bars, rods, and sheets ; and Birmingham industry has then to impart to this iron the countless forms which distinguish it. There are steam-engine makers, mill-wrights, axle-tree makers, boiler-makers, and others, who use iron in large and weighty pieces ; and here the forge, the casting-pit, and the file, are the main appliances for bringing the iron to the required forms.

If we go to the next lower stage in the use of iron, by tracing it to the manufacturer of smaller articles, and if we include the South Staffordshire district generally, instead of confining our attention strictly to Birmingham, the number and variety become perfectly bewildering. Agricultural implements, anvils, hammers, and all kinds of tools, locks and keys, hinges and bolts, springs, stoves, fenders, fire-irons, chains, fences, tubes, presses and vices, saucepans and kettles, gridirons and flat-irons—it would be in vain to try to get to the end of the list. And what is very remarkable is, that each one of these articles is a separate branch of manufacture. Take the lock-manufacture, for example : we find not only that locks form a distinct branch of industry, but that book-case locks, cabinet locks, case locks, dead locks, drawback locks, gate locks, mortice locks, padlocks, pocket-book locks, rim locks, sash locks, spring locks, stock locks, thumb locks, trunk locks, and probably many others,—all form distinct branches, undertaken by different men, and wrought by workmen, each of whom confines himself pretty nearly to one kind. Then again, take keys : some of the men—not merely the workmen, but masters who take orders on their own account,—are key-makers, some key-stampers, some key-filers. Nearly the whole of the iron implements and articles mentioned in this paragraph are made in workshops containing only a small number of men : but they are more closely connected with the environs of Birmingham than with Birmingham itself ; so we will defer to a future page a sketch of the manufacturing system which distinguishes them.

If we descend to a next lower scale in the use of iron, we find that though the articles themselves are smaller, the establishments in which they are made are generally larger. This arises from the circumstance that the steam-engine can be used in this group of manufactures; whereas the group noticed in the last paragraph are almost wholly made without the aid of this mighty worker. This precisely illustrates the comparison which we before made between factories and workshops. Wire, nails, and screws, are three classes of products that especially come under the operation of this remark: they are all made in enormous quantities in Birmingham, and for the most part in large establishments. In the making of wire on the improved modern system, rods of iron are drawn repeatedly through holes in hardened steel plates, until the thickness of the iron is so reduced as to bring it to the form of wire; smaller and smaller holes being used according as the thickness of the iron diminishes; and as this drawing requires an immense mechanical force, such an operation is a very proper one to be brought within the scope of steam-machinery. Then, when a steam-engine is once provided, every motive of economy leads the manufacturer to make it do as much work as possible; and hence he has many draw-plates, many coils of wire, many drums round which the wire can wind as it is made, and many repetitions of the drawing machinery. All this gives to his workshop the appearance of a large factory.

The nail and screw factories are yet larger exemplifications of the same system. Some of them employ several hundred men, and are fitted up with complicated machinery in every room. The number of nails and screws made in Birmingham is almost beyond belief. The iron for the nails is sent into the factories in the form of sheets; and these sheets are cut into strips, which strips are further cut up into various sizes and shapes of nails. There is one establishment in Birmingham which cuts up from thirty to forty tons of iron per week, to make into nails; the nails, taking one size with another, give an average of about a million to a ton; so that the total yield would amount to *two thousand million* nails in a year!—All this in machine-made nails alone, and in one factory alone! Whether any one has ever attempted to estimate the almost uncountable number made in the whole Staffordshire district, we do not know. *Screws* are not made in such enormous number as nails; but still the produce must be very large, and the establishments in which they are made exhibit highly ingenious specimens of mechanism. The cutting off of a piece from a coil f thick wire, the forging of a protuberance to form the head, the turning or shaping of the head and shank into a symmetrical form, the cutting of the notch or cleft in the head, and the cutting of the thread or worm of the screw,—all are effected by the aid of machinery, some of which is of a very curious kind. It is a remarkable feature in this manufacture, that the machines are attended almost wholly by females: the employment is of a kind that requires steady attention rather than physical strength or great skill; and it is one of many in Birmingham that females can attend to.

If, lastly, we descend to a still lower application of iron in manufacture,—lower in respect to the size of the pieces of iron employed,—we shall find that Birmingham industry becomes more and more interesting. We must here suppose the iron to have undergone that process which converts it into steel; for steel is capable of being employed in smaller fragments than iron. Who does not now use *steel pens*? Who does not remember the time when a steel pen cost as much as a dozen quills? Who is ignorant of the marvellous reduction that has taken place in the market value of these tiny bits of steel? Sixpence a piece, sixpence a dozen, sixpence a gross,—thus have they come down in value. All this could not have been done but for the application of machinery. Men's hands employed in cutting and pressing and shaping the pens, would never have permitted this cheapening to have gone to such an extent. And yet there are actually more men employed in the manufacture than were employed when machinery was less used. The machinery, in fact, has created a demand, which requires large numbers both of machines and of men to supply. Some of the steel-pen manufactories of Birmingham are very large establishments, containing ranges of highly-finished machines, and giving employment to large numbers of workmen. One of these manufacturers, in his advertisements, states his yearly produce at *millions of dozens;* and there is no reason to doubt that it does reach that extraordinary pitch.

Needles are another application of minute pieces of steel, requiring very delicate and beautiful machinery. No fewer than thirty separate and successive processes are involved in the manufacture of a good needle, affording an example of subdivided employment scarcely paralleled in any other industrial process. Birmingham produces its millions of needles; but the manufacture is not one which marks the town particularly. The village of Redditch, in Worcestershire, one of the most extraordinary villages in England, is the home of the needle trade: almost every manufacturer makes needles, almost every workman makes needles; almost every lawyer and doctor, every landlord and householder, every shopkeeper and pedlar, makes his money indirectly by needles or needle-makers: needles are the beginning and the end, the be-all and the do-all, the sinews and the life-blood, of Redditch. Three or four thousand millions of needles travel out of this needle-making Redditch every year. No wonder, then, if Birmingham has to be content with the second place in this department of industry. She has her revenge, however, in steel toys and ornaments. These are produced in exhaustless variety at Birmingham. Studs and rosettes, clasps and buckles, handles and knobs, feet and claws, are made of steel, to a vast extent, and give rise to a constant exercise of ingenuity on the part of the designer to produce patterns which shall please by their gracefulness and beauty.

THE MIXED METAL TRADES.

But large as is the consumption of iron, either in its

6.—THE RAILWAY TERMINUS.

crude form or in the altered state of steel, and numerous as are the distinct varieties in its application, the industrial arrangements of Birmingham are, perhaps, still more remarkably distinguished by the application of other metals in a more or less mixed form. Copper, tin, zinc, lead, and nickel, either in their simple states or mixed and combined so as to form brass, bell-metal, bronze, pewter, and white metal, give rise to an extraordinary diversity of manufactures, in which Birmingham takes the lead of all other towns, beyond the reach of comparison. Look at any correct list of the divisions of Birmingham manufactures, (if such a list can possibly be prepared,) and see how this matter presents itself. Beer-engines, bells, Britannia-metal goods, British plate or nickel-silver, bronze goods, buttons, candlesticks, chandeliers, clock - dials, clock - hands, clock-movements, coach-beading, coach brass-work, coach-plating, coach-ornaments, coffin-furniture, brass cocks and valves, corkscrews, cornice-poles and curtain-rings, brass fire-furniture, gas-fittings, guns and muskets, inkstands, letter-weights, lamps, medals and dies, military ornaments, pewter vessels, pins, plated ware, brass rings and rods and tubes, harness-ornaments, copper vessels, scales and weights, stamped brass-work, tin-plate ware,—here is a list which would put any one out of breath to read; and all of these articles are made wholly, or mainly, of one or other of the metals lately named. Each one, too, is the object of a separate and distinct branch of Birmingham manufacture; and not only so, but many of them are further subdi-

vided. The factor or dealer may receive the finished article from a manufacturer, who has received it in half-a-dozen different parts from half-a-dozen smaller manufacturers; and each of these, again, employs many men, each of whom can do only one part of the work.

The making of muskets and fowling-pieces strikingly illustrates this subdivision of Birmingham industry. Gun-making is one of the best and most extensive of her trades; but we should form a most erroneous estimate of the matter if we interpreted a gun-manufacturer to mean one who makes guns complete within the walls of one establishment. There are gun-barrel makers, gun-case makers, gun-engravers, gun-filers, gun-finishers, gun-furniture makers, gun-percussioners, gun-polishers, gun-screwers, gun-lock makers, gun-stockers. Even these are subdivided among themselves; for among the gun-barrel makers are borers, browners, filers, grinders, ribbers, smoothers, and welders; and the gun-locks are distributed among makers, forgers, and filers. In some of the numerous branches here indicated, the work is done by manufacturers who have tolerably large workshops, and employ a good many hands, and who send in their finished portion of the work to the gun-manufacturer or first-hand employer; while, in other cases, the occupation is more that of a journeyman than of a master. The consequence of this system is, that the parts of a gun are travelling about Birmingham most actively: the fragments are running after each other, and do not come finally together till they are about to reach the warehouse of the manufacturer. Smith, Brown, Jones, Robinson, Higgins, Tomkins, Jenkins,—all are at work, in their respective workshops, and, perhaps, all in different streets, on different parts of the same gun, at the same time; and a good deal of testing is required from time to time, to see that the adjustment of the different parts is correct.

The whole internal economy of the gun-making trade of Birmingham, indeed, is very interesting. During the French war, infantry-muskets were made at Birmingham at the rate of a musket a minute; and the organised system is still maintained, whereby a large order of muskets can be executed in a very short space of time. Many of the processes themselves are highly curious. The common barrels are formed by hammering a heated strip of plate-iron round a mandril, or core, until it assumes a tubular shape; while the best barrels are made by twisting a narrow strip of iron round and round, in corkscrew fashion, and then heating and hammering so as to close the fissures between the successive thread of the spiral. The boring and smoothing of these barrels are subsequent and very carefully conducted operations; for the right discharge of the bullet requires that the axis of the tube shall be in a mathematically straight line, and the sides of the tube perfectly smooth. While the barrel is being made, the 'stock' or woodwork, is progressing in other quarters. This is usually of walnut-wood, and is shaped by saws, planes, chisels, spoke-shaves, and other tools. The Wolverhampton and Willenhall and Walsall men, too, are making the locks in the meantime; for, though Birmingham could make gun-locks as well as other things, yet it seems that all parties agree to locate this trade out of the town—another proof of combination in subdivision: subdivision in the processes themselves, and combination in respect to the workmen in each branch grouping themselves pretty much in one spot. These country-made gun-locks are always cheaper than the Birmingham men could make them for themselves.

Who has ever visited Birmingham by railway without having his ears saluted with a bang and a boom from some spot near the station? This 'bang, bang,' comes from the gun-barrel proof-house, which is within a few dozen yards of the passenger station. In order that the Government might be able to depend on the quality of the infantry muskets supplied from Birmingham, and that the reputation of Birmingham manufacturers might be maintained at an honourable point, an arrangement was made during the war, which empowered the Birmingham gun-makers to establish a barrel-proving-house, under the management of a warden and other officers, selected from among themselves. Every manufacturer is bound, under a heavy penalty, to send all the barrels he may make to this establishment, for trial and proof; and the few pence which he pays for the proving of each barrel defray the expenses of the establishment. This gun-proof-house is a large, dirty, rambling sort of building.

The barrels sent in from the several manufactories are loaded with four or five times as much powder as they will be required to carry in actual practice. They are then ranged side by side on a low stage in a long building, in such a way that all the touch-holes shall rest upon a long train of gunpowder. All the men then leave the place, doors are closed, a light is applied to the extreme end of the train, a hundred barrels are fired at once, and the bullets bury themselves in a large heap of sand provided for that purpose. The smoke is allowed a few moments to dissipate itself, the doors are opened, and the barrels are taken up one by one. A small per-centage of them—we believe from one to two per cent.—yield to this severe test: they burst. The workman who has forged the barrel undertakes that it shall bear the test applied to it; if it does not do so, he repairs or remakes the barrel without extra charge to his employer.

The Government proof-house is a more comprehensive and interesting establishment. It is situated near the Walsall-road, at the northern part of the town. This is a proof-house in the fullest sense of the term, for everything is put to a severe test. Workmen and errand-boys, messengers and carriers, are continually coming to and fro, bringing the several parts of muskets which have been made by different manufacturers, in order that they may be proved by persons belonging to the establishment. Each musket barrel is here proved separately. It is loaded, and put into an oak chest of immense strength, the lid of which is then held down by ponderous iron fastenings: by an ingenious piece of mechanism the barrel is fired:— bullet, smoke, flame,—all are confined within the chest, which is shortly afterwards removed. When the strength of the barrel is thus tested, it is gauged and measured in its diameter, and in the straightness of its bore; and all the little nicks and juts and prominences which are to aid in fastening it to the stock are separately examined. The woodwork is struck and beat and examined, to see that there is no flaw. The locks are taken piecemeal, and screws and springs minutely examined. The bayonets are struck and bent in various ways, to prove their temper; and the sockets which are to receive them in the gun are examined and gauged. In short, every bit of metal and wood in the musket undergoes a separate and severe scrutiny; and if anything fails in the proof, the makers are the losers; for the terms of contract are, that all the articles made shall bear the test applied to them. Most of these provers in the Government establishment receive high wages; great experience, steadiness, and tact are called for in the exercise of their vocation, and are paid for accordingly. It is however, a sad exemplification of the stupid folly of 'strikes,' in mechanical employments, that one class of operatives, engaged in fitting together all the minute portions of a gun, thought proper to 'strike' for higher wages a few years ago, although they were then in receipt of £4 or £5 per week wages. The Government would not submit to this demand; and an ingenious arrangement of machinery was invented,—not for the purpose of dispensing with manual labour, but to enable a workman of moderate skill to make the requisite adjustments: this renders the employers independent of any small clique of high-skilled workmen; and the 'percussioners' as they are called, have since had cause to regret their short-sightedness.

If guns are one of the notable features of Birmingham, *Buttons* are another. Ever since buttons were buttons, Birmingham has been their head-quarters. Birmingham, doubtless, would undertake to button up all the world, if the world wished to be buttoned. You must not say you "don't care a button" to a Birmingham man; for to him a button is a thing of rank and importance: it is not to be laughed at or treated with disrespect. Buttons give employment, and homes, and sustenance to many thousands of persons in this town; and every change of fashion in these tiny products involves large commercial consequences to Birmingham. The demands for 'protection' in buttons have been more numerous than most persons are aware of. In the early part of the last century, coat-buttons usually consisted of a central mould or disc, made of wood or bone, round which threads of gold, silver, or silk, were wound by women and girls, who sat about a table at this employment. But at last, the fashion arose of covering the mould with the same kind of cloth as was employed in the dress. Hence arose a huge outcry; and a petition was presented to Parliament, which, like all similar petitions in all ages, shows how utterly useless is the attempt to legislate on such matters. The Petition held forth thus:—
"It appears by long experience that needle-wrought buttons have been a manufacture of considerable importance to the welfare of this kingdom, insomuch that, whenever such buttons have been disused, the wisdom of the nation hath always interposed, as may be seen by the several Acts passed in the reigns of King William, Queen Anne, and of His Majesty in this present Parliament. Yet, notwithstanding the said Acts, the tailors continue to make buttons and button-holes of the same materials the clothes are made of; and the said Acts cannot be put in execution, because of the great difficulties that attend the detecting and prosecuting the offenders."—Of course, the said Acts *could* not be put in execution. If those incorrigible tailors had been the very models of meekness and kindness, they could not have done it: they were relatively powerless: they had to bend to a greater power—fashion—which runs its circle in spite of all such laws.

Buttons were more showy affairs in Hutton's time, half a century ago, than they are now. He says:—
"Though the original date is rather uncertain, yet we well remember the long coats of our grandfathers covered with half a gross of high-tops, and the cloaks of our grandmothers ornamented with a horn button, nearly the size of a crown piece, a watch, or John-apple, curiously wrought, as having passed through the Birmingham press. Though the common round button keeps in with the pace of the day, yet we sometimes see the oval, the square, the pea, and the pyramid, flash into existence. In some branches of traffic the wearer calls loudly for new fashions; but in this the fashions tread upon each other and crowd upon the wearer." Our buttons are less capricious in shape than were those of Hutton's time; but we have new kinds of which he knew nothing.

The button manufactories of Birmingham are among the largest and most interesting in the town. They are really comprehensive and well-conducted establishments in which supervision and subdivision play their parts effectively. Gilt buttons, silvered buttons, plated buttons, silk buttons, Florentine buttons, shell buttons, horn buttons, bone buttons, wood buttons— all are made in these large establishments; and the processes relating to them are very numerous. For instance, there are, for the common gilt button, the stamping out of the sheet-copper 'blank,' the trimming of the edge, the cutting of a bit of wire for the 'shank,' the bending of this shank to its proper shape, the adjustment and soldering of the shank to the blank, the steeping of the button in a mercurial solution, the gilding by means of gold-amalgam, the fixing of the gold by a heated iron, the cleansing of the button, the burnishing with a piece of blood-stone, and the papering and wrapping up. If, instead of being flat and plain on both sides, the button is curved on the outside, or if it be globular like some of the buttons for boys' dresses, or if it has a raised device like livery or uniform buttons, there are many additional processes besides those here enumerated; and if the button is to exhibit a silvery whiteness instead of a golden yellow, both the original metal and the final chemical processes are different. For a Florentine or silk coat-button, two bits of thin sheet-iron, a bit of pasteboard, a bit of thick canvas, and a bit of the Florentine or silk, are cut out, by stamping each circular disc; and by a most beautiful machine, all these are adjusted and fixed together by two movements of a press—without the aid of glue, cement, riveting, sewing, twisting, screwing, or any other fastening. For buttons of shell, wood, or bone, the chief operations are, the mechanical ones of turning, stamping, and drilling; while, for those of horn, the main process is pressure in a die or mould, while the horn is in a softened state of heat.

As a proof of the commercial largeness of this apparently trivial trade, it has been stated that a new kind of button has been known to cost the manufacturer several thousand pounds, and many months of thought and labour, before it was introduced into the market!

If any one would witness the nimbleness of female fingers, let him ask permission to enter one of the Birmingham button-factories. Many females are there employed, and the celerity with which they cut out the small circular pieces of metal and other material by means of a cutting-press, is almost inconceivable. Some of the circular convex discs of copper are stamped out at the rate of thirty in a minute; each stamping involving three distinct operations—the placing of the strip of metal, the movement of the stamping-press, and the removal of the little disc from the cell or die where it lies!

A very wide range is taken of articles made by somewhat similar means to buttons. Stamping-works are numerous at Birmingham; and at these works an exhaustless variety of articles is produced from sheet metal, applicable to various purposes of use and ornament. The supply of dies and stamps is a remarkable feature at such establishments. It is said that some of the Birmingham stamping-works possess as many as a quarter of a million separate dies, all of which are liable to be thrown into disuse by the changes of fashion!

Buttons, and guns, and stamped goods, are among those examples of the use of mixed metals at Birmingham, which we alluded to in a former page. But they are not the only examples: brass tubing, curtain rods, bedsteads, telescope tubing, candlesticks and chandeliers, bronze gates, railings, vases, tripods, statuettes, ornaments, Britannia-metal—or would-be silver—articles of use and ornament; these, and a hundred others, help to swell the list of industrial products of this remarkable town. Pins, too, though small in size, are large in manufacturing importance. They are made in large establishments; and the cutting, the pointing, the head-cutting, the whitening, and the papering, give employment to a large number of hands, of which the chief are boys and girls.

THE GOLD AND SILVER TRADES.

But even yet we have not done with Birmingham metals: we must go to gold and silver, of which a large quantity is used in the town. If we enter the shop of a London silversmith and jeweller, and look around at the tempting bits of glitter that meet the eye, we should be pretty safe in saying that much of the store came from Birmingham. Cheap articles in gold and silver can in no other town in England be made so cheaply as in Birmingham. She has all the machinery wanted, all the manual skill wanted, all the trading organization wanted, for such work. Her principal manufacturers are in a position to show that if costly and highly-artistic productions be required, she can produce them; but the prominent and staple produce is that which meets the requirements of a low-priced market. No one knows better than a Birmingham man, how to make a grain of gold cover a large surface; and it is by carrying this principle to an outrageous extent, that some of the smaller and more obscure manufacturers have given a 'Brummagem' character to Birmingham goods, not without injury to others engaged in the trade.

The gold and silver manufactures of Birmingham exhibit the *workshop* system of that town more, perhaps, than the manufactures in other metals. There are very few or no large factories for these goods. The pencil-cases, pen-holders, thimbles, bodkins, toothpicks,

tweezers, brooches, finger-rings, (25,000 gold wedding-rings have been marked in the Assay-office of Birmingham in one year!) ear-rings, chains, bracelets, armlets, buckles, clasps, and countless other articles in gold and silver, are mostly made in small workshops, or in the attic or back shop of a workman. There are in Birmingham many manufacturers, factors, or warehouse keepers, who supply these goods to the shopkeepers and dealers, but who do not keep premises in which the goods are actually made. Such an employer supplies himself with gold and silver of the requisite thicknesses and standard, and gives out this material either to a workman, or to an intermediate manufacturer, who keeps a small number of men and apprentices under him; and the material so given out is manufactured to a definite size and form, which is returned to the factor, who pays for the labour so bestowed. So subdivided is the employment, that one article of gold and silver is made, perhaps, by a dozen different persons, in as many places; each workman or small master undertaking to make only one fragmentary portion of the complete article. In some cases these fragments are put together on the factor's own premises; while in other instances, a distinct class of middlemen or operatives undertake this sort of putting together. The articles themselves are made by varied applications of the processes of tube-drawing, wire-drawing, rolling, stamping, pressing, turning, filing, punching, chasing, engraving, riveting, soldering, &c., according to the size and nature of the thing to be made; and the little bits of gold and silver are mostly fashioned at small workbenches in small workshops. Hence arises one peculiarity of Birmingham trade. Few towns equal it in the number of small workshops scattered throughout its streets and lanes; or in the number of its small masters.

As Birmingham has found out the art of spreading out a bit of gold to a large superficies, so has she brought to a high state of efficiency that most extraordinary art, by which electricity instantaneously developes a film of gold or silver over a prepared surface. This is not the place to talk about the wonders of the galvanic battery. We must ask the reader to believe the following points: That when a solid substance, properly prepared for the purpose, is immersed in a liquid solution, containing a chemical combination of gold or silver, if the mysterious influence from a galvanic-battery be brought to bear on the solution, the metal separates from it, and becomes spread in a thin film on the prepared body; that the thin film may be rendered permanent and durable; that it may be burnished and otherwise wrought up to a high state of beauty; and that it may then be used as a substitute for real gold and silver plate. All this has been developed at Birmingham within the last few years, partly founded on galvanic discoveries made elsewhere. One of the largest and finest establishments in Birmingham, is devoted to this kind of electro-plating, or electro-metallurgy; and there are several of smaller rank. The kind of work for which the electro-plate is mostly used as a substitute, is silver-plated, or gold-plated, or silver-gilt goods. The real and costly gold and silver goods, of the highest class, which are as pure within as they are without, are either cast in moulds, or stamped and pressed from sheet metal, or both, and are afterwards wrought up to the highest pitch of finish and beauty by hand. The plated goods are made by rolling a sheet of copper and a sheet of silver together with such force as permanently to unite them, and by working up this two-fold sheet into any required form : the silver, which is very much thinner than the copper, being used as the outer or visible surface. Silver-gilt goods are made either of solid silver, or of silver plated on copper, and then coated externally by what is termed the "water-gilding" process, with a thin film of gold. But in the electro process, no solid gold, silver, or plated copper are used. A model, or foundation, varied in its character and material according to the purpose in view, is prepared by the designer, the modeller, and the moulder, and the chaser ; and this being immersed in a vessel containing a chemical solution of gold or silver, a few minutes' application of a galvanic-battery suffices to separate the gold or silver from the solution, and to deposit it in an exquisitely fine and complete layer on the model. This is one of the most surprising and beautiful of all manufacturing processes. It is one which vividly illustrates the debt that art owes to science. Whether rank and fortune will consent to use this substitute for plate instead of plate itself —whether some manufacturers will be tempted to make the thin film of precious metal *too* thin, and thereby damage the good name of this magically-coated material—are points beside our present object. Enough to state what can be done, what has been doing, and what is now doing, in the development of this beautiful department of industry. As one consequence of the spread of this art will be to add to the number and variety of richly adorned articles in the houses of the middle and upper classes, it will lend an impetus to the arts of design ; since no brilliancy in the appearance of the material will ensure for it permanent favour unless it be wedded to that grace and elegance which it is the office of the designer to infuse into it.

Birmingham has contrived to make *paper* do duty as a material for some most attractive and delicate productions. Papier maché—the name and the material both derived from the French—is a pulpy mass prepared by shredding and softening pieces of paper ; and this pulp can be pressed into moulds, and afterwards dried into an uncommonly light, tough, and durable material for ornaments. Another mode of using paper is to paste numerous sheets together so as to form a pasteboard or cartoon, and to use this pasteboard as a material. Tea-trays and other flat articles are made of this pasteboard material ; while more diversified and ornamental forms are better produced on the other method. There is an establishment in Birmingham in which this art is brought to a high pitch of excellence ; for after the actual form is given to the material, the processes of japaning, painting,

gilding, varnishing, and polishing, are carried to an elaborate extent : insomuch that it becomes difficult to believe that so humble a material as paper lies beneath so much beauty. It is possible that this sheet may reach the hands of some who saw the gorgeous sofa at a recent exhibition of specimens of manufacture at the Society of Arts in London : this sofa will suffice to show what Birmingham can do to impart solidity and splendour to—mere paper.

SOCIAL FEATURES.

Let not the reader suppose that we are about to drag him into all the workshops of Birmingham. He will perhaps think that there has been enough of it already ; but to attempt to give anything like a general idea of this busy town, without dwelling a little on the organization and subdivision of its manufactures, would be nearly as bad as enacting 'Hamlet' with the chief character omitted. Further down, deeper and deeper still, goes the subdivision of employments, not only in metallurgic manufactures, but in others in which other materials are employed. When the British Association held its meeting at Birmingham, in 1839, a valuable paper relating to that town was read before the Statistical Section, by Mr. Francis Clark, who from his two-fold position as a manufacturer and a magistrate, has peculiar facilities for obtaining trustworthy information. In this paper he gives an analysis of 791 persons who formed the members of a Provident Institution ; and he found that these members belonged to no less than 110 different branches of trade—an amount of subdivision of labour truly remarkable. He was also able, by examining the condition of a large number of these persons, to form an average which he thinks approaches very near to a correct average of the earnings of *the whole* of the Birmingham operatives, at different ages. These rates he gives thus : from seven to thirteen years of age, boys, 3s. 1d. per week—girls, 2s. 4d. ; from fourteen to twenty years, males, 5s. 9d. —females, 5s. 2d. ; and above the age of twenty years, males, 24s. 3d.—females, 8s. per week. If such an estimate be applicable to an *average* of years, and if the men of Birmingham do really earn and receive 24s. per week as an average of *all* the manufacturing trades, we will venture to express a doubt whether there is another large manufacturing town in the kingdom to equal it ; at any rate, it has but few equals. How must the poor framework-knitters of Nottingham and Leicester envy these Birmingham men ! According to this estimate, a Birmingham metal-worker could buy out three or four cotton-stocking men of Nottingham, or worsted-stocking men of Leicester.

It is one consequence of the mode of conducting Birmingham manufactures, that the wretched cellar-dwellings of many of our large towns are not there met with. There are but few extreme poor, driven down to the verge of starvation. Times may be hard, and trade may be slack, but still the weekly wages distributed are always large and more equable than in most towns. The workmen do not congregate six or eight families in a house : it is more common for one or two families to have a small house to themselves ; and as, luckily for Birmingham, most of the streets incline from one end to the other, on account of the irregular level of the town, the streets undergo a natural drainage, which is of immense importance to the health of the inhabitants. The consequence is, that Birmingham is, for a smoky centre of manufactures, a tolerably healthy town. A little progress is being made by some of the larger firms, in the adoption of smoke-consuming apparatus for the furnaces.; and if Birmingham would go as far as Leeds has gone in this matter, it would be all the better for the inhabitants.

In Birmingham, as elsewhere, a Mechanics' Institution was founded,—flourished for a time,—and decayed. On its ashes arose a Polytechnic Institution, having a somewhat similar object in view : this still exists. Whether by such or by any other means, the raising of the position of the working-classes by education is of immense importance in a town like Birmingham, where such classes form so large a proportion of the whole population. That they become both better workmen and better men by such agency, is now pretty well a settled point. Valuable testimony on this matter was given by Mr. Turner, the eminent button-manufacturer, in 1841, to one of the Commissioners sent down by the Government. His evidence was summed up as follows : " Knows all his work-people personally ; has had constant opportunities of contrasting the conduct of the educated and well-informed with that of the ignorant and ill-informed ; finds that the educated workman is unquestionably of much greater value to his employer than the uneducated ; would not, knowingly, employ even one of the lowest mechanics, who could not read ; finds that exactly in proportion to the extent of a mechanic's information, is he respectful in his behaviour, and generally well-conducted ; and, on the other hand, the ignorant are less respectful, and not so well-disposed towards their employers. In the event of any disagreement between the workmen and their employer, the most ignorant are always the first to complain, and are invariably the most suspicious and untractable." This distinct avowal, by an employer of several hundred persons, is very important.

A remarkable and laudable attempt is being made by Mr. J. G. Brooks, to establish a 'Ministry to the Poor.' A Society has been formed, in co-operation with certain Sunday-schools ; the purpose of which is, to diffuse among the poorest inhabitants a knowledge of and taste for those purifying influences to which they are too often strangers. A humble house in a poor neighbourhood has been rented at a low rate : it has been cleansed and whitewashed and rendered decent : it has been furnished with a few forms and desks, and a few books. Here, at stated times, the broad principles of Christian truth are set forth to whoever will come and listen to them, in a series of simple discourses. At other times the poor and ragged are invited in to learn something of the decencies and usefulness of society : boys and girls are taught to read and write, and girls are taught to hem and sew. Those who, at their own wretched homes (for there are some wretched homes at Birmingham, notwithstanding the circumstances recently touched upon) witness nothing but ignorance, dirt, and profligacy, do here catch a glimpse of something better, a something which may raise them above the level of brutes. At other times the sick and poverty-stricken are visited at their own homes ; and a little pecuniary aid, and that sort of kindness which is often of more value even than money itself, are bestowed. Something of a literary cast, too, is attempted ; for a news-room, library, and lecture-room —forming indeed a sort of humble Mechanics' Institution—are maintained. It is termed the People's Instruction Society, and is, in fact, a distinct and self-supporting institution. Though the payment is so marvellously small as one penny per week from each member, yet by frugality and good management, the Society is enabled to have a news-room, with newspapers and magazines, a circulating library, classes for instruction, and occasional lectures.—Let those who would wish to do much with little means, see what earnestness of purpose can accomplish. This 'Ministry to the Poor' seems to have but small funds at its command ; yet it has set on foot a People's Instruction Society, Sunday-schools, a Provident Institution, Day-schools for children, Evening-schools for adults, and District-visitings to those whom small contributions in money, food, or raiment might benefit. In short, it is an attempt to penetrate down to those classes which Mechanics' Institutions and Benefit Societies have never yet reached.—All honour to such an attempt !

A few words more about the men of Birmingham before we leave them. Institutions have been established, mainly through the instrumentality of Mr. Sanders and Mr. Francis Clark, designed to embrace all the advantages of Benefit Societies, without the pernicious obligation of holding the meetings at public houses, and with sounder financial principles in regard to the apportionment of benefits. One of these, the 'Birmingham Provident and Benevolent Institution,' has been established about fifteen years, and is in connection with Church Sunday-schools. It numbers between two and three thousand members. It embraces a Medical Attendance Club ; an Annuity, Sick Pay, and Funeral Society ; a Saving Club ; an Endowment Society ; a Benevolent Fund ; and a Library. Whatever may be the station in life of a member, of either sex or of any age, some one or other of these benefits may be made available. By paying one penny a week, medicines and medical attendance are ensured during sickness. By making a small weekly payment, a funeral-fund, a sick-fund, a superannuation-fund, or an endowment-fund, may be secured. The other Society, the 'New Meeting Provident Institution,' is very like the former in character and object, and is, like it, primarily connected with certain Sunday-schools. Both proceed on the principle, that the system of co-operation and mutual assistance may be judiciously carried much further than it usually is; that the every-day troubles of life are susceptible of much amelioration, if we would only make to-day think for to-morrow. If sickness be the evil, one penny per week will do what man can do to ward it-off. If prudent saving be the object, sums so small as one penny are received as deposits. If endowment or superannuation allowance be desired, every imaginable facility is offered, to meet the means and wants of all. Two admirable features accompany these institutions—they are self-supporting, deriving no portion of their funds from charity; and they are conducive to length of life; for an extraordinary difference is observable, between the rate of mortality in those who belong to these institutions, and in that of the other inhabitants of Birmingham who move in a similar sphere of life.

The Neighbouring Iron and Coal Towns.

We must now ask the reader to turn his back upon Birmingham, and take a hasty glance at the district by which it is surrounded.

North-westward lies the busy home of iron and coal. Nothing gives a better notion of the region than a ride outside a 'bus' or coach to Wolverhampton or Dudley: especially if we return in the evening, after dusk; we see the daylight scene in one direction, and the extraordinary glare of flames in the other. We can see that the grass of the fields is willing to be green, if the miner will let it alone. We see how towns and villages have grown up where farms and fields were a few years ago. We see that churches, and chapels, and humanizing institutions have settled down in these spots, but generally long after a thick population had been brought together. We see a district in which every town and village, every house, every man and woman and child, every occupation and station, are more or less dependent on, and at the mercy of lumps of coal and lumps of iron.—Very unpoetical, perhaps; but yet there is a good deal of rough stern poetry in these said lumps.

The southern corner of Staffordshire is one huge honey-comb. The ground is perforated and tunnelled and galleried in every direction, insomuch that the surface is continually sinking. Many and many a house requires to be chained round its middle, or propped up by timbers or stones, to prevent it from falling. Many a turnpike-road or path changes its level by sinking. When a new church or other large structure is to be built, great difficulty is sometimes experienced in finding a spot firm enough to bear it. Near Sedgeley there are (or were, a few years ago) a church and parsonage-house made of frame-work, capable of being *screwed-up* when they wander from the perpendicular! Much of the Staffordshire coal lies very near the surface; so that when the coal is extracted by mining, the superficial crust is scarcely strong enough to bear itself up.

If the district underground is a labyrinth of dark passages, so is the district above-ground a labyrinth of red brick houses. It is scarcely an exaggeration to say that the eight miles from Birmingham to Dudley present one continued string of houses. You hardly know what to call it; you meet with but few of the adjuncts of a complete and regular town. It seems as if houses had been jotted down here and there—anywhere—and had shuffled themselves into the order of a street. There is one large parish, West Bromwich, which was a few years ago mostly agricultural ground, belonging in great part to the Earl of Dartmouth. Shafts have since then been opened, galleries wrought, and mines established; and as the crude coal and iron was brought up to the surface, so were smelting and colliery works formed on the surface; and as the works spread around, so were houses rapidly built for the accommodation of the workmen. The consequence is that West Bromwich has become not merely a parish, but a town; and a most extraordinary town it is. You cannot tell where it begins or where it ends. You may walk through two or three miles of houses along the high road, and be all the while in West Bromwich; you may see a clustering village afar off across some fields—still West Bromwich; you may leave the high road altogether, and strike across to the north-east—again and again West Bromwich. Several local names are however, gradually being given to different portions of the group; and we shall probably find the name of West Bromwich by-and-bye applied to a more limited area of ground. Most of the houses inhabited by the workmen are two stories in height, and as all of them are made with red bricks, (red through the impregnation of the clay with iron,) the several groups are very conspicuous when contrasted with the green fields seen from a distance.

The principal manufacturing towns, however, are of older date, and have the usual concomitants of established towns. The whole of them—Wolverhampton, Walsall, Wednesbury, Bilston, Dudley, &c.,—derive their commercial position almost wholly from manufactures in iron: and it is curious to see how particular branches of manufacture have settled in particular spots. Bloxwich supports itself almost wholly on awl-blades and bridle-bits; small matters perhaps, but great by the power of numbers. Wednesfield has its locks, keys, and traps—most of the unlucky rats, mice, foxes badgers, and weasels, have to thank Wednesfield for the means by which they have been or are to be captured; Darlaston, its gun-locks, hinges, and stirrups; Walsall, its buckles, spurs, bits, and saddlers' ironmongery generally; Wednesbury, its gas-pipes, coach-springs, axles, screws, hinges, and bolts; Bilston, its japan-work and tin-plating, but principally the actual smelting and making of iron; Sedgeley and the whole of its neighbourhood, nails, nails, nothing but nails; Dudley, its vices, fire-irons, nails, and chains; Willenhall, its locks, keys, latches, curry-combs, bolts and gridirons; Tipton, its heavy iron-work; and lastly Wolverhampton, the giant of the whole, with its more varied products of locks, keys, nails, tips, screws, hinges, vices, bolts, tin toys, steel toys, tin plate-work, and japan-work. A few towns, farther south, such as Oldbury, Smethwick, Rowley-Regis, Halesowen, and Stourbridge, are also connected with the iron manufacture, but not so exclusively as those named above.

The state of society has assumed many remarkable features in this district. Workers in iron give the tone to everything; and many of the elements of a well-balanced society are in some places almost wholly wanting. In the parish of Darlaston, containing about ten thousand inhabitants, it was said, two or three years ago, that there were no resident gentry whatever; all were engaged either in mining or manufacturing. Walsall is a good town: it is situated on a declivity, which greatly aids in the maintenance of drainage. The Walsall folks keep up an odd old custom on St. Clement's Day, of scrambling for apples and nuts thrown among them from the Town Hall. Bilston is perhaps the blackest of the black: it makes more iron, as is said, than the whole of Sweden, and it must needs be a smoky place. There are many streets of this town where gas-lights are almost useless—so bright is the glare at night from fifty furnace-mouths being within a short distance of it.

In Wolverhampton, Willenhall, and others of these towns, the work is nearly all executed by small masters, who have a few apprentices each, and work hard themselves. They work for factors, or dealers, who procure their supplies from these men and sell to merchants and shop-keepers. There are whole districts of streets and courts almost without names or numbers, in which neither name nor occupation of the inhabitants is written up. A stranger could neither see nor guess what is going on, nor who are the residents; and if he wished to find a particular person, he might have some difficulty so to do—unless he were well-learned in nick-names, in which these Staffordshire folks love to revel. The nameless streets and the non-numbered houses are occupied by the small masters who work in small shops in the rear of their dwellings; and as they know nothing of any employers except the factors whom they supply, they care nothing about the means of publicity which a London tradesman courts. Willenhall is really an extraordinary place. There are scarcely a dozen professional men in it—all the rest being working manufacturers; and two-thirds of all these workmen are employed in making locks. The men are mostly small masters, employing two or three apprentices each; and masters and boys together work on almost incessantly from morning to night. Mr. Horne, one of the Commissioners sent down a few years ago to examine the state of the manufacturing districts, gave the following picture:—" Sometimes men and boys eat their meals at leisure: the former at intervals, between drinking and smoking, the latter while playing at marbles or going on errands. This is on Monday and Tuesday. In the middle and latter end of the week, men and boys eat their victuals while they work, or bolt their victuals standing. You see a locksmith and his two apprentices with a plate before each of them, heaped up (at the best of times when

they can get such things) with potatoes and lumps of something or other,—but seldom meat,—and a large slice of bread in one hand. Your attention is called off for two minutes, and, on turning round again, you see the man and boys filing away at the vice." This filing is the most endless part of the Willenhall work: for the file is the tool that principally gives form and surface to the parts of a lock. Some men file away all their lives, and, in such cases, they acquire what the workmen call a K knee, from the position into which they throw themselves while at the bench. The apprentices, who are sent with a small premium by the guardians of agricultural parishes, have but a hard life of it. Yet do these Willenhall folks manage to pick up some crumbs of comfort out of their rough and toil-worn life. They have quite an *esprit de corps* among them: a Willenhall girl will, for the most part, only marry one of her townsmen, and a stranger-husband would be looked upon with something like doubt and suspicion. The love of home shows itself in a remarkable way; for, a few years ago, a factor sent over twenty-five Willenhall men to Brussels, to establish a lock-manufacture there: their earnings, which at home had not reached 15s. per week, were £3 a week at Brussels: yet they did not like it; they were out of place and out of sorts, and they came back one by one to Willenhall, there to resume their old habits.

Intermediate between the towns of this remarkable district are the hovels and forges of the *nailors*—a class quite as curious as any we have named. For a century and a half—probably much more—have these nailors speckled the district. William Hutton, who contrives to give an odd quaintness to everything he says, tells us, that when he first approached Birmingham, about a century ago, he was surprised to observe the prodigious number of blacksmiths' shops upon the road. "In some of these shops," he remarks, "I observed one or more females, stripped of their upper garments, and not overcharged with their lower, wielding the hammer with all the grace of the sex. The beauties of their face were rather eclipsed by the smut of the anvil, or, in poetical phrase, the tincture of the forge had taken possession of those lips which might have been taken by a kiss. Struck with the novelty, I enquired 'Whether the ladies in this country shod horses?' but was answered, with a smile, 'They are nailors.' "

It is as true in 1848 as it was in 1748, that these sooty beauties make nails. Their cottages are the same, their forges are the same, the anvils and hammers are the same, their fathers, brothers, husbands are the same: scarcely anything in their condition is altered, except that they have to contend against nails made by steam-power. The machine-made nails are mostly what are termed *cut* nails, while those made with the hammer on an anvil are *wrought*; and the wrought-nailors are still able to bear up against the competition. They go to a neighbouring town and buy a bundle of iron rods, or wire, of the requisite thickness, and then they work the iron up into nails in the little, dark, dirty forges attached to their dwellings: father-

7 & 8.—SOHO.

mother, sons, daughters, all frequently working to-gether. The rapidity of their rate of working is quite surprising. Some years ago a man undertook, for a wager, to make thirty-four thousand large nails in a fortnight: he completed his task, and a newspaper-writer took the trouble of making a few statistical calculations on the matter. He estimated that, on an average, twenty-five strokes with a hammer were required for each nail—making nearly a million in all; and that, in addition to this, the man had to give from one to three blasts with his bellows for every nail he made, had to supply the fire with fuel, and had to move from the fire-place to where the nails were made, and *vice versâ*, upwards of 42,830 times!—Curious statistics these! The nailors are a rough set; but we are not obliged to suppose them always amenable to the picture drawn by Hutton.

THE NEIGHBOURING PLEASURE-SPOTS.

When the Birmingham inhabitants wish for a holiday, whither can they go? We have before said that they have no river, no steam-boats, no regattas, no rowing matches, no parks; and the iron and coal towns of the north-west are not exactly the places for a ramble or a pic-nic. Yet is there a goodly sprinkling of pleasant green fields near and around Birmingham, when once we get quit of the streets and factories. A year or two ago, there was an advertisement which looked like a gentle satire on the Birmingham folks, for their do-nothing course in respect to public parks. At the eastern margin of the town is a place of public amuse-ment called Vauxhall Gardens, concerning which an advertisement ran thus:—"Eligible public walks having long been desired and highly recommended, —— feels convinced that those who wish for such a deside-ratum, will find the above rustic retreat a place where they can promenade for hours, among stately trees, flowers, and shrubs, with beautifully designed fountains of crystal water, playing continuously; the whole pre-senting a rich display of nature and of art, refreshing and invigorating, &c., &c., &c."

There are two villages or hamlets almost absorbed within the vortex of Birmingham, but yet still main-taining the character of country spots, Aston and Hands-worth, which are worth a visit for more reasons than one. They are agreeable places in themselves, and they are associated with the names of the departed great. The spirit of James Watt hovers about this neighbour-hood. In the immediate vicinity of Handsworth, at the northern margin of Birmingham, stand the celebrated Soho Works (Cuts, Nos. 7 and 8), which will be asso-ciated with the great engineer long after every brick has been razed to the ground. From the year 1774, when Watt entered into partnership with Matthew Boulton, till 1800, when the partnership ended, the works at Soho were the great scene of operation, whence all Europe was supplied with those steam-engines which so excited the wonder of all; and even after Watt's seces-sion from the firm, his enduring friendship with Boulton

till the death of the latter in 1809, the residence of Watt near the spot till his own death in 1819, and the continuance of the establishment by the sons of these two great men—all tended to fix public attention on the Soho Works as the centre of a mighty social power. It was more than ninety years ago that a rolling mill was built on this spot—previously a barren heath; in 1762, the mill was bought by Boulton; in 1764, he built the large structure which still exists; and for eighty-two years the operations of the establishment have continued uninterruptedly. It is not merely the making of steam-engines and other large pieces of machinery that has made these works famous; other manufacturing pro-cesses have been introduced; or, more properly speak-ing, other manufactures preceded that of steam-engines by ten years. Buttons, buckles, watch-chains, and trinkets, were the first objects of manufacture; then plated ware; then *or molu* vases, candelabra, clock-cases and watch-stands; then pure silver plate, of the highest order of excellence. All this occurred before the introduction of Watt to the firm. The establish-ment was then divided into two parts; one for continu-ing the former manufactures, and the other for making steam-engines and other machines. Their separation has continued down to the present day: but the impor-tance of the place is gone—it has outlived itself. The relations and successors of the two great founders have become wealthy men; and, like the Etruria Works of Wedgwood, and the Cromford Works of Arkwright, the Soho Works no longer possess the rank which per-tained to them in the days of *the* Watt and *the* Boulton. There is even, we believe, mention made of breaking up part of the establishment, and letting the ground on building leases. We must never, however, forget what the Soho has been: its memory must be preserved in pictures as well as in words.

The representative of the Boultons resides in a mansion near the works; while the representative of the Watts lives at Aston Hall, (Cut, No. 10,) a fine old mansion, of which we obtain a peep through an avenue of trees, from the Lichfield Road. This manor-house was erected by Sir Thomas Holt, in the reign of Queen Elizabeth, and is a good example of those comely com-fortable hospitable old Elizabethan structures. Charles the First was sheltered there for two nights, previous to the battle of Edge Hill; for which act of loyalty, the Parliamentarians soon afterwards levied contributions on the then Sir Thomas Holt, and cannonaded his mansion: the impress of some of these republican bullets is still visible on the staircase. Not far from Aston Hall is the church, a picturesque old building, which looks well from all sides. Indeed, the neighbourhood around Aston is sprinkled with many pretty spots. It is well worth a walk, too, to the nice old country church at Handsworth. The church and the village seem to have run away from each other; for while the one is out in the open fields, thoroughly countryfied in all its associations, the other is half a mile off, on the busy Wolverhampton Road! The church is many centuries old, and contains several curious monuments and relics of past days. Some of the redoubtable church-wardens have cut a brave recumbent knight's head in two, in order to make room for a staircase! The gem of the church is Chantrey's statue of Watt, one of the finest works of that artist's chisel. The exquisite purity of the marble which Chantrey was fortunate enough to obtain, the wonderful expression of steadiness and thought in the countenance of Watt, the ease of the attitude, and the skilful placing of the statue in a small chapel built expressly for its reception, (over Watt's grave,) all combine to make this more than commonly interesting among works of its class. Smaller memorials of Boulton and Murdoch are contained in the same church. This Murdoch was the engineer who first applied gas-lighting with success; and the Soho was the first large building where it was so applied. It is something for a church to contain the remains of Watt, Boulton, and Murdoch!

At a distance of three or four miles beyond Aston and Handsworth is the Roman Catholic college of St. Mary's, Oscott. (Cut, No. 11.) Few positions can be more thoroughly free from the associations of smoky towns and busy streets. Nothing but green fields and country scenes lie between this spot and the northern confines of Birmingham; and were it not for the dim haze that hovers in the south, we should not know that any bustling town is near. The iron and the coal-seams do not reach so far eastward as this spot; so that Oscott is as much free from mines below as from factories above: there is a total absence of both. This was the spot selected about ten years ago, by a body of influential Roman Catholics, as the site for a college; and Mr. Pugin has built a large and beautiful structure, in the midst of an equally beautiful park or enclosure. On applying at the entrance gate, (which, like everything else about the spot, is of the Tudor or late perpendicular style,) we are admitted into the park, which presents some lovely walks and terraces, winding round in picturesque curves, bounded by luxuriant trees, shrubs, and flowers. A quarter of a mile of such walking brings us to the college, a very extensive red brick and stone-dressed building. It has its chapel, refectories, oratories, vestries, studies, dormitories—all the requirements for a college in the Roman Catholic form; and it is difficult, while walking through them, to believe that we are in the nineteenth century, and in the vicinity of a rattling, hammering, stamping, steaming town. Everything speaks of past times: the black letter inscriptions over the doors; the encaustic tiles under the feet; the stained glass in the windows; the combination of plain dark oak with polychrome decorations; the ancient relics carefully stored up and displayed in cases; the black collegiate costume of the quiet, pale, calm students; the order and noiselessness that pervade the whole building—all have a sort of impressiveness about them, even to Non-Catholics. The chapel is a most splendid apartment, glittering with devices and ornaments in gold and in every imaginable colour: indeed the chapel seems to be the special object for display, as the other portions of the

building are for the most part plain and simple. A view from the windows of the college shows that the surrounding country, though flat and undiversified by rivers, is thoroughly open, healthy, and in parts really beautiful. It was good judgment that selected such a site for such a building.

There is a large extent of open heathy country to the south-west of Oscott, which affords abundant scope for all sorts of open-air sports; but, unluckily, it is too far off from Birmingham. Even among the mining districts themselves there are a few pleasant spots; and when we come to Dudley, we reach a park which is not only beautiful, but highly picturesque. A considerable portion of Dudley and its mines belongs to Lord Ward, who is also proprietor of the ruined Castle and the large Park named after it. The Castle we have before alluded to: it is a fine old ruin, with its warder's tower, watch-tower, triple gate, keep, vault and dungeons, sally-port, octagon-tower, justice-hall, dining-hall, chapel, all more or less discernible, but all in dilapidation. The view from the summit of the keep is wide-spreading: Lichfield Cathedral in the north-east; Birmingham in the east; Hagley in the south; the Malvern Hills in the south-west—all are visible, forming a back-ground to the busy environs of Dudley. But when we descend from the keep, and enter the grounds of the Castle, we soon become as much shut out from busy and smoky scenes, and as much surrounded by sylvan objects, as if we were a hundred miles away from any manufacturing town. At some very remote period, these grounds appear to have been quarried for limestone; for there are dells, and caverns, and recesses, whose origin we can hardly explain in any other way; but most of them are now clothed with verdure, or bordered by trees and shrubs; and the eye is easily cheated into the belief that they are all natural formations. Some of the limestone caverns are almost as curious as the caves of Derbyshire; and there is a ravine, about half-a-mile in length, which looks so wild, so ancient, so picturesque, that one is inclined to think it *ought* to be one of Nature's productions. It is mortifying to be obliged to descend from such a thought, and to dabble with quarrymen's picks and shovels; yet the opinion seems to be that even this ravine is the work of men's hands. We will try, however, until evidence becomes stronger than it has yet been, to believe that the ravine existed when picks and shovels were not; and we will, moreover, advise the reader, if ever he is within a short distance from Dudley, to go and judge for himself: he will not regret his visit.

South of Dudley there is a very pleasant part of Worcestershire and Shropshire, which can be reached by an hour or two's ride from Birmingham. The *Leasowes* and *Hagley*—the one associated with Shenstone, and the other with the Lyttletons—here lie enticingly open to a ramble of inspection. On the south of the road from Birmingham to Halesowen, in the midst of a very delightful country, a plain white house peeps between the trees. It is a house which, *per se,*

9.—BLUE-COAT SCHOOL.   10.—ASTON HALL.

deserves scarcely a word of praise; but it was once inhabited by Shenstone, and it is surrounded by a lovely park—lovely once through the care bestowed in giving it loveliness, and lovely still though neglected. It is unpleasant, nevertheless, to be obliged to hear that Shenstone spent on this spot the means which might have been appropriated better. Somewhat above a century ago, he came into possession of the place; from which time, as Dr. Johnson says, he began "to point his prospects, to diversify his surface, to entangle his walks, and to wind his waters; which he did with such judgment and fancy, as made his little domain the envy of the great and the admiration of the skilful: a place to be visited by travellers and copied by designers." But what was the consequence? He devoted so much of his means to external embellishment that the house continued to be a dilapidated sort of place, unfit, as he acknowledges, to receive 'polite friends.' His beautiful park did not give him adequate pleasure; for he became, from various causes, disappointed, querulous, and dejected, in his declining years. Of the Poems, Prose Essays, and Letters of Shenstone, a large portion of the latter relate wholly to the Leasowes, and his 'Schoolmistress,' the best and most celebrated of his productions, is an embodiment of his thoughts relating to a primitive dame-school at which he received his early education, near Halesowen. The ground on which the Leasowes stands is very undulating, and these undulations have been so managed as to give the spot a much larger apparent area than it really possesses. Some parts are wild and rugged; some so thickly planted that the light of the sun is almost hidden; some soft and graceful; little streams wander hither and thither, and little bridges cross them in unexpected spots. In bygone times, the last-century taste of statues, and vases, and urns was displayed in decking the grounds; but these have disappeared: these, indeed, we might spare, but there are other indications of neglect which are less welcome. Eighty-five years have elapsed since Shenstone's death; and perhaps it is hardly to be expected that those who have since possessed the estate should in all cases have been imbued with the feeling necessary for its conservation.

Four miles south-westward of the Leasowes stands Hagley Park, the seat of Lord Lyttleton. Hagley itself is a village, but not a manufacturing one; it contains the private residences of many manufacturers and merchants, whose places of business are elsewhere; so that it presents much more of a holiday aspect than other villages whose names we have mentioned. Sir Thomas Lyttleton, father of Lyttleton the poet, lived here in the early part of the last century; but its celebrity began with the next possessor, who was created Lord Lyttleton in the early part of George the Third's reign. This Lord Lyttleton's 'Monody on his Wife's Death;' 'Prologue to the Tragedy of Coriolanus,' and other poetical pieces, attracted a good deal of notice in the last century; but he is perhaps best known to later readers by his 'History of the Reign

of Henry the Second.' In his 'Monody,' he speaks of the 'well-known ground' the 'fountain's side,' the 'waters gliding along the valley,' the 'wide-stretched prospect,' the 'playful fawns,' the 'verdant lawns' —all of which referred to Hagley; and we find all these at Hagley at the present day. As this estate, unlike the Leasowes, has remained the family seat of the founder's successors, it has been well kept up and cared for. The mansion is far larger than Shenstone's, and of more architectural pretensions. Within, it has a fine collection of pictures, and all the adornments of an English noble's house. Without, it has a park of great beauty, with lawns, shrubberies, gardens, woods, walks, pastures, avenues, artificial basins, and all the similar concomitants. The neat little village church, too, is so situated as to seem to form part of the domain. On the opposite side of the high road is a lofty obelisk, erected to the memory of Lord Lyttleton; and near it is one of those little prettinesses, mock temples, which are always in danger of slipping down from the sublime to the ridiculous—a proverbially short journey. It is a miniature Parthenon, perched up among the trees on a hill, which serves as the Acropolis; and so long as no other building is within immediate view, all goes on tolerably well; but, as seen from a portion of the park, there is a provoking cottage gable comes into comparison, and the poor temple loses a good deal of its dignity immediately. We doubt whether the Leasowes, even in its comparative decay, is not a finer bit of landscape, a more delightful place to lose one's-self in, than even its larger and better preserved neighbour.

The country lying southward of Birmingham does not begin to be particularly attractive until we arrive at a considerable distance from that town: but when this distance has been traversed, the charms of the locality are so numerous and so varied, and appeal to such a crowd of associations, that we get almost into a new world. Stratford, and its undying celebrities, Warwick, and its fine old castle,—one of the few real old English castles still kept up and inhabited,—Kenilworth, and all that it suggests to us of the Elizabethan days, Guy's Cliff, and Piers Gaveston's monument, and Stoneleigh Abbey,—all these come upon the sight one by one. But it is only by a stretch of courtesy that we can be permitted to include such a district in the environs of Birmingham; and all attempts to describe these scenes in the present sheet would be out of place. Coventry, too, situated about as far as Warwick from Birmingham, is a host in itself; with its ribbons and ribbon-weavers, its fine old churches and crosses and halls, its pageants of former days, and its Shaksperean associations. But though it does not fall within our present object to describe all these fine things, and to 'lionize' the reader through the beauties of North Warwickshire, it is quite permissible for us to congratulate the good folks of Birmingham on the practical nearness of all these scenes. We say 'practical nearness,' because distance is, in our day, better measured by minutes than by miles. A railway run of some thirty or forty minutes carries us from Birmingham to Coventry, whence a branch line turns off to Kenilworth, Leamington, and Warwick; the result is, that we can reach Kenilworth as early by this conveyance as Dudley by coach: so that, after all, Coventry, and Kenilworth, and Warwick *are* next-door neighbours to Birmingham. Stratford-upon-Avon lies further to the south-west, about eight miles from Warwick, or twenty-three from Birmingham, by coach-road. When the new railway schemes are completed, the Birmingham and Oxford line will give ready access to Stratford from Birmingham; while the Narrow Gauge Company, on their part, are shortening and improving the line from Birmingham to Kenilworth and Warwick. We must beg of the poets, and painters, and anglers, and lovers of the picturesque, to concede to us this point: that if railways sometimes break up a beautiful scene by ugly embankments and yawning cuttings, and disturb the calm serenity of country life by the shrieking tones of the railway whistle, they afford good compensation, by opening up to the denizens of busy towns scenes which they would never have met with but for the aid afforded by these media of communication. It is more fanciful than true to draw the distinction, "God made the country, man made the town;" but it is perfectly true, that if the town-man can become occasionally a country-man, he will be all the better for it.

Birmingham, then, in spite of all its iron and coal, is not without its beauty-spots, as soon as the greenfields are reached. We have named a few of them; and a rambler who is not frightened by a good tough walk, or a railway excursionist who can spare a shilling or two, might easily meet with others.

11.—OSCOTT.

Before leaving Birmingham, it may afford some gratification to speak of WARWICK, LEAMINGTON and STRATFORD-UPON-AVON, which are so celebrated in the history of the county of Warwick, and at the same time so replete with local interest.

The city of WARWICK is one of the most ancient in the kingdom. After having been destroyed by the Danes, it was restored by Ethelfreda, daughter of Alfred the Great, who built a fort there, A. D. 913. It returned Members to Parliament so early as Edward I., and received its first charter of incorporation in the time of Philip and Mary. The city stands on the west side of the river Avon —Shakspere's Avon—from which it is separated by Warwick Castle and grounds. It was formerly a little county metropolis ; many of the families of rank and fortune had winter residences there ; the Warwick balls were frequented by a select and exclusive set ; a small theatre was well supported ; and few races assembled more distinguished company than used to throng the Warwick course once a-year, in family coaches and four-in-hands. All this grandeur has departed. Leamington has absorbed the wealth and fashion of Warwick ; the town mansions have fallen into plebeian hands ; the theatre has ceased to be a training school for the London boards ; and the streets, except on particular occasions, are silent.

Warwick deserves a long journey, if it were only for the sake of the fine woodland scenery which surrounds it for ten miles. But the castle is the especial object of attraction. This interesting edifice rises upon the brink of the river, which foams past over the weir of an ancient mill, where once the inhabitants of the borough were bound by feudal service to grind all their corn. The best approach is from the Leamington Lower Road, over a bridge of one arch, built by a late Earl of Warwick. Cæsar's and Guy's towers rise into sight from a surrounding grove. The entrance is through an arched gateway, past a lodge, where the relics of Earl Guy, the Dun Cow slayer, are preserved ; and a winding avenue cut in solid rock effects a sort of surprise, which, as the castle comes again suddenly into view, is very pleasing. The exterior realizes a baronial abode of the fourteenth or fifteenth century ; the interior has been modernized sufficiently to be made comfortable, still retaining many striking features of its ancient state. A closely-cropped green sward covers the quadrangle, which was formerly the tilting-ground. The date of Cæsar's tower, the oldest part of the building, is uncertain. Guy's tower, of the latter part of the fourteenth century, is in fine preservation. The great entrance hall, a grand old room sixty-two feet by thirty-seven, is adorned with armour and other appurtenances to feudal state.

LEAMINGTON, about two miles distant from the city of Warwick, may be reached by turnpike-roads and a pleasant footpath. Mineral waters, fashion, a clever physician, the Warwickshire hounds, the surplus capital of Birmingham, speculative builders, and excellent sanitary regulations, have contributed to the rapid rise of this picturesque and fashionable watering-place. The waters, which resemble mild Epsom salts, first brought the village into notice, in 1794 ; although the existence of mineral springs at Leamington Priory had been recorded by Camden and Dugdale. At a later period, the talents of Dr. Jephson attracted an army of invalids and would-be-invalids ; Sir Walter Scott's novels brought Kenilworth and Warwick Castle into fashion, just as Garrick, like a second Peter the Hermit, preached up a pilgrimage to Stratford-on-Avon. The number of interesting places within an easy walk or drive of Leamington forms one of its great advantages. Either on foot or in a carriage (and Leamington is extremely well provided with carriages for hire), Warwick Castle, or Stratford-on-Avon, or Guy's Cliff, and Kenilworth, or Stoneleigh Abbey, may be visited in the course of a day.

STONELEIGH ABBEY, the residence of Lord Leigh, is noticeable for its fine woodland scenery— splendid oaks adorn the Park—and as having been the subject of a series of very extraordinary trials at the suit of claimants of the estate and ancient title. In the incidents of the Leigh Peerage are the materials of half-a-dozen romances.

GUY'S CLIFF—where Guy Earl of Warwick, and slayer of the Dun Cow, lived and died as a hermit, fed daily by his Countess, without knowing whom she fed—is situated on the banks of the Avon, about a mile from Warwick, on the high road to Kenilworth, and may be approached by footpaths across the fields leading to the same village.

STRATFORD-ON-AVON (with SHOTTERY, where Ann Hathaway was courted by Shakspere), and CHARLECOTE, the residence of the Sir Thomas Lucy whom the poet immortalized as Justice Shallow, are all within ten miles of Leamington.

1.—EXTERIOR OF SHAKSPERE'S HOUSE, IN 1788, 1807, AND 1824.

WASHINGTON IRVING, in one of his pleasantest papers in the 'Sketch Book,' speaking of the tomb of Shakspere, in the chancel of Stratford Church, says, "There are other monuments around, but the mind refuses to dwell on anything that is not connected with Shakspere. This idea pervades the place." The American essayist could only look upon this fine old church as Shakspere's 'mausoleum.' Through the same predominant association, the pleasant town of Stratford, the gentle river, the quiet meadows, the old woods, the pretty villages, which are as interesting in themselves as many a locality which the topographer has delighted to describe, appear to have no value but in connexion with the memory of him who was born here and died here,—who had knelt in this church, and conversed with neighbours in these streets, and gazed upon this river, and rambled amidst these meadows and woods, and had been familiar with all the features of these scenes that two centuries and a half of change have not yet obliterated. It is the Stratford of William Shakspere that we are about to present to our reader, and nothing more.*

In the custody of the vicar of Stratford is a venerable book—a tall, thick, narrow book, whose leaves are of fine vellum—which contains various records that are interesting to us—to all Englishmen—to universal mankind. It is the 'Register of the Baptisms, Marriages, and Burials of the Parish of Stratford.' The record commences in 1558, the first year of Elizabeth, when the regulation for keeping such registers was strictly enforced. Let us pause on the one entry of that book, which most concerns the human race :

" 1564, April 26.—GULIELMUS FILIUS JOHANNES SHAKSPERE."

John Shakspere, the father of William, was thus unquestionably dwelling in Stratford in 1564. He was dwelling there in 1558, for the same register in that year records the baptism of a daughter. His wife was Mary, the daughter of Robert Arden, of Wilmecote, (a neighbouring village,) who was unmarried in 1556, as we learn from the will of her father. Various have been the stories as to the occupation of John Shakspere :

In 1556, the year that Robert, the father of Mary Arden, died, John Shakspere was admitted at the Court-leet as the purchaser of two copyhold estates in Stratford. In 1570 John Shakspere is holding, as tenant under William Clopton, a meadow of fourteen acres, with its appurtenance, called Ingon, at the annual rent of eight pounds—equivalent to at least forty pounds of our present money. When John Shakspere

* Many of the passages in the following paper will be necessarily repeated from the writer's ' William Shakspere. A Biography.' The local descriptions of that work were the result of diligent observation. They are here condensed and brought together.

married, his wife's estate of Asbies, within a short ride of Stratford, came also into his possession. With these facts before us, scanty as they are, can we reasonably doubt that John Shakspere was living upon his own land, renting the land of others, actively engaged in the business of cultivation, in an age when tillage was becoming rapidly profitable,—so much so that men of wealth very often thought it better to take the profits direct than to share them with the tenant? A yeoman he might call himself, a yeoman he might be called by his neighbours; but he was in that social position that he readily passed out of the yeoman into the gentleman, and in all registers and records after 1569 he was styled Master John Shakspere.

The parish of Stratford, then, was unquestionably the birth-place of William Shakspere. But in what part of Stratford dwelt his parents in the year 1564? It was ten years after this that his father became the purchaser of two freehold houses in Henley-street—houses which still exist—houses which the *people* of England are at this moment called upon to preserve as a precious relic of their greatest brother. William Shakspere, then, might have been born at either of his father's copyhold houses, in Greenhill-street, or in Henley-street; he might have been born at Ingon ; or his father might have occupied one of the two freehold houses in Henley-street at the time of the birth of his eldest son. Tradition says, that William Shakspere *was* born in one of these houses; tradition points out the very room in which he was born.

Whether Shakspere were born here, or not, there can be little doubt that this property was the home of his boyhood. It was purchased by John Shakspere, from Edmund Hall and Emma his wife, for forty pounds. In a copy of the chirograph of the fine levied on this occasion (which is now in the possession of Mr. Wheler, of Stratford) the property is described as two messuages, two gardens, and two orchards, with their appurtenances. This document does not define the situation of the property beyond its being in Stratford-upon-Avon; but in the deed of sale of another property in 1591, that property is described as situate between the houses of Robert Johnson and John Shakspere ; and in 1597 John Shakspere himself sells a ' toft, or parcel of land,' in Henley-street, to the purchaser of the property in 1591. The properties can be traced, and leave no doubt of this house in Henley-street being the residence of John Shakspere. Stratford, in the middle of the 16th century, was a scattered town,—no doubt with gardens separating the low and irregular tenements, sleeping ditches intersecting the properties, and stagnant pools exhaling in the road. Even in the reigns of Elizabeth and James the town was nearly destroyed by fire ; and as late as 1618 the privy council represented to the corporation of Stratford that great and lamentable loss had " happened to that town by casualty of fire, which, of late years, hath been very frequently occasioned by means of thatched cottages, stacks of straw, furzes, and such-like combustible stuff, which are suffered to be erected and made confusedly in most of the principal parts of the town without restraint." If such were the case when the family of William Shakspere occupied the best house in Stratford, it is not unreasonable to suppose that sixty years earlier the greater number of houses in Stratford must have been mean timber buildings, thatched cottages run up of combustible stuff; and that the house in Henley Street which John Shakspere occupied and purchased, and which his son inherited and bequeathed to his sister for her life, must have been an important house,—a house fit for a man of substance; a house of some space and comfort, compared with those of the majority of the surrounding population. John Shakspere retained the property during his life; and it descended, as his heir-at-law, to his son William. In the last testament of the poet is this bequest to his " sister Joan :"—" I do will and devise unto her the house, with the appurtenances, in Stratford, wherein she dwelleth, for her natural life, under the yearly rent of twelve-pence." His sister Joan, whose name by marriage was Hart, was residing there in 1639, and she probably continued to reside there till her death in 1646. The *one* house in which Mrs. Hart resided was doubtless the half of the building now forming the butcher's shop and the tenement adjoining; for the other house was known as the Maidenhead Inn, in 1642. In another part of Shakspere's will he bequeaths, amongst the bulk of his property, to his eldest daughter, Susanna Hall, with remainder to her male issue, "two messuages or tenements, with the appurtenances, situate, lying, and being in Henley-street, within the borough of Stratford." There are existing settlements of this very property in the family of Shakspere's eldest daughter and grand-daughter; and this grand-daughter, Elizabeth Nash, who was married a second time to Sir John Barnard, left both houses; namely, " the inn, called the Maidenhead, and the adjoining house and barn," to her kinsmen Thomas and George Hart, the grandsons of her grandfather's " sister Joan." These persons left descendants, with whom this property remained until the beginning of the present century. But it was gradually diminished. The orchards and gardens were originally extensive: a century ago tenements had been built upon them, and they were alienated by the Hart then in possession. The Maidenhead Inn became the Swan Inn, and is now the Swan and Maidenhead. The White Lion, on the other side of the property, was extended, so as to include the remaining orchards and gardens. The house in which Mrs. Hart had lived so long became divided into two tenements; and at the end of the last century the lower part of one was a butcher's shop. Mr. Wheler, in a very interesting account of these premises, and their mutations, published in 1824, tells us that the butcher-occupant, some thirty years ago, having an eye to every gainful attraction, wrote up,

"WILLIAM SHAKSPEAR WAS BORN IN THIS HOUSE.
N.B.—A HORSE AND TAXED CART TO LET."

It is not now used as a butcher's shop, but there are the arrangements for a butcher's trade in the lower room—the cross-beams with hooks, and the window-board for joints. We are now told by a sign-board,

"THE IMMORTAL SHAKSPERE WAS BORN IN THIS HOUSE."

Twenty-five years ago, when we made our first pilgrimage to Stratford, the house had gone out of the family of the Harts, and the last alleged descendant was recently ejected. It had been a gainful trade to her for some years to show the old kitchen behind the shop, and the honoured bed-room. When the poor old woman, the last of the Harts, had to quit her vocation (she claimed to have inherited some of the genius, if she had lost the possessions, of her great ancestor, for she had produced a marvellous poem on the Battle of Waterloo), she set up a rival show-shop on the other side of the street, filled with all sorts of trumpery relics pretended to have belonged to Shakspere. But she was in ill odour. In a fit of resentment, the day before she quitted the ancient house, she whitewashed the walls of the bed-room, so as to obliterate the pencil inscriptions with which they were covered. It has been the work of her successor to remove the plaster; and manifold names, obscure or renowned, again see the light. The house has a few ancient articles of furniture about it; but there is nothing which can be considered as originally belonging to it as the home of William Shakspere.

The engraving which occupies the first page exhibits John Shakspere's houses in Henley-street under three different aspects. No. 1 (the top) is from an original drawing made by Colonel Delamotte in 1788. The houses, it will be observed, then presented one uniform front; and there were dormer windows connected with rooms in the roof. We have a plan before us, accompanying Mr. Wheler's account of these premises, which shows that they occupied a frontage of thirty-one feet. No. 2 is from an original drawing made by Mr. Pyne, after a sketch by Mr. Edridge, in 1807. We now see that the dormer windows are removed, as also the gable at the east end of the front. The house has been shorn of much of its external importance. No. 3 is from a lithograph engraving in Mr. Wheler's account, published in 1824. The premises, we now see, have been pretty equally divided. The Swan and Maidenhead half has had its windows modernised, and the continuation of the timber-frame has been obliterated by a brick casing. In 1807, we observe that the western half had been divided into two tenements;— the fourth of the whole premises, that is the butcher's shop, the kitchen behind, and the two rooms over, being the portion commonly shown as Shakspere's House. Some years ago, upon a frontage, in continuation of the tenement at the west, three small cottages were built. The Royal Shaksperian Club of Stratford-upon-Avon have purchased the whole of this portion of the property. In their address, dated the 2nd of

August, they make the following statement :—"There are within the area of the property on the western side, belonging to Mrs. Izod, four tenements, three of which were apparently erected or converted into habitations, at the beginning of the last century; for before that period they seem to be unnoticed; and the fourth, which, from the continuation of the framed timber front, and from the old doorways communicating internally, evidently forms part of the birth-place; but which, in 1771, was separated from it. The Committee have much satisfaction in stating, that they have within the last few days purchased of Mrs. Izod the four tenements above-mentioned, for the sum of £820; which, as it puts them in actual possession of a part of the house in which Shakspere was born, cannot but be regarded as a most important acquisition at the present moment." The property, whose future destination is to be decided by the auctioneer's hammer, comprises the remainder of the original two messuages. How far the one messuage extended, in which John Shakspere lived, which William Shakspere, his heir, gave to his sister for life, and which did not pass out of the hands of Shakspere's descendants till 1807, cannot, we think, be exactly determined without a professional inspection of the internal walls. It is evident, from the plan, that in some parts doors have been stopped up, and in others doors have been cut through; and we are inclined to think that the second messuage, which became the public-house in 1642, occupied less of the frontage than it now claims. At any rate the Shaksperian Club have done wisely in purchasing one isolated portion of the property. If the public obtain the remainder, there can be no difficulty in restoring the whole to its condition at the end of the sixteenth century. The Shaksperian Club assume, without hesitation, that in these premises William Shakspere was born. Mr. Wheler says, "In this lowly abode it has been the invariable and uncontradicted tradition of the town, that our inimitable Bard drew his first breath." Disturb not the belief. To look upon this ancient house,—perhaps one of the oldest in Stratford, votaries have gathered from every region where the name of Shakspere is known. Washington Irving says, "I had come to Stratford on a poetical pilgrimage. My first visit was to the house where Shakspere was born; and where, according to tradition, he was brought up to his father's craft of wool-combing. It is a small mean-looking edifice of wood and plaster,—a true nestling-place of genius, which seems to delight in hatching its offspring in by-corners. The walls of its squalid chambers are covered with names and inscriptions in every language, by pilgrims of all nations, ranks, and conditions, from the prince to the peasant; and present a simple but striking instance of the spontaneous and universal homage of mankind to the great poet of nature. The house is shown by a garrulous old lady, with a frosty red face, lighted up by a cold blue anxious eye, and garnished with artificial locks of flaxen hair, curling from under an exceedingly dirty cap. She was particularly assiduous in exhibit-

ing the relics with which this, like all other celebrated shrines, abounds." The engravings at page 233 exhibit the room, whose walls "are covered with names and inscriptions in every language," as it existed with some of its "relics," about the period when Washington Irving made his visit to Stratford. He had a true poet's faith even in the relics:—"What is it to us whether these stories be true or false, so long as we can persuade ourselves into the belief of them, and enjoy all the charm of the reality?" The American pilgrim found a representative of the matter-of-fact portion of the world in the old sexton of Stratford, and a superannuated crony named John Ange: "I was grieved to hear these two worthy wights speak very dubiously of the eloquent dame who shows the Shakspere House. John Ange shook his head when I mentioned her valuable and inexhaustible collection of relics, particularly her remains of the mulberry-tree; and the old sexton even expressed a doubt as to Shakspere having been born in her house. I soon discovered that he looked upon her mansion with an evil eye, as a rival to the poet's tomb; the latter having comparatively but few visitors. Thus it is that historians differ at the very outset; and mere pebbles make the stream of truth diverge into different channels, even at the fountain-head." For ourselves, we frankly confess that the want of absolute certainty that Shakspere was born in the house in Henley-street produces a state of mind that is something higher and pleasanter than the conviction that depends upon positive evidence. We are content to follow the popular faith, undoubtingly. The traditionary belief is sanctified by long usage and universal acceptation. The merely curious look in reverent silence upon that mean room, with its massive joists and plastered walls, firm with ribs of oak, where they are told the poet of the human race was born. Eyes now closed on the world, but who have left that behind which the world "will not willingly let die," have glistened under this humble roof, and there have been thoughts unutterable —solemn, confiding, grateful, humble—clustering round their hearts in that hour. The autographs of Byron and Scott are amongst hundreds of perishable inscriptions. Disturb not the belief that William Shakspere first saw the light in this venerated room.

————

Pursuing the associations connected with Shakspere, we naturally turn from the home of his childhood to his school, and his school-boy days.

In the seventh year of the reign of Edward VI., a royal Charter was granted to Stratford for the incorporation of the inhabitants. That charter recites, "That the borough of Stratford-upon-Avon was an ancient borough, in which a certain Guild was theretofore founded, and endowed with divers lands, tenements, and possessions, out of the rents, revenues, and profits, whereof a certain Free Grammar-school for the education of boys there was made and supported." The charter further recites the other public objects to which the property of the Guild had been applied;—that it was dissolved; and that its possessions had come into the hands of the King. The charter of incorporation then grants to the bailiff and burgesses certain properties which were parcel of the possessions of the guild, for the general charges of the borough, for the maintenance of an ancient almshouse, "and that the Free Grammar-school, for the instruction and education of boys and youth, should be thereafter kept up and maintained as theretofore it used to be." The only qualifications necessary for the admission of a boy into the Free Grammar-school of Stratford were, that he should be a resident in the town, of seven years of age, and able to read. The Grammar-school was essentially connected with the corporation of Stratford; and it is impossible to imagine that, when the son of John Shakspere become qualified by age for admission to a school, where the best education of the time was given, literally for nothing, his father, in that year, being chief alderman, should not have sent him to the school. We assume, without any hesitation, that William Shakspere did receive, in every just sense of the word, the education of a scholar; and as such education was to be had at his own door, we also assume that he was brought up at the Free Grammar-school of his own town.

The Grammar-school is now an ancient room, over the old Town-hall of Stratford—both, no doubt, offices of the ancient Guild. We enter from the street into a court, of which one side is formed by the Chapel of the Holy Cross. Opposite the chapel is a staircase; ascending which we are in a plain room, with a ceiling. But it is evident that this work of plaster is modern, and that above it we have the oak roof of the sixteenth century. In this room are a few forms, and a rude antique desk. But it appears that the Chapel of the Guild was also used as a school-room. This chapel is in great part a very perfect specimen of the plainer ecclesiastical architecture of the reign of Henry VII.; —a building of just proportions and some ornament, but not running into elaborate decoration. The interior now presents nothing very remarkable. But upon a general repair of the chapel in 1804, beneath the whitewash of successive generations, was discovered a series of most remarkable paintings — some in a portion of the building erected by Sir Hugh Clopton, and others in the far more ancient chancel. If this was the school-room of William Shakspere, those rude paintings must have produced a powerful effect upon his imagination. Many of them in the ancient chancel constituted a pictorial romance—the History of the Holy Cross, from its origin as a tree at the creation of the world to its rescue from the pagan Cosdroy, king of Persia, by the Christian king, Heraclius; and its final exaltation at Jerusalem,—the anniversary of which event was celebrated at Stratford at its annual fair, held on the 14th of September.

There is a passage in one of Shakspere's sonnets, the 89th, which has induced a belief that he had the misfortune of a physical defect, which would render him peculiarly the object of maternal solicitude:

"Say that thou didst forsake me for some fault,
And I will comment upon that offence:
Speak of my *lameness*, and I straight will halt;
Against thy reasons making no defence."

These and other lines have been interpreted to mean that William Shakspere was literally lame, and that his lameness was such as to limit him, when he became an actor, to the representation of the parts of old men. Of one thing, however, we may be quite sure—that, if Shakspere were lame, his infirmity was not such as to disqualify him for active bodily exertion. The same series of verses that have suggested this belief that he was lame, also show that he was a horseman. His entire works exhibit that familiarity with external nature, with rural occupations, with athletic sports, which is incompatible with an inactive boyhood. It is not impossible that some natural defect, or some accidental injury, may have modified the energy of such a child; and have cherished in him that love of books, and traditionary lore, and silent contemplation, without which his intellect could not have been nourished into its wondrous strength. But we cannot imagine William Shakspere a petted child, chained to home, not breathing the free air upon his native hills, denied the boy's privilege to explore every nook of his own river. We would imagine him communing from the first with Nature, as Gray has painted him,—

"The *dauntless* child
Stretch'd forth his little arms, and smiled."

Much of the education of William Shakspere was unquestionably in the fields. A thousand incidental allusions manifest his familiarity with all the external aspects of nature. He is very rarely a descriptive poet, distinctively so called; but images of mead and grove, of dale and upland, of forest depths, of quiet walks by gentle rivers,—reflections of his own native scenery,—spread themselves without an effort over all his writings. All the occupations of a rural life are glanced at or embodied in his characters. The sports, the festivals, of the lone farm or the secluded hamlet, are presented by him with all the charms of an Arcadian age, but with a truthfulness that is not found in Arcadia. The nicest peculiarities in the habits of the lower creation are given at a touch; we see the rook wing his evening flight to the wood; we hear the drowsy hum of the sharded beetle. He wreathes all the flowers of the field in his delicate chaplets; and even the nicest mysteries of the gardener's art can be expounded by him. All this he appears to do as if from an instinctive power. His poetry in this, as in all other great essentials, is like the operations of nature itself; we see not its workings. But we may be assured, from the very circumstance of its appearing so accidental, so spontaneous in its relations to all external nature and to the country life, that it had its foundation in very early and very accurate observation. Stratford was especially fitted to have been the "green lap" in which the boy-poet was "laid." The whole face of creation here wore an aspect of quiet loveliness. Looking on its placid stream, its gently swelling hills, its rich pastures, its sleeping woodlands, the external world would to him be full of images of repose: it was in the heart of man that he was to seek for the sublime. Nature has thus ever with him something genial and exhilarating. There are storms in his great dramas, but they are the accompaniments of the more terrible storms of human passions: they are raised by the poet's art to make the agony of Lear more intense, and the murder of Duncan more awful. But his love of a smiling creation seems ever present. We must image Stratford as it was, to see how the young Shakspere walked "in glory and in joy" amongst his native fields. Upon the bank of the Avon, having a very slight rise, is placed a scattered town; a town whose dwellings have orchards and gardens, with lofty trees growing in its pathways. Its splendid collegiate church, in the time of Henry VIII., was described to lie half a mile from the town. Its eastern window is reflected in the river which flows beneath, as it is at present reflected (Cut, No. 2); its grey tower is embowered amidst lofty elm-rows. At the opposite end of the town is a fine old bridge, with a causeway whose "wearisome but needful length" tells of inundations in the low pastures that lie all around it. We look upon Dugdale's Map of Barichway Hundred, in which Stratford is situated, published in 1656, and we see four roads issuing from the town; as these are amongst the principal roads at the present day. (See Map.) The one to Henley-in-Arden, which lies through the street in which Shakspere may be supposed to have passed his boyhood, continues over a valley of some

breadth and extent, unenclosed fields undoubtedly in the sixteenth century, with the hamlets of Shottery and Bishopton amidst them. The road leads into the then woody district of Arden. At a short distance from it is the hamlet of Wilmecote, where Mary Arden dwelt; and some two miles aside, more in the heart of the woodland district, and hard by the river Alne, is the village of Aston Cantlow. Another road indicated on this old map is that to Warwick. The wooded hills of Welcombe overhang it, and a little aside, some mile and a half from Stratford, is the meadow of Ingon, which John Shakspere rented in 1570. Very beautiful, even now, is this part of the neighbourhood, with its rapid undulations, little dells which shut in the heart of the scattered sheep, and sudden hills opening upon a wide landscape. Ancient crab-trees and hawthorns tell of uncultivated downs which have rung to the call of the falconer or the horn of the huntsman; and then, having crossed the ridge, we are amongst rich corn-lands, with farm-houses of no modern date scattered about; and deep in the hollow, so as to be hidden till we are upon it, the old village of Snitterfield, with its ancient church and its yew-tree as ancient. Here the poet's maternal grandmother had her jointure; and here, it has been conjectured, his father also had possessions. On the opposite side of Stratford the third road runs in the direction of the Avon to the village of Bidford, with a nearer pathway along the river-bank. We cross the ancient bridge by the fourth road (which also diverges to Shipston), and we are on our way to the celebrated

THE NEIGHBOURHOOD OF STRATFORD.

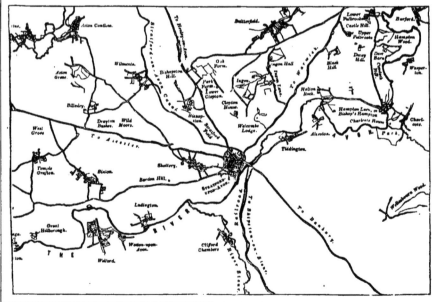

house and estate of Charlcote, the ancient seat of the Lucys, the Shaksperian locality with which most persons are familiar through traditions of deer-stealing. A pleasant ramble, indeed, is this to Charlcote and Hampton Lucy, even with glimpses of the Avon from a turnpike-road. But let the road run through meadows without hedge-rows, with pathways following the river's bank, now diverging when the mill is close upon the stream, now crossing a leafy elevation, and then suddenly dropping under a precipitous wooded rock, and we have a walk such as poet might covet, and such as Shakspere did enjoy in his boy rambles.

On the road to Henley-in-Arden, about two or three hundred yards from the house in Henley-street, where John Shakspere once dwelt, there stands even now a very ancient boundary-tree—an elm which is recorded in a Presentment of the Perambulation of the boundaries of the Borough of Stratford, on the 7th of April, 1591, as "The Elme at the Dovehouse-Close end."[*] The boundary from that elm in the Henley road continued, in another direction, to "the two elms in Evesham highway." Such are the boundaries of the borough at this day. At a period, then, when it was usual for the boys of grammar-schools to attend the annual perambulations in Rogation Week of the clergy, the magistrates, and public officers, and the inhabitants, of parishes and towns, might William Shakspere be found, in gleeful companionship, under this old boundary elm. A wide parish is this of Stratford, including eleven villages and hamlets. A district of beautiful and varied scenery is this parish—hill and valley, wood and water. Following the Avon upon the north bank, against the stream, for some two miles, the processionists would walk through low and fertile meadows—unenclosed pastures then, in all likelihood. A little brook falls into the river, coming down from the marshy uplands of Ingon, where, in spite of modern improvement, the frequent bog attests the accuracy of Dugdale's description. The brook is traced upwards into the hills of Welcombe; and then, for nearly three miles from Welcombe Greenhill, the boundary lies along a wooded ridge, opening prospects of surpassing beauty. There may the distant spires of Coventry be seen peeping above the intermediate hills, and the nearer towers of Warwick lying cradled in their surrounding woods. In another direction a cloud-like spot, in the extreme distance, is the far-famed Wrekin; and turning to the north-west are the noble hills of Malvern, with their well-defined outlines. The Cotswolds lock, in the landscape on another side; while in the middle distance the bold Bredon-hill looks down upon the vale of Evesham. All around is a country of unrivalled fertility, with now and then a plain of considerable extent; but more commonly a succession of undulating hills, some wood-crowned, but all cultivated. At the northern extremity of this high land, which principally belongs to the estate of Clopton, and which was doubtless a park in early times, we have a panoramic view of the valley in which Stratford lies,

[*] The original is in the possession of R. Wheler, Esq., of Stratford.

with its hamlets of Bishopton, Little Wilmecote, Shottery, and Drayton. As the marvellous boy of the Stratford Grammar-school looked upon that plain, how little could he have foreseen the course of his future life! For twenty years of his manhood he was to have no constant dwelling-place in that his native town; but it was to be the home of his affections. He would be gathering fame and opulence in an almost untrodden path, of which his young ambition could shape no definite image; but in the prime of his life he was to bring his wealth to his own Stratford, and become the proprietor and the contented cultivator of some of the loved fields that he now saw mapped out at his feet. Then, a little while, and an early tomb under that grey tower—a tomb so to be honoured in all ages to come,

"That kings for such a tomb would wish to die."

For some six miles the boundary runs from north to south, partly through land which was formerly barren, and still known as Drayton Bushes and Drayton Wild Moor. Here,

"Far from her nest the lapwing cries away."

The green bank of the Avon is again reached at the western extremity of the boundary, and the pretty hamlet of Luddington, with its cottages and old trees standing high above the river sedges, is included. The Avon is crossed where the Stour unites with it; and the boundary extends considerably to the south-east, returning to the town over Clopton's Bridge.

As we become familiar with the neighbourhood of Stratford we find it associated with traditions of Shakspere's early manhood. The world has for the most part received these traditions as it found them, and has cared little to examine whether the stories were baseless that described the youth of the great master of wisdom as one of gay revelry, of bold adventure, and of rash love. We may take these associations as they present themselves, without very scrupulously examining into their historical value. Eight villages in the neighbourhood of Stratford have been characterized in well-known lines by some old resident who had the talent of rhyme. It is remarkable how familiar all the country-people are to this day with these lines, and how invariably they ascribe them to Shakspere:

"Piping Pebworth, dancing Marston,
Haunted Hillborough, hungry Grafton,
Dudging[*] Exhall, Papist Wickaford,
Beggarly Broom, and drunken Bidford."

It is maintained that these epithets have a real historical truth about them. The neighbourhood of Bidford is associated with a "drunken" tradition. About a mile from the little town on the road to Stratford was, some twenty years ago, an ancient crab-tree, well known to the country round as Shakspere's Crab-tree. The tradition which associates it with the name of Shakspere is, like many other traditions regarding the poet, an attempt to embody the general notion that his social qualities were as remarkable as

[*] Sulky, stubborn, in dudgeon.

his genius. In an age when excess of joviality was by some considered almost a virtue, the genial fancy of the dwellers at Stratford may have been pleased to confer upon this crab-tree the honour of sheltering Shakspere from the dews of night, on an occasion when his merrymakings had disqualified him for returning homeward, and he had laid down to sleep under its spreading branches. It is scarcely necessary to enter into an examination of this apocryphal story. Indeed, although the crab-tree was long ago known by the name of 'Shakspere's Crab-tree,' the tradition, that he was amongst a party who had accepted a challenge from the Bidford topers to try which could drink hardest, and there bivouacked after the debauch, is difficult to be traced further than the hearsay evidence of Mr. Samuel Ireland. In the same way, the merry folks of Stratford will tell you to this day that the Falcon Inn in that town was the scene of Shakspere's nightly potations, after he had retired from London to his native home; and they will show you the shovel-board at which he delighted to play. Harmless traditions, ye are yet baseless!—The Falcon was not an inn at all in Shakspere's time, but a goodly private dwelling.

Charlcote:—the name is familiar to every reader of Shakspere; but it is not presented to the world under the influence of pleasant associations with the world's poet. The story, which was first told by Rowe, must be here repeated: "An extravagance that he was guilty of forced him both out of his country, and that way of living which he had taken up; and though it seemed at first to be a blemish upon his good manners, and a misfortune to him, yet it afterwards happily proved the occasion of exerting one of the greatest geniuses that ever was known in dramatic poetry. He had, by a misfortune common enough to young fellows, fallen into ill company, and, amongst them, some, that made a frequent practice of deer-stealing, engaged him more than once in robbing a park that belonged to Sir Thomas Lucy, of Charlcote, near Stratford. For this he was prosecuted by that gentleman, as he thought, somewhat too severely; and, in order to revenge that ill-usage, he made a ballad upon him. And though this, probably the first essay of his poetry, be lost, yet it is said to have been so very bitter, that it redoubled the prosecution against him to that degree, that he was obliged to leave his business and family in Warwickshire for some time, and shelter himself in London." The good old gossip Aubrey is wholly silent about the deer-stealing and the flight to London, merely saying, "This William, being inclined naturally to poetry and acting, came to London, I guess about eighteen." But there were other antiquarian gossips of Aubrey's age, who have left us their testimony upon this subject. The Reverend William Fulman, a fellow of Corpus Christi College, Oxford, who died in 1688, bequeathed his papers to the Reverend Richard Davies, of Sandford, Oxfordshire; and on the death of Mr. Davies, in 1707, these papers were deposited in the library of Corpus Christi. Ful-

2.—STRATFORD CHURCH.

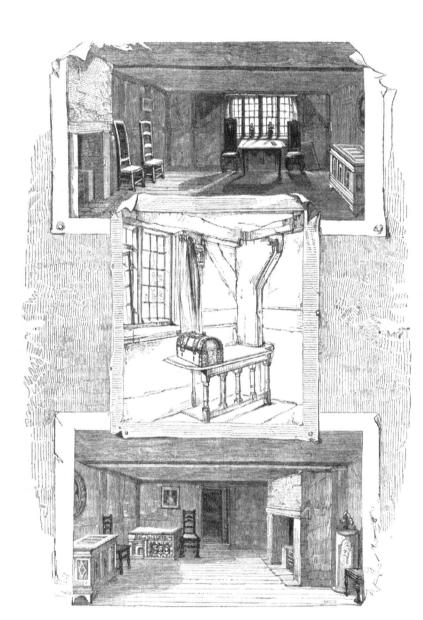

3.—INTERIOR OF SHAKSPERE'S HOUSE.

man appears to have made some collections for the biography of our English poets, and, under the name Shakspere, he gives the dates of his birth and death. But Davies, who added notes to his friend's manuscripts, affords us the following piece of information: "He was much given to all unluckiness, in stealing venison and rabbits; particularly from Sir Lucy, who had him oft whipped, and sometimes imprisoned, and at last made him fly his native country, to his great advancement. But his revenge was so great, that he is his Justice Clodpate, and calls him a great man, and that, in allusion to his name, bore three louses rampant for his arms." The accuracy of this chronicler, as to events supposed to have happened a hundred years before he wrote, may be inferred from his correctness in what was accessible to him. Justice Clodpate is a new character; and the three louses rampant have diminished strangely from the "dozen white luces" of Master Slender. In Mr. Davies's account we have no mention of the ballad—through which, according to Rowe, the young poet revenged his "ill-usage." But Capell, the editor of Shakspere, found a new testimony to that fact: "The writer of his 'Life,' the first modern (Rowe), speaks of a 'lost ballad,' which added fuel, he says, to the knight's before-conceived anger, and 'redoubled the prosecution;' and calls the ballad 'the first essay of Shakespere's poetry:' one stanza of it, which has the appearance of genuine, was put into the editor's hands many years ago by an ingenious gentleman (grandson of its preserver), with this account of the way in which it descended to him:' Mr. Thomas Jones, who dwelt at Tarbick, a village in Worcestershire, a few miles from Stratford-on-Avon, and died in the year 1703, aged upwards of ninety, remembered to have heard from several old people at Stratford the story of Shakespere's robbing Sir Thomas Lucy's park; and their account of it agreed with Mr. Rowe's, with this addition,—that the ballad written against Sir Thomas by Shakespere was stuck upon his park-gate, which exasperated the knight to apply to a lawyer at Warwick to proceed against him. Mr. Jones had put down in writing the first stanza of the ballad, which was all he remembered of it, and Mr. Thomas Wilkes (my grandfather) transmitted it to my father by memory, who also took it in writing." This, then, is the entire evidence as to the deer-stealing affair. According to Rowe, the young Shakspere was engaged more than once in robbing a park, for which he was prosecuted by Sir Thomas Lucy; he made a ballad upon his prosecutor, and then, being more severely pursued, fled to London. According to Davies, he was much given to all unluckiness, in stealing venison and rabbits; for which he was often whipped, sometimes imprisoned, and at last forced to fly the country. According to Jones, the tradition of Rowe was correct as to robbing the park; and the obnoxious ballad being stuck upon the park-gate, a lawyer of Warwick was authorized to prosecute the offender. The tradition is thus full of contradictions upon the face of it. It

necessarily would be so, for each of the witnesses speaks of circumstances that must have happened a hundred years before his time. The state of the law, as to the offence for which William Shakspere is said to have been prosecuted; the state of public opinion, as to the offence; and the position of Sir Thomas Lucy, as regarded his immediate neighbours—all these circumstances go very far to destroy the credibility of the tradition.

Charlcote, then, shall not, at least by us, be surrounded by unpleasant associations in connexion with the name of Shakspere. It is, perhaps, the most interesting locality connected with that name; for in its great features it is essentially unchanged. There stands, with slight alteration, and those in good taste, the old mansion as it was reared in the days of Elizabeth. A broad avenue leads to its fine gateway, which opens into the court and the principal entrance. We would desire to people that hall with kindly inmates; to imagine the fine old knight, perhaps a little too puritanical, indeed, in his latter days, living there in peace and happiness with his family; merry as he ought to have been with his first wife, Jocosa (whose English name, Joyce, sounded not quite so pleasant), and whose epitaph, by her husband, is honourable alike to the deceased and to the survivor: "All the time of her life a true and faithful servant of her good God; never detected of any crime or vice; in religion, most sound; in love to her husband, most faithful and true; in friendship, most constant; to what in trust was committed to her, most secret; in wisdom, excelling; in governing her house, and bringing up of youth in the fear of God, that did converse with her, most rare and singular. A great maintainer of hospitality; greatly esteemed of her betters; misliked of none, unless of the envious. When all is spoken that can be said, a woman so furnished and garnished with virtue as not to be bettered, and hardly to be equalled, of any. As she lived most virtuously, so she died most godly:

"Set down by him that best did know
What hath been written to be true.—Thomas Lucy."

We can picture Sir Thomas planting the second avenue, which leads obliquely across the park from the great gateway to the porch of the parish-church. It is an avenue too narrow for carriages, if carriages then had been common; and the knight and his lady walk in stately guise along that grassy pathway, as the Sunday bells summon them to meet their humble neighbours in a place where all are equal. Charlcote is full of rich woodland scenery. The lime-tree avenue may, perhaps, be of a later date than the age of Elizabeth; and one elm has evidently succeeded another from century to century. But there are old gnarled oaks and beeches dotted about the park. Its little knolls and valleys are the same as they were two centuries ago. The same Avon flows beneath the gentle elevation on which the house stands, sparkling in the sunshine as brightly as when that house was first built. There may we still lie

"Under an oak, whose antique root peeps out
Upon the brook that brawls along this wood,"

and doubt not that there was the place to which

"A poor sequester'd stag,
That from the hunter's aim had ta'en a hurt,
Did come to languish."

There may we still see

"A careless herd,
Full of the pasture,"

leaping gaily along, or crossing the river at their own will in search of fresh fields and low branches whereon to browse.

The village of Charlcote is now one of the prettiest objects. Whatever is new about it—and most of the cottages are new—looks like a restoration of what was old. The same character prevails in the neighbouring village of Hampton Lucy; and it may not be too much to assume that the memory of him who walked in these pleasant places in his younger days, long before the sound of his greatness had gone forth to the ends of the earth, has led to the desire to preserve here something of the architectural character of the age in which he lived. There are a few old houses still left in Charlcote; but the more important have probably been swept away.

In the 'Two Gentlemen of Verona,' which we hold to be one of Shakspere's very early plays, he has denoted some of the characteristics of the Avon of his boyhood:

"The current, that with gentle murmur glides,
Thou know'st, being stopp'd, impatiently doth rage;
But, when his fair course is not hindered,
He makes sweet music with the enamell'd stones,
Giving a gentle kiss to every sedge
He overtaketh in his pilgrimage;
And so by many winding nooks he strays,
With willing sport to the wild ocean."

Very lovely is this Avon for some miles above Stratford; a poet's river in its beauty and its peacefulness. It is disturbed with no sound of traffic; it holds its course unvexed by man through broad meadows and wooded acclivities, which for generations seem to have been dedicated to solitude. All the great natural features of the river must have suffered little change since the time of Shakspere. Inundations in some places may have widened the channel; osier islands may have grown up where there was once a broad stream. But we here look upon the same scenery upon which he looked, as truly as we gaze upon the same blue sky, and see its image in the same glassy water.

The Avon necessarily derives its chief interest from its associations with Shakspere. His contemporaries connected his fame with his native river:—

"Sweet swan of Avon, what a sight it were,
To see thee in our waters yet appear,
And make those flights upon the banks of Thames,
That so did take Eliza and our James!"

So wrote Jonson in his manly lines, "To the Memory of my Beloved, the Author, Mr. William Shakspere, and what he hath left us." After him came Davenant, with a pretty conceit that the river had lost its beauty when the great poet no longer dwelt upon its banks:—

"Beware, delighted poets, when you sing,
To welcome nature in the early spring,
Your numerous feet not tread

The banks of Avon; for each flow'r,
As it ne'er knew a sun or show'r,
Hangs there the pensive head.

Each tree, whose thick and spreading growth hath made
Rather a night beneath the boughs than shade,
Unwilling now to grow,
Looks like the plume a captain wears,
Whose rifled falls are steep'd i' the tears
Which from his last rage flow.

The piteous river wept itself away
Long since, alas! to such a swift decay,
That, reach the map, and look
If you a river there can spy,
And, for a river, your mock'd eye
Will find a shallow brook." *

Joseph Warton describes fair Fancy discovering the infant Shakspere "on the winding Avon's willowed banks." Thomas Warton has painted the scenery of the Avon and its associations with a bright pencil:—

"Avon, thy rural views, thy pastures wild,
The willows that o'er-hang thy twilight edge,
Their boughs entangling with the embattled sedge;
Thy brink with watery foliage quaintly fring'd,
Thy surface with reflected verdure ting'd;
Soothe me with many a pensive pleasure mild.
But while I muse, that here the Bard Divine,
Whose sacred dust yon high-arch'd aisles enclose,
Where the tall windows rise in stately rows
Above th' embowering shade,
Here first, at Fancy's fairy-circled shrine,
Of daisies pied, his infant offering made;
Here, playful yet, in stripling years unripe,
Fram'd o' thy reeds a shrill and artless pipe:
Sudden thy beauties, Avon, all are fled,
As at the waving of some magic wand;
An holy trance my charmed spirit wings,
And awful shapes of leaders and of kings,
People the busy mead,
Like spectres swarming to the wizard's hall;
And slowly pace, and point with trembling hand
The wounds ill-cover'd by the purple pall.
Before me Pity seems to stand,
A weeping mourner, smote with anguish sore
To see Misfortune rend in frantic mood
His robe, with regal woes embroider'd o'er.
Pale Terror leads the visionary band,
And sternly shakes his sceptre, dropping blood." †

The well-known lines of Gray are among his happiest efforts:—

"Far from the sun and summer gale,
In thy green lap was Nature's Darling laid,
What time, where lucid Avon stray'd,
To him the mighty mother did unveil
Her awful face: the dauntless child
Stretch'd forth his little arms, and smil'd.
'This pencil take,' she said, 'whose colours clear
Richly paint the vernal year:
Thine too these golden keys, immortal boy!
This can unlock the gates of joy;
Of horror that, and thrilling fears,
Or ope the sacred source of sympathetic tears.'" ‡

These quotations sufficiently show that the presiding genius of the Avon is Shakspere. But even without this paramount association, the river, although little visited, abounds with picturesque scenery and interesting objects.

Shottery, the prettiest of hamlets, is scarcely a mile from Stratford. Here, in all probability, dwelt one who was to have an important influence upon the destiny of the boy-poet. We cannot say, absolutely, that Anne Hathaway, the future wife of William Shakspere, was of Shottery; but the prettiest of

* In Remembrance of Master William Shakspere. Ode.
† Monody, written near Stratford-upon-Avon.
‡ The Progress of Poesy.

maidens (for the veracious antiquarian boldly says there is a tradition that she was eminently beautiful) would have fitly dwelt in the pleasantest of hamlets. Shakspere's marriage bond, which was discovered a few years since, has set at rest all doubt as to the name and residence of his wife. She is there described as Anne Hathwey, of Stratford, in the diocese of Worcester, maiden. Rowe, in his 'Life,' says:— "Upon his leaving school he seems to have given entirely into that way of living which his father proposed to him; and in order to settle in the world, after a family manner, he thought fit to marry while he was yet very young. His wife was the daughter of one Hathaway, said to have been a substantial yeoman in the neighbourhood of Stratford." At the hamlet of Shottery, which is in the parish of Stratford, the Hathaways had been settled forty years before the period of Shakspere's marriage; for in the Warwickshire Surveys, in the time of Philip and Mary, it is recited that John Hathaway held property at Shottery, by copy of court-roll, dated 20th of April, 34th of Henry VIII. (1543).* The Hathaway of Shakspere's time was named Richard; and the intimacy between him and John Shakspere is shown by a precept in an action against Richard Hathaway, dated 1579, in which John Shakspere is his bondman. Before the discovery of the marriage-bond Malone had found a confirmation of the traditional account that the maiden name of Shakspere's wife was Hathaway; for Lady Barnard, the grand-daughter of Shakspere, makes bequests in her will to the children of Thomas Hathaway, "her kinsman." But Malone doubts whether there were not other Hathaways than those of Shottery, residents in the town of Stratford, and not in the hamlet included in the parish. This is possible. But, on the other hand, the description in the marriage-bond of Anne Hathaway, as of Stratford, is no proof that she was not of Shottery; for such a document would necessarily have regard only to the parish of the person described. Tradition, always valuable when it is not opposed to evidence, has associated for many years the cottage of the Hathaways at Shottery with the wife of Shakspere. Garrick purchased relics out of it at the time of the Stratford Jubilee; Samuel Ireland afterwards carried off what was called Shakspere's courting-chair; and there is still in the house a very ancient carved bedstead, which has been handed down from descendant to descendant as an heirloom. The house was, no doubt, once adequate to form a comfortable residence for a substantial and even wealthy yeoman. It is still a pretty cottage, embosomed by trees, and surrounded by pleasant pastures: and here the young poet might have surrendered his prudence to his affections:—

"As in the sweetest buds
The eating canker dwells, so eating love
Inhabits in the finest wits of all."†

* The Shottery property, which was called Hewland, remained with the descendants of the Hathaways till 1838. Amongst the laudable objects proposed by the Shaksperian Club was the purchase and preservation of this property.

† 'Two Gentlemen of Verona,' Act i. Scene 1.

The very early marriage of the young man, with one more than seven years his elder, has been supposed to have been a rash and passionate proceeding. Upon the face of it, it appears an act that might at least be reproved in the words which follow those we have just quoted:—

"As the most forward bud
Is eaten by the canker ere it blow,
Even so by love the young and tender wit
Is turn'd to folly; blasting in the bud,
Losing his verdure even in the prime,
And all the fair effects of future hopes."

This is the common consequence of precocious marriages; but we are not therefore to conclude that "the young and tender wit" of our Shakspere was "turned to folly"—that "his forward bud" was "eaten by the canker"—that "his verdure" was lost "even in the prime" by his marriage with Anne Hathaway before he was nineteen. The influence which this marriage must have had upon his destinies was no doubt considerable; but it is too much to assume, as it has been assumed, that it was an unhappy influence. All that we *really* know of Shakspere's family life warrants the contrary supposition.

Stratford and its neighbourhood are not less associated with the Shakspere of middle and later life. He left Stratford, as we believe, about 1585 or 1586. If he were absent alone during a portion of the year from his native place, his family probably lived under the roof of his father and mother. His visits to them would not necessarily be of rare occurrence, and of short duration. The latter part of the summer and autumn seem to have been at his disposal as far as theatrical performances were concerned, during the first seven or eight years of his career. In 1597 he bought "all that capital messuage or tenement in Stratford, called the New Place." In 1602 he made a large addition to his property at Stratford, by the purchase of a hundred and seventy acres of arable land, and also a house in Stratford, situated in Walker-street. In 1603 he purchased another messuage in Stratford, Barne's gardens and orchards. In 1605 he accomplished a large purchase of the moiety of the lease of the great and small tithes of Stratford. There could be no doubt from these circumstances, and from documents that show that he dealt in corn, that he was a cultivator of his own land in his native place. At what period he entirely gave up his profession of an actor it is difficult to say. We believe it was earlier in the seventeenth century than is commonly imagined. There can be no doubt that for several years previous to his death, he had returned, wealthy and honoured, to the bosom of those who were dearest to him—his wife and daughters, his mother, his sisters and brothers. The companions of his boyhood are all around him. They have been useful members of society in their native place. He has constantly kept up his intercourse with them. They have looked to him for assistance in their difficulties. He is come to be one of them, to dwell wholly amongst them, to take a deeper interest in their pleasures and in their cares, to receive their sympathy. He is come to walk amidst his own fields, to till them, to sell their produce. His labour will be his recreation. In the activity of his body will the energy of his intellect find its support and rest. A pleasanter residence than Stratford, independent of all the early associations which endeared it to the heart of Shakspere, would have been difficult to find as a poet's resting-place. It was a town, as most old English towns were, of houses amidst gardens. Built of timber, it had been repeatedly devastated by fires. In 1594 and 1595 a vast number of houses had been thus destroyed; but they were probably small tenements and hovels. New houses arose of a better order; and one still exists, bearing the date on its front of 1596, which indicates something of the picturesque beauty of an old English country town. Shakspere's own house was no doubt one of those quaint buildings which were pulled down in the last generation, to set up four walls of plain brick, with equi-distant holes called doors and windows. His garden was a spacious one. The Avon washed its banks; and within its enclosures it had its sunny terraces and green lawns, its pleached alleys and honeysuckle bowers. If the poet walked forth, a few steps brought him into the country: near the pretty hamlet of Shottery, by his own grounds of Bishopton, then part of the great common field of Stratford. Not far from the ancient chapel of Bishopton, of which Dugdale has preserved a representation, and the walls of which still remain, would he watch the operation of seed-time and harvest. If he passed the church and the mill, he was in the pleasant meadows that skirted the Avon on the pathway to Ludington. If he desired to cross the river, he might now do so without going round by the great bridge; for in 1599, soon after he bought New Place, the pretty foot bridge was erected, which still bears that date. His walks and his farm labours were his recreation. We believe that his *higher* labours continued till the end.

It would be something if we could now form an exact notion of the house in which Shakspere lived; of its external appearance, its domestic arrangements. Dugdale, speaking of Sir Hugh Clopton, who built the bridge at Stratford and repaired the chapel, says: "On the north side of this chapel was a fair house, built of brick and timber, by the said Hugh, wherein he lived in his later days, and died." This was nearly a century before Shakspere bought the "fair house," which, in the will of Sir Hugh Clopton, is called the "great house." Theobald says that Shakspere, "having repaired and modelled it to his own mind, changed the name to New Place." Malone holds that this is an error:—"I find from ancient documents that it was called New Place as early at least as 1565." The great house, having been sold out of the Clopton family, was purchased by Shakspere of William Underhill, Esq. Shakspere by his will left it to his daughter, Mrs. Hall, with remainder to her heirs male, or, in default, to her daughter Elizabeth and her heirs male, or the heirs male of his daughter Judith. Mrs. Hall died in 1649;

surviving her husband fourteen years. There is little doubt that she occupied the house when Queen Henrietta Maria, in 1643, coming to Stratford in royal state with a large army, resided for three weeks under this roof. The property descended to her daughter Elizabeth, first married to Mr. Thomas Nash, and afterwards to Sir Thomas Barnard. She dying without issue, New Place was sold in 1675, and was ultimately repurchased by the Clopton family. Sir Hugh Clopton, in the middle of the eighteenth century, resided there. The learned knight thoroughly repaired and beautified the place, as the local historians say, and built a modern front to it. This was the first stage of its desecration. After the death of Sir Hugh, in 1751, it was sold to the Rev. Francis Gastrell, in 1753.

The total destruction of New Place in 1757, by its new possessor, is difficult to account for upon any ordinary principles of action. Malone thus relates the story:—"The Rev. Mr. Gastrell, a man of large fortune, resided in it but a few years, in consequence of a disagreement with the inhabitants of Stratford. Every house in that town that is let or valued at more than 40s. a-year is assessed by the overseers, according to its worth and the ability of the occupier, to pay a monthly rate toward the maintenance of the poor. As Mr. Gastrell resided part of the year at Lichfield, he thought he was assessed too highly; but being very properly compelled by the magistrates of Stratford to pay the whole of what was levied on him, on the principle that his house was occupied by his servants in his absence, he peevishly declared, that *that* house should never be assessed again; and soon afterwards pulled it down, sold the materials, and left the town. Wishing, as it should seem, to be 'damn'd to everlasting fame,' he had some time before cut down Shakspere's celebrated mulberry-tree, to save himself the trouble of showing it to those whose admiration of our great poet led them to visit the poetic ground on which it stood." The cutting down of the mulberry-tree seems to have been regarded as the chief offence in Mr. Gastrell's own generation. His wife was a sister of Johnson's correspondent, Mrs. Aston. After the death of Mr. Gastrell, his widow resided at Lichfield; and in 1776, Boswell, in company with Johnson, dined with the sisters. Boswell on this occasion says—"I was not informed till afterwards, that Mrs. Gastrell's husband was the clergyman who, while he lived at Stratford-upon-Avon, with Gothic barbarity cut down Shakspere's mulberry-tree, and, as Dr. Johnson told me, did it to vex his neighbours. His lady, I have reason to believe on the same authority, participated in the guilt of what the enthusiasts of our immortal bard deem almost a species of sacrilege." The mulberry-tree was cut down in 1756; was sold for firewood; and the bulk of it was purchased by a Mr. Thomas Sharpe, of Stratford-upon-Avon, clock and watchmaker, who made a solemn affidavit some years afterwards, that out of a sincere veneration for the memory of its celebrated planter he had the greater part of it conveyed to his own premises, and worked it into curious toys and useful articles. The destruction of the mulberry-tree, which the previous possessor of New Place used to show with pride and veneration, enraged the people of Stratford; and Mr. Wheler tells us that he remembers to have heard his father say that, when a boy, he assisted in the revenge of breaking the reverend destroyer's windows. The hostilities were put an end to by the Rev. Mr. Gastrell quitting Stratford in 1757; and, upon the principle of doing what he liked with his own, pulling the house to the ground in which Shakspere and his children had lived and died.

There is no good end to be served in execrating the memory of the man who deprived the world of the pleasure of looking upon the rooms in which the author of some of the greatest productions of human intellect had lived, in the common round of humanity—of treading reverentially upon the spot hallowed by his presence and by his labours. It appears to us that this person intended no insult to the memory of Shakspere; and, indeed, thought nothing of Shakspere in the whole course of his proceedings. He bought a house, and paid for it. He wished to enjoy it in quiet. People with whom he could not sympathize intruded upon him to see the gardens and the house. In the gardens was a noble mulberry-tree. Tradition said it was planted by Shakspere; and the professional enthusiasts of Shakspere, the Garricks and the Macklins, had sat under its shade, during the occupation of one who felt that there was a real honour in the ownership of such a place. The Rev. Mr. Gastrell wanted the house and the gardens to himself. He had that strong notion of the exclusive rights of property which belongs to most Englishmen, and especially to ignorant Englishmen. Mr. Gastrell was an ignorant man, though a clergyman. We have seen his diary, written upon a visit to Scotland three years after the pulling down of New Place. His journey was connected with some electioneering intrigues in the Scotch boroughs. He is a stranger in Scotland, and he goes into some of its most romantic districts. The scenery makes no impression upon him, as may be imagined; but he is scandalized beyond measure when he meets with a bad dinner and a rough lodging. He has just literature enough to know the name of Shakspere; but in passing through Forres and Glamis he has not the slightest association with Shakspere's Macbeth. A Captain Gordon informs his vacant mind upon some abstruse subjects, as to which we have the following record:— "He assures me that the Duncan murdered at Forres was the same person that Shakspere writes of." There scarcely requires any further evidence of the prosaic character of his mind; and if there be some truth in the axiom of Shakspere, that

> "The man that hath no music in himself,
> Nor is not moved with concord of sweet sounds,
> Is fit for treasons, stratagems, and spoils,"

we hold, upon the same principle, that the man who speaks in this literal way of the "person that Shakspere writes of," was a fit man to root up Shakspere's mulberry-tree, and pull down his house,

being totally insensible to the feeling that he was doing any injury to any person but himself, and holding that the wood and the stone were his own, to be dealt with at his own good pleasure.

It is a singular fact that no drawings or prints exist of New Place as Shakspere left it, or at any period before the alterations by Sir Hugh Clopton. It is a more singular fact that although Garrick had been there only fourteen years before the destruction, visiting the place with a feeling of veneration that might have led him and others to preserve some memorial of it, there is no trace whatever existing of what New Place was before 1757. The representation of 'New Place' given in some variorum editions of Shakspere, is unquestionably a forgery. A modern house is now built upon the spot. Part of the site is still a pleasant place of garden and bowling-green.

Pass we to Stratford Church—the last and most solemn association with the name of Shakspere. We transcribe a brief description of this honoured pile from the 'Rambles by Rivers' of our friend Mr. James Thorne:—"Stratford church is a structure of large size and unusual beauty. The bold free hand of the old English architect is seen to advantage here. It is placed on the banks of the Avon, which is fringed by a few willows, and from the river our church appears of surpassing gracefulness. It has transepts, nave, chancel, and aisles, a fine tower and steeple. The tower, transepts, and some other portions are of the early English style, and very perfect; the remainder belongs to a later period, and is not less graceful. Its windows are some of them full of rich tracery. The approach from the town is by a curious avenue of lime-trees. The whole appearance of the pile, with the surrounding objects, is extremely pleasing. Beautiful as is the exterior, the interior is even more so. It has very recently been fully restored, and with very great skill—so great skill, indeed, is displayed, that little is left to desire. All the barbaric refinements and embellishments of the last two centuries have been swept away—would they were in every church in the country—and there is really now a fair restoration of the whole to its original state, with some little concessions, indeed, to modern requirements, but all done in the spirit of its original contrivers. The monuments in the church are many, and, besides, *the* monument, are interesting. One chapel is entirely filled with those of the Clopton family, and many of them are handsome. On the north of the east window is a marble tomb to the memory of John Combe, the friend of Shakspere, and whom he has been charged with libelling in some rhyme that would have disgraced a Thames waterman. The statue of Combe was executed by Gerard Johnson, the sculptor of Shakspere's bust. But all else sinks into insignificance before the monument of Shakspere, rendered, too, so doubly interesting by the likeness of him it has preserved."

The sculptor of *the* monument was Gerard Johnson, whose name we learn from Dugdale's correspondence, published by Mr. Hamper in 1827; and we collect from the verses by Digges, prefixed to the first edition of Shakspere, that it was erected previous to 1623 :—

> "Shakspere, at length thy pious fellows give
> The world thy works; thy works by which outlive
> Thy tomb thy name must: when that stone is rent,
> And time dissolves thy Stratford monument,
> Here we alive shall view thee still. This book,
> When brass and marble fade, shall make thee look
> Fresh to all ages."

The fate of this portrait of Shakspere, for we may well account it as such, is a singular one. Mr. Britton, who has on many occasions manifested an enthusiastic feeling for the associations belonging to the great poet, published in 1816 'Remarks on his Monumental Bust,' from which we extract the following passage :— "The Bust is the size of life ; it is formed out of a block of soft stone ; and was originally painted over in imitation of nature. The hands and face were of flesh colour, the eyes of a light hazel, and the hair and beard auburn ; the doublet or coat was scarlet, and covered with a loose black gown, or tabard, without sleeves ; the upper part of the cushion was green, the under half crimson, and the tassels gilt. Such appear to have been the original features of this important but neglected or insulted bust. After remaining in this state above one hundred and twenty years, Mr. John Ward, grandfather to Mrs. Siddons and Mr. Kemble, caused it to be 'repaired,' and the original colours preserved, in 1748, from the profits of the representation of Othello. This was a generous, and apparently a judicious act ; and therefore very unlike the next alteration it was subjected to in 1793. In that year Mr. Malone caused the bust to be covered over with one or more coats of white paint ; and thus at once destroyed its original character, and greatly injured the expression of the face." It is fortunate that we live in an age when no such unscrupulous insolence as that of Malone can be again tolerated.

The following lines are inscribed beneath the bust :—

> "Jvdicio Pylivm, genio Socratem, arte Maronem,
> Terra tegit, popvlvs mæret Olympvs habet.
>
> Stay passenger, why goest thov by so fast,
> Read, if thov canst, whom envious death hath plast
> Within this monvment, Shakspeare, with whome
> Qvick natvre dide; whose name doth deck ye tombe
> Far more than cost; sith all yt. He hath writt
> Leaves living art bvt page to serve his wit.
> Obiit ano. doi. 1616. ætatis 53. die 23 ap."

Below the monument, but at a few paces from the wall, is a flat stone, with the following extraordinary inscription :—

> "Good frend for Jesus sake forbeare,
> To digg the dust encloased heare;
> Bleste be ye man yt spares thes stones,
> And cvrst be he yt moves my bones."

In a letter from Warwickshire, in 1693,* the writer, after describing the monument to Shakspere, and giving its inscription, says, " Near the wall where this monument is erected lies the plain freestone underneath which his body is buried, with this epitaph made by himself a little before his death." He then gives the epitaph, and subsequently adds, " Not one for fear of the curse above-said dare touch his gravestone, though his wife and daughters did earnestly desire to be laid

* Published from the original manuscript by Mr. Rodd. 1838.

in the same grave with him." This information is given by the tourist upon the authority of the clerk who showed him the church, who " was above eighty years old." Here is unquestionable authority for the existence of this freestone seventy-seven years after the death of Shakspere. We have an earlier authority. In a plate to Dugdale's ' Antiquities of Warwickshire,' first published in 1656, we have a representation of Shakspere's tomb, with the following :—" Neare the wall where this monument is erected, lyeth a plain freestone, underneath which his body is buried, with this epitaph :

> " Good frend," &c.

But it is very remarkable, we think, that this plain freestone does not bear the name of Shakspere—has nothing to establish the fact that the stone originally belonged to his grave. We quite agree with Mr. De Quincey, that this doggrel attributed to Shakspere is " equally below his intellect no less than his scholarship ;" and we hold with him that, " as a sort of siste viator appeal to future sextons, it is worthy of the gravedigger or the parish-clerk, who was probably its author."

The wife of Shakspere died on the 6th of August, 1623, and was buried on the 8th, according to the register. The gravestone is next to the stone with the doggrel inscription, but nearer to the north wall, upon which Shakspere's monument is placed. The stone has a brass plate with the following inscription :— " Heere lyeth interred the bodye of Anne, wife of Mr. William Shakspeare, who dep'ted this life the 6th of Avgvst, 1623, being of the age of 67 yeares." Some Latin verses then follow, which are intended to express the deep affection of her daughter, to whom Shakspere bequeathed a life-interest in his real property, and the bulk of his personal. The widow of Shakspere, in all likelihood, resided with this elder daughter. It is possible that they formed one family previous to his death. That daughter died on the 11th of July, 1649, having survived her husband, Dr. Hall, fourteen years. She is described as widow in the register of burials. Ranging with the other stones, but nearer the south wall, is a flat stone now bearing the following inscription :—

> " Heere lyeth ye body of Svsanna, wife to John Hall, Gent. ye davghter of William Shakspeare, Gent. She deceased ye 11th of Jvly, Ao. 1649, Aged 66."

On the same stone is an inscription for Richard Watts, who had no relationship to Shakspere or his descendants. Fortunately, Dugdale has preserved an inscription which the masons of Stratford obliterated, to make room for the record of Richard Watts, who has thus attained a distinction to which he had no claim :

> " Witty above her sexe, but that's not all,
> Wise to salvation was good Mistris Hall,
> Something of Shakespere was in that, but this
> Wholy of him with whom she's now in blisse.
> Then, passenger, ha'st ne'ae a teare,
> To weepe with her that wept with all?
> That wept, yet set herselfe to chere
> Them up with comforts cordiall.
> Her love shall live, her mercy spread,
> When thov hast ne'ae a teare to shed."

Judith, the second daughter of Shakspere, lived till 1662. She was buried on the 9th of February of that year. On the 10th of February, 1616, she was married to Thomas Quiney, of Stratford. The last will of Shakspere would appear to have been prepared in some degree with reference to this marriage. It is dated the 25th of March, 1616; but the word " Januarii" seems to have been first written and afterwards struck out, " Martii" having been written above it. It is not unlikely, and indeed it appears most probable, that the document was prepared before the marriage of Judith; for the elder daughter is mentioned as Susanna Hall—the younger simply as Judith. To her, one thousand pounds is bequeathed, and fifty pounds conditionally. The life-interest of a further sum of one hundred and fifty pounds is also bequeathed to her, with remainder to her children; but if she died without issue within three years after the date of the will, the hundred and fifty pounds were to be otherwise appropriated. We may here fitly mention the mode in which Shakspere disposed of the great bulk of his property, subject, as we have elsewhere shown, to the dower of his wife upon the freehold estates. All the real estate is devised to his daughter, Susanna Hall, for and during the term of her natural life. It is then entailed upon her first son and his heirs male; and in default of such issue, to her second son and his heirs male; and so on: in default of such issue, to his granddaughter, Elizabeth Hall, (called in the language of the time his "niece"); and in default of such issue, to his daughter Judith, and her heirs male. By this strict entailment it was manifestly the object of Shakspere to found a family. Like many other such purposes of short-sighted humanity, the object was not accomplished. His elder daughter had no issue but Elizabeth, and she died childless. The heirs male of Judith died before her. The estates were scattered after the second generation; and the descendants of his sister were the only transmitters to posterity of his blood and lineage. WITH REFERENCE TO THE ONE UNDOUBTED AND MOST INTERESTING PROPERTY THAT BELONGED TO WILLIAM SHAKSPERE, LET THE PEOPLE OF ENGLAND BECOME ITS POSSESSORS AND ITS " HEIRS FOR EVER.'

4.—CHANCEL OF STRATFORD CHURCH.

STAFFORDSHIRE.

THE BLACK COUNTRY.

THE first diverging railway, after leaving Handsworth on the road to the north, is what, for want of a better name, is called the South Staffordshire, which connects Birmingham with Dudley, Walsall, Lichfield, and Tamworth; thus uniting the most purely agricultural with the most thoroughly manufacturing districts, and especially with that part of the great coal-field which is locally known as the "Black Country." In this Black Country, including West Bromwich, Wednesbury, Dudley, and Darlaston, Bilston, Wolverhampton, and several minor villages, a perpetual twilight reigns during the day, and during the night fires on all sides light up the dark landscape with a fiery glow. The pleasant green of pastures is almost unknown; the streams, in which no fishes swim, are black and unwholesome; the natural dead flat is often broken by huge hills of cinders and spoil from the mines; the few trees are stunted and blasted; no birds are to be seen, except a few smoky sparrows; and for miles on miles a black waste spreads around, where furnaces continually smoke, steam-engines hiss, and long chains clank, while blind gin-horses walk their doleful round. From time to time you pass a cluster of deserted roofless cottages of dingiest brick, half-swallowed up in sinking pits or inclining to every point of the compass, while the timbers point up like the ribs of a half-decayed corpse. The majority of the natives of this Tartarian region are in full keeping with the scenery;—savages, without the grace of savages, coarsely clad in filthy garments, with no change on week-days and Sundays, they converse in a language belarded with fearful and disgusting oaths, which can scarcely be recognised as the same as that of civilized England.

On working days few men are to be seen; they are in the pits or the ironworks; but women are met on the highroad clad in men's once white linsey-woolsey coats and felt hats, driving and cursing strings of donkeys laden with coals or iron rods for the use of the nailers.

WALSALL, eight miles from Birmingham, the first town in our way, which may be reached directly by following the South Staffordshire line, or by omnibus, travelling half-a-mile from Bescot Bridge, lies among green fields, out of the bounds of the mining country, although upon the edge of the Warwickshire and Staffordshire coal-field,—indeed the parliamentary borough includes part of the rough population just described. It is very clean, without antiquities or picturesque beauties, and contains nothing to attract visitors except its manufactures, of which the best known is cheap saddlery for the American, West Indian, and Australian markets. They make the leather and wooden parts, as well as stirrups and bridles; also gun-locks, bits, spurs, spades, hinges, screws, files, edge tools; and there is one steel-pen manufactory, besides many articles connected with the Birmingham trade, either finished or unfinished, the number of which is constantly increasing. Walsall is celebrated for its pig-market, a celebrity which railroads have not destroyed, as was expected, but rather increased. Special arrangements for comfortably disembarking these, the most interesting strangers who visit Walsall, have been made at the railway station. The principal church, with a handsome spire, stands upon a hill, and forms a landmark to the surrounding country. The ascent to it, by a number of steps, has, according to popular prejudice, produced an effect upon the legs of the inhabitants more strengthening than elegant, which has originated the provincial phrase of "Walsall-legged."

WEDNESBURY, pronounced Wedgbury, and spelt Wednesberie in Domesday Book, stands in the very heart of the coal and iron district, and is as like Tipton, Darlaston, Bilston, and other towns where the inhabitants are similarly employed, as one sweep is like another. Birmingham factors depend largely on Wedgbury for various kinds of ironwork and "heavy steel toys." The coal pits in the neighbourhood are of great value, and there is no better place in the kingdom to buy a thorough-bred bull dog that will "*kill or die on it*," but never turn tail. The name is supposed to incorporate that of the Saxon god Woden, whose worship consisted in getting drunk and fighting, and, to this day, that is the only relaxation in which many of the inhabitants ever indulge. The church stands upon a hill, where Ethelfleda, Lady of Mercia, built a castle to resist the Danes, A.D. 914, about the time that she erected similar bulwarks at Tamworth and other towns in the Midland counties; but there are no antiquities worth the trouble of visiting.

WOLVERHAMPTON formerly lay away from railroads, at a convenient omnibus distance; but competition has doubly pierced it through and through. One line connects it with Shrewsbury; another with Dudley, Birmingham, and Oxford; and another with Worcester. Add to these means of communication the canals existing before railroads commenced, extending to Hull, Liverpool, Chester, and London, and it will be seen that Wolverhampton is most fortunately placed.

Wolverhampton, and all the towns and villages in the coal and iron district, are only so many branch-Birminghams; in that hardware metropolis the greater part of the goods made are ordered and sold. The town is of great antiquity, although with as few remains as most flourishing towns built of brick, where manufactures have chased away mansions. The name is derived from Walfrana, a sister of King Edgar, who founded a monastery there in A.D. 996, and collected a village round it named Wanfrana Hampton, which was eventually corrupted into Wolverhampton. In the oldest Church, St. Peter's, there is a pulpit formed of a single stone, elaborately sculptured, and a font, with curious bas-relief figures of saints. The Church is collegiate, and the College consists of a dean, who holds the prebend of Wolverhampton, which was annexed by Edward IV. to his free chapel of St. George, within the Chapel of Windsor. A Free Grammar School, supported by endowments, affords a head-master £400 a-year; the second master £200; and a third master £120. Close to the town is a good race-course, well frequented once a year, formerly one of the most fashionable meetings in the country.

From Wolverhampton there are two grand lines leading to Chester; the one through Stafford, and the other through Shrewsbury. On the former line is PINKRIDGE, a rural village of considerable antiquity, ten miles from Wolverhampton, adorned with a Gothic church, and several picturesque houses of the Elizabethan style of domestic architecture.

STAFFORD is a borough town of some antiquity; but it now appears to have lost all semblance of its ancient importance, and quietly realizes the idea of a borough which at every election is for sale to the highest bidder. Its principal manufacture is that of shoes for exportation.

STAFFORD CASTLE, on the summit of a high hill, whose slopes are clothed with forest trees, gives, in the romantic associations it awakens, a very false idea of the town to be found below. The towers of the Castle built by the son of Robert de Tonsi, the Standard Bearer of William the Conqueror, have survived the Wars of the Roses and the contests of the Great Rebellion, while the remainder has been restored in an appropriate style by the family of the present possessors,—representatives of the ancient barony of Stafford.

Beside the old Grand Junction line to Crewe, the Trent Valley line ends, strictly speaking, at Stafford, after passing by Atherston, Tamworth, and Lichfield; but, since the construction of the North Staffordshire, which joins the Trent Valley at Colewich, the most direct way to Manchester is through the pottery district and Macclesfield, instead of by Stafford and Crewe.

On leaving Staffordshire for Crewe we pass, on the right, Ingestrie Park, the seat of the Earl of Talbot; the ruins of Chartley Castle, the property of Earl Ferrers, the defendant in the action brought by Miss Smith for breach of promise of marriage; and Sandon Park, the seat of the Earl of Harrowby, who for many years, before succeeding his father, represented Liverpool in the House of Commons as Lord Sandon.

Near the WHITMORE Station the railway winds for two miles through an excavation in solid stone, enclosed by intermediate slopes of turf, ending, as it were, in an arch, which, spanning the road, forms a sort of frame to a wild region that stretches on beyond.

CHESHIRE, SHROPSHIRE, AND NORTH WALES.

Without anything very important to induce a halt by the way, the train runs into Crewe. Eighteen years ago it was the quietest of country-villages, and now it is intersected in every direction with iron roads pointing from it to almost every point of the compass. Crewe Hall is picturesquely situated on a rising ground, well wooded, near a small lake, and contains, among other pictures, portraits of Fox, " Coke of Norfolk," and several other political friends with whom the first Lord Crewe was closely associated.

NANTWICH, about five miles from Crewe, is one of the towns which supplies Cheshire's salt exports; Middlewich and Northwich being the other two. In all, rich brine springs are found; but the celebrated mines of rock-salt are found at Northwich only. At the Nantwich yearly fairs, samples of the famous Cheshire cheese made in the neighbourhood, of the best brands, may be found.

Just before reaching the HARTFORD BRIDGE Station, on the way to Chester, we pass Vale Royal Abbey, the seat of the Cholmondeley family, pronounced Chumleigh, whose representative, in 1821, was created Lord Delamere.

The third line, which diverges westward from Stafford, is the branch to Shrewsbury. The first station, after leaving the town of Stafford and crossing into Shropshire, is NEWPORT,—a small market town and borough, with a corporation, which can be traced to Henry III. The church is of the fifteenth century, with an interior of great beauty; but it has been frightfully disfigured by aisles built of bricks in a common builders' style of architecture. There is a free grammar school founded by one William Adams in 1756, which has a library attached to the school and five scholarships. The best, of £80 a-year, to Christchurch, Oxford.

WELLINGTON stands at the base of the Wrekin, and is the centre of the Shropshireman's toast. It is the chief town of the coal and iron district, and the point where the line from Wolverhampton makes a junction, which affords the nearest road from Birmingham to Shrewsbury. It was here that Charles I., on his march from Wellington to Shrewsbury, assembled his troops, and, in order to allay the growing disaffection among them, declared that he would "support the reformed religion, govern by law, uphold the privileges of Parliament, and preserve the liberty of the subject."

From Wellington you may proceed by omnibus to Coalbrookdale, where the first iron bridge was built over the Severn, where the Darbys and Dickensons have carried on iron works for more than a century, where coal was first applied profitably to smelting iron, and where the fine iron castings of Berlin have been rivalled, and successful attempts made to introduce the principles of the fine arts into domestic manufactures.

SHREWSBURY, ten miles from Wellington, is, in more respects than one, an interesting town, situated partly on a precipitous peninsula formed by the swift clear waters of the Severn, and united to the opposite side by bridges. The manufactures of Shrewsbury are not very important; they chiefly consist of thread, linen, canvas, and iron-works in the neighbouring suburb of Coleham. A considerable and ancient trade is carried on in Welsh flannel and cloths from the neighbouring counties of Denbigh, Montgomery, and Merioneth, and markets and fairs are held for the benefit of the rich agricultural district around, in which, besides fine butter, cheese, poultry, and live stock, a large assemblage of the blooming, rosy, broad-built Shropshire lasses show the advantage of a mixture of Welsh and English blood. But Shrewsbury is most celebrated for its school, its cakes, its ale, and the clock mentioned by Falstaff, for which on our last visit we found an ingenuous Frenchman industriously searching. The royal free grammar school, endowed by Edward VI., was raised, by the educational talents of the late Dr. Butler, afterwards Bishop of Lichfield and Coventry, to a very high position among our public schools; a position which has been fully maintained by the present master, Dr. Kennedy.

In the history of England and Wales, Shrewsbury plays an important part. It is supposed that " the town was founded by the Britons of the kingdom of Powis, while they were yet struggling with the Saxons, or rather the Angles, for the midland counties, and, it is probable, was founded by them when they found Wroxeter (the Uriconium of the Romans) no longer tenable. On the conquest of the town by the Anglo-Saxons it received the name of Scrobbes-byrig; that is to say, Scrub-burgh, or a town in a scrubby or bushy district, and, in the Saxon Chronicle, Scrobbesbyrig-scire is mentioned, now corrupted or polished into Shropshire. Ethelfleda, whose name we have so often had occasion to mention as the builder of castles and churches, founded the collegiate church of St. Alkmund; and Athelstan established a mint here. It is evident that the "Athelstan the Unready" mentioned in Ivanhoe, must have very much degenerated from the ancestor who established a mint for ready money.

According to Domesday-Book, Shrewsbury had, in Edward the Confessor's time, two hundred and fifty-two houses, with a resident burgess in each house, and five churches. It was included in the Earldom of Shrewsbury, granted by William the Conqueror to his kinsman, Roger de Montgomery, who erected a castle on the entrance of the peninsula on which the town now stands, pulling down fifty houses for that purpose. In the wars between Stephen and the Empress Maude, the castle was taken and retaken; and in the reign of John the town was captured by the Welsh under Llewellyn the Great, who had joined the insurgent Barons in 1215. It was again attacked, and the suburbs burnt by the Welsh in 1234. Shrewsbury was taken by Simon de Montfort and his ally, Llewellyn, grandson of Llewellyn the Great, in 1266, the year before de Montfort fell on the field of Evesham. Here, in 1283, David, the last prince of Wales, was tried, condemned, and executed as a traitor; and here, too, in 1397, in the reign of Richard II., a Parliament was held, at which the Earl of Hereford (afterwards Henry IV.) charged the Duke of Norfolk with treason. The charge was to have been decided by a trial of battle at Coventry. On the appointed morning, " Hereford came forth armed at all points, mounted on a white courser, barded with blue and green velvet, gorgeously embroidered

MARKET-PLACE, SHREWSBURY.

with swans and antelopes of goldsmiths' work. The Duke of Norfolk rode a horse barded with crimson velvet, embroidered with lines of silver and mulberries."

At that time it took more days to travel from Shrewsbury to Coventry than it now does hours. The cloth of gold was as splendidly, perhaps more splendidly, embroidered than anything we can do now ; but in the matter of shirts, shoes, stockings, and the clothing necessary for health and comfort, and of windows and chimneys, and matters necessary for air and shelter, mechanics and day labourers are now better provided than were the squires and pages of those great noblemen. Five years after, Harry of Hereford having become Henry IV. of England, assembled an army at Shrewsbury to march against Owen Glendower, and the following year he fought the battle of Shrewsbury against Hotspur, and his ally the Douglas, which forms the subject of a scene in Shakspere's play of *Henry IV.* At that battle Percy Hotspur marched from Stafford towards Shrewsbury, hoping to reach it before the king, and by being able to command the passage of the Severn to communicate with his ally Glendower ; but Henry, who came from Lichfield, arrived there first, on the 19th July, 1403. The battle was fought the next day at Hateley Field, about three miles from the town.

In the Wars of the Roses, Shrewsbury was Yorkist. In the great Civil War, Charles I. came to Shrewsbury, there received liberal contributions, in money and plate, from the neighbouring gentry, and largely recruited his forces ; and in the course of the war the town was taken and retaken more than once. Thus it will be seen that Shrewsbury is connected with many important events in English history. The first Charter of incorporation extant is of Richard I.

From Shrewsbury to Chester there are many places of interest. The town of OSWESTRY is situated about eighteen miles from Shrewsbury. It was formerly enclosed by walls. It has a venerable and picturesque church, an ancient grammar school, a national school, several considerable charities, a town hall, theatre, and some remains of a strong castle erected in the reign of Stephen.

The DEE VIADUCT, across the Vale of Llangollen, is a noble work, simple in its design, but of massive strength and beautiful proportions. Its length is 1508, its height 147 feet, and the span of its arches (19 in number) 50 feet each. Its construction occupied about two years and a half, and cost £72,346. This arched road, crossing the river Dee under circumstances of great difficulty, is justly regarded as one of the most signal triumphs of engineering skill to be found amongst the magnificent railway works of the British isles.

Pursuing the railway route from CHIRK, the tourist arrives in a few minutes at the LLANGOLLEN ROAD station, whence he can be conveyed by one of Mr. Moses's cars, along the smooth bowling-green surface of the Holyhead road, to the celebrated town of Llangollen, the poetical birth-place of Charles Mathews' " Sweet Jenny Jones." During the summer season there are coaches running daily between this station, Llangollen, Corwen, Bala, Dolgelley, Aberystwith, and other places. This far-famed town consists principally of a long straggling street of small shops, public-houses, and private dwellings. There is not an architectural beauty in the place. All its charms are derived from the surrounding scenery, which has been celebrated both in prose and verse, and roused the enthusiasm of scores of painters and musical composers. The church, which is dedicated to St. Collen, whose Latin legend is extant, is in Early English, and possesses a fine ceiling of carved oak, two richly-coloured paintings of stained glass, by Egginton and Evans, and an ancient chased brass tablet to Magdalen Trevor, of Trevor Hall. The churchyard contains a monument to the memory of the two " Ladies of the Vale," the Hon. Miss Ponsonby and Lady Eleanora Butler, with their faithful servant, Mary Carrol. They all three occupy one spacious tomb, railed off and planted with yew-trees. The selection of Llangollen for a dwelling-place by these ladies, and the description, by various writers, of their residence, PLAS NEWYDD, with their mode of life, give a celebrity to the place which will doubtless long exist.—[For further details see the " Tour through North Wales."]

CASTELL DINAS BRAN (or Crowe Castle, as it is frequently called, from its elevated position) is about a mile from the town. It stands on the summit of a high conical hill, about 910 feet above the Dee. It is believed to be one of the earliest castles of North Wales.

PENGWERN HALL, once the residence of Tudor Trevor, Earl of Hereford and Lord of Bromfield, about 924, and from whom the Mostyn family are descended, is situated in a retired valley near Plas Newydd. It is now the property of the Hon. E. M. Lloyd Mostyn. Several of the windows are entire. A coffin-lid of Goronwy ab Jorwerth, from Valle Crucis Abbey, is built into a wall here.

RHUABAN is a little village, in the midst of a cluster of gentlemen's seats, and in the immediate vicinity of some extensive iron-works and collieries. The most important of the mansions upon which the eye rests is WYNNSTAY, once the residence of Madoc ab Grufydd Maelor, the founder of the Abbey of Valle Crucis. It is surrounded by a park more than eight miles in circumference. The domain is now in the possession of Sir W. W. Wynn, Bart., M.P. for Denbighshire. The grounds are of matchless beauty, and command diversified views of great extent. There is an extensive cold bath; not far from which is a fine fluted column or obelisk, 100 feet in height, erected to the memory of Sir Watkin's grandfather. A spiral staircase in the interior leads to the top, which is protected by a balustrade. Near the south end of the grounds is a cenotaph, erected by the late Sir W. W. Wynn, recording the names of his brother officers and privates who were slain in the Irish Rebellion in 1798. It stands on an eminence, overlooking a deep ravine called Nant-y-Bele (the Dingle of the Marten), through which the Dee urges its rapid course along a narrow channel rich with impending woods. From this elevated spot are seen the distant hills of Caernarvon, Denbigh, Flint, Chester, and Salop; the fairy arches of Pont Cysylltau, the Railway Viaduct across the Dee, with the Vale of Llangollen spreading far away before the sight. Castell Dinas Brân can be seen to the right, whilst the Berwyn range of hills to the left stretches to the utmost point of vision. Near the Park the Dee makes a horse-shoe bend, and pursues its course through the Marten Dingle, which lies immediately before the beholder. It was this scene which produced such enchantment on the mind of Lord Lyttleton when he first beheld it. The Waterloo Tower, within the grounds, and near the railway, was erected by the late Sir W. W. Wynn to commemorate that victory.

WREXHAM is twelve miles from Chester. It is a large and important town; and the residences of the numerous gentry who have settled here may be seen studding the beautiful country around. The markets and fairs here are always crowded; and the mineral district around sends forth large numbers of people to Wrexham on such holiday occasions. The church, formerly collegiate, is a noble structure, and the glory not only of the place but of the Principality. It is ranked among the Seven Wonders of North Wales. Browne Willis, in his Survey of St. Asaph, says that the stately gothic tower of Wrexham church is exceeded by very few in England. The old church was destroyed by fire in 1457; the present church was completed in 1472; and the tower in 1506. The tower is 140 feet high, and is richly ornamented on three sides with rows of saints placed in rich gothic niches: among them is St. Giles, the patron saint of the church, with the hind which, according to the legend, miraculously nourished him in the desert. Within the church are several handsome monuments: one by Roubiliac, in memory of Mary, daughter of Sir Richard Myddleton, of Chirk Castle, who died in 1747. She is represented as rising from the tomb in the fulness of youth and beauty.

In the neighbourhood of Wrexham the tourist will derive much pleasure from his visits to several remarkable places.—ACTON PARK, one mile on the Chester road, for a long period the property of the Cunliffe family, and now occupied by Sir R. H. Cunliffe, Bart. The village of GRESFORD is only two miles farther in the same direction. It may be reached by the railway from Wrexham, Gresford station being placed beneath the church. This village place of worship is seated on the brow of a lofty eminence, commanding an extensive view, commencing with the picturesque Vale of Gresford, and terminating with the vast expanse of the Vale Royal of Cheshire, the seed-plot of " Cheshire's Chief of Men." The bells of Gresford church are reckoned among the seven wonders of North Wales.—OVERTON CHURCHYARD (eight miles from Wrexham, and close to BANGOR ISCOED) is also included in the seven wonders; its celebrity having been gained by its fine yew-trees, twenty-five in number, and one, it is said, that grew on the church tower.—ERDDIG, the seat of Simon Yorke, Esq., about two miles from Wrexham, is a lovely residence, and rendered historically interesting, from having been occupied for many years by Philip Yorke, Esq., author of " The Royal Tribes of Wales."

In the immediate neighbourhood of the ROSSETT station some objects of interest may be seen. Trevallyn Hall, built by Sir John Trevor, is a fine Elizabethan structure on the left; and on Mount Alyn, on the right, is the house of the late Colonel Maxwell Goodwin. The site takes its name from the river Alyn, on the banks of which Germanus and Lupus, the great opponents of the Arian heresy obtained their miraculous Hallelujah Victory, in the fifth century.

PULFORD is a small village, three miles and a half distant from Saltney, and a mile from Eaton Hall, the seat of the Marquis of Westminster.

SALTNEY is about two miles from CHESTER, and is the last station on that route. The extensive establishments seen on the left, just before reaching the station, are where the railway carriages are manufactured. The tourist then passes by the Brewer's Hall Hill (from an elevated position of which Oliver Cromwell bombarded the city), and shortly afterwards enters the ancient and interesting city of CHESTER.

NORTH WALES.

NORTH WALES is more frequently compared with the mountain district of Westmoreland and Cumberland than with any other locality, either at home or abroad. Comparisons are proverbially odious; and, to our thinking, comparisons of scenery are almost invariably unjust. There are usually more points of distinction than of agreement; and different things cannot fairly be compared with each other. We have no intention to institute invidious comparisons between these beauteous rivals, and certainly none of awarding the palm to either. But there is a difference between them, which the visitor to each should bear in mind, and which, therefore, it may be proper to call attention to. Cumbria has few historical or romantic recollections, and possesses, consequently, hardly an historical memorial. It is a region of beauty, which owes all its charms to Nature: even the poetry that is connected with the lakes and fells is of recent date, and but a reflex of the native loveliness. With Cambria it is otherwise. Everywhere exist the monuments or the traditions of an ancient and entirely different condition of society. Throughout Wales occur places which are associated with tales of British prowess, or are celebrated in antique legend. The stories are often fabulous; and where the events they describe are real, the relations possess no very powerful attraction for 'Saxon' ears and hearts—at least, as they have been hitherto told: were there a Welsh Walter Scott to vivify his native records, and re-people his native fastnesses, they might be found to have for all nations equal interest with the history and the romance of Scotland. Still, as it is, those ancient memories serve at least to invest these scenes with that indefinite charm, which ever lingers over the spot whose name has been inscribed on the historic or poetic page. And the ruined castle and monastery, while they add something of elevation to the mind which is most susceptible to the sublimity and the grace of Nature, seldom fail to receive the homage even of those whose hearts the mountain and the cataract alike speak to in vain.

We are not going, here or hereafter, to inflict upon the reader any details of Welsh history, or to plunge into the depths of its legendary lore: all we desire is, to have it remembered that our tour lies through an historic region; and to suggest to the tourist that it will add to the charm of even Cambrian scenery, if it be kept in mind that every hill and every valley abounds with recollections and relics; and that the humble tradition of mythic hero, the incoherent tale of national glory and valour, the rude vestiges of faëry legends, and the superstitions and observances which are yet lingering on, though in the latest stages of decay, all speak of those ancient manners which were created and fostered by the peculiar insulation of the

people during so many centuries, and of that national pride, which, in early times, the example of the chief and the exhortations of the priest and the bard, made a part of the popular character and creed.

There are many ways of approach to Wales; and the chief features may, of course, be visited in various order and succession. The tourist will be guided in the selection of his route by convenience. We propose, in the first place, to look at so much of North Wales as lies along the line of the Chester and Holyhead Railway, and of the old coach-road through the Vale of Llangollen—staying by the way as we please, and making short excursions from the principal stations. In this manner we shall see the leading features of the northern coast, the district lying between it and the valleys of the Dee and the Conway, and have also a cursory view of the Isle of Anglesea. We shall then be at leisure to examine the interior of the Principality and the remainder of the coast; and thus readily visit whatever is most worth visiting in the entire district. Chester will consequently be our starting-place; our journey will terminate at Holyhead. Concerning the character of the country and the people, and of the main objects of interest that lie in the route, it is not necessary to make any further general remarks now: it will be as well to leave them to speak for themselves when we come upon them.

CHESTER.

Before giving an account of North Wales itself, we must look awhile at Chester: for the old city, though it lies just outside the boundary of the Principality, always forms an essential part and main attraction of a Welsh tour. Indeed it thus becomes one of the many advantages of this tour, that not only is the tourist led to investigate a grand mountain tract, with a people in many respects so remarkable as are the Welsh, but he also has the opportunity of examining three or four old towns of almost unique character, and of singular interest.

Chester is one of the most curious cities in the kingdom, as well as one of the most ancient. Nothing can be better in its way than Thomas Fuller's notice of it: "Chester is a faire city on the north-east side of the river Dee, so ancient, that the first founder thereof is forgotten. . . . . It is built in the form of a quadrant, and is almost a just square; the four cardinal streets thereof (as I may call them) meeting in the middle of the city, at a place called the Pentise, which affordeth a pleasant prospect at once into all four. Here is a property of building peculiar to the city, called the Rows, being galleries, wherein the passengers go dry, without coming into the streets, having shops on both sides and underneath; the fashion whereof is somewhat hard to conceive. It is therefore worth their pains, who have money and leisure, to make their own eyes the expounders of the manner thereof; the like being said not to be seen in all England; no, nor in all Europe again." (*Worthies, Chester.*)

Fuller is no doubt correct in affirming that "the first founder of the city is forgotten in its antiquity :" but the citizens in former days cherished a tradition that the first founder was a very famous personage. Bradshaw, the writer of the old metrical ' Life of St. Werburgh,' the patron saint of Chester, tells, in melodious strains, what was in his day the received opinion :

> "The founder of this city, as saith Polychronicon,
> Was Leon Gaur, a mighty strong giant,
> Which builded caves and dungeons many a one,
> Ne goodly building, ne proper, ne pleasant."

But Master Bradshaw is scandalized at having such a parentage affixed on his native place; and accordingly repudiates the claim of Leon Gaur to be founder of the city of Chester, notwithstanding that the original name of the city bears an affinity to that of this Patagonian. He is naturally averse to ascribe the title of founder of a city to one who merely selected the site, in order to excavate vile caves and dungeons,—not as dwellings for a peaceful sodality, but doubtless only that he might imprison in them unhappy wanderers, with a purpose, at his leisure, to pick their bones ;—for we may be sure, by his name, that like one of John Bunyan's giants, " he was of the nature of flesh-eaters." Such, our poet evidently thinks, was an odd mode of founding a city. Rather, he declares,

> " King Lear, a Briton stout and valiant,
> Was founder of the city by pleasant dwellings."

And it was in honour of him, he adds, that it was called Guar Lear. All that authentic history can venture to say of its foundation is, that it may have been a British town; but it was certainly an important Roman station. The plan of the city, and the arrangement of the principal streets — answering, in some measure, to those of a Roman camp—are thought to bear witness to its Roman origin. Its Roman name was Deva, or the station of the Dee. The 20th legion —the *Legio vicesima valens victrix*—had its station, according to the ' Antonine Itinerary,' on the Dee ; and, in all probability, Chester was the place. The British (or Welsh) name, Caer Leon Gawr, the City of the Great Legion, appears plainly to bear evidence to this ; and it is confirmed by the discovery at Chester of a votive altar, bearing an inscription to the effect that it was raised by an officer of the 20th legion, named the Victorious.[*] Of the residence of the Romans here many vestiges of all descriptions usually classed together as ' Roman remains,' have been at different times discovered. Among others, is a tolerably

[*] " It appears from the inscriptions, that the 20th legion remained here till the third century, but removed some time before the final abandonment of Britain by the Romans in the fifth."

complete hypocaust, which may be seen by the visitor at the sign of ' The Roman Bath.'

On the departure of the Romans, Chester, then the most important place in these parts, appears to have fallen into the hands of the Britons; but as the Saxon power became consolidated in England it was finally gained by that people. The reader will, doubtless, recollect the story of the Saxon monarch, Edgar,[*] holding his court there, and of his boat being rowed on the Dee by six or eight tributary kings. Chester was, however, for a while wrested from the Saxons by the Danes : and Alfred was once compelled to raise the siege while it was held by the famous sea-king, Hasting. Bede, writing early in the eighth century (Hist. Ecc., b. ii., c. 2), styles Chester " the city which is called by the English, Lega Caester, but by the British more correctly, Carlegion." We have here an early approach to the present name ; the *lega* was dropped in the course of time, but as there were other Caesters or Chesters, this was called West to distinguish it from them. Richard of Cirencester wrote the name West Chester in the fourteenth century, and so it continued to be written down to the nineteenth by those who affected extreme precision.

Under the Normans the importance of Chester was greatly increased. William I. created his nephew Hugh, surnamed Lupus, Earl of Chester, granting him at the same time sovereign jurisdiction over the county of Cheshire, which he erected into a county palatine. Lupus made Chester his place of abode, and held there his courts and parliaments, to which he called the barons and landholders with the superiors of the religious houses of the county.[†] In order to secure the city from the attacks of the Welsh, Lupus erected a castle, and built, or rebuilt, the city walls. It was now made the head-quarters of the army which it was found necessary to maintain in order to keep in check the Welsh, against whom he was obliged on several

[*] The story is differently told : in some recent descriptions of Chester we see Edwin incorrectly named as the Saxon king. William of Malmesbury's account is as follows : " Scarcely does a year pass in the Chronicles in which he did not perform something great. . . . Kinad, king of the Scots, Malcolm, of the Cumbrians, that prince of pirates, Maccus, all the Welsh kings whose names were Dufnal, Giferth, Huval, Jacob, Judethil, being summoned to his court, were bound to him by one, and that a lasting oath; so that, meeting him at Chester, he exhibited them on the river Dee in triumphal ceremony. For putting them all on board the same vessel, he compelled them to row him as he sat at the prow : thus displaying his regal magnificence, who held so many kings in subjection."—(' *Gesta Rerum Ang.,*' c. viii.—*Sharpe's Translation.*) The ' Saxon Chronicle' mentions (sub anno 972) the meeting of " six kings with Edgar, at Chester, to plight their troth to him ;" but makes no reference to their rowing of him. Malmesbury wrote early in the twelfth century.

[†] The title of Earl of Chester, with all its vast privileges, remained in the descendants of Lupus for nearly two hundred years : it was then annexed to the crown by Henry III.; and the title has ever since been held by the eldest son of the sovereign.

occasions to lead a considerable force. Indeed, it is affirmed by Camden, that "in those early Norman times, the skirmishes between the Welsh and English were so numerous, the inroads and incursions, and the firing of the suburbs of Hanbrid beyond the bridge, so frequent, that the Welshmen called it Treboeth, that is, Burnt Town. They tell us also that there was a long wall made there of *Welshmen's skulls.*" Truly a pleasant dwelling-place must Chester have been in those days!

We need not pursue the history of the city further: enough has been said to show its great antiquity and early consequence. It is foreign to the purpose of this sketch to trace its commercial prosperity and decay; or to speak of the eminent literary rank of several of its inhabitants during the period when English literature was emerging from the condition of mere monkish chronicles. Nor can we do more than refer to the Chester miracle-plays which the trades were accustomed to perform on holy days, and which have in some instances been preserved along with the still more famous Coventry mysteries, till the present time.

Chester is the only English city which retains its walls in a complete state. They are, of course, no longer of use as military works, but they afford an excellent public walk for the citizens; and for that purpose they are kept in repair. Ormerod, in his elaborate 'History of Cheshire,' (vol. i., p. 278), says of them:—"The walls enclose an oblong parallelogram, and most undoubtedly stand, for a large portion of their extent, on Roman foundations, as is indisputably proved by the remains of the ancient east gate discovered in erecting the present arch, and some relics of Roman masonry near, still existing, but concealed from public view by the houses adjoining . . . The present circuit of the walls is somewhat more than a mile and three quarters: the materials are a red stone; the exterior elevation is tolerably equal, but the interior is in some places nearly level with the ground, and in others with the tops of the houses. The entire line is guarded with a wooden rail within, and a stone parapet without; and the general line which is kept in repair as a public walk, commands interesting prospects . . . At the sides of the walls are the remains of several ancient towers, which have either been made level with the walls, been completely dismantled, or been fitted up as alcoves by the citizens. At the north-east angle is a lofty circular tower, erected in 1613, and called the Phœnix Tower, observable from the circumstance of Charles I. having witnessed a part of the battle of Rowton Heath from its leads in 1645. Another tower of higher antiquity, and the most picturesque of the military remains of Chester, projects out at the north-west angle, and is approached by a small turret, called Bonwaldesthorne's Tower, which forms the entrance to a flight of steps leading to an open gallery embattled on each side. Below this is a circular arch, under which the tide flowed before the embankment of the Dee. At the end of the gallery is the principal tower, a massy circular building of red stone, embattled; the principal room is an octagonal vaulted chamber, in the sides of which were pointed arches for windows. This tower, now called the Water Tower, and formerly the New Tower, was erected in 1322, for £100, at the city expense, by John Helpstone."

The stranger should let the circuit of the walls be one of his first strolls. It shows to considerable advantage the general features of the city, exhibiting it in very various aspect, and displaying alike the meaner and poorer as well as the better parts. The views too, outwards, are extensive, and some of them very fine. The prospect from the vicinity of the Water Tower may be specially noted; the eye is carried along the valley of the Dee over a fertile and diversified tract, which is bounded by the nearer Welsh mountains. The Water Tower itself will, of course, claim attention. In it is now deposited a small collection of antiquities and geological specimens—the museum of the Chester Mechanics' Institute; it will repay examination, but it might be greatly improved by the addition of *local* objects:—a good local museum ought to be found in every town in the kingdom. The tower which is passed through in order to reach the Water Tower, contains in the upper story a camera, whose vivid pictures will amuse the visitor. The Phœnix Tower is also open to inspection, being occupied during the day by a retired veteran of the histrionic art, who has a telescope pointed out of the window, wherefrom, as he tells you, the unfortunate Charles watched the defeat of his army on Rowton Heath,—a spot that now wears very little of the appearance of a battle field.

We ought to mention, that with the citizens the walk along the walls by moonlight is in high repute; and the stranger who is at Chester about the time of full moon will do well to remember this. The appearance of the old city as it is then seen, separated into masses of bold light and shadow which bring out with strong effect the peculiarities of the gable-fronted houses, with their dark line of 'Rows,' is certainly very striking; the cathedral too, (which lies close under the walls, and can only be fairly seen from them,) is never else seen to so much advantage (Cut, No. 1); and the contrast which the broad moonlit landscape, bounded by the Welsh mountains, presents to the close dark city, is as pleasing as it is uncommon.

But Chester is so remarkable a city, that at no time can it be looked on without peculiar interest by the stranger. No other city, perhaps, in the kingdom, carries so singular an air of antiquity. Unlike most of the other old towns in which the streets are narrow and irregular, the main streets are here broad and straight, and set at right angles to each other. The houses generally are of the quaint, old-fashioned, half-timber kind, with roofs of high pitch, and having the ornamented gables turned towards the street. Some of them display good examples of that kind of enriched plaster-work called pargetting, while in many the main beams of the gables are carved, and there is also a good deal of carving about the lower stories. But that which gives to them the peculiar character which

1.—CHESTER CATHEDRAL.

distinguishes the principal streets of Chester from those of every other town, is what is called the 'Rows,' which have already been referred to. These are covered galleries of unequal height and width, open towards the street, supported in front by carved wooden pillars, and having a low railing or balusters, but instead of projecting, like balconies from the houses, they are cut out from them : they are, in fact, walks along what in ordinary towns would be the first-floors of the houses. If the reader will fancy that the ground-floors remain untouched, while the front and partition-walls of the first-floors have been removed, and the space converted into a public walk, he will comprehend, by the help of the engraving which we have given of one of the streets (Cut, No. 2), the situation and external appearance of these Rows. But it will be necessary further to understand that there is a line of shops within them, at the back of the Rows (and among them are the best shops in the city), while towards the street are spaces for stalls or open shops (but which are now not so used except in the poorer parts); and at the same time the ground-floors, on the top of which the passengers along the Rows walk, are themselves shops, having their entrances as in ordinary towns, from the street pavement. Wherever the main streets are intersected by other streets, there is a flight of steps to be ascended and descended in passing along the Rows,

and these add to their general singularity of appearance. Altogether, the Rows are what mainly contribute to render Chester, what it is generally admitted to be, one of the most picturesque as well as remarkable cities in the kingdom.

There is some difference of opinion as to the origin of the Rows. Pennant and others think them to be a sort of relic of the Roman occupation of the city, they "having the form and being derived from the ancient vestibules." Others again have fancied that they were a kind of construction adopted in order to enable the citizens to attack with advantage the Welsh marauders who so frequently made incursions into the town ; and it is added, that during the encounters which took place between the partizans of Charles I. and the Parliament, they were found serviceable to the party which had possession of them. It might almost as feasibly be suggested, that the old spectacle-loving inhabitants constructed them for the sake of being able to see to advantage their famous pageants ! At any rate, we may well imagine that in those gay old times, Chester streets must have afforded a notable sight when old and young were congregated in the Rows on one of the high-days, to see the pageant pass along "according to ancient custom," with "the four giants and the unicorn, and the dromedary, the luce, the camel, the ass, snap-the-dragon, the four hobby-

2.—WATERGATE-STREET, CHESTER.

horses, and sixteen naked boys," as the Cupids and juvenile angels are somewhat irreverently styled by the dry old chronicler, who, perhaps, had in himself a spice of the spirit of that Puritan mayor who, as he tells, caused "the giants to be broken, the devil in his feathers to be sent into limbo, and the dragon and the naked boys to be whipped away."

The richness of Chester in an architectural point of view, as well as in a picturesque, consists in the abundance of its examples of early urban domestic buildings: it has very few public structures of any consequence. The chief, of course, is the Cathedral; and it is in almost every respect inferior to the greater number of English cathedrals.

Chester in very early times had splendid ecclesiastical establishments. The chief of these was the Benedictine Abbey of St. Werburgh, which was of great extent, and very wealthy: at the suppression of monasteries, its annual income was found to exceed £1000. Chester was made the seat of one of the bishop's sees, created by Henry VIII., at the dissolution of religious houses. The Abbey Church became the cathedral, and the incomes of the bishop, the dean, and six prebendaries were provided out of the abbey property. The church was enlarged and altered, to adapt it to its new purpose; but the Reformation which so speedily followed is believed to have put a stop to the completion of the works. It was evidently intended to erect a stone roof over the nave and choir, but an ordinary wooden one was substituted. The cathedral is wholly in the perpendicular style of Gothic architecture; and though the western front is rather grand, and the Lady Chapel elegant, it is, on the whole, by no means a favourable specimen of that style. Externally it is plain and heavy, and the interior, though more pleasing, is not at all striking. There is little of the religious majesty and impressiveness of some other of our glorious cathedrals: yet there is much that is interesting in the interior, especially in the choir, with its stalls and bishop's throne; and an hour will be well spent in examining it, and the conventual remains connected with it. The most noticeable point in the general external view is the unusual length of the south transept, which is nearly as long as the nave—a peculiarity, as far as we know, without parallel. The cathedral is built of the ordinary red sandstone of the neighbourhood, which is of a very friable nature, and the whole body of the edifice appears to be, in consequence, fast crumbling away. Parts of it have been of late carefully and judiciously restored.

The Chapter-house is much older than the cathedral, its builder being said to be Randal de Blundeville, who lived in the early part of the thirteenth century. It is of the early English style of architecture—and is, internally at least, the most beautiful architectural object in Chester. The form is a plain oblong, but the arrangement of the pillars in the entrance-chamber imparts something of originality to the general effect, while the details are all excellent. The ancient conventual buildings covered a very large space; and what remains of them will repay the examination of those curious in this class of objects. There are eight or nine parish churches in Chester, and some have points of interest; we can only mention that some ruins of Norman date, attached to the Church of St. John, without the walls, are worth visiting.

Of the castle built by Hugh Lupus, hardly a fragment is left. The present Castle is of the last century. It is very large; and from its size rather imposing, but heavy. It is used as the Shire Hall, the county jail, and military barracks. To make way for it a portion of the old wall was pulled down; but the walk is continued, a new wall being carried somewhat farther out. The very handsome New Bridge which is carried across the Dee, close by the castle, must not pass unnoticed. It was erected from a design by the architect of the castle, Mr. T. Harrison, of Chester; it consists of but one arch, of 200 feet span, being the largest stone arch which had then been constructed; and it still we believe remains so, unless it has been rivalled by any of the vast structures raised by railway engineers. This bridge was opened in 1832 by her present Majesty, then Princess Victoria. In passing, we ought to mention perhaps the celebrated spot called the Roo-dee, or Chester race-course, which lies just under the wall, at no very great distance from the castle. The stranger will be sure to notice it in making the circuit of the walls, and be ready to acknowledge that the citizens are right in asserting that there is not such another convenient race-course to be found by any other English city. The Roo-dee is one of the oldest English race-courses. Strutt quotes from a native author of the time of Henry VIII., a passage to the effect, that "a bell of silver, valued at three shillings and sixpence, or more, was to be annually given by the Company of Saddlers, to him who shall run the best and the farthest on horseback." The running was to take place on Shrove-Tuesday, in the presence of the mayor, and some of the city companies, "on the Roo-dee." This was in 1540; in 1624 the silver bell was "of a good value, of eight or ten pounds or thereabout;" a striking instance of the change in the value of money in that interval.

Chester, we have mentioned, was once a place of great commercial importance. It was a considerable port when Liverpool was hardly a port at all: but as the new one rose, the old one declined; and now hardly any shipping comes to Chester. Quite remarkable is the quiet, almost listless, aspect of the city and its inhabitants, to one who has just been observing the feverish and almost preternatural activity of Liverpool. With such a neighbour, it is surprising that Chester should have gone on so long in its dull old-fashioned course. But it cannot be expected to remain much longer as it is, now that it has become the centre of a considerable railway traffic. There are, indeed, so many symptoms of what is called improvement already noticeable, that we cannot help recommending the lovers of antiquity to follow honest old Fuller's advice, "to make their own eyes the expounders" of its aspect, and not to delay their visit long, lest they lose some characteristic feature.

While at Chester, the stranger will doubtless visit Eaton Hall, the magnificent seat of the Marquis of Westminster: it lies within a rich park, about three miles from the city, on the Shrewsbury road. It has long been one of the most celebrated of the mansions of the nobility, as well on account of its architectural claims as of its internal splendour, and the collection of pictures which it contains. For some time past it has been undergoing extensive alterations and embellishments; and, consequently, has not been open to the public: when these shall be completed, access to it will, we hope, be as liberally granted as it was during the life of the late Marquis.

FLINT.

Crossing the "Wizard Dee," we now enter fairly upon the Welsh country. The best plan for the tourist will be, not to loiter by the way, looking at the lesser hills and meaner streams; but to proceed directly from Chester to Holywell or Conway, by the Holyhead Railway, or to Llangollen by the Shrewsbury line, according as he may intend to pursue his journey, along the coast, or through the interior: in either case, he enters at once upon a scene of great interest, and will be able to continue his route through a tract of increasing grandeur. For us, however, it seems necessary, lest our sketch should appear too imperfect, first to glance at two or three spots that perhaps ought not to be omitted in a notice of North Wales.

Hawarden is the first of these places. The pedestrian will find the walk to it by the Dee a very pleasant one; and if he have a little leisure, the place itself will repay the visit. It is usually visited for the sake of the ruined Castle, which will be seen, just out of the road, within the grounds of Sir S. R. Glynne, close by the modern mansion, called Hawarden Castle. The ruins are now carefully preserved; but they are slight, and, though not unpicturesque, are of little interest in comparison with many of the noble castellated remains which will hereafter be met with. The castle was first erected in Norman times; it was dismantled after its capture by the Parliamentarians in 1645. From the summit of the keep there is an extensive prospect. The richly-wooded park within which it stands also affords many pleasing views. Hawarden, or, as the natives call it, Harden, is apparently a thriving little town, with very little that is Welsh in the appearance of it or of its inhabitants. But generally, it may be remarked that Flintshire is by far the most English county in North Wales.

About a couple of miles beyond Hawarden are a few ivy-covered fragments of another of those strongholds which the Norman and early English conquerors raised wherever they obtained footing in Wales. Ewloe, or Owloe Castle, however, hardly ought to be termed a castle; it is rather one of those lesser fortresses, which in the north country are called peels. It stands on the edge of a woody glen, in a wild and picturesque spot. The glen below the castle is famed as the scene of the defeat of a branch of the army of Henry II. by the sons of Owen Gwynedd,—a victory the more grateful to the Welsh, inasmuch as it led to one of still greater moment; for Henry, incensed at the defeat of his soldiers, led the main body of his army against Gwynedd, who was encamped a few miles farther on, at a place called Coleshill, near Flint: but the English army was again routed, and the king himself escaped with some difficulty.

Mold, which is situated four or five miles to the westward, is one of the most important towns in Flintshire. Its situation in the midst of a district rich in minerals, has caused the accumulation of a considerable population: — some 9000 persons reside within its boundaries. Little can be said for the beauty of the town, but there is a new county hall, of rather ambitious design, wherein the assizes are held; and the church is larger, and of a superior character to those generally seen in Welsh towns. The church was erected in the sixteenth century: the style is perpendicular, and it has a good tower. In the interior are a great many monuments, the most noticeable being a marble statue of a Welsh squire, hight Davies of Llanerch, who is very appropriately clad in a Roman habit. In the neighbourhood of Mold are coal and lead mines, iron-works, and the like. Celtic remains, including a gold torque, have been found here. At the village of Northop, not far from Mold, is another church, of a much better class than the ordinary parish churches in Wales.

A mile from Mold is a spot called Maes Garmon, whereon the Scots and Picts, who had invaded the land of the Britons, sustained a notable defeat: the particulars are told by venerable Bede, in his 'Ecclesiastical History,' and by other monkish chroniclers, with great unction. On the invasion of the Picts, the "fearful Britons" had assembled here in a valley surrounded by mountains: it was the holy season of Lent, which inspired in all religious thoughts; and in their distress they listened with devout attention to the teaching of the holy St. Germanus and Bishop Lupus, who had come amongst them to instruct them in the true doctrine, and who were now in the midst of the army. So efficacious did their exhortations prove, that the hardy warriors thronged in crowds to be baptized. The enemy having been duly informed by their spies of this unmartial employment of the army, hastened to the place, intending to surprise them while thus engaged; nothing doubting of an easy victory. But Germanus, aware of their approach, selected the most active of the British soldiers, and placing himself at their head, conducted them to the pass by which the heathen army must enter the valley. As the savage multitude drew near the spot where Germanus had secreted his followers, the holy man, raising the rood in his hands, thrice shouted aloud Hallelujah! The Britons, as they had been directed, repeated the cry, which the mountains on all sides re-echoed; and the enemy, struck with dread by the sound, which appeared suddenly to peal forth, not alone from the surrounding rocks, but from the very sky itself, cast down their arms, and fled in fearful disorder. Many of them were drowned in the neighbouring river, and more slain by their relentless pursuers. Without the loss of a single man did the pious Britons thus achieve a perfect victory. In memory of so marvellous an event, the field has ever since borne the name of Maes Garmon,—the Field of Germanus. This memorable victory was gained in 429: in 1736, an Obelisk was erected by a modern Briton, Nathaniel Griffiths, of Rhual, to mark the site; and the particulars of the event are recorded upon it in sounding Latin. Mr. Griffiths, by the way, has chosen to call the vanquished "Picts and *Saxons,*" which is certainly not as written in the 'Chronicles:' he has also placed the date in 420, which is also not according to the early scribes. While speaking of monuments, we may mention that the one seen on Moel Famau, the loftiest mountain in this vicinity, being 1840 feet above the level of the sea, was erected in commemoration of the jubilee, as it was called, of George III. The monument is a pyramid, 60 feet broad at the base, and 125 feet high. From its magnitude and lofty site, it is a conspicuous object for miles around, and even from the walls of Chester. Not far from Maes Garmon, a portion of the celebrated boundary, 'Offa's Dyke,' may be readily traced.

From Flint its ancient glory has entirely departed. Situated in a convenient nook at the estuary of the Dee, before the channel of that river filled with silt, Flint boasted of great commercial aptitude. The strong castle served to protect it from any sudden assault; a large and busy population filled its streets. When the navigation of the Dee was diverted, and the Mersey attracted the vessels which used to enter the wizard stream, Flint gradually declined. It still boasted itself the county town, but even that local eminence was lost when, in the last century, the assizes were removed from it to be held in future in the rising town of Mold. Yet Flint has a strong attraction for the English visitor. In Flint Castle, "which," says old Hall, "a man may call Dolorous Castle, because there king Richard declined from his dignity, and lost the type of his glory and pre-eminency"—in Flint Castle it was that the meeting so often related by our old historians, and immortalized by Shakspere, took place between Richard II. and "the banished Bolingbroke."

The castle stands on a low rock which rises bluffly from the marshy shore. The banks generally are low and bare; when the tide is out, the broad estuary—it is here three miles across—presents the appearance of a naked sandy waste. Hall states that Richard, who had wandered from Carnarvon to Conway, and even to Beaumaris, in hope of finding a fortress strong enough and sufficiently provisioned to afford a prospect of a lengthened resistance, when apprised that Bolingbroke "was coming toward the Castle of Flint, . . . departed out of the castle and took the sands by the river Dee, trusting to escape to Chester, and there to have refuge and succour; but or he had far passed, he was forelayed and taken, and brought to the duke." Of the meeting itself—

"King Richard's night, and Bolingbroke's fair day"—

it behoves us not here to speak.

Flint Castle was erected by Henry II. or his successor, and must have been, for the time, a place of enormous strength; yet it is said, that it was more than once taken by the Welsh princes, and retaken by the English. During the great civil war, Flint Castle was garrisoned for Charles by Roger Mostyn. It endured a long siege by the forces of the Parliament, and only surrendered when the garrison was reduced to the extremity of famine. Flint Castle was dismantled, by order of the Parliament, at the same time as those of

3.—FLINT CASTLE.

Rhyddlan and Hawarden. It was a square castle, with large round towers at the angles; one angle having a second and larger tower, intended, no doubt, to serve as the keep. All that remains of it now are portions of several towers, and a part of the walls—all in the most ruinous condition. (Cut, No. 3.) One of the towers fell, as lately as last winter; those that remain, as well as the walls, are full of rents. The governor of Flint Castle was also mayor of the borough: and the half-civil half-military officer is still duly appointed, though the castle and the borough are alike decayed. A part of the site of the castle is occupied by the prison, a plain edifice, erected some sixty-five years back.

The town, as we have said, is now of little consequence and no comeliness: it is a very dirty sample of an inferior Welsh town. It has some fishing trade; in the neighbourhood are smelting-works; the parish contains above two thousand inhabitants, and it is resorted to by a few strangers for the benefit of bathing. A neat church has recently been erected, and also a market-house.

HOLYWELL.

There is little beauty in the scenery around Flint; and indeed it may be said, that the tameness extends the whole distance of the line of the railway by the Dee-side from Chester to Holywell. Between Flint and Holywell the pedestrian will find little to arrest his attention, unless it be in the dirty-looking smelting village of Bagilt. All along here, by the way, occur at intervals smoky and ungainly ' works' of one kind and another—important and interesting enough, of course, in their way, but which we gladly hasten by.

On approaching Holywell, however, the scenery improves, and there is a good deal that is observable in the vicinity. Not far from the Holywell station (and in rather too close proximity to a modern factory) are the remains of the once flourishing abbey of Basingwerk. They stand in what must once have been a very pretty spot, close by where the stream which flows from the wonder-working well falls into the estuary of the Dee. The foundation of this abbey is ascribed to Ranulph, Earl of Chester, who lived in the early part of the 12th century: at the dissolution of monasteries, the annual revenue was estimated at above £150. Close by the abbey stood Basingwerk Castle, of which however hardly a fragment is now left. This castle, it is said, was erected by Richard, son of Hugh Lupus, the first Earl of Chester. According to the tradition, or legend, Richard had been on a pilgrimage to St. Winefred's Well, and on returning from it was attacked by a body of Welshmen, too numerous for his small band of retainers to withstand. He happily succeeded in reaching Basingwerk Abbey, where he sought sanctuary. But the Welsh closely beset the abbey; and the soldiers of his father were on the opposite side of the Dee, separated from him by some miles of deep water. In his emergency he supplicated the aid of St. Winefred (or as some say of St. Werburgh, but Chester

and Holywell must settle that), when suddenly the sands were raised above the waters, and his father's troops marched over them, speedily dispersed his enemies, and released him from his dangerous position :— in commemoration whereof the sands have ever since been called the ' Constable's Sands.' The reader will see that there is a little confusion in the chronology here. If Basingwerk Abbey were founded in the 12th century, Richard could not well have taken refuge in it in the 11th; but it may have been, as was often the case, that the monastery was refounded, or rebuilt then, at the cost of Earl Ranulph, who, for his liberality, received the title of founder. Be that as it may, the story adds that Richard, in grateful recompense to the good monks, erected a castle by their house, in order henceforward to afford to them the protection which, in his emergency, they had extended to him. Not far from the castle the antiquary may discern traces of Watt's Dyke, a portion or continuation of the better known Offa's Dyke.

About a mile from the ruins of Basingwerk Abbey stands the town of Holywell, on the summit of a steep hill. On the way to it, where the hill rises abruptly, is the Well of St. Winefred, which we must turn aside to look at. The stranger is surprised by seeing a singularly graceful Gothic edifice, the purport of which he is at first at a loss to comprehend. On entering he sees that it covers a bath of goodly proportions, wherein perchance some in suitable garments are very deliberately moving about, while around it are others, halt, and lame, and withered, waiting as it should seem for some one to lift them into the water. Over head is a vaulted stone roof, of elaborate design and richly ornamented ; but, among the ornaments, he observes some which, in the dim light, appear to him quite inexplicable. He looks at them with increasing wonder, till, when his eye has become accustomed to the obscurity, he discerns that they are crutches fixed in the groinings, and on inquiry he is informed that they are votive offerings placed there by those who have experienced the efficacy of the waters. Altogether the scene is an unusual one :—but then the well itself is of no ordinary kind. We must relate its origin.

In the seventh century the lord of these parts was one Thewith ; by his wife, Wenlo, he had an only daughter, whose name was Winefred. Now the brother of Wenlo was a man of saintly character, who had devoted his life to the service of religion. Bueno, for so he was named, had founded a monastery, and built a church at Clynoeg, in Carnarvon, and there he had dwelt as abbot till the work of his hands had become firmly established, and the monks were well grounded in doctrine and discipline. Then he removed to where his sister abode, and begged of his brother-in-law a small piece of land, at the foot of the hill on which stood his palace, and thereon he erected for himself a cell, resolving to devote the remainder of his days to pious meditation, and to the instruction of his niece. The maiden was extremely beautiful, and under his teaching she became no less remarkably devout. Attracted by her surpassing loveliness, Caradoc, the son of king Alen, sought her hand; but Winefred had already devoted herself to a life of celibacy. Finding her unmoved by all his entreaties, Caradoc—as Welsh knights were in ancient times but too apt to do—determined on a rougher mode of courtship. The maiden, however, escaping from his hands, fled for refuge, as was natural, towards her uncle's cell. Caradoc maddened at the frustration of his purpose, drew his sword and pursued her; and having overtaken her as she was about to descend the hill, struck off her head at a blow. Her body fell where the blow was struck, but the head bounded forward till it reached the feet of the horror-stricken Buenô. In those times saints were not confounded at what would overwhelm common folk in our unbelieving days: Bueno, therefore, caught up the severed head, and hastening to the place where the body lay, he replaced it in its proper position. When a saint did such a thing, it may be supposed it was followed by the junction of the divided parts. Winefred, accordingly, to the great edification of the bystanders, arose, hale as ever, having apparently suffered no inconvenience from her decapitation ;—it is not said whether the narrow crimson circlet was visible, which was the insignia of those saintly ones who had undergone this species of martyrdom. Caradoc, it may be believed, after so manifest a miracle, did not care to renew his suit, or to repeat his violence; and Winefred lived henceforward for fifteen years, in the bloom of maiden purity, and died in the odour of sanctity.

But the violence of the wicked Caradoc was the occasion of lasting good. For from the spot where the head of the holy Winefred rested, there burst forth a spring of the purest water: and the valley, which hitherto had been arid and barren, was now irrigated and fertilized by a perennial and abundant stream. And as though to proclaim wherefore the waters thus flowed, the stones which formed the channel of the stream were spotted as with blood, though the water itself was clear as crystal; and the moss which covered the sides of the fountain exhaled a grateful odour. Nor did the miracle end here. It was speedily discovered that whoever bathed in that fountain soon lost all his ailments, and became every whit whole. Wherefore, in process of time, a shrine was erected over the hallowed spring, and dedicated to the now sainted maiden to whose intercession it owed its healing properties, and a priest was maintained out of the offerings of the pilgrims who resorted thither.

So runs the legend; and doubtless it is as worthy of credence as such legends usually are. The building which now covers the well is said to have been erected by Margaret countess of Richmond, the mother of Henry VII.; it is light and elegant in design, and rich and tasteful in its ornamentation; altogether it is a very pleasing specimen of the early perpendicular style. (Cut, No. 4.) In the chapel over the well-room, divine service is once a week performed in the English language: it is also used as a school-room.

The water rises in a basin six feet deep, whence it flows into a paved channel, wherein, as well as in the basin, the patients bathe. The water is perfectly pellucid, and flows in such abundance as to be capable of working a large mill immediately it leaves the enclosure; while during its short course of only a mile it turns several others. Pennant asserts, "that by two different trials made for his information, it was found that twenty-one tons of water rose from the spring in a minute." According to the same naturalist, the blood-spots on the stones are produced by the *Byssus Jholitus*, which produces the appearance of blood on the stones to which it adheres; while the odoriferous moss is the well-known *Jungermannia Asplenoides*.

Recently the shrine of St. Winefred has been restored, and the facilities for bathing are increased. A small well, which had long been filled up, has been re-opened: it rises near to the principal one, and is apparently connected with it. This is thought to be efficacious for ophthalmic diseases; the larger well is chiefly resorted to in cases of lameness, or rheumatism. For about a couple of hours in the morning and evening the outer doors are closed, "that strangers and visitors may bathe in private,"—the remainder of the day it is free to all comers.

Among those who have visited St. Winefred's Well, either out of devotion or curiosity, is included a long array of notable persons, ranging from William the Conqueror to the late Duchess of St. Albans. Towards the close of the last century the well appears to have attracted few pilgrims, for Warner, who visited it in 1798, says, "Much of its celebrity has long since vanished, and either from a decrease of faith in patients, or from the waters having lost their sanative powers, the saint is now sinking fast into oblivion, and her well into neglect." And again: "the resort of Roman Catholics to the well has ceased." But either the saint has recovered her fame, or the waters have regained their sanative powers, or the faith of patients has revived, or all these things have combined—but at any rate the well is not *now* neglected. We saw there this summer a goodly number of bathers—and in the roof a stock of crutches, amply sufficient to evidence that not a few were cured, or fancied they were. And certainly the resort of Roman Catholics has not yet ceased: indeed the greater number who resort here we were assured are of that faith. Many of the patients are poor Irish, who have come over mainly to visit the shrine. We saw them of both sexes and all ages—some come to bathe and some to beg. "And have you derived any benefit from the waters?" said we to a shrewd-looking 'boy' who had volunteered a long story of the mystery of the well. "Sure it's myself that have," said he, "a mighty dale—considering the time I've been here, which is only five days, more's the sorrow—or else I'd be well entirely if I'd bin long enough. But it would have done yer honour good to have seen Fin Kahll, who went home again only last Saturday that ever was. When he first came to this, it was the world and all of throuble he had to drag himself to the holy wather be his crutches; but Fin had

4.—ST. WINEFRED'S WELL, HOLYWELL.

the faith, yer honour; and Father Hale, God bless him, the good priest of Fin's own parish in Connaught, wher' he came from, sent him here, and gave him good advice, and the papers that should tell all Christen people what he came to the blessed well for—and so before he had been here for six weeks, Fin was as sound and clane as your honour, saving your presence, is at this blessed moment—may the sweet saint be ever praised for the same. And now if ye will but just look up there for a minute, I'll show you the very sticks that Fin put up in the roof, as was only right and proper he should do, to testify to the same." Among the subscribers to the restoration of the building we noticed several Irish names—and one or two from Maynooth College: a circumstance, by the way, at which some Welshmen shake their heads rather gravely.

Close against the well—the tower of it is seen in the engraving—stands the parish church, a large plain building not at all noteworthy on its own account, but remarkable for the singular method adopted to summon the congregation. Not having ourselves heard the church-bell rung, we shall borrow the account we find reprinted from Perry (who took it from Bingley, who took it from Warner, who took it from Pennant, who took it from et cetera,) in the circular issued by the committee of management for restoring the well: its accuracy is attested by the circumstance of its being now published by the townsmen, and it is repeated almost verbatim in all the works we can turn to from the newest to the oldest; we may say that the practice has "come down from time immemorial." "The situation of the church is so low, that the prayer-bell cannot be heard in the town; the congregation is therefore assembled by a *walking steeple*: a man has a leathern strap fastened round his neck, to the end of which is suspended a bell of tolerable weight, and over one of his knees is buckled a cushion; thus accoutred, he sets out just before the hour of prayers, and walks around the principal parts of the town, jingling the

bell every time his cushioned knee comes forward."
The strange 'accoutrement' of the man, and the
gravity with which he goes through his duty is said,
by those who have witnessed it, to be very comical.

The town of Holywell, though it boasts itself " for
population, wealth, commerce, and manufactures, . .
at present the principal town in North Wales," must be
content with brief notice here. It is a straggling sort
of place, seated as was said, on the slope and the
summit of a hill. In 1841 it contained nearly 11,000
inhabitants. The houses are substantial; there are
excellent hotels, good shops, a couple of banking
establishments; a second church of recent erection;
a Roman Catholic chapel, and several meeting-houses
belonging to the various sects of dissenters. Altogether
the place wears a more business-like and flourishing
appearance than any other town in this part of the
principality. In the town and its immediate vicinity
are numerous mines of lead and calamine, works of
copper, brass, shot, paper, zinc, and lead; and yet it
is stated that the town is greatly resorted to by invalids
on account of the salubrity of the air.

THE VALE OF CLWYD.

We might, keeping to the line of railway, continue
our journey as hitherto along the coast, by Air Point
and Rhyl to Conway; and in our way visit Mostyn
Hall and Downing, which lie only three or four miles
from Holywell—the former a baronial hall partly of the
Tudor period, the latter noted as having been the residence of the literary veteran Thomas Pennant. Mostyn
Hall, the seat of the noble family of the same name,
is interesting on account of the collection of British
antiquities which it contains, as well as for its architectural character. It has, too, some historical associations. Downing was described by its owner as
being " Cowley's wish realized, a small house and a
large garden." It was indeed a choice retreat for the
diligent naturalist and indefatigable student. Pennant
was not a man of very powerful mind, but he was a
careful observer, and not apt to write for the sake of
effect. Johnson went little beyond the mark when he
said, " The man's a Whig, sir, a sad dog, but he's the
best traveller I ever read; he observes more things
than any one else does." His description of his native
country (' Tour in Wales,' 1778) has served as a
quarry for all his successors. Both Mostyn Hall and
Downing stand in good situations. Mostyn is
approached by a noble avenue of " old patrician trees,"
and the park affords some fine views of mingled sea
and land; the grounds of Downing yield excellent
prospects. They are worth visiting, therefore, by those
who have leisure and feel interested in celebrated
houses. It is time, however, that we turned our steps
a little inland. There is a short detour which will
carry us through a more beautiful country than any we
have yet seen, and enable us also to visit some localities
that must not be overlooked.

Our course for the present lies south-west, Caerwys

being the first town we are to halt at, and the Vale of
Clwyd our day's journey. We strike right up the hills,
ascending higher and higher as we pass from one
summit to another till we reach the top of Pen-y-bant
(or some such name), where we gain a prospect that is
perfectly refreshing after having been so long confined
to a comparatively low strip of land. Far away the
view extends over hill and valley till it is on the one
hand bounded by a bold and varied mountain-range;
on the other, reaches over river and strait to the opposite
coast; and again, on turning northwards, to the ocean
horizon. This, as far as we know, is the finest walk
out of Holywell, and though there are many far finer in
Wales, we should deem him a sorry companion who
under a favourable sky could gaze upon this without
delight.

Caerwys is now but a poor place: once it was a
town of importance. Happily it has yet a comfortable
inn, where the rambler will be able to obtain a breakfast
such as he will know how to appreciate after his walk
over the hills from Holywell. While it is getting
ready he may see all that is to be seen in the town
—as it is called, but as he would style it, village.
Caerwys is believed to have been a Roman station, and
Roman coins are said to have been found there; and
until a comparatively recent time it was a busy market
and assize town. The market-place yet remains, and
so too does the jail, but both are converted into dwelling-houses. Still though the market be lost and the
assizes removed, Caerwys retains its fairs,—which are
said to have the best display of cattle of any in the
county of Flint. What most dignifies Caerwys, however, in the eyes of the natives, is that it was the
theatre of the last of the royal Eisteddvodau—and that
of the first of these revived national festivals. It was
in the ninth year of the reign of Elizabeth that the last
royal summons was issued for all those who intended
to follow the profession of bard, to appear before
the queen's commissioner to give proof of their skill.
Fifty-five of the persons who obeyed the summons, it
is said, gave satisfactory evidence of their ability, and
received the official testimonial. Henceforward, if the
harp was not silent, the minstrel was unhonoured. It
was not till near the close of the last century that a
society of Welsh gentlemen determined to endeavour
to re-establish the ancient bardic meetings. They
accordingly announced an Eisteddfod to be holden at
Caerwys, in May, 1798, when prizes were adjudicated
to the best poet, the best harper, and the best singer
in the national tongue and music. Since then, these
meetings have been held with tolerable regularity—but
Welsh bards, like the English philosophers, are now
ambulatory: the Eisteddvodau being held successively
in the chief towns of ancient date. The great object
now of these meetings appears to be to encourage the
diligent study of the Welsh language,—and to keep
alive a national Cambrian spirit.—We shall again
come upon the trail of these wanderers, when we may
perhaps find space for a word or two further on their
doings.

The neighbourhood of Caerwys affords some pleasant strolls: the wooded dell, called Maes-mynan Wort, is a local celebrity: at the end of it the last native prince, Llewellyn ap Gruffydd, is said to have had a palace—the site is marked by Pandy Mill.

When the Vale of Clwyd first opens upon the eye from the heights by this its lower end, it is almost sure to extort an exclamation of surprise and delight. Exquisitely beautiful does it appear as it stretches far away rejoicing under the beams of the soft morning sun: yet travellers often declare that they are disappointed when they visit it, and many of the books assert that it scarcely deserves its fame. The complainers are in error. Clwyd is not less beautiful than it is pronounced to be by those who know it best, but they are estimating it by a standard which is inapplicable. Travellers must "learn to distinguish rightly:" all fine scenery is not savage—or Claude was but a poor judge of a landscape. Clwyd is an open valley, some six or seven miles across, bordered by hills that are not to be ranked as mountains, and watered by a stream which only swells into a river as it arrives towards the end of its course. But this broad valley is gently undulated in surface; fertile and well cultivated; clad in part with rich foliage; spotted over with barn and byre, humble cottage and noble mansion, rude village, castle-crowned rock, cathedral town; bare hills border it, and low craggy mountains rise like a barrier at the further end. It is possible that all this may appear tame to one who has been wandering among the majestic mountain passes farther in the principality, or is familiar with Alpine grandeur or Italian splendour. It may appear also far from striking to one who views it in dull weather, or in expectation of something 'wonderful' in peaked mountain-summits, foaming cataracts, and rushing streams: but let it be only looked on with a heart alive to the milder graces of Nature, and its loveliness will be felt like that of some sweet passage of poetry, into which is breathed the living spirit of humanity and civilization.

The broad open vale is above twenty miles long; the narrow part above Ruthin is some five or six miles more. It may be well seen by entering it, as we have done, at the lower end, and then proceeding upwards on the north side as far as Ruthin (or farther, if there be time); descending on the southern side,—not keeping servilely by road or river, but deviating as either stream or fell promises a fairer prospect, a kindlier shade, or more grateful change.

Ruthin is a good object to set before you as the goal of a day's ramble. In front, the vale seems to terminate in a bay of mountains, which serves as a back-ground to the town with its lofty castle, which

"Rests on a mount and looks o'er wood and plain."

The town is said to owe its name to the colour of the rock on which the castle was built—Rhudd-din being the Welsh for the Red-fort. Ruthin is a very respectable town, and has some excellent buildings, among which the Shire-hall is prominent. The church, too,

will repay the time spent in its examination. The town contains about 4000 inhabitants, who are chiefly supported by agriculture. Ruthin Castle was erected by Reginald de Grey, in the reign of Edward I. In the struggle between Charles I. and the Parliament it was garrisoned for the king; but it was forced to yield, in 1646, to Cromwell's army, though not till it had withstood a siege of two months' duration. It was soon after dismantled. Originally it must have been a place of great strength, as well as extent; but now only a few fragments remain. Churchyard, who saw it before its demolition, speaks with much admiration of its design, which, he says, as here "set forth full fine by heart and hand," shows

" A deep device did first erect the same ;
    It makes our world to think on elder days,
    Because one work was form'd in such a frame."

If it were to be built again, he thinks

" The work itself would shake a subject's bag."

Within the walls of the old fortress, but not occupying nearly the whole of the area, a modern castle has been erected, which, at a distance, has a picturesque if not a very formidable appearance. An old mill, with a cross on its gable, is thought by some to have been the chapel belonging to the White Friars, who are said by Leland to have had a cell at Ruthin. The river Clwyd is here quite a trivial stream, scarcely sufficing to turn the two or three mills which are scattered along its banks.

The head of the valley above Ruthin is entirely different in character to the open part below: it is greatly narrowed, and closed in by rougher hills, but is no less picturesque—or even more, according as the word be understood. The little streamlet would be found a pleasant guide to the Bronbanog Hills, by one who had leisure to wander among the lesser-known localities,—often the most enjoyable,—and from the source a path might be struck over the hills to Valle Crucis and Llangollen.

But we must return. As we descend the valley it gradually expands, ever presenting some new feature. Many a picturesque homestead or village, or rich prospect, tempts the wayfarer to linger. Generally, the lower ground is enclosed for the purposes of cultivation, and the views are limited; but the uplands afford sufficient recompense. The time to wander down the valley, so as to see it to most advantage, is as the evening is drawing on. Then, when the sun is sinking before you in the west, and some tall old tree rears its black head proudly against the sky, while Denbigh Castle on its rocky height imparts an air of grandeur to the wide vale and golden stream, the Vale of Clwyd might tempt even the pencil of a Turner or a Claude. There, too, as from some eminence the eye wanders from castle to castle, which, in the uncertain light, present no image of desolation, will the imagination strive to realize the Clwyd Valley of the fierce conqueror of France and Wales.

The town of Denbigh climbs up the rugged sides of

a steep insulated hill, the summit of which is crowned by the vast ruins of the castle. In itself the town is almost naught—at least in the eyes of the tourist. The castle alone will engage his attention. It is related that the builder of the castle was Henry Lacy, Earl of Lincoln, to whom the lordship of Denbigh was granted by Edward I. He, however, left it unfinished. His son, it is said, fell into the castle well and was drowned; and the unhappy father could not afterwards endure the sight of the building which reminded him of his bereavement. Denbigh Castle has had some royal tenants in its time. Edward IV. was here besieged by the army of Henry VI. " Had he been taken there," says old Leland, rather quaintly, " *debellatum fuisset* :" fortunately, he managed to make his escape before the castle surrendered. Charles I. came here on his flight from Chester, after the battle of Rowton Heath. The governor, though a royalist, must have made, as the phrase is, a clean breast of it, if the tradition may be trusted that the unfortunate monarch exclaimed, at the close of their interview, " Never did king hear so much truth *at once* !" Fallen kings, of all kinds, do doubtless hear a quite surprising amount of this unpleasant sort of truth : the pity is, that these truth-speakers save their commodity for such seasons ; to their own great discomfort, as it must be, (their consciences the while bending under such a burden,) and to no one's profit, even when they discharge themselves of it.

Denbigh Castle covers an area of great extent, and must in its perfect state have been a place of immense strength. It withstood the Parliamentarians for above two months, and then only surrendered by order of the king. For the demolition of this fortress Cromwell is not responsible. It was dismantled after the Restoration : and this was pretty much the order of things in Wales. Cromwell dismantled most of the castles which fell into his hands, but spared and garrisoned a few of the strongest—and those, when he ascended the throne, Charles II. destroyed. Owing to the excessive thickness of the walls of Denbigh Castle, they were blasted by gunpowder, and hence the shattered fragmentary condition in which it now appears. From the grandeur of its appearance, as seen from the valley below, some disappointment is felt when, close at hand, it is found to be so utterly ruinous. Still it is a noble ruin, and perhaps none the less impressive for having been so mutilated. The grand gate-house, with its massive towers, and the statue of the founder over the gateway, is the most perfect part—and the most picturesque. From it a tolerable estimate may be formed of the original magnificence of the entire structure. The walls of the citadel encompassed the old town, but the modern street has extended beyond the pale. Within the walls is a curious old chapel, dedicated to St. Hilary, which, till within the last three or four years, served as the parish church : the proper parish church—now ruinous—is at Whitchurch, a mile from the town. There will be noticed, close by the entrance to the castle, the shell of an ecclesiastical building of rather large size. It

is a church, the erection of which was commenced by Elizabeth's Earl of Leicester, to whom the queen had made a grant of Denbigh. The earl dying before the church was completed, the townsmen, for whose use it was intended, raised a sum of money sufficient to carry on the work; but the Earl of Essex called at Denbigh on his way to Ireland, and ' borrowed ' the money— and the church was suffered to remain unfinished.

From the castle there is an admirable prospect of the Vale of Clwyd, and the mountain range of which Moel Famau is the chief. About twenty years ago the Eisteddfod was held in the extensive area of the castle ; and the townsmen yet dwell with some pride on the memory of that day, when the whole beauty and dignity of the principality were assembled here on the summit of their own Caled-Vryn. The attraction was increased to an unusual degree by the presence of the Duke of Sussex and many other eminent persons; and we have heard the spectacle described as most brilliant.

The city of St. Asaph—less in size and population than many a village in England—consists of one street, and contains somewhat under 800 inhabitants. Especially to be admired, however, is the beauty of its situation. It stands near the lower end of the vale, on an eminence, the base of which is washed on the one side by the river Clwyd, and on the other by the Elwy. The houses are built for the most part on that side of the hill which inclines to the Elwy ; abundant foliage waves at the base and on the slopes of the hill, the roofs of the houses rise picturesquely one above the other, while over all, on the brow of the hill, stands the cathedral.

The foundation of the see dates from a very early period. One of the most famous saints of the British Kalendar was St. Kentigern, the patron saint of Glasgow. Whoso lists to read the legend of his marvellous birth, and equally marvellous life and death, will find it told by Southey, in his own inimitable style, in the second volume of his ' Colloquies.' Here it must suffice to say that Kentigern, who was bishop of Glasgow and all Cumberland, being driven from his see by a barbarous prince, sought shelter in Wales. At first he dwelt with the great saint of Wales, the renowned David; but King Cadwallon, moved by the advice of St. David, gave him a piece of ground at Elwy, that he might erect a monastery thereon, and establish an episcopal see. The reputation which the northern saint had already gained, soon attracted around him a community worthy of their chief. The establishment numbered nine-hundred and sixty-five brethren. " Three hundred of these were uneducated men, whose office it was to till the lands and tend the cattle belonging to the convent; three hundred more, of the same description, were employed within the building in preparing food and other domestic concerns ; the remaining three hundred and sixty-five were literates, whose business it was to perform divine service. They were divided into companies or watches; when one set had finished their service, another was ready immediately to begin, so that an everlasting course of prayer and thanksgiving was kept up without intermission night and day." (*Southey*.)

Kentigern, during a sojourn of several years on this pleasant hill, brought the community into a state of the most edifying devotion, while his own fame extended far and wide. He went also seven times from hence to Rome, in order to obtain the Pope's assent to the establishment of the diocese, and confirmation of his own consecration as bishop. Among the monks of Elwy was a young man named Asaph, who was the especial disciple and favourite of Kentigern, and under his guidance was graduating with every prospect of success for the degree of saint. It happened on one occasion that, from remaining too long in the bath, the bishop became chilled, and requested Asaph to bring him some fire. Having no utensil near him, Asaph placed the live coals on his hand, and carried them, without suffering any injury, to his master. Kentigern was at length summoned back to Glasgow, in order, if possible, to reclaim the inhabitants who had relapsed into paganism, and to avert the calamities that were impending over the land on account of their wickedness. He carried with him six hundred and sixty of the monks, leaving his scholar to succeed him in his offices here. Accordingly Asaph became bishop of Elwy, and he governed the see with so much wisdom till his death, which occurred near the close of the sixth century, that both city and diocese received the name of their canonized bishop. The cathedral is dedicated (like that of Glasgow) to St. Kentigern, while the parish church is dedicated to master and pupil. The history of the early cathedrals is a history of alternate buildings and burnings, and is too long to repeat here.

This present cathedral is in part of the early English, and partly of the decorated style and period. It is cruciform, with a heavy central tower; small in size, plain (having no more "whigmaleeries and curliwurlies, and open-steek hems about it," than its namesake and kinsman at Glasgow), and while it has a nave, choir, and transept, is without any superfluous additions. It has neither crypt, cloisters, chapter-house, nor Lady Chapel: yet there is something pleasing in its simplicity and regularity, and also in its neatness. Parts of it, too, as the eastern window, are really fine. Of the interior not much must be said. Restorations in *plaster*, are hardly what we look for in a cathedral, yet it is proper to recollect that quite recently, enriched roofing has been "restored" in a wealthy English cathedral in *paper*. The choir, with its handsome window filled with coloured glass, and rich canopied stalls, certainly has a pleasing look.

The fate of the cathedral during the Commonwealth affords a curious instance of the tyranny of fanaticism. It was rented by a person who must have studied hard to convey his hatred of "superstitious uses." The choir he converted into a calf-pen, the nave served for cattle-stalls, one transept he made a stable, the other he employed for a post-office; the font he carried to his own yard, and used for a hog-trough.

Within these few years the episcopal palace and the deanery have been rebuilt at the cost of the bishop and dean, and now add considerably to the beauty of the place. Several new dwelling-houses have also been erected of a better class than are usually erected in the smaller Welsh towns.

We ought, perhaps, to have spoken of the pleasantness of the walk from Denbigh to St. Asaph; but it was hardly needful, for the whole neighbourhood affords agreeable walks. The upper valley of the Elwy is particularly pleasing. And there are objects of curiosity as well as of beauty. There are, for instance, the caverns of Cefn Meriadog, with their contents, which the geologist and palæontologist find very interesting, and the proprietor has found very profitable;—for the fossil bones in some of these caverns are so plentiful, and so fertilizing, that the gain would hardly have been greater had a bed of guano been discovered there. There are also some slight remains of small religious edifices to be found by searching for. All around here, too, are the mansions and parks of the wealthy and noble. Here, as may be remembered, was Mrs. Piozzi's house; and the neighbourhood, consequently, is associated with the memory of Johnson, who spent a week or two there, and whose visit is commemorated at one place by the preservation of the chair in which he sat, at another by a monument, and again by an inscription. Of the seats in the vicinity, among the most celebrated are Pengwern and Bodelwyddan—the latter, a modern castellated structure, having perhaps the finest grounds in this part of Wales.

Three miles below St. Asaph is seen on the right bank of the Clwyd another castle — and one which appears hardly less striking than those we have already visited. Rhyddlan Castle (pronounced Ruthlan) was an important fortress, and has a history—too long to tell. A castle or fortress of some kind appears to have existed here at a very early period. By the Welsh, Rhyddlan was regarded as one of the most important of their military stations, and its possession, therefore, was disputed with more energy than perhaps any other place in North Wales. The present castle was erected by Edward I., and formed a main link in the great chain of fortresses commenced by the first Norman invaders of Wales, and perfected by the skill and caution of Edward—the several members being so disposed as mutually to sustain and strengthen each other.

It was at Rhyddlan that Edward I., in 1283, consolidated by his policy the success of his able but merciless and remorseless campaign, by the promulgation of the celebrated 'Statute of Rhyddlan,' which while it engaged to secure the judicial rights and privileges of the principality, served effectually to subjugate it to English rule. At this parliament of Rhyddlan it was that Edward is said to have outwitted the Welsh notables by the somewhat apocryphal artifice of proposing that Wales should be governed by a native prince, whose character no one should be able to gainsay. The Welsh accepted the offer with exclamations of unbounded joy and gratitude, when the king pre-

5.—CONWAY CASTLE

sented to them his own infant son recently born at Carnarvon Castle, and whom he had already created Prince of Wales. Near the centre of the town is the fragment of an old house, which the inscription on a stone tablet inserted in the wall, by a late dean of St. Asaph's, states to be that in which Edward held his parliament.

Rhyddlan Castle was dismantled in 1646, by order of the Parliament: merely the shell is now standing. In form it is a quadrangle with massive towers at the angles: at two of the corners are double towers. Seen from the river, in connection with the bridge and part of the town, the appearance is highly picturesque: the effect being increased perhaps by the general flatness of the neighbourhood. The Clwyd is a tidal river up to Rhyddlan, and vessels of sixty tons ascend as far as the town, which has in consequence some little commerce. The town itself is but a poor place, without anything beside the castle to interest the stranger.

Beyond Rhyddlan is a broad marsh, known as Morva Rhyddlan, whereon was fought a battle between the Mercians and British, when the latter were defeated, and Caradoc their king with the flower of his nobility, and a vast number of the people, were slain. The memory of the battle is preserved in one of the most plaintive and beautiful of the Welsh melodies, named after the fatal field, Morva Rhyddlan.

About a couple of miles east of Rhyddlan are the ruins of Dyserth Castle. They are not very remarkable on their own account, but the situation is fine: they stand on a lofty eminence, which commands a splendid view of the Vale of Clwyd. The church lies in a hollow, and is often mentioned on account of its old yews, and some curious monuments.

The Clwyd falls into the sea at Rhyl about a couple of miles below Rhyddlan. Rhyl is a small watering-place, a good deal frequented by the people of Liverpool. A mile or so on the other side of the estuary of the Clwyd is Abergele some such another place. Tourists often visit both, but we cannot guess why.

CONWAY.

Many an English traveller, who has run over half the globe to see rare towns, has not deigned to visit Conway. Many another who has visited it thinks it needful to excuse or confirm his admiration of it by declaring that it bears a marked resemblance to some Syrian, or Moorish, or other foreign and far distant town. Its real attraction is its *originality* : it is unique. And it is the most romantic town in this kingdom, and, of its kind, perhaps in any other. It is idle to praise Conway in measured terms. He who does not admire it may be sure, however respectable and useful a member of society he may be, he has no eye for such objects. He who does truly admire it must admire it thoroughly.

Conway is a nearly perfect example of a walled and fortified English town of mediæval date. This is its main peculiarity. Chester is a remarkable place, and,

as we said when there, the walls are complete; but then, Chester is a good-sized city: half of it, nearly, lies outside the walls; and there are extensive suburbs; the walls and castle, too, were only intended to guard the city. Conway is a sort of garrison town; is still wholly confined within the walls; has no suburbs; and the castle was a great military station, intended to guard an important pass, and serve as a grand centre for offensive as well as defensive operations.

The situation and external appearance of Conway are very striking. The ground on which the town is built slopes up rapidly from the estuary of the Conway river, which flows around two sides of it. The walls of the town form a triangle, or, as some will have it, a Welsh harp,—a form given to it, they add, in compliment to the natives of the Principality. The broadest base of the triangle lies along the river ; at one angle is the majestic castle, seated on a bold rock ; while the town walls rise inland to the apex, which is on the highest point of ground, and terminates in a large round tower. Twenty other towers are placed at intervals along the walls. The entrances to the town are through rude old gatehouses. Across the river, just under the castle, is a long light suspension-bridge ; and alongside that, is the tubular railway-bridge : the last structures are of course both recent, and so far interfere with the antique aspect of the town and castle. (Cut, No. 5.)

Within the walls Conway is equally noteworthy. The streets are irregular ; the houses, nearly all humble in rank, are generally rude, old-fashioned, overhanging, gable-fronted, half-timber ones, for the most part differing from each other, and many of them semi-ruinous. At every turn there is some quaint old structure, or picturesque bit of a street, terminated by a tower and fragment of the walls, a portion of the castle, or one of the gatehouses : just such a picture, in short, as Prout might paint without changing a feature. Nor are fitting ' figures' wanting to give animation and completeness to the picture. Welsh peasants, countrymen from neighbouring villages, miners, or market-women with their jackets and odd tall hats, and perhaps a sailor or two, are strolling about the streets : while on a market or fairday, the lively groups in their best native costumes, talking, at the top of their voices, in their strange guttural language, increase not a little the uncommon character of the scene. Tourists and tourists' books (by which, indeed, tourists usually speak), complain generally that the town inside is " mean and rude ; and, consequently, uninteresting :" but it is because it is so rude and unpretending that it is really interesting. It wears the more truly the genuine antique air. Here is no modern antique : no smooth-polished and pretty revival or imitation of what an old place might have been. It is the old place itself, decayed indeed, but still itself ; not defaced by modern embellishment, nor softened into insignificance by modern taste.

Conway Castle was erected by Edward I., in 1283. Of all his Welsh castles,—except, perhaps, Carnarvon, this was the most magnificent ; and hardly a finer was there, probably, in England. Edward himself held his court here; and here, on one occasion, kept his Christmas festivities: and once, cut off from the main body of his army, was shut up in it, and had to endure a short but sharp siege, the Welsh having unexpectedly descended from the mountains in large numbers, in the hope of surprising and seizing the king. In the great civil war, Conway Castle was garrisoned for Charles; but in May, 1645, the town of Conway was stormed by a Parliamentary force, commanded by Colonel Mytton; and a few days after the castle was compelled to surrender. The Irish who were among the garrison were tied back to back and flung into the river: an instance of the furious national and religious, as well as political, animosity, which became engendered in the course of that terrible struggle. Charles II. granted the castle to the Earl of Conway. The castle was dismantled; all the timber, iron, and lead being removed and shipped to Ireland.

The castle is in form a simple parallelogram: the walls, which are of immense thickness, are flanked by eight circular towers, some forty feet each in diameter, and carrying light turrets—of which, however, only four remain: they are machicolated, and greatly relieve the heaviness of the towers. The towers at the grand entrance, called respectively the King's and Queen's, were of richer character than the others. The great strength of the masonry is rather remarkably evinced by one of the towers. About a century ago a large portion of the lower part of the tower, which rises from a steep rock, fell down, owing to the incautious quarrying of the rock on which it rested; and yet though only supported by the adhesion of the inner wall to the main building, the upper part of the tower has remained ever since suspended far aloft unmoved. The barbicans, the outworks which were carried into the river, and the drawbridge, are gone. Although on entering it the castle is found to be very ruinous, it yet is very imposing. The remains of the grand hall attest its ancient splendour: it is a noble apartment, 130 feet long and 30 wide; some of the arches remain—but time and the negligence (or worse) of its keepers have despoiled this and the other parts of all semblance of grandeur, and hardly enough is left to enable even the antiquary to restore to the imagination the inner castle of Edward's time. From the terrace which overlooks the river, and from the towers, there are fine views of the town and vicinity. The singular figure of the town is well seen from these castle towers; and with its walls and old houses appears as remarkable seen thus under the eye as any way. When looking down from the castle upon the river, Gray's lines will be sure to recur to the memory:

" On a rock, whose haughty brow
Frowns o'er old Conway's foaming flood."

They describe well enough the site of the castle, which we may suppose occupies the place from which the Bard poured forth his maledictions and his prophecies; but the epithet applied to the river is so far unfortunate

that it has given the small critics occasion to point out that old Conway is here a quiet stream: in fact, it would be about as characteristic to talk of " the foaming flood of Father Thames."

The houses in the town, as we mentioned, are only individually noticeable as examples of the ordinary dwelling-houses of the olden time: but there is one exception. Near the middle of the High Street is one that cannot fail to arrest attention. It is known as the Plas Mawr, or Great Mansion, and was erected in 1576 by Robert Wynne, Esq., of Carnarvon. It is of the quaintest fashion of that time, but is handsome as well as quaint in appearance. Both externally and internally it is elaborately ornamented with figures, coats of arms, scrolls, etc. Over the chief entrance is a Greek inscription; while the initials of Elizabeth and those of the Earl of Leicester are frequently repeated. From the turret there is a capital view over the city. Plas Mawr is now the property of the Hon. — Mostyn: it is let out in humble tenements, and is in a sad condition—crumbling, in fact, to pieces. There is little observable in the church, though old, besides a monument to a worthy native, who was the forty-first child of his father; and himself the parent of twenty-seven children:

" Of a notable race was Shenkin!"

The suspension-bridge, which connects Conway with the opposite bank, is a very graceful structure. Objections have been raised against it as being too light and frail in appearance to accord with the massive form of the castle; but this is refining: in truth, there is much propriety in this characteristic. It seems as though it were just the bridge (one being requisite in such a position) which the builder of the castle might have chosen, on account of the ease with which (as would seem) it might be destroyed before an approaching foe.

But no such apology can be made for the railway-bridge which has been within the last year or two placed alongside of it. This—in itself a mass of unmitigated deformity—has at once effectually destroyed the beauty of the suspension-bridge, and also the grandest view of the castle. It is placed parallel to and in the closest proximity with the former, and runs directly in front of and under the latter. Even here the mischief perpetrated by the railway vandals does not end. The line is continued just under the broken tower, which, in consequence, is left, unsupported, to bear the constant vibrations caused by the passing trains; with what ultimate (and probably not very distant) result may be imagined. However we may, perhaps, be thankful that the railway lords contented themselves with these things, and with merely making an ugly gaping arch in the town walls. The railway was commenced while the mania was in its hottest fit, and whatever had been asked, " the houses" would doubtless have granted. Seeing that the chief aim of engineers just at that time appeared to be the doing of some strange thing, one may be glad it did not occur to the projector of this

THE VALE OF LLANGOLLEN.

line to plough right through the old castle. But in all seriousness, and sadness too, for every week almost some irreparable mischief is being done, how strange does it seem that there is nowhere in the Government an official conservator of our national monuments! Monuments, in the preservation of which every one has an interest, for they are an open book, a living picture, for every one's delight and instruction. Were there such an officer (or were it the duty of any particular official) the sense of individual responsibility would intervene to preserve from preventable injury what even a nation's wealth cannot replace.

As examples of engineering skill, both of these works deserve attention; and both are on a very important scale. The suspension-bridge was constructed in 1826, by Telford, and forms a portion of the great Irish line of road constructed by order of the Government. Before the erection of this bridge, the passage across here was effected by means of a ferry,—from the nature of the place always an inconvenient and often a dangerous passage. The river is here, at high-water, three quarters of a mile over; but when the tide is out, the stream is confined within a narrow channel. On the eastern side of this channel is an insulated rock, on which the farther pier of the bridge is built. The length of the bridge between the supporting piers is 327 feet: an embankment of clay, faced with stone, is carried along the sands on the eastern side for 2015 feet. The tubular railway-bridge is precisely similar in character (though, of course, of much smaller magnitude) to that which is now being carried across the Menai Straits: we may therefore defer for the present any remarks on its peculiarities. The length of the tube of the Conway Bridge is 400 feet. Trains have passed regularly through it for above a year, without producing any sensible effect: it is only by means of instruments that a slight deflection can be detected during the passage of a train. Both the tubular and suspension bridges are 18 feet above high-water mark.

While at Conway the visitor may walk over to the famous promontory of Great Orme's Head—a rock which lifts its grim black mass to a vast height from the waves. When a fierce sea is running and dashing into spray against the base, its appearance is sufficiently impressive, even from the shore; but its stern majesty is only properly understood in sailing around it when the sea is not too smooth. The riven face of the rock is the chosen home of the sea-birds, whose wild cry and ceaseless evolutions add not a little to the character of the scene. From the summit there is a fine sea-view. On the western side is a copper-mine, which employs two hundred men, and on the eastern side is the village of Llandudno, whose church serves as a valuable beacon. Orme's Head appears to have been the theatre of Druidic rites, as there are still some of the rude circles of stones usually considered to have been employed for the purpose. A rocking-stone is called Cryd Tudno—the Cradle of St. Tudno, a famous Welsh saint, who, as we might expect from such a cradling on this bleak height, when he became a saint, proved one of no common kind. The village bears his name, Llandudno, the church of Tudno.

THE VALE OF LLANGOLLEN.

We shall now conduct the tourist to Conway by another route; and one which, though possessing few reverend castles or other objects of antiquity, is very far superior to the former in landscape beauty.

The road lies by way of the Chester and Shrewsbury Railway to the Llangollen-road station, whence there is a beautiful walk of four miles to the village; which latter may of course be saved by means of omnibus or fly. The ride by railway is very much more pleasant than such rides usually are. Every mile till Llangollen is within ken the scenery improves; and probably there is hardly another view obtainable from a railway equal to that of the Vale of Llangollen, when the train is halting on the Dee viaduct, in order to stop at the Cefn station. The beautiful vale is seen from a quite new point of view,—the spectator being placed on an elevation of 150 feet above the level of the river, with the Cysylltan aqueduct carried boldly across the valley at a short distance in front, and serving by its rigid outline to impart vigour to the foreground, and a more aërial grace to the distant mountains.

Several places that are passed in the ride to Llangollen station wear a tempting look to the tourist; and in particular the town of Wrexham will seem to deserve a visit, as the really noble tower of its church is caught sight of. But the church is almost the only thing there that is worth seeing; and it is unquestionably one of the very finest in Wales. It is of the perpendicular style, and was erected at the close of the fifteenth and commencement of the sixteenth centuries. The exterior, which is least injured, is quite florid in its ornamentation; but from a distance, sufficient to see it as a whole has an effect of exceeding richness. In the interior are very interesting monuments: among the rest is the celebrated one, by Roubiliac, of Mrs. Myddleton, in which she is represented rising from the tomb. The town is a place of considerable business, and has a rather large population.

The Vale of Llangollen is one of those places which suffer from the excessive praise which has been lavished upon them. Something more is anticipated than almost any spot will supply. Tourists who just come, take a glance, and are away again, are often, as they pretty loudly exclaim, "disappointed." So, too, are those who have been rambling among the wilder scenery of the Principality: "Llangollen," say these, "does not do after Snowdonia." But to such as come hither without expectations too highly raised, and before they have seen the wilder country, Llangollen affords a satisfying pleasure at the first, and grows more and more delightful as it is more thoroughly known. She is a fair one, fitted for daily familiar intercourse, ever pleasing to one willing to be pleased, but whose many charms unfold fully only to him who is content patiently to watch and woo.

It is, perhaps, hardly fair to set Clwyd and Llangollen in rivalry, as is constantly done : their attractions are essentially different. Clwyd is an ample open placid valley, which may occasionally rise into an almost Claudean grace or grandeur, under favouring "skyey influences ;" but which owes its chief secondary charm to the numerous ruins of castles and strongholds, and the recollections of the age to which they belong, which clothe with the purple haze of antiquity alike the hills and the valley. Llangollen has no historical relics of any importance, and no imposing associations ; but it has natural charms which abundantly compensate. The valley is narrow and winding : the hills on either hand are steep and lofty : the crystal Dee, a copious stream, winds along the bottom of the vale,—now resting in a deep pool, embosomed in trees, which hardly allow the summits of the distant hills to be discerned ; and presently, as it careers along a more open space, forcing its way between scattered masses of rock, or rushing over a blue ledge in sparkling waterbreaks. Thus, while Clwyd, if regarded as a landscape, must be viewed as a whole,—the interest of the parts depending rather on some ruined castle, to which the surrounding objects serve but as a foil,—Llangollen affords a continued succession of altogether independent and various scenes. From the heights, if the eye be turned westward, there are often exquisite views over a long stretch of valley, closed by a grand array of distant mountains ; while, eastwards, a softer but even more extensive and delightful prospect extends. And in the valley the companionable river, differing at every turn, serves as the centre of an unfailing succession of charming pictures.

The village of Llangollen*—the centre from which the valley must be explored—is in itself by no means attractive, though its situation is pleasing. The houses are dropped down almost at random ; while the picturesqueness that might be expected to result from this chance arrangement, is prevented by their want of character. The church is an old one ; but, like the generality of Welsh village churches, is quite plain and poor. It is noteworthy, however, inasmuch as it covers the remains of the saint to whom it is dedicated, and who has given his name to church, village, and valley. Llangollen is the church of Collen. Pennant says, his full name—and it is worth while having the full name of one Welsh saint—is Saint Collen ap Gwynnawg ap Clydawg ap Cowrda ap Caradoc Freichfras ap Lleyr Merion ap Einion Yrth ap Cunedda Wledig !

"Bless us ! what a name for a holy saint is this !"

Old Fuller, speaking of a certain Welsh gentleman of many aps, whose name was called at full on the panel of a jury, says that he "was advised by the judge, in the reign of King Henry VIII., for brevity sake, to contract his name ;" and that he did so accordingly. "This leading case," he adds, was "precedential

* This, in the books, is generally said to be pronounced Thlangothlen ; but the sound is somewhat more like Chlancothlen,—the *chl* being a strong guttural.

to the practice of other gentry in Wales, who (leaving their pedigrees at home) carry only one surname abroad with them, whereby much time (especially in winter) is gained for other employment." Perhaps it was usual, once, to call Welsh demons, as well as Welsh saints and Welsh gentlemen, by their ancestral names ; (on the ground that "his Honour was a gentleman !") and this may explain what Hotspur said of Owen Glendower's catalogue of serviceable spirits :

"I tell you what—
He held me, last night, at least nine hours,
In reckoning up the several devils' names
That were his lackeys."

If Llangollen village be not in itself very attractive it proves a capital first station whereat the tourist may make his early essays in Welsh rambling, and obtain induction into Welsh characteristics. The people of the village talk English pretty generally, but all around the Welsh language prevails : and if he wish to hear it in continuous discourse he may do so by attending the service at either church or chapel on Sunday afternoon. The hills and the crags will serve as exercise-ground on which the incipient pedestrian may test and train his budding powers of walking and climbing. Then there are, moreover, two excellent inns, at either of which, after his day's wanderings, he may solace himself with Welsh fare—prime mountain mutton, Dee trout or salmon (which will be all the better, of course, if he catch them), and for a beverage some genuine cwrw (and that of mine host of the Hand is eminently cwrw dha): while he will be cheered during the breakfast, or dinner-hour by the melody of Welsh tunes, played on a Welsh harp, by a thoroughly Welsh harper.

This custom, by-the-way, of having a harper stationed in the hall, prevails pretty generally at the hotels through the touring districts. Of the agreeableness or otherwise of the practice, opinion seems to differ considerably among both tourists and writers. All who discourse in the high musical dialect laugh it to scorn : to the unlearned, however, while only Welsh tunes are played with merely the simple national variations, the harping is usually not merely pleasing, but the simplicity of structure and frequently plaintive tone of the airs appeal to the feelings in a way that the bewildering compositions of profound contra-puntists never do. For our part we should be very sorry to lose the harp,—but heartily glad if the harpers would give up polkas and waltzes, and stick to their national tunes. Mayfair melodies are sadly out of place among the Welsh mountains.

The harp itself, as the national instrument, claims a word of passing notice ; we therefore borrow Mr. Bingley's description of it, which we hope will satisfy our musical readers, acknowledging ourselves 'ignorance itself' in the matter :—"The harp has been always esteemed the principal musical instrument among the Welsh. Anciently it was strung with hair, and this continued in use until the commencement of the fifteenth century, up to which period it had only a single row of strings, but the performer was able to produce a flat or sharp by a peculiar arrangement of the finger and thumb; an artifice, it is believed, no longer known. The harp now in common use, is the triple harp. It extends in compass to five octaves and one note. The two outside rows of strings are the diatonics, which are both tuned in unison, and in any key that the performer means to play in. The treble row comprises twenty-seven strings, and extends from A in alt down to C in the bass; and the opposite row or unisons comprises thirty-seven strings, and extends from A in alt down as low as double G in the bass. The middle-row, which is for flats and sharps, comprises thirty-four strings."

So much for the harp. Of the music we will only further remark, that the airs so familiar in England, such as 'Of a noble race was Shenkin,' 'Jenny Jones,' (Yr Gwdlas, and Cader Idris), and the like, are very different in the Welsh version: and it is much to be regretted that some Welsh Moore does not arise to marry the music of his national melodies to verse which shall echo the original sentiment, instead of degrading it by ludicrous or puerile associations.

Llangollen, it was said, affords an abundant variety of those short loitering strolls, which are so pleasant to take in a hilly country. These the tourist will best discover for himself—he can seldom go wrong, if he direct his way to the uplands, or, with pencil or rod in hand, betake himself to the fishermen's paths beside the Dee. But two or three of the more noted spots must be mentioned. The few fragments of a building, which are seen cresting the brow of the lofty hill on the north of Llangollen, are the remains of a fortress; but when built or at what time dismantled are alike unknown. They are too much decayed to be picturesque, or even to afford much clue to their age; and they are of little interest, for, as old Leland said in the time of Henry VIII., "the castle was never big thing." Still Castell Dinas Bran should be visited. The hill stands nearly insulated, and the summit being more than 900 feet above the Dee at Llangollen bridge, there is from it a remarkably fine view of the valley; moreover, the climb will be an excellent fillip to the appetite against the hour of breakfast—for, as the hill-top is only a mile or so from the inn, and the prospect is much the finest as the mists are dispersing, the early morning is assuredly the proper time for the ascent. As far as the prospect is concerned, fine as it certainly is, it is by no means so fine as that obtained from the brow of the Eagles' Crag (Greigiau Eglwysegle), as the remarkable bare scarp is called, which a little farther north towers far above Dinas Bran. This crag consists of a vast limestone cliff, which rises in a range of irregular ledges to a great height. It is very difficult to climb directly from Dinas Bran—and to find an easy ascent will require a rather long walk; but the prospect will repay the labour. The view of the valley downwards with the stream winding through the centre, and crossed by aqueduct and viaduct, and extending

into the open plain beyond, is very fine: while upwards, reaching far away to the lofty mountains, it is really grand. The view of the village and upper Vale of Llangollen, which we have given in the steel engraving, was sketched from the hill that rises immediately behind Llangollen Church.

A day will be well spent in a ramble to Chirk and Wynnstay, returning by the aqueduct and thence along the vale.

Chirk is a neat little village, and the village church, with the solemn old yews that stand in the churchyard, has a venerable air. But it is Chirk Castle, with its magnificent park, which the stranger comes to see. The house is a modern mansion of great size and splendour, which has been formed in part out of the old castle that was dismantled by the Parliamentarians, after they had well battered it with their cannon. The interior of the house is permitted to be seen by the stranger: but as we have not seen it, we shall merely say that it is highly spoken of by those who have; and that it contains some very good pictures. One landscape—a view of the famous Montgomery Waterfall, Pistyl Rhaider—is universally popular; not on account of its faithfulness. It was painted by one of the many Dutchmen who practised their craft in England prior to the rise of the English school of landscape painters. Mynheer was commissioned to paint the cataract by one of the Middleton family, who, when the picture was brought home, sought to display his connoisseurship by proposing 'a slight alteration.' "It is very pretty indeed—but don't you think it would give it more animation if a few sheep were added?" "A few sheeps!" exclaimed the astonished artist; "a few sheeps by the waterfall!—ah well, you shall have a few sheeps if you wish for them." Accordingly the picture when sent home again, had the old rocky foreground painted out, and replaced by the sea, on which "a few *ships*" are sailing, and into which the cataract is made to fall.

There is something finer to be seen at Chirk Castle than the interior of the mansion, however splendid that may be. From the terrace there is a prospect of surpassing beauty and of extraordinary extent: on a clear day seventeen counties, it is said, may be seen from it. The park itself is well wooded, has a handsome lake, and affords pleasing views. The valley of the Ceiriog, (the little river which flows below, and is here the boundary between England and Wales), is a scene famous in Welsh annals: the army of Henry II. having been there defeated by the renowned Welsh prince Owen Gwynedd—to the estate of whose descendant we are now to direct our steps.

From Chirk a walk of two or three miles leads to New Bridge, near which is a lodge by which Wynnstay Park may be entered. The path leads along the beautiful glen through which the Dee here makes its way. Nant-y-Belan, or the Glen of the Marten, as it is called, is one of the loveliest in this part of the country. The steep banks are richly clad with light foliage, while the river runs along the bottom, now foaming over broken and projecting rocks, and presently flowing smooth and noiseless, and reflecting with a softened lustre the rich tints of the pendant trees and grassy knolls. From the end of the glen a path will be found to Belen Tower, a circular building, erected by Sir Watkin Wynne to the memory of the Cambrian officers and soldiers slain in the Irish rebellion of 1798. The building is a conspicuous object for a great distance in every direction: and glorious is the view from it. The whole Vale of Llangollen stretches at your feet. Cysylltau Aqueduct gives a distinctive character to the nearer part of the landscape; Dinas Bran is an important feature in the middle distance; the Dee is traced at intervals along the valley; a lofty barrier of mountains closes the prospect. As the sun is declining in the westward sky, and clothing hill and vale with a milder radiance, the scene is one that might well inspire poet or painter, and which it is hardly possible to gaze upon unmoved. Equally delightful in its way is the prospect over the Marten's Glen. Other parts of the park yield very fine views, but none comparable with these. The park itself is of great extent, and very varied in surface. It has many grand old trees; and noteworthy are the noble avenues. There are also several monuments and buildings in the park besides that we have named. One, a column, 110 feet high, is to the memory of the mother of Sir Watkin: the summit commands a wide and splendid prospect. Another conspicuous structure is the Waterloo Tower, raised to commemorate the great victory. The mansion is very large, and the interior is befitting the position and affluence of its owner. The collection of pictures, which includes a good many capital Wilsons, is celebrated. Altogether Wynnstay is a splendid domain—almost the only drawback being that it is too closely neighboured by the mines and works, which emit enormous and everlasting volumes of smoke.

Until the last year or two the Cysylltau Aqueduct was the wonder of the lower valley of Llangollen; now it has a rival: we may as well look at them together, only giving precedence, as is fitting, to the elder. The Cysylltau Aqueduct was constructed for the purpose of carrying the Ellesmere Canal across this part of the Vale of Llangollen. Telford was the engineer. The watercourse, which is wholly of cast-iron, is 1,007 feet in length; and is supported on eighteen stone piers. Its height above the surface of the Dee is 120 feet. It was commenced in 1795, and completed in 1805, at a cost, including the embankment, of £47,000.

The other structure to which we referred is the Viaduct which carries the Chester and Shrewsbury Railway over the valley. This is of even more surprising proportions than the Aqueduct. In length it is 1,530 feet; and its height is 150 feet above the level of the Dee. Nineteen arches, each having a span of 90 feet, support the roadway. The cost of construction was upwards of £100,000. In beauty as well as in magnitude, the Aqueduct must unquestionably yield the palm. This Viaduct is in truth a noble structure. Generally the viaducts are the most successful architec-

tural objects which railway engineers erect: but this probably surpasses in elegance as well as size all that have yet been raised. It is built almost wholly of stone; the arches are circular; and while there is no unsuitable display of ornament, enough has been done to impart an appearance of architectural character and finish. It is certainly the finest viaduct we have seen, and we believe it is the finest in the kingdom. The lover of beautiful scenery will feel grateful that what might have been a grievous disfigurement is really made an additional ornament to the beautiful vale.

To perceive clearly the vast size of these two structures, the stranger should descend into the valley between them: indeed he should do so if he is regardless of that matter. It is a singular spectacle to stand by the river-side and behold far aloft in the air, on the one hand, a barge floating slowly along; and on the other, a train of carriages flying as on the wings of the wind. It is a singular spectacle, and one suggestive of many thoughts. We were struck too with the view from the towing-path of the Aqueduct: it has a curious effect to stand beside a stream on which heavily-laden vessels are floating, and at the same time see a river a hundred and twenty feet beneath you. From this aqueduct too the viaduct has a graceful appearance, seen as it is in connection with the distant landscape.

There is only one place up the vale which we need speak of: namely, Valle Crucis Abbey. (Cut, No. 6.) The ruins will be found in the Vale of Crucis, which meets the Vale of Llangollen about two miles from the village. It is one of those delicious spots the old monks knew so well how to select. Here in this secluded valley did they build their house; where, snugly embayed under sheltering mountains, with a brawling rivulet behind their dwelling, and the well-stored Dee close at hand, they needed to "fear neither winter nor rough weather." The mountain-sides and the clear stream would afford them sufficient fare, as well as walks where they might indulge in solitary meditation. Valle Crucis was a Cistercian monastery founded by Madoc-ap-Griffith, in the beginning of the twelfth century. It flourished till the spoliation of religious houses; when the annual revenues were estimated by the Royal Commissioners at upwards of £200.

The chief portions remaining of the abbey are now the east and west gables: both of which prove that when complete it must have been a handsome pile. The western end (which is shown in the engraving), as seen half-hidden by the tall ash-trees which have grown up around it, and within the walls since the desecration of the church, is remarkably pleasing and picturesque. The long lancet windows, and the tolerably-complete circular window above, are of very good design. The eastern end is not quite so picturesque, but it has some peculiarities which will render it more interesting to the architectural antiquary. The remaining transept and arches add not less to the picturesqueness than to the architectural value of the ruin. Some portions of the conventual buildings are preserved by being

6.—VALLE CRUCIS ABBEY.

included in the adjoining farm-house; but they are of little interest compared with the church and connected parts—which, let us add, are now carefully preserved.

The ruins of Valle Crucis Abbey are now merely thought of as a pleasing addition to the beauties of Llangollen: but they must once have been regarded with very different feelings by the solitary wanderer. Here on the one hand he saw a secluded dwelling, whose inmates were a band of men who had professedly devoted their days to the service of their Maker, and who lived here in the quiet performance of their religious duties, the instruction of those who sought their aid, the contemplation of Nature, and the pursuit of literature and of art—as those things were then understood and studied—and whose doors were ever open to afford shelter and refreshment to the traveller, and succour and refuge to the distressed and the oppressed. On the other hand he saw, perched on an almost inaccessible rock, a building whose approaches were guarded by every military contrivance, and whose whole appearance, as well as its history, spoke aloud of strife, and tyranny, and rapine. Every castle would not then wear so forbidding an aspect as Castell Dinas Bran, nor every monastery appear as grateful as Valle

Crucis; but with all the faults and all the shortcomings of these religious houses—and even at the best their faults and shortcomings were necessarily very many—it must have been a consolatory thought to the reflective mind, that, as the world then was, there were scattered all over the land places which gave a home to the homeless, and while they proffered to the man of fervid religious spirit a better and more humanising retreat than the solitary hermitage, afforded also to the studious man a place where, undisturbed by anxious forebodings, he might prosecute his researches for the general good. Well is it that the monastic system is with us for ever gone; but let us acknowledge that in its better day it has done our country good service.

A little beyond the ruins of the abbey is a stone cross, which is by some antiquaries thought to have given its name to the valley, and by others to the lofty crags which skirt the vale. It is now known as the Pillar of Eliseg; it is said to have been erected above a thousand years ago, in memory of a British hero, Eliseg, father of Brochwel Ysythroc, Prince of Powis, by his grandson Congen: but we do not, of course, vouch for the truth of the saying. The cross, which had been defaced and thrown down as a popish relic, was replaced on its pedestal towards the close of the last century. It stands in a lonely spot, surrounded by a network of bare mountains ; and was, in all probability, erected in commemoration of some deed of blood—either of battle fought or of prince who fell here.

When at Valle Crucis, the visitor will find it a pleasant short extension of his walk to continue along the Dee, past the Chain-bridge, to the place where the canal unites with the river. The channel of the river is filled with massive blocks of stone and slate ; and indeed, the rock and river scenery is unusually bold : while the spot where the canal joins the Dee is a broad smooth semicircular bay, with a wide weir on one side of it.

CORWEN.

The ten miles between Llangollen and Corwen are very pleasant and very varied. For the entire distance the Dee runs beside, and generally somewhat below the road, which is carried along the base of the Moel Ferna Mountains. Where the Vale of Llangollen ends—by the huge Rhisgog—the tourist will instinctively halt to take his parting glance of the famous vale. It is a well adapted to leave on the memory a favourable impression—especially if the hill be ascended. The valley is then seen in one of its grandest as well as fairest aspects. Dinas Bran stands out majestically from the Eagle Crags ;—which in their turn exhibit to perfection their bold shattered cliffs. The river glitters under the bright morning sun. The light blue smoke curls up unbroken from one homestead and another, and hangs like a vapour over the half-concealed village.

Onwards is the Valley of the Dee, Glyn Dyfrdwy. The road now keeps at some height above the stream ; but it affords no very extensive prospects ; for the valley makes many sharp curvatures, and on the left the hill-side rise abruptly from the road. On the right, however, owing to the many tributary dales, there are more open prospects and distant peeps. Still there is a continuous variety of scenery forwards, and no feeling of weariness is likely to creep on. The river lies in a sort of glen on the right ; and, as it emerges now and then into view, or sends up a cheerful sound as it leaps along its rocky bed, it is sadly tempting to one who prefers a river side to the main road ; and heartily will he repent if he be an angler that he has not brought his rod with him, that he might whip the stream to Corwen, and at the same time enjoy its delicious succession of close, quiet scenery.

This Valley of the Dee was the patrimony of the redoubted Owen Glyndwr—Shakspere's Glendower—and with many a mountain side and summit do the natives delight to associate his name. Just beyond the seventh mile stone will be seen a kind of tumulus crested with a clump of firs ; this is Glyndwr's Mount, and is, we believe, fixed on as the site of his palace,

which his bard described as "a fair timber structure on the summit of a green hill." On the brow of the Berwyn Mountain, behind Corwen, is Owen Glyndwr's Seat, and the fine prospect from the stone chair might lead one to fancy him a lover of beautiful scenery, as well as a hardy warrior, but the prosaic guide assures you that he delighted most in the prospect, because it showed him forty square miles of his own land. On one of the walls of Corwen church they show a hole made by the fiery chief's dagger, which he flung from this chair on some occasion when the townsmen had offended him.

Before reaching Corwen the valley opens ; the hills recede further apart, are less abrupt, and though not less rocky, the rocks are plumed with wood ; and Dee is smooth and dull—you would hardly fancy he could be so buoyant and sprightly a mile or two lower. Just a momentary tarriance will be made at the picturesque village of Llansantffraid, and then nothing will occur to arrest the attention till Corwen be reached.

Corwen is not at all a place to interest the stranger on its own account. But it has an hotel (named after the mighty Owen) whose fame is widely spread ; it is a convenient centre from which to explore some very good (though not remarkable) scenery ; and it is a favourite fishing station. The town is one of the quietest of its size in Wales—at least of those which lie in a great line of road. It has no manufactures, and only the trade of an agricultural district, with that produced by a wealthy resident gentry, and the summer visitors.

A short distance beyond Corwen, the Dee bends sharply to the left, and the tourist might ascend it to Bala along the Vale of Eideyrnion—one of the loveliest in the principality. Our course however lies forward : we must diverge little either to the right hand or to the left till we arrive at Conway.

Hardly have we parted company with the Dee when its affluent, the Alwen, comes to the road-side and gives us for some miles its pleasant company. It breaks away to the right just by its confluence with a smaller stream, the Geirw—which in its turn runs alongside the road for half a dozen miles. But Geirw provides a spectacle which the larger rivers did not offer. Close by the sixty-first milestone from Holyhead, the little stream rushes over a series of rocky slopes into a deep glen. The sides of the glen are thickly clothed with trees—too thickly perhaps, for in consequence of the narrowness of the glen and the quantity of foliage, it is difficult to see more at once than a small portion of the waterfall. High above the stream the glen is spanned by a bridge, which is named with the happy descriptiveness so often observed in Welsh nomenclature, Pont-y-Glyn, the Bridge of the Glen.

Three or four miles farther is Cerig-y-Druidon, now only noticeable as a tolerably fair example of a thoroughly Welsh village ; but which in Camden's time contained two Kist-vaens, as they were called ; Camden seemed to think they were "solitary prisons." These, "and the name of the parish," he says, "are all the memorials left of the residence of those ancient philosophers the Druids here." These are gone now; but the tradition is preserved. There is a tumulus called Pen-y-Caer, about a mile south-east of the village, and near it is another spot bearing the same name, which we fancy to be the places Camden speaks of. Somewhere in the neighbourhood, too, is a hill of unmanageable title, whereon is said to have stood the castle at which, according to the Welsh version, Caractacus was delivered into the hands of the Romans by a Cymric Delilah.

The road here is in dull weather sufficiently dreary. The mountains lie somewhat away, and are lumpish in form. No sparkling rivulet meanders on either side; instead is a level peat-bog, unvaried by house or tree. But there is one scene which would repay thrice the extent of dreariness. You come almost suddenly, where the left-hand mountains open, upon a view of the entire range of the Snowdon Mountains. (Cut, No. 9.) Under almost any aspect it must be a grand sight, for nowhere else is the entire range so fairly seen: but it was truly a thing to remember as we beheld it at the close of a day of remarkable beauty. The sun had just descended behind the most northern of the hills, when suddenly the summits in that direction became as it were incandescent, while those at the opposite extremity, and the giant Snowdon himself, rapidly changed in hue from a blueish purple into the deepest gloom,—their bases meanwhile being concealed by a pinky vapour, out of which the mighty hills rose like islands from a foaming sea,—and over-head the fleecy clouds gathered into a canopy of crimson and gold: it was a glorious vision; but it retained only for a moment its full splendour, and then fled swiftly into the darkness.

THE VALLEY OF THE CONWAY.

At Pentre Voelas—where, as well as at Cernioge, which has just been passed, there is a good tourist's inn —the river Conway comes down from the mountains, and will be our guide and companion for the day's ramble. It has its source only a few miles higher, a little above Llyn Conway, and is in its early course a beautiful stream: but it is in the few miles from Pentre Voelas to Bettws-y-Coed that it appears to feel its strength, and there it exhibits best its daring and frolicsome spirit. As it advances it grows soberer, and at length settles down into a dignified gravity. Gray should not have written " Old Conway's foaming flood:" it would have been applicable enough to its youthful career.

The scenery as well as the river is full of beauty for all this distance: but in one part it is eminently fine. About seven miles from Capel Curig, there opens a view of an uncommon kind even in this region of splendid views. (Cut, No. 7.) The valley is bounded by lofty hills, which send their projecting roots far into the vale, where they terminate in rugged cliffs; a narrow stream plays along the bottom; groups of handsome trees are in the foreground; while the enormous form of Moel

Siabod is seen in all its vastness filling the distance. We have given an engraving of the view, but it is impossible to represent the fitful play of light and shadow along the slopes, the gloom of the hollows, and the creeping mists on which so much of the effect of such a scene depends. (Cut, No. 8.)

Immediately beyond this occurs another famous scene,—the Falls of the Conway. They will be found just out of the main road, where that to Ffestiniog is carried by a lofty arch across a chasm:—but the ear will be a sufficient guide to the spot. The Conway, a stream of considerable volume, is here pent within a narrow ravine, through which it rushes with tremendous impetuosity, and after making a short sharp turn— seeming indeed as though it burst *through* the rock— flings itself over a long slope of riven rocks into a deep pool below. The rocky banks, as well as the fallen fragments which check the progress of the stream, are of the grandest forms. The cataract altogether is of the finest kind; but there are two things which detract a good deal from its grandeur, the thick plantation of trees which has a formal air, and the proximity of the road, together banishing effectually what most befits such an object—the feeling of solitude, of standing alone in the presence of the untouched handiwork of Nature.

Not far from this cataract is another formed by the Machno river, a short distance before its junction with the Conway. The Falls of the Machno are not comparable with those of the Conway, either for magnitude or grandeur; but they are eminently picturesque and beautiful. The mass of water foams and dashes from rock to rock in every variety of form and curve, before it takes its grand plunge, and then quickly recovering from the shock starts forward again, making in its rapid way a multitude of wild waterbreaks. From every clift spring self-planted trees and shrubs. On one side is seen a pandy (or fulling) mill, sufficiently rude and informal to add to the effect as a picture.

From the Falls to Bettws-y-Coed, the Conway continues to maintain the wild beauty of its character. Now passing along a close wooded glen, again, through a more open but still wild valley, and occasionally crossed by bridges noticeable both for their fine forms and often striking positions. This part of the stream is the delight of the skilful angler, with whom the Oak at Bettws-y-Coed is a favourite little hostel. The sketch (Cut, No. 10) will show better than words the kind of scenery which the fisherman meets with in here pursuing his gentle craft along the margin of Conway. The spot represented is a wild rocky passage, about a mile above Bettws-y-Coed,—well known to artists and anglers, but from the difficulty of access not often seen by the tourist; though, as the engraving shows, well worth scrambling down to.

Bettws-y-Coed—or, as cockney tourists resolutely pronounce it, ' Betsy Code,'—is a quiet, thoroughly Welsh village (with something of English neatness superadded), seated in a beautiful neighbourhood, just by the confluence of the Llugwy with the Conway.

1.—SNOWDON, FROM CAPEL CURIG.

The only thing in the village which aspires to a place in tourists' books, is the mutilated statue of Gruffydd ap Davydd Goch, a nephew of the last of the Welsh princes : it is set in a niche in the church wall. But the village itself will find a place in the tourist's memory : it is one of the spots which is not likely to be quickly forgotten. The bridge which crosses the Llugwy just before it falls into the Conway, is one of the Welsh notabilities : it is somewhat rude in form, and consists of five arches, the piers of which rest on separate rocks, which stand in the bed of the river. The river here forms a cascade, of no great height, but one that appears eminently picturesque, as seen in connection with the singular bridge and the detached masses of rock which strew the channel. When the river is in flood, and pours at once through all the arches, the effect must be very striking : ordinarily one or two arches suffice for the passage of the waters.

The road through the village soon brings the wanderer to Capel Curig, and into the heart of the mountain district ;—a tempting route, but one that we must leave for a while. Our way is still beside our river. There is a road on each side of the Conway to Llanrwst ; that on the right is the main road, but the other, which lies along the foot of wild craggy slopes and steep cliffs, is the quieter and the pleasanter. Just before Llanrwst is reached, is Gwydyr, the patrimony of an ancient branch of the Wynne family, now extinct. Gwydyr House, now the property of Lord Willoughby d'Eresby, stands in beautiful grounds, and is permitted to be seen.

The steep bridge by which we cross the river to Llanrwst, erected by Inigo Jones, is said to have the peculiar property that "if a person thrusts himself against the large stone over the centre of the middle arch, the whole fabric will vibrate ;" but we neglected to test its vibratory capabilities. The Gwydyr Chapel attached to Llanrwst Church, is also the work of Inigo, and tempts one to say of him, as did crabbed Ben Jonson, "He had a monstrous medley wit of his own." In the chapel are some interesting monuments ; and both it and the old church, to which it is joined, merit attention.

Llanrwst is a town of some importance in the locality. It has considerable trade, and contains some 4000 inhabitants. The houses are small and plain ; but the situation of the town renders it an important object in the landscape ; and it is not an unpicturesque one. The Vale of Llanrwst, as this part of the valley of the Conway is called, is often said to be the finest in Wales—uniting in itself the beauties of the Vales of Clwyd and Llangollen ; and tourists fortify the assertion by quoting from the guide-books, that " Burke declared it to be the most charming spot in Wales ;" and that Windham said something to the same effect. But here is a very pretty blunder. These are not the Burke and Windham, but a couple of nobodies, who wrote accounts of Wales that have been forgotten long ago, and whose names would never be mentioned, but that, having once got into the guide-books, they are as a matter of course, repeated in all succeeding ones. We fancy that, if tourists knew this, " Burke and

9.—THE SNOWDON RANGE, FROM CERNIOGE.

Windham" would not be rung out so authoritatively. Be it understood, however, that we say not a word in depreciation of the Valley: it is not equal to either Clwyd or Llangollen; but it is as charming a spot as a man could wish to light upon for a few days' tarriance, or to spend the evening of his days in. The mountains which border the valley are among the loftiest in Wales — the companions, Carnedd Llewellyn and Carnedd Davyd, attaining an altitude, the one of 3469, and the other of 3427 feet above the sea. The slopes are varied; the vale is cultivated and flourishing, and thickly sprinkled over with lordly and lowly dwellings; and the river which flows through the midst is broad and shallow, and rendered more lively by the numerous coracles* that are moving nimbly to and fro.

The Conway is navigable, for vessels of 50 or 60 tons burden, as high as Trefriew,—a village, a mile or so below Llanrwst. They bring hither coal, lime, and timber; and carry back the produce of the farm, and of the mines and quarries in the neighbourhood. Trefriew is an unpretending village, but a very pretty one. The neighbourhood, too, is rich in the kind of objects which usually find a place in the sketch-book. There is a mill close by, which is unrivalled in Wales: it stands in a most picturesque spot; and the water falls in succession over two wheels, placed one immediately above the other; while the surplus supply finds its way over a number of huge moss-covered blocks of stone. The singular-looking mill and the waterfall, together with the wild scenery around, form a noticeable scene, which has been often painted. In this vicinity are several waterfalls: the chief is the Rhaidr Porthlwyd, or Rhaidr Mawr (the Great Waterfall), as it is commonly called by the peasantry. It is situated far up in the mountains: the path to it must be taken somewhere near Porthlwyd Bridge, about seven miles from Conway. The fall is one of the largest class of Welsh cataracts, and the accompaniments are on a grand scale. Many tourists and writers pronounce it to be the finest waterfall in the principality; but it is seldom that there is a sufficient body of water to give it due importance. Another fall, about a mile from this, is formed by the Dolgarrog, a lively but not very ample stream. This, which is known as Rhaidr Dolgarrog, is on a smaller scale than the last, but is exceedingly pretty. On the mountains may be found two or three Llyns which, if there be time, will repay the labour of ascending to them,—if only by the views that will be had on the road. Llyn Geirionydd is the most celebrated, Taliesin, 'Prince of Bards,' having dwelt on its margin—as is often repeated in the Welsh bardic verse. Lord Willoughby d'Eresby has erected a column there, in memory of the famous minstrel.

About five miles from Conway is the village of Caer Rhun,—a place which is by most antiquaries fixed on

* These are light boats, formed of skin or tarred canvas, stretched over a wicker frame in the manner described in our notice of 'The Wye,' vol. i., p. 247. They carry only one person, are moved and guided by means of a paddle, and are chiefly used by fishermen.

as the site of the Roman station, Conovium; though some think Conway the more probable locality. Certain it is, that Caer Rhun was a Roman settlement of some kind; for at various times numerous Roman remains—some of them of much interest and value—have been discovered there. Now it is merely a plain Welsh village, charmingly situated, indeed, by the river side, and "celebrated for containing three of the most magnificent yews that are now to be found in the principality."

The vale maintains its character for richness and for beauty quite up to Conway; and when, at length, the old town comes fairly into sight, it affords a noble termination to the prospect; while from the heights the backward view, extending over the valley, now changed in character by the frequent passage of boats and small craft to and fro on the smooth stream, and closed by magnificent mountains, is scarcely less interesting and more impressive. A more delightful day's ramble could hardly be found, of its kind, than this of the Vale of Conway, or a more fitting resting-place, at the close of such a day, than the fine old town.

BANGOR.

In the good old times, the fifteen miles from Conway to Bangor were thought rather a serious journey: one at any rate not to be undertaken without due consideration. The road lay along the brow of the precipitous Penmaen Mawr; and to traverse it was often really dangerous. The only means of avoiding this road by a land passage was to proceed along the sands, which could only be ventured upon when the tide was out. Even as late as 1774, after a better road had been constructed, it appears to have been regarded as sufficiently formidable. Dr. Johnson was here with the Thrales in that year, and he has this entry in his Diary: "Aug. 18.—We would have stayed at Conway, if we could have found entertainment; [it was race-day, and the inns were full;] for we were afraid of passing Penmaen Mawr, over which lay our way to Bangor, but by bright daylight. . . . There was no stay, however, on any other terms than of sitting up all night. . . Our coach was at last brought, and we set out with some anxiety, but we came to Penmaen Mawr by daylight; and we found a way lately made, very easy and very safe." This road was afterwards improved, and in 1827 was re-constructed by Telford, and rendered one of the finest in the kingdom—a remark applicable, by-the-way, to the great Holyhead lines of road which that eminent engineer formed by order of the Government throughout the principality, on a scale of greatness and excellence till then unseen in this country. Even now, some portions of the road along Penmaen Mawr wear, in stormy weather, a rather startling appearance; especially where it is in part cut out of the face of the beetling cliff, with the sea at a considerable distance below, and the grim precipice towering high over head. Never for a moment, however, does a feeling of insecurity obtain: the substantial character of every part impresses on the mind too much confidence in the skill of the engineer for that. There would, indeed, be little heed given to the sign-board advice,—did it exist now —which is said to have once been put forth at the two public-houses which then stood at either end of this formidable pass. The verses are affiliated by the guide-books on Dean Swift, who often had occasion to experience the terrors of the road in his journeys to and from Dublin. On the side of either sign-board which greeted you as you approached the dreaded road, the lines ran thus:

"Before you venture hence to pass,
Take a good refreshing glass."

As you escaped from it, you saw—

"Now you're over, take another,
Your frighten'd spirits to recover."

And the advice was no doubt often taken on both sides. Now the railway-train whisks you by Penmaen Mawr so swiftly, that you hardly are aware of his existence.

Bangor is a more busy-looking town than Welsh towns usually are. The streets are filled with an active population; new houses are being erected and old ones altered and smartened; and, generally, there are the signs of a considerable and increasing traffic. The main street is above a mile long, and as it lies just under a steep rock, the town seems capable of little lateral extension. If the business and the population continue to increase as they are said to have done of late, the town must expand into some rather curious form; though that will be a matter of small moment if it continue to prosper. Within the town, the only building of any importance is the Cathedral. The handsomest of the public establishments is the Bank, a substantial stone building, in the Elizabethan style, as yet unfinished.

Bangor Cathedral is comparatively small in size, and of no great architectural merit. It stands, too, in a low site, and is itself so low, and altogether so unimportant in appearance, that it might almost pass unnoticed were not the attention directed to it. A cathedral existed here at an early period; but the present building is only of the sixteenth century. The choir was erected about 1500 by Bishop Dean, at his own cost: the nave and tower were added in 1532 by Bishop Thomas Skevington—as is recorded by an inscription on the tower. The entire length of the cathedral is 214 feet; the nave is 34 feet, the tower 60 feet high. If, externally, the cathedral presents no very splendid appearance, the interior will not make amends: it is bald and mean to a degree that will surprise the English visitor. The only thing to be said in its favour is, that it appears to be kept in a state of substantial repair. In the nave the English service is performed: a Welsh church occupies the chief remaining part of the cathedral; and both look pretty much as Welsh churches usually look.

Bangor is in some repute as a bathing-place, and as a summer residence; and for the latter purpose it has many advantages. The surrounding country is very beautiful; the heights afford splendid views; there are considerable facilities for reaching almost any point; and, though last not least, there is good society. The heights around appear to be becoming sprinkled over with neat villas, wherever practicable. Bangor is a place at which tourists almost always make some stay; and it is accordingly well supplied with suitable accommodation for them. The 'Penrhyn Arms' is one of the largest hotels in the principality, making up, it is said, a hundred beds; and there are others of good size in the town and by the bridge.

The lion of Bangor is Penrhyn Castle, the seat of the Pennant family. It occupies the site of an old castle, but the present building is almost entirely of recent date: it stands in a commanding position, and has a striking appearance from many points of view; and there are almost matchless prospects from it. In size and splendour it is one of the chief mansions in Wales, and the interior fittings are on a magnificent scale. The owner derives a large part of his wealth from the famous slate quarries of Cae Braich-y-Cefn, four or five miles from Bangor, on the road to Nant-Francon. These quarries are generally among the things which tourists 'do' in their Welsh journey:—they are well worth a visit by those who feel (as every one ought) an interest in such matters. They are of great extent, as will be supposed, when it is said that 2,000 persons are employed at them. The quarrying is conducted in ledges up the the whole front of the mountain—which is carved out in an amazing manner. The scarified face of the mountain, with the multitude of men hacking away at every part of it—the many 'shoots' of shattered slates which seem in constant motion as fresh loads are being poured down—the enormous heaps of debris— the regular piles of trimmed slates—the incessant activity visible over the entire area—the noise of the multifarious processes, and that also of the loud talking and shouting of the workmen, which like that of all Welsh men—and here all the workmen are Welsh—has to a Saxon ear a sound very like that of quarrelling; all these things combined have a quite remarkable effect when the works are entered. The works are maintained in the highest state of efficiency. Every mechanical and scientific contrivance which is available is said to be employed, as well as every means of lightening the labour and lessening the danger of the workmen. From the quarries a railway has been constructed, at an expense of £170,000 for conveying the slate at once to the sea-side, where a convenient harbour and wharf have been formed. This spot, called Port Penrhyn, lies a little to the east of Bangor, just under Penrhyn Castle. Two hundred and fifty tons of slates are said to be shipped there daily. Altogether, the quarries, railway, port, and castle, to say nothing of houses and land, form a very pretty property. We are glad we can conclude by adding, that the owner of it all has the reputation of using his wealth nobly:—in the promotion of industry, the diffusion of refinement and the encouragement of skill and art, and the improvement in all ways of his numerous dependents.

10.—FORS NOTHYN.

THE BRITANNIA BRIDGE.

Bangor lies towards the northern end of the Menai Strait. Until 1826, the communication was carried on by means of ferry-boats, and in stormy weather was both uncertain and dangerous. Holyhead being the nearest point of the British coast to Dublin, and the speediest and least uncertain means of reaching Dublin, being an important object, a bridge across the Menai Strait was long desired; but the difficulty and costliness of erecting one in so exposed a situation, and at a height sufficiently great not to interfere with the navigation, prevented its erection, although many plans had at different times been proposed. When, however, the construction of the great lines of road from Shrewsbury and Chester to Holyhead were entrusted to Telford, a bridge across the Strait was considered a necessary part of the plan:—and his project of a suspension bridge was approved of.

The site he selected was about two miles and a half west of Bangor, at a place known from a rocky point on the Anglesea side as Ynys-y-Moch, "where the opposite shores are bold and rocky, and allow the roadway of the bridge to be 100 feet above high water-mark." The first stone of the bridge was laid in August, 1819; it was opened in January, 1826. The piers which support the suspended portion of the bridge are 560 feet apart; and there are seven stone arches, each of 60 feet span; four on the Anglesea coast, and three on that of Carnarvonshire. The entire length of the bridge is 960 feet; the height above high water-mark is 102 feet. At the time of its erection this was in every way the most important bridge that had been constructed on the suspension principle, and it was justly regarded as one of the greatest triumphs of modern engineering. Suspension-bridges of greater magnitude have since been built, but, all things considered, it may be doubted whether this does not maintain its first rank. It is unquestionably one of the chief monuments of the genius of Telford, and is, indeed, in every way a noble work. Noticeable it is, moreover, as an ornamental as well as a useful structure. It hangs there, in its lofty position, light and graceful almost as a living thing. So symmetrical are its proportions, that its magnitude is one of the last things thought of in looking at it: you need to sail under it to observe the scale of the surrounding objects, or to walk over it and see a goodly ship with its masts unstruck sailing beneath your feet, before fully recognising its great elevation and vast size.

From the configuration of the banks and other circumstances, the action of the wind during gales is here extremely great. Soon after its opening the Menai Bridge suffered considerably from a storm; and subsequently it was again a good deal injured. But experience has suggested some methods of in a measure obviating the peculiar evils attached to this kind of bridge—especially that of making joints in the lower part of the rods, thereby lessening the rigidity—and it appears to be now capable of withstanding any ordinary storm.

Great as the Menai Bridge was as an engineering achievement, it must in that respect yield to the Britannia Bridge, which has been lately erected about a mile nearer Carnarvon. The problem to be solved in this case was to carry the Chester and Holyhead Railway across the Strait, at such a height as to allow of a clear way for shipping of at least 100 feet; and of course without placing piers so as to interfere with the channel. A suspension bridge will not sustain the motion and weight of a railway train: and an arch or arches would require the roadway to be 150 feet above high-water mark, in order to satisfy the requirements of the Admiralty Commissioners. The plan adopted by Mr. Stephenson was novel and simple. It was merely that of laying across the channel a covered trough or hollow beam, through which the trains should pass, letting the ends of the beam rest on piers of adequate height, and supporting it in the middle. There was a convenient site, which seemed fashioned by Nature for such a bridge,—the opposite shores being bold steep rocks, and there being just about mid-channel a rocky island which would afford a perfect foundation for the central pier.

So far all was well. But now even the rudimentary difficulties attending the erection of a bridge, so much greater both in span and bulk than any rigid bridge of iron which had yet been erected, had to be pre-determined and provided against. The mechanical difficulties arising from the nature of the materials—difficulties that appeared to be almost insuperable—the necessity of providing not merely for the support of its own immense weight, and the additional weight of a train in motion, but also of increasing the strength sufficiently to withstand the action of the fiercest gales upon so vast a resisting surface; and finally floating the gigantic tubes, which were to be constructed by the shore, and lifting them, thus completed into their position, a hundred feet above the water;—these things have called into exercise a union of the highest mechanical and mathematical skill, which has not only sufficed for the immediate purpose, but will serve to facilitate considerably the labours of future engineers. An account of the elaborate experiments and investigations, which were deemed necessary in order to determine the exact form of the tubes, with a narrative of the progress of the works, has been published by Mr. Fairbairn, — to whom, with Mr. Hodgkinson, an eminent mathematician, the preliminary experiments were intrusted; and it will be read with interest and admiration by those conversant with such pursuits. A full history of the bridge, with working plates, has been given by Mr. Edwin Clark, the acting engineer; and the work will be found replete with interesting details.

The few particulars we annex are taken from the semi-official 'General Description of the Britannia and Conway Tubular Bridges, by a Resident Assistant'— (Mr. Latimer Clark.) They will suffice to give some notion of the structure; for fuller particulars the reader will do well to refer to the work itself, which is clear and brief in its explanations, and moderate in price.

And first for the general form of the bridge:

"When the whole structure is completed, it will consist of two immense wrought-iron tunnels or tubes, each considerably upwards of a quarter of a mile in length, placed side by side, through which the up and down trains respectively will pass. The ends of these tubes rest on abutments, the intermediate portions being supported across the Straits by three massive and lofty stone towers. The centre tower stands on a rock, which is covered by the tide at high water. The side towers stand on the opposite shores, each at a clear distance of four hundred and sixty feet from the centre tower. The abutments are situated inland, at a distance of two hundred and thirty feet from the side towers."

The following dimensions of the piers, or towers, as they are called, will give a tolerable idea of the amazing scale on which the whole is constructed: — "The Britannia (or central) Tower is 62 feet 52 feet at the base; it has a gentle taper, so that where the tubes enter it is 55 feet by 45 feet. Its total height from the bottom of the foundations will be, when completed, nearly 230 feet; it contains 148,625 cubic feet of lime-stone, and 144,625 of sandstone, weighing very nearly 20,000 tons, and there are 387 tons of cast-iron built into it in the shape of beams and girders. The land towers are each 62 feet by 52 feet at the base, tapering to 55 feet by 32 feet at the level of the bottom of the tubes; their height is 190 feet from high water; they contain 210 tons of cast-iron in beams and girders." In other words, each of the land towers is nearly as high as the London Monument, and much larger; while the central tower is higher as well as larger.*

We may now let Mr. Clark describe the tubes which these vast piles of masonry are intended to support:

"The bridge, as we have seen, is divided into four spans—viz., the two small spans at each end, which are over the land, and are each 230 feet wide; and the two principal spans which are over the water, and are each 460 feet wide. The small tubes, as they are termed, or those which cross the land, being constructed on the platforms, at their ultimate level, do not require any removal. Although called the 'small tubes,' their span is vastly greater than that of any other railway bridge in existence, the Conway tubes alone excepted. But the large tubes, which are to cross the water, are constructed on timber platforms along the beach, on the Carnarvon shore, just above the level of high water. These have consequently to be removed, and elevated to their final position on the towers; and to these the principal interest attaches.

"The length of one of these tubes, as constructed on the platform, is 472 feet; this additional length is

* The height of the monument is 202 feet; the pedestal is 20 feet square: the diameter of the column is 15 feet at the base.

intended to afford a temporary bearing of six feet at each end, after they are raised into their places, until there is time to form the connection between them across the towers. Our London readers will better appreciate the great length of these tubes by remembering that if one of them were placed on end in St. Paul's Church-yard, it would reach 107 feet higher than the top of the cross!"

Plain tubes of this size could not sustain the pressure of their own weight: an extremely ingenious modification of the form, and distribution of the materials was therefore ultimately adopted, which, strange as it may appear to those unacquainted with mechanics, necessitated a great increase of both size and weight—the additional weight being accumulated at top and bottom, but most on the top. For the full particulars and explanation of this we must refer the reader to the work from which we have quoted, or to the lively description of the bridge in the recent number (170) of the 'Quarterly Review'—no doubt by the skilful hand of the author of 'Stokers and Pokers'—here it must suffice to say, that the tube is strengthened by having six smaller tubes constructed along the bottom of the main tube, and eight along the top. Another important point consists in making the height of the tubes increase towards the centre. "It is greatest at the centre, in the Britannia Tower, where it is 30 feet outside, and diminishes gradually towards the ends, at which, in the abutments, the external height is only 22 feet 9 inches; the top forms a regular arch (a true parabolic curve), and the bottom is quite straight and horizontal. The clear internal height is, on account of the double top and bottom, less by four feet than the external. . . . . The internal width from side to side is 14 feet.

"The general method of the construction of the tubes is readily seen. They consist of sides, top, and bottom; all formed of long narrow wrought-iron plates, varying in length from twelve feet downwards, and in width from two feet four inches to one foot nine inches. The direction in which these plates are laid is not, as may at first sight be supposed, arbitrary or immaterial, but is governed by the directions of the strains in the different parts of the tube." The iron plates are fastened together by iron rivets, each rather more than an inch in diameter; about 2,000,000 of them will be employed in the bridge.

"The plates are joined together (at the sides), and greatly strengthened and stiffened at the joints by T shaped irons both inside and out, reaching from top to bottom, and forming a complete pillar at every two feet." Of this T iron and of angle iron there are about sixty-five miles in the whole bridge. "The weight of the wrought-iron in one of the large tubes is estimated at about 1,600 tons; of which 500 are in the bottom, 600 in the sides, and 500 in the top." (Clark.)

But amazing as the separate portions of the tubes seem, it is only when they are regarded in their united form that the stupendous mass which the piers have to sustain is properly comprehended. "When all the tubes have been raised, and the small ones completed, their ends will be joined . . . The exact length of each of the two tubes will then be one thousand five hundred and thirteen feet, and the weight *five thousand tons,*—in size far surpassing any piece of wrought iron-work ever before put together, and in weight nearly double that of a hundred and twenty gun ship ready for sea." And these two prodigious 'tubes,' be it remembered, are to be suspended aloft a hundred and two feet above high water. Provision is made for the expansion and contraction of these enormous masses of metal from changes of temperature by *fixing* the middle of each tube in the Britannia Tower, and leaving the ends free to travel to and fro upon rollers inserted in the land towers. The variation in length of one of the tubes between summer and winter is nearly twelve inches.

It is almost needless to mention, what every one is familiar with from the ample accounts which have been published in the newspapers, that the first of the great tubes was, in June last, safely floated on pontoons to its position at the foot of the towers, whence it was to be raised by means of hydraulic presses. The tempo-rary suspension of the 'lifting,' owing to the breaking of the case of the large hydraulic press, is also well known; as well as the resumption of the proceedings. The press (in itself a wonder) lifts six feet at each stroke, when the masonry is built up under the tube, the end of which lies within a groove in the tower. The tube is thus raised six feet in the morning, and the remainder of the day is occupied in building up to it. The first tube is now raised to its proper place, and ships are probably sailing beneath it.

While the works connected with the bridge were in their greatest activity—that is while the construction of the tubes and of the towers was advancing simulta-neously—the Carnarvon shore presented a remarkable scene. Along the bank stretched a strong wooden platform half a mile in length, upon which the tubes were constructed. A large area was covered with long lines of workshops, for the masons and the workers in iron; those belonging to the latter exhibiting, in constant and noisy action, some of the most ponderous and some most complicated machinery. Fifteen hun-dred workmen were employed while the works were in full operation. The quartering of such an army in the neighbouring towns and villages, if even they had been sufficiently near, would have been impracticable. A temporary village was therefore built, consisting of rows of wooden cottages. Suttlers followed the camp, and shops of course were opened, at which provisions might be purchased; and it is said that all kinds of provisions rose considerably in price in this part of Carnarvon subsequently to the irruption of this army of artizans. A medical man was resident, to afford immediate assistance in case of accidents — which happily have been far from numerous considering the magnitude and nature of the undertaking. A chaplain was found to minister to the religious wants

of the community.* A school was established for the children. Occasionally, at least, the mental culture of the adults was sought to be advanced by an itinerant lecturer : their amusement by the visit of a travelling show. Altogether the village, regarded in itself, and surrounded as it was by the symptoms of a recent clearance, in the midst of a wild mountain tract, and beside a bold rapid river—for such the Strait appears to be—appeared to us to wear some such strange aspect, as one might expect to witness in the incipient town of an American settlement.

"What will the bridge look like when complete?" was a question commonly asked : the answer, though unsatisfactory, is not difficult. The tube itself is quite unornamented; and it appears exactly like a gigantic rectangular-covered trough made of iron plates, fastened together by rivets in the manner of steam-engine boilers, and supported on piers or towers; which themselves are nearly plain masses of masonry carried to a consider-able height above the trough. The land towers are surmounted each by two couchant lions, of colossal size, and "in the Egyptian style;" that is, with big ears, and a close-cropped judge's wig. The central tower was intended, originally, to have been sur-mounted with a statue of Britannia some sixty feet high; but that is abandoned. In all this it will be seen that there is very little of what can be called 'art' in the design; and, in truth, not much beauty. We have seen and heard it gravely spoken of as "light and graceful in appearance," and its "elegance" even has been eulogised. It is really too bad. To praise too highly the engineering skill displayed on the bridge is perhaps impossible, but in the name of all the Muses let us hear nothing of its beauty. In sad verity, we must confess it to be our conviction that, although the Britannia Bridge is certainly the most wonderful bridge in the world, it is probably the ugliest ever erected.

ANGLESEA.

The Isle of Anglesea need not detain us long. For one who can make a leisurely survey of it, there is a good deal that will be found of interest :—the antiqui-ties, the mines, the scenery of the coast, well deserve investigation. For one who is willing to connect the present with the past, the Sacred Isle of the Druids,— the Mona of the Romans,—the residence and the seat of government of the native Princes of Wales,—the battle-field of the Britons with Romans, Picts, and Saxons,— could not be a barren ground. Where, however, only a general glance over the entire district of Cambria can be taken, it is a different matter. Few tourists spend more than an exceedingly brief time in Anglesea; and certainly, if they have come to Wales for the enjoyment of mountain scenery, they do well

* It deserves mention, that the masons have erected a small stone obelisk on the Anglesea coast, "to the memory of those of their companions who have been killed during the progress of the undertaking."

to devote their time almost or altogether to the really mountainous region. Anglesea is not by any means a level country, especially northwards; but its hills—though some of them are called mountains—are comparatively low, and characterized neither by majesty nor beauty; while the general face of the country is seldom interesting.

A journey is almost always made from Bangor to Beaumaris. The sail thither along the Strait is a delightful one. The Carnarvon coast, with Penmaen Mawr, and the lofty mountains of Snowdonia—though the giant himself is hardly seen, if seen at all—form a grateful addition to the delight which the sail along a bold river or arm of the sea is sure in itself to excite. The enjoyment derivable from the sail will be much increased, if it be continued to Great Orme's Head, and around the rough wild rock. Priestholme, or Puffin's Island—the little island situated at the eastern extremity of Anglesea, should also, if possible, be thus visited. It abounds, during the summer, with the bird from which it has received its local name, and with vast numbers of other aquatic birds, which give to its bluff black cliffs a singularly wild appearance. But the distance between Bangor and Beaumaris should also be gone over by land. The road lies along the top of a high bank, from which there is a noble prospect across the Strait; and the mountains beyond, from Penmaen and Llewellyn to Snowdon, are seen to great advantage. Indeed it may be said, generally, that the finest views *in* Anglesea are views *from* it.

Beaumaris is a fashionable and thriving watering-place, with an excellent pier, terraces of large and handsome houses, hotels of more than common size and style, good shops, and all the appliances of a well-frequented bathing-town. The streets, too, are more regular, and neater and better kept, than those in most Welsh towns. The town itself is pleasantly situated in the hollow of Beaumaris Bay; and there are beautiful rides and walks in the vicinity. The steamer which plies between the Menai Bridge and Liverpool calls at Beaumaris, so that a constant and easy intercourse is kept up with the great northern port; from which a large proportion of its summer residents come.

The town appears to owe its origin to the Castle, which was erected by Edward I., in 1295. From its dilapidated condition, and the lowness of the site—it having been built on a marsh, partly, no doubt, for the convenience of surrounding it with a moat—Beaumaris Castle by no means presents so imposing an appearance as either Carnarvon or Conway Castle. It is of considerable size: when it was in a perfect state it consisted of an outer ballium, or envelope, surrounded by a moat, and flanked with ten circular bastion-towers, of which those at the angles are the largest; and it had on the east side an advanced work, called the 'Gunner's Walk.' Within this fortified enclosure was the body of the castle, which was nearly square, with a round tower at each angle, and another in the centre of each face. This inner castle rose much above the ballium, and must, before the building was dismantled,

have had a grand effect from a distance, appearing, as it did, to rise from so broad a base. Now Beaumaris Castle is chiefly interesting to examine in detail. The grand entrance, which is still in tolerable preservation, is between two massive round towers; and forms perhaps the most "picturesque bit" remaining of the entire building. But the grandest portion is the Great Hall—a spacious apartment, 70 feet long by 23 feet wide. The front, which is turned towards the inner area of the castle, has five handsome windows; and the hall must once have been a splendid structure. The most curious remaining portion of the castle is the chapel; and it is also the most perfect. It is very small in size, with a handsome groined roof, supported by attached pillars: at the eastern end are three lancet-windows, so narrow and oilet-like, as to give to the gloomy little edifice quite a military character. Around the entire area are carried narrow galleries, cut out, as it were, from the walls of the ballium.

Beaumaris Castle has not a very important history. In the great civil war, it was taken, after a short siege, by Colonel Mytton, the Parliamentary general, and was not long after dismantled. The castle is the property of the crown; and some use is found for a part of it: opposite the Great Hall is a tennis-court, for the recreation of the lord of Baron Hill. This abomination has been permitted for many years, in spite of the continued remonstrances of the books; and it is likely to be continued much longer: for when we were there, two or three months back, it was being carefully repaired and strengthened. One might have hoped that a little more respect would be shown in the present day for the grand old pile.

On the eminence behind Beaumaris is Baron Hill, the seat of Sir R. B. W. Bulkeley: the mansion is of no mark; but it commands an almost unrivalled view over the Strait and the Snowdon mountain chain beyond. It has also a noble sea-view.

Plas Newydd is another mansion, which is frequently visited from Bangor. It lies in the opposite direction to Beaumaris, being situated a mile or so beyond the foot of Britannia Bridge. The chief objects of interest here are two cromlechs, which stand just behind the house. The top stone of the larger one is a block, 12 feet long, 10 feet broad, and 4 feet thick: it was supported by seven upright stones; but two of them have fallen. The smaller cromlech adjoins the larger. Of these strange objects there still remain twenty-eight in Anglesea: there were once many more. Four or five hundred yards from the cromlechs, at Plas Newydd, is a carnedd, or tumulus, covered with loose irregular stones: it was opened in the last century; but "being found to contain human bones, the workmen were ordered to desist." In the present day, the greatest inducement to open it would be the hope of finding human bones. Of this kind of tumulus there are a great many in North Wales; and generally, we believe, they are found on the heights.

On an eminence just above the Britannia Bridge stands the Anglesea Column, a pillar erected in commemoration of the military exploits of the Marquis of Anglesea : the first stone was laid on the first anniversary of the battle of Waterloo. The pillar is 100 feet high ; the hill on which it stands is 260 feet above the sea—so that it is a conspicuous object for a considerable distance.

Holyhead is a small island, divided by a narrow strait from the western extremity of Anglesea. It is generally believed that Anglesea once formed a portion of the mainland ; and Holyhead was doubtless in the same way united with Anglesea : and as the larger island, though cut off by Nature from the parent land, has been again united with it by the hand of man, so has Holyhead been joined to Anglesea ; being connected with it by the embankments and bridges of the great Irish coach-road and of the Chester and Holyhead Railway.

The chief interest attaching to Holyhead arises from its being the station for the Dublin mail packets. For the use chiefly of the packets, there have been constructed a harbour-pier and graving-dock, with all suitable appliances, at a cost of upwards of £140,000. They were designed by the late Mr. Rennie. The pier is nearly a thousand feet in length ; at the extremity of it is a lighthouse ; at the commencement is an arch of ' Mona marble,' erected to commemorate the visit of George IV. in 1821. The harbour, though sufficient for the purpose of a packet-station, and though it has been of much service to shipping, is far from answering the end of a harbour of refuge. One more sheltered and of greater area was needed for this dangerous coast, into which it would be comparatively easy for a ship of the largest size to run in any weather, and to ride at anchor in any state of the tide. A site adapted for such a harbour was found somewhat to the westward of the present one ; and the construction of it was commenced some time back. But the progress of the works has been very irregular.

The town of Holyhead is a straggling collection of streets, rows, and single houses. It has not much trade, and ordinarily has little to interest the stranger. But one who is there on a Saturday morning may find some amusement in strolling through the principal street. It is the market-day, and Holyhead is the market-town which supplies all this part of Anglesea. Every variety of article for domestic use is displayed on the stalls, as well as all the ordinary articles of food ; and stalls with gilt gingerbread and toys are there also. Towards noon, the open space where the market-cross stands begins to be thronged with farmers and farmers' wives and daughters, and the wives and daughters of the peasantry, who bring for sale their baskets of butter and eggs, and so forth, or come to purchase their stores for the ensuing week. Then the market-place presents a curious sight. On the steps of the cross are seated a dozen very old and (according to Price's reading of the phrase) very picturesque women, dressed in the quaintest of Welsh costumes, with their several stores at their feet. Of the fair ones who crowd the market-place, many are very young,

and, as Welsh maidens often are, very pretty. These all talk Welsh—and Welsh never sounds so well as from feminine lips—but do not by any means all dress Welsh ; and the mingling of costume increases the liveliness of the scene. It is, like almost every Welsh market, worth seeing ; and, to our fancy, Holyhead appears quite another and more likeable place on Saturday than any other day.

It will not be expected that a little out-of-the-way town like Holyhead will have any buildings of much importance. The church, however, is not uninteresting. It is of the perpendicular style, and has been a good deal enriched with carvings on the exterior ; but these being executed in soft stone, and exposed to the sea, are almost mouldered away ; under the porch, however, where sheltered from the weather, they are much more perfect. They are rude, but curious ; and the church altogether will repay the time spent in its examination.

The same, indeed, may be said of the whole island of Holyhead. There are yet remaining in it a cromlech, and some other vestiges of British antiquities ; Roman remains have at different times been found here ; and there are fragments still existing of a ' capel ' or two of mediæval date ; the rocky shores will furnish employment for the naturalist : while, as far as we have seen, the most striking scenery of Anglesea may be found in this its satellite. Holyhead Mountain, a bare, craggy hill, two or three miles from the town, affords some glorious sea views. Far and wide in every direction stretches away the bright blue ocean ; mingling near at hand with the broken coast of Anglesea, and bounded by the mountains of Snowdonia ; while in the dim distance may be discerned Ireland, and sometimes even Scotland. We saw from it, on a clear morning of June, the Wicklow Mountains quite distinctly. From the mountain you may descend to the shore, or to the South Stack Lighthouse, which stands on a detached fragment of rock, or islet, and is reached by a suspension-bridge that has been thrown across the dark narrow chasm. When the light-house was first erected, the only means of access to it from the land was by a basket and rope ; afterwards a rope-bridge was made ; but this, though less hazardous than the former rude contrivance, was found to be unsafe, and about twenty years ago the present neat chain-bridge was constructed. As it is, the approach is not very tempting ; you have to descend nearly four hundred steps before reaching the foot of the bridge : it is said that this step-road is three-quarters of a mile long ; but the wearisomeness of the way is relieved by the fine rock scenery that opens to you in winding down it. A strange wild spot is this South Stack. The sea beats heavily against it, and against the cliffs which tower up behind it grim, black, and all over deeply riven. On every ledge, and in every rent, are numerous auks and gulls and divers, and other aquatic birds ; while the entire surface of the Stack Rock is literally whitened with them. The black rocks rise grandly from the sea, which, incessantly

11.—NEAR SOUTH STACK, ANGLESEA.

beating against them, has hollowed out their bases into deep caverns, and appears to be eating away the whole coast. Hardly elsewhere will a more impressive or romantic piece of rocky coast scenery be found, than this deeply-indented and shattered promontory, with its lonely lighthouse, fairy-like bridge, and the countless multitudes of sea-fowl which are mocking the eye with their rapid and ceaseless evolutions, and mingling their plaintive wild cry with the regular sullen beat of the waves upon the rocky cliffs.

The entire coast of Anglesea is studded with islets. The most important, after Holyhead, are those to the north-east, called the Skerries. Upon the largest of these there is a lighthouse, which, with that of the South Stack, guides the packets to Holyhead Harbour, and warns the mariner of the dangers of the coast. But, notwithstanding the light, the Skerries are often fatal to the seaman.

To one desirous of witnessing mining operations, the neighbourhood of Amlwch may be attractive. The town of Amlwch is situated on the north-eastern coast: it is of modern growth, having been almost entirely built since the opening of the mines in 1768. The only noticeable thing about it is the harbour, which was cut entirely out of the solid rock: it is of ample size, and capable of containing vessels of 200 tons burden. Parys Mountain, in which are the famous copper-mines, is situated about two miles south of the town. The Parys mine was opened, as was said, in 1768; and with the Mona mine, which was opened two or three years later, in the same mountain, at one time produced annually from 60,000 to 80,000 tons of copper ore—a quantity greater than was at any time obtained elsewhere, and equal, it is believed, to the amount raised from all the Cornish mines at the same period. But this extraordinary productiveness has

long ceased, and for some years the Parys Mountain has yielded but a small amount of mineral wealth.

A pedestrian, who had sufficient time, might find it a not uninteresting, though somewhat rough walk, to proceed from Holyhead by the west coast of Anglesea to the Carnarvon ferry. The coast along this part of the great Carnarvon Bay is indented with numerous lesser bays, some of which, with the distant Carnarvon mountains, are singularly beautiful. The engraving (Cut, No. 11) will serve to impart a notion of the character of the scenery of these lesser bays. The small lonely farm-houses and scattered cottages are rude and humble, but frequently picturesque—though the common habit of lime-washing the exterior (often roofs and all) is somewhat annoying to an artistic eye.

Aberffraw, three or four miles from Carnarvon, is the only place on the way that calls for particular notice—and that only for what it was. In the days of Welsh independence, it was there that the princes of Wales had their palace and held their court. Of course, upon the conquest of Wales by the first Edward, its importance passed away, and now nothing remains but the memory of its ancient glory. This present year, however, it received the greatest dignity which the Welsh notables could confer, it having been selected as the theatre for holding the Eisteddvod of 1849, which was celebrated there with all the honours.

CARNARVON.

The site of the old town of Carnarvon, a sort of peninsula just by the confluence of the river Seiont and the Cadnant brook with the Menai Strait, might seem to have been chosen as well for its commercial as its military convenience. Yet the original town, the Segontium of the Romans, the Caer Segont of the

12.—EAGLE TOWER, CARNARVON CASTLE.

Britons, was seated at least half a mile inland. The present Carnarvon was founded by the conqueror of Wales, who, in 1286, caused walls to be constructed around the town that was growing into existence under the shadow of the castle which he had built a year or two before. Carnarvon was the first town in Wales to which Edward I. granted a charter of incorporation: it bears date, September, 1286. It is therefore an old town; and yet in itself—apart, that is, from the walls and the castle—it has preserved little of its antique character. Straight streets and plain houses are all it can show, and these are not particularly interesting to a stranger. In its way, however, it is an important place, being the second if not the first town for extent and population in North Wales. At the census of 1841, the inhabitants of Carnarvon numbered 7,356: but that number must be taken with some allowance; for that is the census of the parish, which, as is usual in Wales, is much more extensive than the town; a circumstance that somewhat "extenuates the populousness," as Gibbon said of ancient Rome. Carnarvon has considerable trade. The shipping of slates is largely carried on; the slate-wharfs under the castle, to which the slates are brought by railway direct from the quarries, are generally an active scene, and afford a lively contrast to the old castle, which frowns grimly above.

It was in 1283 that Edward I. commenced the erection of the castle of Carnarvon, the largest and fairest of all his Welsh castles; but, though it was soon, perhaps, completed for all military purposes, it was many years before the more ornamental parts were finished. Only the year after the commencement of the works, the wife of Edward gave birth, within the walls of Carnarvon Castle, to the son who succeeded him—the first prince of Wales—the miserable Edward II. In 1294, the Welsh, under Madoc, seized and burnt the town; and having forced the castle to surrender, put the whole of the garrison to death. Twice (in 1402 and 1403) did the "renowned Glendower" besiege Carnarvon; but both times without success, though on the last occasion he had the aid of some French auxiliaries. It is not worth while to notice how often it changed masters during the war of the roses: in the war between Charles I. and the Parliament, it was three or four times assaulted by the two parties, and thrice taken. It was dismantled in 1660, by order of Charles II.

Fallen as is Carnarvon Castle from its high estate, it is yet magnificent in its decay. Among the ruined castles of our land it holds a high rank. Whether for size or grandeur, few can compare with it. "I did not think there had been such buildings," wrote Johnson, in his 'Diary,' on the day of his visit to Carnarvon: "it surpassed my ideas:" and few who survey it for the first time will wonder at the unusually warm terms in which he speaks of "the stupendous magnitude and strength of this edifice." One is half inclined to fancy, by the way, that this visit of Johnson to it is not the least pleasing association connected with the grand

old pile. It is a picture worth recalling to the imagination—that of the sturdy moralist, attended by Paoli and the Thrale, exploring with unchecked amazement the "mighty ruin," as he styles it,—mounting the Eagle Tower, and carefully numbering, as he mounts, the "one hundred and sixty-nine steps, each of ten inches," by which it is ascended,—listening, too, all the while with respectful heed to the explanations of "one Troughton, an intelligent and loquacious wanderer," who, though on half-pay, has donned his uniform as lieutenant of the navy, that he may the more fitly do the honours to such a visitor.[*]

The external walls of the castle form an irregular oblong, and enclose an area of three acres. Originally it was surrounded by a moat, but that has been long filled in, and is now not even traceable. The walls are nine or ten feet thick; and within their thickness, as at Beaumaris, runs a gallery or covered-way, which is at intervals pierced with loop-holes for the discharge of arrows. The castle walls were connected with those of the town; and strong outworks were thrown forward to strengthen the fortifications. The approaches to the castle were by two grand entrances; there was also a small postern, which led from the Eagle Tower by a flight of stairs to the strand. Along the walls are many stout and lofty towers—hexagonal, octagonal, and pentagonal, with tall light turrets rising above them. Many of these towers, with their turrets, appear to be tolerably perfect, till you see them close at hand. Altogether the old ruin looks best at a distance. From the Strait, where you can take in the whole building at a glance, it has yet a tolerably complete and very noble aspect. The recent repairs add somewhat, no doubt, to the perfectness of its appearance. The red bands which relieve the gray stone, of which it is mainly built, add somewhat more. From the opposite side of the Seiont, the grand Eagle Tower rising boldly from the water appears very striking. (Cut, No. 12.) Enter the gates, however, and the desolation is at once perceived. Only the walls and the towers remain. Both the buildings of state and the apartments for ordinary use are destroyed, or only exist as a few crumbling ruins. The towers and the grand entrances alone are left to attest the magnificence, as the walls declare the extent of the edifice. Some of the towers are mere shells; the stairs have long been destroyed, but the case has, in consequence, generally escaped with less mutilation. In the Eagle Tower, however, the stairs remain, and the summit may be ascended. There is a splendid prospect from it of the country around: moreover, the general plan of the castle, and the town walls, may thence be readily comprehended. This is called the Eagle Tower, from a carved figure of an eagle that once was fixed upon it,—if Pennant may be believed, a real Roman eagle, brought from the ancient Segontium; but the fact may be doubted. There were also other eagles on the battlements. The fragments are now quite indistinguishable. Tradition asserts

* See 'Boswell's Johnson,' v., p. 208, ed. 1835.

LLANBERIS.

that in this tower Edward II. was born; and a small rude room is pointed out as his birth-place: but it is certain that this tower was erected several years after his birth. A room in another tower is shown as that in which the stout-hearted William Prynne—the persecuted alike of churchman and independent, of Laud and of Cromwell—was imprisoned till the number of sympathizers who resorted to Carnarvon in order to catch sight of him caused his removal to a less accessible spot. The grand entrances are the most perfect portions of the castle. The King's Gate, on the northern side, with its barbicans and portcullises, must once have been of great strength: over the doorway is a seated figure of the mighty founder—too much defaced now, however, to be at all decypherable. The Queen's Gate, on the eastern side, is chiefly remarkable for its extraordinary height and apparently inaccessible situation. It is not easy to see where the roadway could have gone, even when the moat was undrained and the drawbridge was standing. Probably there were considerable outworks, a long inclined road, and a steep flight of steps.

As was said, it is the interior that proclaims the work of the destroyer. Gloomy, desolate, and solitary, are the broken walls and mouldering fragments; harsh-voiced ravens are the only occupants; ruin, in its sternest form, broods over all. Strangely irksome and depressing is it to wander alone about the crumbling pile: you hasten to the mountains for relief from the crowd of sombre phantasies that seize hold upon you.

The stranger who is of an antiquarian turn will, however, hardly leave the neighbourhood of Carnarvon without visiting the site of Segontium,—according to local imagination, or tradition, the birthplace of Constantine the Great, and the burial-place of his father, and also the theatre of other memorable circumstances. These are wild fancies, but Segontium was unquestionably a rather important Roman station. The road to Llanbeblig traverses the site. Some fragments of a wall, and rather extensive remains of a fort, are the visible relics of the Roman station; but underground, the relics are more numerous. At the depth of a few feet occur foundations of buildings, broken pottery, ashes, and so forth; while numerous coins, personal ornaments (some of them of gold), and other Roman remains, have, at various times, been exhumed. An account of the more important discoveries may be seen in the 'Archæologia Cambrensis,' the repository of much valuable information concerning the antiquities of the principality. The name of the old town is preserved in that of the river which flows at the base of the hill —the Seiont.

SNOWDONIA.

There are excellent mountain rambles within easy reach from Carnarvon; but it is better to quit the town, and go at once to some quiet mountain home for a few days,—or weeks, if practicable,—and thence explore at leisure the heights and the fastnesses of Snowdonia. Llanberris is almost always made a rest-

ing-place and a centre of exploration by tourists, for whom a couple of good hotels—one of large and another of smaller size—are provided. Thither let us turn our steps.

The road from Carnarvon to Llanberris is of increasing grandeur; and when the lower lake is reached, a magnificent prospect bursts on the eye. Lofty hills are on either hand; a broad sheet of water, black with the shadows of the neighbouring crags and fells, stretches at your feet, and a grand array of huge mountains rise up and encompass the head of the lake. These are the Snowdon mountains; but the patriarch himself is not seen from the road. A good view of him, as well as of the juniors that surround him, is obtained from the bridge at the foot of the lake; but a far finer prospect, embracing, perhaps, the finest view of Snowdon, with the Llanberris lakes and Dolbadern Castle, can be had from the slopes beyond, on the north side of the lake. Thence was taken the sketch from which the steel engraving was made. In continuing along the road to Llanberris, the tourist will not fail to halt on the eminence called Cwm-y-clo, from which another of the more celebrated of the views of the lakes and mountains is obtained. On Cwm-y-clo was a British fortress; and in the days when roads were not it must have been a commanding one.

The Vale of Llanberris is of some half-dozen miles length, and nowhere of very great breadth. The Seiont flows through it—a wild streamlet, gliding quickly but quietly in its channel, or foaming over the rocks which impede its way; till where the valley opens the little river expands into a couple of lakes, which, at some distant day, have doubtless formed but one: they are now divided from each other by a narrow neck of land. The upper lake, Llyn Peris, is less than a mile in length; the lower, Llyn Padern, is nearly a mile and a half long; neither is, in any part, half a mile wide. On the northern side are steep slate rocks, which are the roots of the Glydyr Fawr mountains, while on the south are the lower slopes of the Snowdon giants. The village of Llanberris—a rude rustic gathering of cottages—is at the upper end of the valley; nestled there, in a most romantic (but rather uncomfortable) situation, near the mouth of the Cwm-Glas, the famous Pass of Llanberris. The tourists' resting-place is a mile or so lower, by Dolbadern Castle.

And a thoroughly enjoyable resting-place it is. Commend us, after all, to a good inn, on the evening (or even morning) of a stiff mountain ramble. A rough hostel and rude fare are what a hardy tourist ought to be able not merely to endure, but to enjoy; but when he can have a snug home, an ample repast, and perhaps meet a pleasant and social stranger or two—and we have met such assembled here at the same time from Kent and Cornwall, from Warwick and Wexford, from Germany and from America, — if he is not ready then to make the most of the passing hour, take his ease in his inn, and felicitate himself on his good fortune, he is a very poor traveller, if not a very dull fellow.

K

This Llanberris itself is a place not soon to tire of. There are short walks for showery days, and long ones for fine: the lakes, as well as the mountains, change their hue with every change of weather as well as hour of the day. Light, gay, and cheerful are they, as the noontide sun plays over them, and the green slopes, and the gray tower are reflected in the tremulous water, while the mountains stand out with a firm outline against the deep azure of the sky. Illumined by the rising or touched by the sinking sun, they rise into exceeding beauty. In the evening, when white mists are creeping along the valley, and the summits of the mighty mountains are crested with clouds, while the sides are of a deep brownish purple hue, except where gilded by the last rays of the sun, and the water lies still and gloomy, or curls in sullen black waves,—then it wears an aspect of sombre grandeur that might almost be called sublime. But if the tourist hesitate to apply that epithet then, he will no longer doubt of its appropriateness, if he be fortunate enough to be at the lower end of the Vale as night is drawing on, and a storm is gathering and ready to burst over the mountains. We have seen only a 'little' storm here, and can only imagine what must be the effect of a great one; but for it we could be content to endure a good deal. It is hardly necessary to say that the lakes and the valley will be but imperfectly seen, if not seen from the lake as well as from the shore; or that the mountain slopes should also be ascended, or some of the choicest scenes will be missed. On the effect of moonlight, too, we will be silent.

The steep high crags on the northern side of the lake are peopled during the day with a busy army of quarrymen, whose works add to the wild look, though but little to the beauty, of the place. There are here very extensive slate-quarries, and a rail-road winds along the side of the lake, and down the valley of the Seiont, to the wharf under Carnarvon Castle. Only at intervals is anything seen of this railway, unless you are close to it; but it is not a little curious, while you are gazing over the seemingly solitary landscape, to hear the puffing of a locomotive engine, and then to behold it, with its train of heavily-laden wagons, emerge from behind some huge crag, and come panting along the edge of the lake. On the opposite side of the lake is another but less extensive slate-quarry; there are also two or three copper-mines in the valley. These works together give employment to some two thousand workmen. A large proportion of them live at a distance; and it is amusing to watch them, after work is done, returning to their homes in the evening. Many, to save the labour of walking, skim rapidly along the railway by means of machines which run on the rails, and are propelled by the action of the feet upon treadles; while others descend the lake in boats, forming quite a little procession. The large hotel, by the way, was built by the owner of the chief slate-quarry, and, somewhat characteristically, is built of slate.

Dolbadern Castle, which has been mentioned more than once already, is a round tower, or peel, which stands on a rock between the two lakes: its date is not known; it has no history; and not even a tradition that is worth repeating, or that may not be easily surpassed by the invention of any tourist who likes the occupation of tradition making. However, it is a very picturesque object standing just where it does; and there is, moreover, a capital view from it of the two lakes and the surrounding mountains. It therefore deserves the place it invariably finds in the sketch-books of lady sketchers.

About three-quarters of a mile from the hotel, in a deliciously cool and secluded spot, is a waterfall, that it is quite a pleasure to stroll to on a sunny afternoon. Caunant Mawr is the name of it, which is, being interpreted, "the cataract of the great chasm:" the name pretty well expresses the character of it; but it is hardly so grand an affair as it is sometimes described to be. The water breaks through the rocks, and then rushes down a long diagonal ledge into the deep chasm; it has a somewhat peculiar and certainly a very beautiful effect, when there is a good deal of water, and the slanting rays of the sun are glancing upon it. The rocks are lofty and wild; abundant foliage starts from the crevices, and overhangs the noisy current. This is one of the pleasant short strolls: others may be found wherever there is an opening in the mountains; and especially wherever there is a streamlet, though of the smallest size. From some of the narrow openings on the north side of the upper part of the valley there are glorious views of Snowdon. But the grandest feature of this neighbourhood, apart of course from Snowdon, is the Pass of Llanberris. It is an extremely narrow pass, above three miles long, between lofty and precipitous mountains. Huge masses of rock have fallen, and others are threatening to fall. The rocks are black, bare, and deeply shattered. A narrow brook forces its way along the gloomy bottom. Not very many years ago there was only a rough horse-road through the Pass; and travellers described it as " a tremendous hollow," and with one voice pronounced it "sublime." Now that an excellent carriage-road is carried through it, it has lost somewhat of its terrors and of its sublimity: it needs to be traversed at night-fall to realize its former grandeur; yet is it at all times a most impressive scene; more impressive, perhaps, than any similar spot in this region of grandeur. The look-out from the Pass upon Dolbadern Castle and the lakes—a peep singularly beautiful in itself—is quite a relief when first beheld. It will remind the tourist (though a far grander scene) of the Winnats of the Derbyshire Peak. Here, up the openings on either hand, may be found walks impossible to enumerate, but many of them far finer than those along which ordinary tourists follow each other, sheep-like.

Snowdon—the chief mountain of Wales, the highest mountain south of the Forth—will of course be ascended. There are several points from which the ascent may be made; and either may be chosen, as best suits the convenience of the visitor: neither of them is very difficult; that from Dolbadern is the easiest. The tourist must not reckon on a perfectly clear day; for Snowdon might, in Homeric phrase, be styled the cloud-former: but if one does occur while anywhere in the neighbourhood, the tourist should on no account neglect to avail himself of it; another may not offer. Yet a dull day need not deter any one. If a guide be employed—and, unless accustomed to the mountains, it is scarcely prudent to go without one—his judgment as to the fitness of the day may be trusted: a wet or cloudy morning often clears off, so as to afford the most brilliant prospects. The road commences near the hotel by Dolbadern Castle, and is, for the better part of the way, a well-beaten one. Horses ascend to within three-quarters of a mile of the summit: and they will of course be used by ladies and dandies; but men, who can climb a mountain, will not require their assistance. There is a perennial spring some distance short of the summit, where the thirsty climber may refresh himself.

The prospects on this side of Snowdon are not considered equal to those met with in ascending from Beddgelert; but there are some glorious views notwithstanding. Exquisite prospects are occasionally obtained of the lakes and valley of Llanberris; and, presently, noble ones of Glydyr Fawr, and the vales beyond. Snowdon himself, with his enormous buttresses, is often a magnificent object: and as one and another of the shadowy cwms opens with an inky tarn lying in its bosom, and a far-reaching glimpse of distant country is caught sight of, you are tempted to wonder what the finer prospects on the other side can possibly be.

The summit of Snowdon—Yr Wyddfa, the Conspicuous, is the name of the highest peak—is 3,571 feet above the sea. The view from it embraces the Ingleborough mountains in Yorkshire; the mountains of Westmorland and Cumberland; the Highlands of Scotland; the Isle of Man; the mountains of Wicklow, and a good deal of the Irish coast; a large part of the principality, with the sea of mountains, and five-and-twenty lynns; and a wide range of country besides. All, of course, cannot be seen at any one time while the sun is above the horizon; but a large portion may be seen on a clear, calm day. We have not been fortunate enough to be on the summit on a clear day, yet the views from Snowdon will dwell in our memory among the most cherished of our recollections of mountain prospects. Marvellously beautiful is the scene, when, in a moment, the clouds are rent asunder, and let in the view of a wide stretch of distant country smiling softly in the gentle sunshine: it is like the revelation of a new land. Then, too, what a magnificent gathering of majestic mountains are around you, the clouds rolling away one after another, and displaying ever new wonders—peaks and chasms and glassy lakes! Again, as the shadows fly swiftly over the seemingly level champaign, how does one and another mountain appear to rise into existence, as a shadow rests upon it, while all around is vivid light—

or a gleam of sunshine touches it, and causes it to start forth from the neighbouring gloom! And then the soft, almost invisible distance—the glittering sea—the placid llyns—no, we do not envy those who have only been here on a clear day.

It is said to be a noble spectacle to behold the sunrise from Snowdon: and so doubtless it is. But we never saw Snowdon clear of clouds in the morning, and are a little sceptical whether it ever has been seen, though we once met one person who vowed he saw a glorious sunrise from the summit. The tourist may try his fortune. There are a couple of huts on the summit, erected especially for the accommodation of wanderers, wherein all plain provision is made for their comfort. And there may be compensation found, if the sunrise be not witnessed; for it is affirmed that the Druids proclaimed that the man who stayed all night on Yr Wyddfa would certainly become, for the nonce, inspired. These huts are really pleasant things to find in this bleak spot, even in the day-time. A snug fire-side, with a cigar and a noggin of whisky, if that way inclined; or a cup of coffee, if it be preferred, is a real luxury, while the mountain-top is wrapped in a dense damp cloud. We will whisper to the traveller, however, that he had better carry his own cigars; for the host's are of detestable flavour, and —sixpence a piece.

The descent from Snowdon may be very well made to Beddgelert, if it be desired to visit that place. The views in that direction are very different from those on the side by which we ascended, and exceedingly fine. You have to pass over on one side of what Mr. Bingley describes as "a tremendous ridge of rock, called Clawdd Coch, the Red Ridge. This narrow pass," he continues, "not more than ten or twelve feet across, and two or three hundred yards in length, was so steep that the eyes reached, on each side, down the whole extent of the mountain. And I am persuaded that in some parts of it, if a person held a large stone in each hand, and let them fall both at once, each might roll above a quarter of a mile; and thus, when they stopped, they might be more than half a mile asunder." Clawdd Coch is certainly a rough bit, but far less "tremendous" than Striding Edge on Helvellyn. And as for what is said of the falling stones, we carried some with us— good rollers—and hurled them with all our might;— and though not so strong or so skilful as in our younger days, our arm has not quite lost its cunning;— yet we could not induce them to go, even one at a time, within a mortifying distance of a quarter of a mile: and we are constrained to say that this is, like the difficulties and dangers of the way, much magnified.

We have two or three times spoken of Snowdonia: it may be as well to explain the term. What is generally known as Snowdonia is the mountain district, of which Snowdon is the highest point and leading feature. Its boundaries are not very precisely defined; for our purpose it may be enough to say that it includes the whole of the mountains of Carnarvonshire, from Penmaen

Mawr on the north to Moel Hebog on the south,—or from sea to sea. In this range are the highest and the most magnificent mountains of Wales: it is a tract of wild rocky passes and ravines, of lofty precipices, deep chasms, foaming rivers, bold waterfalls, numerous llyns, gloomy and gay vallies. Now it is traversed in every direction by good roads, though between them lie yet many secluded and seldom-visited spots. Once a vast and thick forest spread over a considerable portion of the district, and the whole was a savage and unreclaimed region. Snowdonia was the last stronghold of the Britons. To its fastnesses, inaccessible to the foe, the princes and the warriors of Wales retreated, and there held out, long after the open country was wrested from them. Every pass was fortified; and it was a difficult undertaking to beard the native lion in such a den: but Edward united caution and perseverance with military skill. The stronghold of the Britons was rather blockaded than forced, and the last Prince of Wales was at length compelled to submit. When Snowdonia was gained, Edward felt that his conquest was assured. He celebrated his victory by gathering here the chivalry of Europe to a magnificent tournament.

It was only in comparatively recent times that strangers penetrated into the district—if they could keep out of it. Old Speed shows pretty plainly in what light it was regarded in his day: "But for the heart of Carnarvonshire," he says, "it is altogether mountainous, as if Nature had a purpose here, by rearing up these craggy hills so thick together, strongly to compact the joints of this our island, and to frame the inland part thereof for a fit place of refuge to the Britons, against those times of adversity which afterwards did fall upon them; for no army, though never so strongly, or scarce any travellers, though never so lightly appointed, can find passage among these so many rough and hard rocks, so many vales and pools here and there crossing all the ways, as ready obstacles to repel any inroads of foreign assailants." Again, after speaking of some of the marvellous tales told by Giraldus Cambrensis, of this part of Wales, he adds: "Touching those two other miracles, famoused by Giraldus and Gervasius, that on those high Snowdon hills there are two pools, called the Mears, the one of which produceth great store of fish, but all having only one eye; and in the other there is a moveable island, which as soon as a man treadeth thereon, it forthwith floateth a great way off, whereby the Welsh are said to have often 'scaped and deluded their enemies assailing them: these matters are out of my creed," writes Master Speed, intending to wind up with a smart hit: "and yet, I think, the reader had rather believe them than go to see whether it be so or no."* Times are

* Giraldus has some other marvels quite equal to that of these monoculous fishes, belonging to this district; but it is the mountains of Merionethshire which he affirms are so lofty, and yet so precipitous, that two choleric shepherds upon neighbouring summits may, from their proximity, very easily fall at odds in the morning, and challenge each

changed since then: "I really can't make out what so many ladies and gentlemen come into this rough wild place to see," said a Snowdon farmer to us one day: "if all the mountains were polished silver, I doubt if more fine folks would come to stare at them; and if all the crevices were full of gold, I don't think some of them could pore closer into them . . . there they go, climbing, and toiling, and chipping at the crags, as if they were paid for it; instead of paying, as they do, pretty smartly at our hotels into the bargain. . . . . Prospects! Beauty! well, I was once in Lincolnshire, and there *was* a prospect, if you like! My heart! it was all as flat and smooth as your hand as far as you could see in every direction: and such crops! I call that beauty." As Crabbe sings:

"It is the soul that sees: the outward eyes
Present the object, but the mind descries—
And thence delight, disgust, or cool indifference rise."

The forest spoken of above was chiefly around Snowdon. It was so dense, in the tenth century, that Howell Dha is reported to have offered to any one who would clear any portion of it, the freehold of the land so cleared; notwithstanding, it is said by native authorities, that it might already be the property of any other individual. This was a part of "the good old plan." As late as the time of Henry VIII., a keeper of Snowdon Forest was duly appointed; and it continued to be a deer forest some time later. Now all that remains of Snowdon Forest is the name: its existence is matter of history and tradition.

Every one comes to Wales mainly for the sake of the mountains and the mountain scenery; and whatever is grandest and most characteristic in Welsh mountain scenery is brought together and concentred in Snowdonia. A month devoted to this district alone would provide food for the intellect and the imagination for years to come. Few tourists are able or willing to give more time than this to the whole of North Wales, and that time is expended in visiting in succession every object that, for any reason, is celebrated; and the arrangements are so made, as to devote to every place and object as little time as it can possibly be examined in. Not so can a mountainous country be fitly explored or understood. It is not merely bare

other to fight, and yet the day would be spent before they could meet to settle the quarrel: a happy thing, Speed thinks, as thereby many a broken head is spared. By the way, it would seem that Giraldus's marvels tempted some to visit Snowdon in search of them, long before touring was fashionable. Thomas Fuller, mentioning the floating island, remarks: "But it seemeth that it either always swimmeth away from such who endeavour to discover it, or else that this vagrant, wearied with long wandering, hath at last fixed itself to the continent." He adds, moreover, that "the one-eyed fishes are too nimble for any men with two eyes to behold them." The rising of a buoyant island to the surface of a lake is by no means an uncommon phenomenon; there may have been one here: its floating away, so as to enable the Welsh to escape from an enemy, may stand out of our creed, as it did out of honest Speed's.

hills and white waterfalls that are of interest and value. The poetry of the mountains lies more in the ever-changeful phenomena that are their inseparable attend-ants. A mountain is in itself the same to-day that it was yesterday; but the appearance it presents to an observant eye is very different: it has become another, though the same. Many of the circumstances which are most annoying to the mere sight-seer are really what afford the richest enjoyment to one watchful of the varying phases of Nature. The grandeur and the gloom of the mountains and the lakes, the most glorious phenomena of which the mind, in such localities, is cognizant, are transitory, evanescent, fitful. If you would enjoy them, you must wait for them in patience; be abroad at all seasons to observe; and then, often when least anticipated, and in places seemingly the least likely, they reveal themselves to the willing eye and heart. Day and night, summer and autumn, fair weather and foul, every hour and every season has its own charms and utters its own voice. Stormy weather, against which, not unreasonably, tourists generally declaim, is, in truth, a thing to be especially coveted. Never do the mountains and the shadowy valleys so emphatically speak home to the heart as then. Whether it be as the gathering clouds herald the coming storm; or when half the landscape is wrapped in darkness and in tempest; as the lightning is breaking upon the sharp peaks and the thunder echoing along the hollows; when the struggle between sunshine and gloom pro-claims that the storm is passing away; or later, when a soft rainbow is spanning the valley—alike is there in the sublimity or the loveliness a power which is never felt amid the quiet beauty attendant on an unclouded sky. And though the mists are hardly to be admired when they envelope both hill and vale in a garment of uniform gray; yet he knows little of mountain scenery, who does not recognize in them perhaps the most valuable of poetic and picturesque auxiliaries. Let but a gleam of sunlight into the landscape, and how beautiful do the mists appear, whether congregating about the summits or rolling along the slopes of the mountains, hanging over the watercourses, or filling the hollow ravines. What knows he of the mountains, who has not wandered alone in some solitary nook,

" When underneath the young gray dawn
A multitude of dense white fleecy clouds
Were wandering in thick flocks among the mountains,
Shepherded by the slow unwilling wind?"
SHELLEY.

But we repeat, thoroughly to enjoy and appreciate this district, it is not enough to keep merely to the beaten roads. Let the tourist wander at will wherever he can find a way, and everywhere he will discover unanticipated wealth. Scenes, whether of grandeur or beauty, or solitary desolation, will be alike recognized as of distinct individuality, complete and perfect in themselves, yet linked by imperceptible gradations into harmony with surrounding scenes.

Capel Curig is another of the chief centres for exploring Snowdonia from. The road to it from the last station lies through the Pass of Llanberris, and then by the valley of Nant-y-Gwryd, and consequently along much splendid scenery. But the Pass we may suppose to have been already sufficiently seen, and Nant-y-Gwryd Vale will be traversed on the way to Beddgelert. It will be better, therefore, for the pedes-trian to make his way from Llanberris over the shoulder or summit of Glydyr Fawr, and thence by Llyn Idwall, or along somewhat more to the right. He will obtain some new and very grand views; those from the summit of Glydyr Fawr are among the very finest in the dis-trict; but it is a rough route, and hardly to be hazarded, perhaps, by a timid traveller, or one unused to wander alone about the mountains.

Capel Curig, so called from its little chapel, dedi-cated to the Welsh saint, Curig, is a wild, lonely spot—a tiny village of half a dozen houses, about half a mile from the Holyhead-road, but having a capacious hotel, where is good accommodation, good fare, and an inde-fatigable harper. From it, as a centre, an almost endless variety of mountain strolls may be made: moreover, in the rivers and llyns close at hand or within easy distance, there is as good trout-fishing as, perhaps, anywhere in Wales. From the garden of the hotel, or still better from the picturesque old bridge, a little farther on, there is a splendid view of Snowdon, with the double lake—the Llyniau Mymbyr—in front. (Cut, No. 7, ante, p. 124.) The walks beside these llyns, in themselves an exquisite picture, and on the hills which border them, are singularly beautiful.

Moel Siabod, which lies just on the south, may be ascended from Capel Curig: the summit is 2,878 feet above the sea: it is reckoned to be nearly four miles from the inn—a rough climb, but the view on a fair day will repay the labour. On the summit is a tarn; and in a hollow just under the summit on the east, is a curious little llyn, with three islets in it. Either over or round Moel Siabod a way may be found to Dolwyddelan; by the direct road, the distance is about five miles. Dolwyddelan itself is a rude and quite sequestered village. Tourists come into the vale merely to visit the remains of Dolwyddelan Castle,—a picturesque ruined tower, standing on a bluff rock, and encompassed by bold mountains. The castle was in the 12th century the residence of Iorwerth Drwndwn—Edward Brokennose. The disfigurement of his prominent feature was a double misfortune to him; for not only was he thereby rendered less amiable in the eyes of the ladies—no small evil in the days of Welsh chivalry—but he was pronounced to be, in consequence, disqualified to wear the Welsh coronet; to which, else, he would have been entitled, as eldest son of Owen Gwynedd. He retired to Dolwyddelan, to conceal at once his chagrin and the cause of it. His son, famous in Welsh history as Llewellyn the Great, was born at Dolwyddelan Castle. Through the long winding valley the Afon Lledr flows from its source on Moel Lledr,—the huge mountain mass which blocks up the head of the valley. This is not exactly a drawing-room district, but there is much characteristic scenery to be found by those who will search after it. Running directly south from the village of Dolwyddelan, there is a Roman road distinctly traceable for some miles. The are also other objects of archæological interest in the immediate vicinity. Hereabout, too, are several copper-mines.

On entering the Holyhead road from Capel Curig, and turning to the right with the little river which issues from the Llyniau Mymbyr, you have before you the valley of the Llugwy, a vale well known to the artist and the angler : it leads to Betwys-y-Coed. The Llugwy is, throughout its short course, a lively, changeful, rapid streamlet; at one moment careering gaily along in broad daylight, presently hiding itself in a narrow glen, or beneath a rich canopy of trees, and again leaping over rocky barriers in sparkling water-breaks or bolder cascades. So it goes on, gathering strength in its way, till it reaches a spot where it flings itself fearlessly down a deep ravine : and thither the tourist must not fail to bend his steps to witness the spectacle.

Rhaiadr-y-Wennol, the Cataract of the Swallow, is not only one of the largest, but, to our thinking, the finest of the waterfalls in Wales : but so much depends on the circumstances under which such places are seen, that we would not have our meaning extended beyond the literal expression; other of the Welsh waterfalls may be even grander; this is our favourite. Except when in flood, the river breaks over the highest ledge of rocks, in three or four distinct streams, which re-unite before plunging into the pool below ; then in one wide foaming mass it rushes over the next rocky ledge, and down a long and broad slope shattering into spray, as it descends against the black projecting crags. Its base is veiled by a shifting cloud of mist, over which, as a straggling sunbeam glances upon it, plays the tremulous iris. Fragments of black rock, gemmed with many-coloured mosses, contrast with the trans-lucent water and snowy spray. The sides of the ravine are steep, and grandly formed. Rich foliage impends from them above the chasm, and climbs along the ledges of purple slate. Nought is seen that inter-feres with the impression of solitary grandeur and majesty; nought is heard but the roar of the falling waters.

This waterfall may be readily compared with one of very different character, but of equal height and extent, though not of equal quantity of water. Let us visit it. You return past Capel Curig by way of the Vale of Llugwy. The valley appeared very beau-tiful in descending it, but it is much finer in ascending. Lofty mountains are on either hand : on the left is the vast form of Moel Siabod ; on the right are the Carn-eddiau David, and Llewellyn; but at every turn, one or the other of them seems to march out directly before you. On passing from the Llugwy, you enter upon a more open and somewhat boggy tract, lying at the base of the bare, precipitous, and broken Trevaen

13.—LLYN OGWEN.

Mountain; from which, and from the opposite mountain, huge blocks of stone have fallen, and lie scattered over the valley; a stern and desolate scene, rendered, if possible, more so, from the presence of two or three wretched cottages which, far apart, spot the boggy level. This leads to Llyn Ogwen—which, as we shall return to it presently, we may pass unnoticed now.

The Ogwen river, which issues from Llyn Ogwen, flows through a short but close and savage gorge, called the Pass of Benglog, and then precipitates itself over a lofty wall of broken rocks, forming the famous Falls of Benglog—the object of our journey. The entire height is said to be, and no doubt is, above a hundred feet; but it is broken up into a number of separate falls. Nothing hardly can exceed the severe rugged character of the scene. On either hand are the grim black slate rocks, and along the bed of the stream are huge detached fragments of a similar kind: in front tower the lofty sides of the Pass, while the shattered Trevaen fills up the opening, lifting its dark bare peaks to the clouds. Not a tree, hardly a shrub, is within ken: all is barren, naked, shattered rock. Were there a sufficient body of water to unite the separate falls into one mighty cataract, Benglog might most fearlessly compare with any waterfall in the kingdom for a savage grandeur approaching to sublimity. As it is, the Fall appears almost insignificant from the magnitude of its accompaniments. A waterfall around which plays rich and graceful foliage, while the bright wild flowers start from every crevice of the rocky sides, and cluster on the margin of the channel below, may be lovelier and more pleasing when only a comparatively small stream is leaping lightly from ledge to ledge, and all the surrounding beauty is reflected in the deep and lustrous pool, into which the pellucid water gently falls, than when, swollen by storms, the broader bed is filled by a discoloured and almost unbroken flood: but one where all around is naked rock, and all the permanent forms are on a scale of vastness and grandeur, requires that the water shall be of correspondent greatness and force, or a feeling of incompleteness is inevitably experienced. Hence it is, that while Benglog never fails to produce a powerful impression, it is yet unsatisfactory and disappointing—at least in ordinary seasons: we can easily imagine that, during or immediately after a great storm, or on the melting of the snows, it must be, with the surrounding objects, a magnificent scene.

The valley into which the Ogwen flows from Benglog is the celebrated Nant-Francon—the Hollow of Beavers. The scenery along it is very striking. On both sides rise to a great height bare and precipitous crags; in the hollow lies a strip of marshy meadow of brightest verdure, with the stream winding quietly through the midst. As you descend towards Bangor the vale becomes gradually tamer; but upwards it increases in boldness and majesty at every step, as the Pass of Benglog, with the Glydyr and Trevaen Mountains beyond, rise into importance, and at length seem to close in the head of the valley. When Pennant wrote, the road through Nant-Francon was scarcely practi-

cable, while the Pass of Benglog was " the most dreadful horse-path in Wales;" now the great Holyhead road runs through it, and the way is as level as along almost any of the roads out of London: to the loss, unquestionably, of much of the ancient grandeur.

Llyn Ogwen, though not one of the largest, is one of the very finest lakes in Wales. It is encompassed with mountains of bold form and noble proportions, which rise abruptly from its shadowy surface. Like the scenes we have just left, all is barren, desolate, savage grandeur. Not a tree waves on either bank: only here and there a scanty herbage obtains lodgment on the sides of the mountains. The occasional movement of a boat, in which a busy angler is plying his craft, almost alone breaks the perfect quiet, without, however, disturbing the repose of the scene. (Cut, No. 13.)

This Llyn Ogwen we ought, perhaps, to mention in passing, is famous for a trout of small size, but delicious flavour, which is taken in it in large quantities. The tourist may partake of some of them (or of others as good) at Capel Curig; and we suppose it is hardly needful to remind him that it is "matter of breviary," as Friar John des Entommeures would say, to order a dish of lake trout when they can be transferred direct from the lake to the pan—that is, of course, if he esteem such a dish a dainty.

But to come back to the lakes. A mile or so from Llyn Ogwen, up the Glydyr mountains, there is a smaller lake, Llyn Idwal, which, except in magnitude, is of even nobler character. Of its size, Llyn Idwal is probably without a rival. It lies in a deep gloomy hollow; bare rocks rise precipitously from it, and darken by their heavy shadows and sombre reflections its calm and quiet surface into intensest blackness. On one side the vast rock is split, as though cleft by a giant's blow: it bears the name of the ' Black Chasm' —Twll ddu. There is something almost awful in the stillness, the solitude, and the gloom. The native tradition that the lake received its name from a youthful prince of Wales, who was murdered here by his foster-father, seems but appropriate to the place.

These lesser mountain lakes are an important and characteristic feature of Snowdonia, which the tourist who can wander at leisure over the district ought not to neglect. To notice all of them, if desirable, which it is not, would be quite impossible; for there are in the district some fifty, of various sizes. But a few general remarks may not be out of place. In Wales all the lakes and pools, of whatever size, or wherever situated, are called llyns; but it would be as well if, as in Cumberland, the small mountain lakes bore a different title: there they are called tarns. They are too much neglected by the mountain rambler, these mountain llyns. Happy would it be if the young tourist would learn to draw from such objects the enjoyment and the poetry they are capable of inspiring. In Wordsworth's 'Scenery of the Lakes,' there is a passage descriptive of the Cumberland tarns, so beautiful in itself, and with the change of that one word so exactly applicable to the Welsh mountain llyns, that we are tempted to extract it, instead of enlarging on the subject in our own feeble phraseology : admirably will it instruct the tourist who has not been used to regard steadily and thoughtfully, the various classes of natural objects, how much of beauty and poetry there is in every piece of Nature's handiwork, if contemplated in the light of a trustful imagination. He says:—" The *mountain* tarns can only be recommended to the notice of the inquisitive traveller who has time to spare. They are difficult of access and naked; yet some of them are, in their permanent forms, very grand; and there are accidents of things which would make the meanest of them interesting. At all events, one of these pools is an acceptable sight to the mountain wanderer; not merely as an incident that diversifies the prospect, but as forming in his mind a centre or conspicuous point to which objects, otherwise disconnected or insubordinate, may be referred. Some few have a varied outline, with bold heath-clad promontories; and, as they mostly lie at the foot of a steep precipice, the water, where the sun is not shining upon it, appears black and sullen; and, round the margin, huge stones and masses of rock are scattered; some defying conjecture as to the means by which they came thither; and others obviously fallen from on high— the contribution of ages ! A not unpleasing sadness is induced by this perplexity and these images of decay; while the prospect of a body of pure water, unattended with groves and other cheerful rural images by which fresh water is usually accompanied, and unable to give furtherance to the meagre vegetation around it, excites a sense of some repulsive power strongly put forth, and thus deepens the melancholy natural to such scenes. Nor is the feeling of solitude often more forcibly or more solemnly impressed than by the side of one of these mountain pools : though desolate and forbidding, it seems a distinct place to repair to; yet where the visitants must be rare, and there can be no disturbance. Waterfowl flock hither; and the lonely angler may here be seen ; but the imagination, not content with this scanty allowance of society, is tempted to attribute a voluntary power to every change which takes place in such a spot, whether it be the breeze that wanders over the surface of the water, or the splendid lights of evening resting upon it in the midst of awful precipices.

> There, sometimes does a leaping fish
> Send through the tarn a lonely cheer;
> The crags repeat the raven's croak
> In symphony austere :
> Thither the rainbow comes, the cloud,
> And mists that spread the flying shroud,
> And sunbeams, and the sounding blast."

We now turn towards Beddgelert, the next and last of the Snowdonian centres of exploration. There we shall not need to sojourn long: indeed, having already examined with sufficient tediousness examples of the chief classes of objects which are characteristic of the Welsh tour, we may hasten over the remaining ground

without staying to bestow on any thing or place more than a passing and cursory glance.

On leaving Capel Curig you proceed along Nant-y-Gwryd, and by the Llyniu Mymbyr—a vale of whose beauties we have already spoken. When Gorfwysfa is reached, the tourist will not do amiss to make it, for a few moments, his ' resting-place ;' for that is the meaning of the name of the eminence. From it there is a fine peep into the Pass of Llanberris. Onwards is the Nant-y-Gwynant,—a vale that lies quiet and peacefully under the shadow of the mighty Snowdon : a pleasant vale as a man might desire to wander about at leisure, and penetrate at will into its recesses. Up high on this side it is that the grim black Cwm Dyli lies—one of the deepest cwms on old Snowdon— nursing in its ample bosom Llyn Llydaw, the largest and finest of the giant's tarns. The huge mountain, with its dark red precipices, is a noble object as seen from many parts of this vale. The stream that comes down from Llyn Llydaw forms a cataract in its descent, then flows along the bottom of Nant-y-Gwynant, and presently expands into one of the very loveliest little lakes in Wales. Llyn Gwynant is not above a mile in length, and about a quarter of a mile broad, but is of the richest character. The mountains around are of fine and pleasing form ; the banks of the llyn are gently varied and clad in many places with luxuriant foliage ; the water is clear and silvery ; the whole aspect is one of soft, graceful, and placid beauty. Just below the fine woods of Plas Gwynant is another lake, Llyn-y-Dinas, also very beautiful, but not equal to Gwynant. By the river-side, along here, there are many admirable passages of river scenery, with the vast mass of Snowdon rising up as a noble background.

On the right, a short distance below Llyn Dinas, will be seen a rocky eminence : this is Dinas Emrys, and is affirmed to be the spot whereon Vortigern attempted to erect a tower, and met with such strange hindrances, and where he was sitting when the two dragons, white and red, came out of the lake and fought before the British king till the red dragon was beaten and forced to take to flight. Then the king, being troubled at what he saw, called unto Merlin, son of the Devil, and commanded him to declare what these things portended ; and Merlin, seeing in this combat foreshadowed the misfortunes that were about to befall his country—for though his father was a demon, his mother was a very worthy Welsh princess—lifted up his voice and wept, and made haste to tell the king all those things which are written in the book of the prophecies of Merlin, as contained in the Chronicle of Geoffrey of Monmouth.

The first view of Beddgelert, as you approach the village on this side, is certainly very picturesque. Before you is the clear shallow river, spanned by the rude old ivy-clad bridge, with a tall clump of dusky trees beyond, and the bulky form of Moel Hebog rising high above all, its summit partaking of an aërial hue, while the lower slopes are black and strongly defined against the bright south-western sky. By the bridge are the irregular unpretending houses of the villagers; and if it be morning or evening, most likely there will be seen down by the water-side a group of old village wives and young children, come there to fetch water, or to dabble their clothes in the clear stream, and to exchange some village scandal. (Cut, No. 14.) But Beddgelert hardly maintains its promise; in itself it is neither picturesque nor beautiful: yet as it has an hotel of general popularity among Welsh tourists, and there is a great deal both of picturesque and beautiful scenery in the vicinity, it is not at all surprising that it is a general halting-place.

Here was once a residence of the famous Llewellyn the Great; and it received its name—if song and story may be trusted—from the circumstance in his history which painters, and poets, and story-tellers, have so much delighted to commemorate. The reader will doubtless recollect the tale. The prince, returning one day from hunting, was met at the door of his house by Gelert, his favourite hound, smeared over with blood. On entering, he saw his child's cradle overturned and empty, with blood upon it and about the room. Supposing the dog had destroyed his son, he drew his sword and slew him. Hardly had he done so, when he heard the child's voice, and then discovered that the faithful hound had really killed a wolf which had attempted to seize the child. The prince erected a church upon the spot where he killed his dog, and raised a tomb over the creature's remains. The village which grew up around the church in time received the name of Bedd-Gelert—the grave of Gelert; and so perpetuated the memory of the faithfulness of the animal and of the rashness and remorse of the prince. In a field behind the village the grave is still pointed out: a couple of stones mark the spot, which a few trees overshadow; a path leads to it from the 'Goat' Inn. In the village itself, it has been said, there is little to be found. Once there was a considerable monastery there; but no vestiges of it are left. Near the inn is a small waterfall.

A day may be agreeably spent in a ramble to Nantle Pools and Carnarvon Bay. You take the Carnarvon road, along which are some good views, though the scenery generally is not remarkably interesting. About three miles up this road, near the rock which is called Pitt's Profile, from a fancied resemblance it bears to that great statesman, is the place whence the ascent of Snowdon from Beddgelert is generally made: we should prefer that on the other side of the village, near Llyn Gwynant. Somewhat farther, on the left of the road, will be noticed a small circular lake, Llyn-y-Gader, and soon afterwards the bye-road which leads over to Nantle Pools. But it is certainly worth while to proceed a mile farther to Llyn Llewellyn, a fine lake, somewhat above a mile in length, and encompassed with wild craggy mountains. Some way farther is Nant Mill, where is a singularly picturesque waterfall; and still farther, about four miles from Carnarvon, is Bettws Garmon, whence may be found a road over to the coast, or by the low mountains to the Pools. The

more picturesque route, however, is unquestionably that before-mentioned.

Here, on the western side of Drws-y-Coed Mountain, will be observed a small tarn, called Llyn-y-Dywarchen, in which we have been told there is a buoyant mossy islet, that occasionally rises to the surface: this has been thought to be the floating island Giraldus speaks of; which is quite possible, as there is frequently some foundation for popular stories; and the stories of Giraldus were mostly gathered from the natives. The Nantle Pools are three or four miles further, by a mountain road. The Nantle Valley is close and narrow, yet a good deal varied in character, and in places affords some remarkably fine views. It is comparatively little visited; but, to the pedestrian at any rate, it affords much more interesting and characteristic scenery than many of the more popular and beaten tracks. The swelling mountain sides are bold, and often grand. Nantle Pools, as they are usually termed by Englishmen, but which the Welsh call the Llyniau Nant-y-llef, are only separated by a narrow slip of land, through which the connecting streamlet flows. Seen together, and in connection with the surrounding scenery, they are very beautiful. The finest view of them is from the lower end, where Snowdon is seen rising in all his majesty in the distance. In some respects this is without an equal among the Welsh llyn scenery. Wilson is always said to have painted his view of Snowdon from this spot; but if the painting belonging to Sir R. W. Vaughan be meant, we confess to having fancied, when looking at it, that it must have been from the other side of the mountain—from the Llyniau Mymbyr, at the back of Capel Curig. Be that as it may, this is a very fine view, and the whole neighbourhood abounds in fine views. Here, too, are extensive slate-quarries; and the blasting of the rocks causes some fine reverberations among the mountains and over the lakes. About the mountains are two or three copper-mines. There is a considerable population in this wild, sequestered valley, consisting almost entirely of miners and quarrymen, and those connected with them.

This, and the return by a somewhat different route, will perhaps be quite enough for a day's stroll, especially if the road be occasionally quitted, as it will be, of course, by any one used to mountain walks. This side of Carnarvon Bay may be very well visited from Carnarvon. But it should be visited. It is best seen from the water. Delightful is the sail in Carnarvon Bay and some distance out to sea. The semicircular bay would be considered, in itself, very beautiful; but with the magnificent amphitheatre of mountains, including the Rivals (Yr-Eifl) and the Snowdon range, it is without rival in this country for picturesqueness. During the summer, excursions are occasionally made from Carnarvon in steam-vessels to the end of the promontory: allowing the passengers to land, and remain for awhile ashore on Bardsey Island—the island famous for its ancient monastery and fabulous population of saints. Ten, or, as some say, twenty thousand saints

14.—BEDDGELERT.

were buried in it. The coast-scenery is, in parts, very striking. The same might be said of the coast of the noble Cardigan Bay, on the other side of the promontory, but it must remain unnoticed here.

FFESTINIOG.

It is hardly needful to point out other walks around Beddgelert: we will renew our journey. About a mile from the village commences the famous Pass of Aberglaslyn. It is a narrow gorge between lofty precipitous rocks. The cliffs of bare purple rock rise to an immense height—some five or six hundred feet—on either hand; a rapid stream runs along the bottom in a channel full of scattered blocks of stone which have fallen from the heights above. The winding of the Pass precludes a distant prospect, and adds to the savage character of the scene. As the evening draws on, and the deep hollow lies in the heavy shadow, while the highest portions of the rocky wall are illumined by the declining sun, the appearance is exceedingly grand. But it is still more grand—in truth, magnificent—if seen by the light of a full autumnal moon. In the broad daylight one is apt to feel a little disappointment after having heard so much of the sublimity of the Pass. The excellent level mail-coach road that is carried through it, has, in truth, taken off a good deal of that appearance of the terrible which the earlier tourists used to emphasize.

At the end of the Pass is Pont Aberglaslyn, a bridge which spans the stream where it breaks finely down the sloping rocky channel. The banks are high rocks, of most picturesque character, and richly varied with trees and shrubs which find lodgment in the crevices. It is a charming scene: the more so from its contrast with the grim bare Pass just quitted, whose rugged crags, indeed, form a striking feature in this picture. The lover of river scenery will do well to scramble down the bank, and make his way for a little distance along the bed of the river. (Cut, No. 15.) The appearance of the scene varies a good deal according to the quantity of water in the river; when " roaring in spate" it is a furious torrent; but commonly it is a gladsome, changeful, transparent streamlet. With anglers it is a favourite for both trout and salmon.

The mail-coach road leads to Tremadoc, a modern town, built by W. A. Madocks, Esq., whence its name, which is equivalent to Madocks' Town. Mr. Madocks carried the great embankment across Traeth Mawr, and recovered about seven thousand acres of land from the sea : the embankment was only partially successful, as the sea soon found a way through it, and the land remains marshy, but a good part of it is cultivated. Before the embankment, when the sea covered Traeth Mawr, it is said that the view up it was of surpassing splendour. Traeth Mawr at full tide presented the appearance of a great lake, some five or six miles long and a mile across ; on each side were precipitous mountains, and the head of the lake was encompassed by a magnificent array of mountains, rising tier above tier,

and crowned by the lofty Snowdon. If in the kingdom it had a rival, it must have been sought for in Scotland. The mountains of course remain; but in place of the blue water is a sickly-looking marsh, and an air of formality has been imparted to the whole scene ; but the unquestionable utility of the undertaking must overweigh any regret that may be felt for the change. Tremadoc, Port Madoc, and the works around have a busy appearance.

The nearer and pleasanter road from Pont Aberglaslyn to Maentwrog is to leave the river on the right and to keep the road, which winds under the mountains : but this way Tremadoc will not of course be seen. There is a good deal of rich and varied mountain scenery along this road, but it is needless to particularize. A hardy walker would prefer to make his way over the mountains, taking either the summit or shoulder of Moelwyn : the views are grand, but the way is rough. Just before reaching Maentwrog, is Tan-y-Bwlch, a spot celebrated for its beauty. The mansion is the residence of the Ockleys, who permit access to the grounds under certain restrictions.

The Vale of Ffestiniog is very beautiful. It varies greatly in breadth and character; hardly anywhere, perhaps, grand, but beautiful in every part. The mountains rise high on both sides, but slope gently away ; the vale is soft, verdant, cultivated, and fertile. All along are scattered villas with their cheerful grounds, farm-houses, which seem to be inhabited by prosperous tenants, and cottages, either clustered in little hamlets, or standing singly and apart. The stream which flows through the midst, at first but small in size, in the course of a few miles opens into a broad river, and from that passes rapidly into an arm of the sea. A good deal of nonsense has been talked, about Ffestiniog being quite Italian in character—a Frascati, a Tivoli, another Tempé, nay, even a St. Helena ! and one hardly knows what besides. The plain truth is, that it is a thoroughly Welsh valley, and a very lovely one too. It is about as much like an Italian or a Greek scene as a Welsh peasant is like one of the Abruzzi or an Albanian.

The village of Ffestiniog is seated on the summit of a high hill, at the head and a little on one side of the vale. It is quite a little place, with a neat church and school-house, which have been recently erected on the highest piece of ground ; a couple of inns, and a few poor houses. The scenery all around is full of interest. Besides the vale and the divergent valleys there is in every direction a good wild mountain tract to ramble over, and one that may be traversed without danger by the most inexperienced mountain traveller. Not far from the village are the famous Falls of Cynfael. The stream is one of the wildest and most romantic of Welsh mountain streams. It comes rattling down the mountain side in right joyous mood, till it enters the long close dingle, where it has to surmount many a bold barrier, and force its way through or over many a shattered mass of stone. There are a couple of falls, both of great beauty and wildness ; neither rocky bank, mossy stone, nor feathery tree is wanting, and there is a sufficient volume of water to give a character to the fall worthy of the accompaniments. The stranger will find himself often wandering involuntarily down to the Rhaiadr Cynfael. In one part of the glen will be noticed a great misshapen block of stone, standing high out of the centre of the stream: it is Hugh Lloyd's Pulpit, so called because when that famous Welsh worthy was about to summon a certain personage, who, though sufficiently ready to come when called, is rather a dangerous one to have dealings with, he used first to ensconce himself safely on this seat, where, surrounded by the stream, he was secure from the clutches of the ancient, if he should happen to provoke him overmuch. From this seat Hugh would discourse to him for a whole summer's day at a time. There are other traditions connected with the stream, which the tourist will be able to collect and piece-up for himself. We are tired of telling them.

From the mountains beyond Rhaiadr Cynfael there are very extensive and noble prospects. From Y-Foel Fawr the mountain prospect is particularly fine. The wide-ranging rugged chain on the opposite side of Ffestiniog, of which the triple peak of Moelwyn is the culminating point, is seen in all its grandeur, stretching away to the sea, while the giant Snowdon chain rises surge-like beyond and over it. More to the left, Cardigan Bay, with the low mountains bordering it, is a glorious object, as it lies glittering under the cloudless sky. On the other side is another mountain-tract which is crowned by the lofty Cader Idris. About these mountains are a good many small llyns. Just on the other side, towards the Dolgelley road, may be seen several objects of archæological interest. There are three or four barrows; the British fortress, Castell-Tomen-y-Mur, whose site is easily traceable; and the station, Heririmus, a little to the south-west of it, which is not quite so apparent. Moelwyn, the huge mountain-mass on the west of Ffestiniog, may be ascended without much difficulty: the summit affords prospects better known and more celebrated than those from the Foel Fawr chain, of which we have spoken. North of Ffestiniog there are also bold and lofty mountains, and about them are a good many llyns. In the vicinity are extensive slate-quarries: a railway for the conveyance of the slates to the ships, runs through the Vale of Ffestiniog.

Bala Lake will of course be visited: and as we did not turn aside to it when at Corwen, perhaps Ffestiniog is the best place to visit it from. It is a capital walk of about sixteen miles by a good mountain road; but the tourist may very well lengthen it a few miles by turning occasionally to the mountain side. The best way is to go down to Rhaiadr-Cynfael, and then proceed beside the stream to Pont Newydd (New Bridge). We need not repeat what we have just said of the beauty of this part of the Cynfael; but we may recommend the tourist not to miss that portion of it which is near Pont Newydd; for though it is not often visited, there are along here some as choice passages of the scenery characteristic of Welsh mountain streams as Creswick ever painted. From the bridge, keep by the river (on the left of it) to Cwm Cynfael, and then look ahead for another waterfall—not like Rhaiadr Cynfael, for here the little stream comes right down the steep mountain-side for a considerable distance, leaping from rock to rock in a narrow dark cleft or gulley. It is a bare wild spot, but, under favourable circumstances, both striking and romantic: no one will regret having followed the guidance of Cynfael thus far. This fall bears the name of Rhaiadr Cwm. By the road it is about three miles; by the way we have pointed out it may be a mile further from Ffestiniog; but no one who has the least feeling for river-scenery will hesitate a moment which route to choose, or be likely to measure the distance. Somewhat less than a mile to the north of Rhaiadr Cwm is a lonely lake, called Llyn-y-Morwynion, the Lake of the Maidens, from the maidens who attended that naughty dame, Blodewedd, the treacherous wife of Llaw Gyffes, having been drowned in it. Blodewedd herself escaped drowning, being changed into an owl; whence that bird of ill omen has ever since borne her name. The curious wanderer may even now see standing down by Cynfael side, the slate-rock through which Llaw Gyffes thrust his lance in order to reach her paramour. And so there is a fragment of another tradition about Cynfael, though we have just declared we would repeat no more: however it is only a fragment: if the reader wish to read the whole story, he will find it told at length in the 'Mabinogion,' that old Welsh story-book, which Lady Guest has translated into such graceful English, and illustrated with so choice and rich a collection of notes.

We need not describe the road further: it is mountainous all the way; and towards the latter part it runs between the mountains Arenig and Carnedd-y-Filiast; the former 2,809, and the latter 2,127 feet above the sea. If the pedestrian choose to keep the right-hand road when near the eighth milestone from Bala, and then bear up the mountain side, he may visit Llyn-Arenig, a circular mountain set in a frame of rough crags. He may also gain some wide views by the way.

The road leads into the town of Bala, which lies at the lower end of the lake. Bala is a good-sized and populous Welsh town, but is not a place in itself to interest the visitor. Bala Lake—in Welsh, Llyn Tegid—is the largest in Wales. As its dimensions are sometimes over-stated, it may be as well to give them accurately. The lake is nearly straight: a line through the centre measures rather more than three miles and a half: the broadest part is nearly five-eighths of a mile across. In size, therefore, it will not take rank alongside of the larger of the lakes of Cumberland and Westmorland—to say nothing of Scotland. And it will hardly bear to be compared with them for grandeur. Yet it will certainly remind the traveller of the secondary lakes of Cumberland, and not unpleasantly. Bala, especially from the lower end, is assuredly very beautiful. The broad dark lake, and the soft graceful

15.—PONT ABERGLASLYN.

frame of mountains, with the verdant slopes, the woods, a church or two, and a few villas and humbler houses, all repeated in the depths of the serene water, clear and perfect as they appear above, save where lines of silver stream across the blue expanse, form a picture which cannot be looked on without delight, or remembered without pleasure. A road is carried quite round the lake, and the circuit should be made: it will yield a grand diversity of prospects. Some of the very finest views of Bala are those obtained from the east side, looking towards Arenig. If it be perambulated, and afterwards a boat be taken upon the lake for an hour or two—and especially towards evening or by moonlight—Bala will not only be thoroughly seen, but certainly remembered. Seen from the heights at a little distance, the lake, lying nestled in the bosom of the mountains, has quite a new and most beautiful appearance.

Several streamlets flow down from the mountains, and enter the head of Bala Lake: the largest of them is known as Dwfrdwy, and is generally considered to be the head stream of the Dee; but it is difficult to imagine how that can be, unless, as old writers (and Camden among others) affirmed, the waters of the Dee passed through Pimble Mere (for so English writers used to call Llyn Tegid), without mingling with it. The river, which flows out of Bala Lake, is the Dee; and the vale along which it flows is known as the Vale of Edeirnion—by many considered to be one of the most lovely of the Welsh valleys. Bala Lake and the Dee here are both well known to anglers. In Bala great numbers of a fish called the gwyniaid, so named, it is said, from the whiteness of its scales, are taken; they are much esteemed for their delicate flavour. Bala is a good fishing station. Besides the lake, there are numerous mountain-llyns in the vicinity, which yield fair sport to a skilful artist.

We must not quit the banks of Bala without reminding the reader that they are classic ground. Llywarch Hen, one of the most famous of Welsh bards—the author of the 'Triads,' translated by Mr. William Owen —spent the last years of his life here, seeking to solace himself under his misfortunes; and perhaps finding comfort in repeating them. Llywarch had been a soldier before he became a bard: he took up his pen only when he laid aside his lance. When he wrote, he was "old and he was alone." There is something majestic in his statement of his grief:

> " Four-and-twenty sons, the offspring of my body ;
> By the means of my tongue they were slain :'
> Justly come is my budget of misfortunes.
>
> .   .   .   .   .   .
>
> Wretched is the fate that was fated
> For Llywarch on the night he was born,
> Long pains, without being delivered of his trouble."

His sorrows did not abbreviate his days much, if the tradition may be credited which makes him to have lived to the age of a hundred and fifty years. It is said that a spot in this neighbourhood is still shown as the place where he died, and that it bears his name. If the reader have not formed an acquaintance with the ancient Welsh triads, this translation of Llywarch Hen is the best he can turn to : it is full of real poetry.

Which is the best place to visit the famous cataract Pistyll Rhaiadr from is not easy to say : from no place is it very accessible. From Bala there is a way to it over the Bearwyn mountains ; but the distance is above fourteen miles of a rough mountain road. If the Vale of Edeirnion be descended, the road from Llandrillo, over the mountains, may be taken : the distance is some nine miles. The nearest village on the Denbigh-shire side is Llanrhaiadr, which is only about four miles from the fall. Pistyll Rhaiadr, the Spout of the Cataract, is formed by the little river Rhaiadr, which falls over a mountain side at the end of a close valley. It is a wild and lonely spot, and the waterfall has a most remarkable appearance. The water is said to fall the height of 240 feet. The rocky scarp down which it tumbles is bare, black, and precipitous, and contrasts well with the woody hollow ; but there is a want of water, unless after stormy weather ; and altogether it is hardly so fine an object as, from its height, would be expected. There is a little inn close by ; and the neighbourhood, we imagine, would be worth devoting a day or so to.

DOLGELLEY.

The road from Bala to Dolgelley it would be tedious to describe ; and, indeed, we believe the tourist would find it best to avail himself of the coach which runs during the summer months between these places. From Ffestiniog there is a very interesting road by the coast. Dolgelley is, like most Welsh towns, nought in itself. The houses are mean, irregular, and hardly picturesque ; the streets are narrow and dirty : it has a considerable population, and some trade. The manufacture of flannel, once carried on to some extent, has declined ; but of late the weaving of finer woollen cloths has been tried with success.

The interest of the place to tourists, however, consists altogether in its admirable situation as a centre from which to examine the beauties of this part of Merioneth-shire. Old Camden was moved to declare that Meri-oneth was matchless alike for the loveliness of its

women and the beauty of the country ; and what was indisputably true in the days of Elizabeth is no less certainly true in those of Victoria. So every native asserts ; and the stranger, though his means of judging are unhappily but limited, seldom hesitates to admit and corroborate the assertion. Great is the pity, there-fore, that we can make but brief tarriance in this land of loveliness ; but as we have indicated what is to be looked for, the visitor will not complain. We lingered too long at Ffestiniog and Bala to stay long here.

In whatever direction the stranger turns, he will find beauty on every hand : and the little town itself, though anything but beautiful when in it, is really a beautiful object when seen from a distance. More than in most parts of the mountainous districts, the ancient woods seem to have been preserved around Dolgelley : hence there is what is always so beautiful and cheerful,—a succession of rich prospects, formed by the combination of grand old trees with mountains and running streams. This may be witnessed to perfection by turning towards Nannau, the seat of Sir R. W. Vaughan : a spot famous for its almost matchless scenery, ancient hospitality, old traditions, and almost equally for its modern splen-dour. The park is extensive, broken into hill and dingle, well stored with venison, lively streams run through it, and it abounds in those

> " Old patrician trees
> And plebeian underwood"

that so distinguish English parks ; what kind of scenery it may exhibit, therefore, when the distant and finely-formed mountain summits—and old Cader is among the number—are added, will readily be conceived. Passing through Nannau, or taking the road, the next visit will be made to the waterfalls. The first of them, Rhaiadr Ddu, the Black Cataract, is about four miles from Dolgelley, on the road to Maentwrog : it stands within private grounds, but access is granted to it ; a path has been formed to the bottom, whence it can be best seen. The fall is said to be sixty feet ; there is a tolerable sheet of water ; the rocks around and above are crested with luxuriant wood ; and the scene alto-gether is striking and beautiful. Two or three miles farther is another fall, Pistyll-y-Cain, the Spout of the Cain. Here the water is precipitated from a height of 150 feet ; but the stream is comparatively small, the rocks are flat and regularly stratified ; and though there is wood, it, too, seems to partake of the prevalent formality. However, it might not always appear so, and Pistyll-y-Cain is at any rate sufficiently remarkable to deserve a visit. Not far from it is another but less important fall, the Rhaiadr-y-Mawddach, so called from the river by which it is formed. The neighbourhood is very picturesque.

This road to Maentwrog is not, as will be seen, lacking in interest : yet the road by the sea is the preferable one, as Barmouth and Harlech may be thus visited. We must run rapidly over the ground to Harlech. The road lies along the north bank of the Maw river, or Afon Mawddoch. A mile below Dolgelley a boat may be had, and the passage to Barmouth be made by water. It is a pleasant sail at full tide, but the scenery from the bank of the river is so fine that the tourist should go one way on foot. At Llanelltyd, two miles from Dolgelley, a little to the right of the long bridge, are the ruins of Kymmer Abbey : they are very slight, little more than a battered gable; but with the surrounding scenery, especially if made to form a foreground object to Cader Idris, abundantly picturesque —at least a clever painter would see how to make a good picture of them.

We have noticed in the book of a lady-tourist the remark, that in the journey between Barmouth and Dolgelley "it is difficult to decide as to which bank is to be preferred, both offering so much to be admired." In a coach it may be difficult (though, by the way, there is no coach-road on the south bank, and any road on that side to or from Barmouth will be found rather roundabout), but on foot the difficulty would quickly vanish. The scenery along the south bank cannot but be pleasing, but it cannot be more—along the north it is of almost indescribable beauty, and of the richest variety. After awhile (we are supposing that the tourist has chosen the time of full tide, else there is a muddy swamp) the stream expands rapidly into a broad and noble river ; the banks are richly wooded ; and looking across the river, southwards, you have the glorious range of mountains, of which Cader Idris is the chief, and which is of course invisible from the opposite bank ; whence you see a comparatively tame tract. About Glyn-dwr, eight miles from Dolgelley, the river makes a bold bend, and appears like an inland lake, of above a mile and a quarter broad, and several miles long. From the heights just by, you have a well-wooded foreground, then this fine sheet of water, and beyond, towering high above the lesser mountains, the magnificent form of Cader Idris. There are several other views hardly inferior. The views, too, up the river are very beautiful ; while downwards, the estuary of the Mawddoch, with the sea beyond and the high banks on either hand, is extremely fine.

Barmouth is a watering-place : whether as flourishing as it used to be we really do not know. It is a strange little town. The houses are oddly dotted about, here and there, in all sorts of queer and awkward situations; some by the beach, some on the hill-side almost on the top of each other, some in every out-of-the-way nook and corner. And they are as odd-looking as odd-placed. The town stands at the confluence of the river; in front stretches a long waste of shifting sand. The sand fills the roadway, fills the houses, promises to fill up the town. It is nevertheless a pleasant place, after its kind. There are boarding-houses and a library ; baths and a good beach ; also a pier. There is a capital hotel, wherein is a strenuous harper. There are young ladies and ladies of a certain age ; and there are gentlemen of the kind who commonly dawdle about at watering-places : and all are ever laudably watching for some new arrival, some new scandal, or some new thing, that may afford them some new occupation or topic of conversation. What more can the watering-place lounger desire ?

Very dull is the road between Barmouth and Harlech : every body says so, and every body is doubtless right. Yet there is the sea on one hand, and on the other is many an opening in the too monotonous mountain-slopes, which might well tempt aside a leisurely wanderer : and there are moreover many villages, Llan somethings or other (there are at least half a dozen of these Llans between Barmouth and Harlech), with their humble churches and churchyards, with the curiously inscribed grave-stones, calling you aside to rest or to moralize. There is, in truth, a good deal of quiet rustic character about some of these villages, and we cannot help thinking that he must be a somewhat fastidious person who finds this road quite intolerable. A little way past Lord Mostyn's house there are a couple of cromlechs at a short distance from the road.

Harlech Castle was built by Edward I.,—as native historians assert, on the site of an old British fortress. The situation is a strong one—and, what is more important at present, a picturesque one. The Castle stands on a lofty cliff, whose base was at one time washed by the sea, though now a marshy tract intervenes. The building is nearly a square, of two hundred feet each way, with round towers at the angles, and on each side of the chief entrance. On some of the towers slight fragments of the light turrets which rose from them yet remain. The castle is quite ruinous. Seen from the marsh below, its appearance, raised aloft on the edge of the steep rock, is very striking. But it appears even finer from the summit of the rocks just outside the road wall, a hundred yards or two before you reach the castle : there the building and the cliff on which it stands are both seen to perfection, while beyond is the broad Traeth Mawr, backed by a low dark range of mountains, above which are the cloud-capt peaks of Snowdon. (Cut, No. 16.)

MALLWYD is a pretty little village, and a favourite station for artists and anglers. It is seated on the Afon Dyfi, just in the loveliest part of its course, and is an excellent centre from which to visit some delightful scenery. Should the visitor determine to ascend Cader Idris, near Mallwyd, he may obtain a guide at Dolgelley, from which place the ascent will be best made. It is a noble-looking mountain, from whichever side beheld. The height above the sea is 2,914 feet. The sketch from which the wood-cut was engraved (Cut, No. 17) was taken from Brafch Coch, an eminence at the end of the valley through which the Machynlleth road is carried.

Having thus taken a cursory view of the principal places of interest in the mountainous districts of North Wales, we shall now direct the attention of the tourist to other scenes, which, though of a different character, will not prove the less interesting.

16.—HARLECH CASTLE.

17.—CADER IDRIS, FROM BRAFCH COCH.

DUBLIN AND ITS ENVIRONS.

THERE are just now many circumstances combining to direct the English tourist to Ireland rather than to those localities whither he has heretofore more commonly turned. The continent is no longer the pleasant land it lately was: Rome, Venice, Baden, and like places —almost the second homes of English fashionables— are closed against them; and everywhere, nearly, is heard the harsh voice of war or tumult warning away elegance and gaiety. Touring, it may be expected, will be for a brief while on native soil; and Ireland will have its full share of popularity. The tourists who are lovers of natural scenery will probably be tempted by the splendid mountains and lakes of Wicklow and Killarney, by Glengariff and the Giants' Causeway; but many besides the ordinary tourists will wend thitherward likewise. The grand EXHIBITION, and the unusual facilities offered by the Railway Companies, will doubtless attract numerous strangers to Ireland; while the hopeful calm which has succeeded the long dreary tempestuous season there, will induce not a few to acquaint themselves, by personal observation, with the scenes and circumstances which have engaged so long and so anxiously the public attention. Well will it be if it happen so. Assuredly the most serviceable and instructive, if not altogether the most pleasant, tour that English men and women can make just now, is the tour of Ireland. It is, indeed, almost a duty, for those who have any weight or influence in the country, to go there: and it is most desirable that every one who can go should do so. Notwithstanding all that he may have read and heard about Ireland, it is only when he has seen it for himself that an Englishman comes to comprehend distinctly its condition and its character. A short tour may not teach him much, but it will teach him something—and something of value, too, if he guard against hasty impressions and mere impulses. Ireland offers to one who visits it for the first time a field of observation as new and curious as almost any European country, and infinitely more interesting and suggestive. He must indeed travel to small purpose who gains nought by a journey there.

And there are no lions in the path. Often, even now, do you hear a journey in Ireland spoken of as a hazardous thing: it is certainly otherwise. Travelling, there, is as easy and safe, and almost as pleasant, as in England or Scotland—while it is very much cheaper. We say almost as pleasant, because there is the drawback of beholding the poverty, the wretchedness, and the mendicancy of the peasantry—which, we believe, are now rapidly passing away: but the very visiting may do something, and ought to do much, towards alleviating this state of things. Kindlier feelings must grow with increasing intercourse; and with mutual knowledge something will be done towards removing or softening the suspicion and distrust with which the inhabitants of the two countries unhappily regard each other. Only good can arise from more familiar acquaintance. Happy shall we be if we are able in some measure to promote so desirable an end—if we can induce more of our summer and autumn ramblers to visit the sister island, or, still better, if we can lead some thither who travel with other and nobler purposes than the mere gratification of curiosity, or the search after change of scene and personal enjoyment.

Our intention in the present part of our Tourist's itinerary is to notice briefly the Irish metropolis, and then to guide the reader to the more picturesque or celebrated parts of Wicklow: in a following part we shall continue the tour to Killarney and the south. We shall, of course, — as we have always done — carefully abstain from political and religious, or, at least, from party and sectarian, allusions; but before concluding we shall glance freely at the condition of the people and of the country: a sketch made at the present moment of any part of Ireland would be imperfect indeed in which that were omitted. The reader must not expect from us specimens of Irish wit or Irish brogue. Of the wit, we met with but very little: it seems, in truth, if a stranger may venture to say so, pretty well exhausted—starved out, it may be, as some native apologists affirm; or smothered by political passions, as others suggest. As for the brogue, that, though well enough to listen to from Patrick himself—especially when expressing some of those quaintnesses which only Patrick can utter—is hard to endure in print even from an Irish writer, and is utterly unbearable from an English or Scotch one. We therefore shall not make any assaults in this way on the reader's patience, and we shall leave Irish legends to Irish pens. In a word, not to bestow too much of our tediousness at the outset, all we propose is, to endeavour, in a few rough sketches, to convey the general impression derived from visits, unhappily far too hurried, to the spots we are to illustrate.

DUBLIN.

The first glimpse of the Green Island is well calculated to put the visitor into good humour with it. He will sail from the fine harbour of Holyhead in one of the admirable packet steamers. At first, the rugged South Stack rock and lighthouse, with the amazing flocks of gulls and divers that are in constant motion about them, engage his attention. Then the noble range of the Snowdon mountains comes into view. These presently disappear; but long before the eye becomes tired of the unbroken expanse of ocean, the mountains of Wicklow rise on the westward horizon.

More and more grandly they continue to rise as the steamer cleaves its swift way through the waters, until the heights of Howth and Killiney, which form the opposite boundaries of Dublin Bay, are plainly distinguished : when the distant mountain summits are hardly noticed, even as a part of the general view. Dublin Bay never fails to impress the stranger with unexpected delight. It is one of the most beautiful, if not the most beautiful, bay in the kingdom. The points of the semicircle, nearly seven miles apart, form bold headlands, enclosing a splendid bay, six or seven miles deep, which is pretty thickly besprinkled with ships of various sizes, with yachts, and steamers, and fishing-boats ; the fine sweep of coast being bordered with neat villages, terraces of handsome houses, and scattered villas ; in the centre the estuary of the Liffey guides the eye towards the city ; while beyond are the pointed summits of graceful mountains. It is a scene which every Irishman is, as he well may be, heartily proud of, and of which every one who has beheld it cherishes the memory.

Kingstown, where the steamer disembarks its passengers, is nearly seven miles from Dublin. Here the stranger, as he makes his way to the railway-station, catches his earliest bit of Irish experience from the clamorous crowd which beset him, all proffering service, or exposing their wants, abusing each other and bothering him, in a quite new dialect. By the help of a few stray coppers (and of the policemen, who seem in a perfect fever of anxiety to keep a clear road,) he soon gains the railway that as quickly forwards him to the city, and an outside-car speedily deposits him at his hotel.

These outside-cars, by the way, are excellent things ; and we must give them a passing word of commendation. A stranger cannot desire a better means of making a rapid general survey of the city before he proceeds to examine it in detail, than that of driving on one of these conveyances through the principal streets. Some travellers recommend ascending to an elevated spot which commands a good view of a town, as the best means of getting the *coup-d'œil*; and, doubtless, it is a plan which has its advantages. You come to understand readily the topography of a place which is thus spread, as it were, in ground-plan, at your feet : but you get an unfair and unfavourable notion of it : the buildings appear distorted, the nearer parts assume an undue prominency. In driving at a moderate pace through the main streets of a city, the relative importance of its parts is tolerably well understood, and the chief objects are fixed in the memory as landmarks which effectually direct you in future explorations. For such a ride a solitary stranger will find the Irish car a capital contrivance, and the carman, who sits with him so comfortably *dos-à-dos*, a very useful and amusing commentator and guide, if he only be treated with a little sociality. Of course some care must be exercised in crediting what he says. Carmen and guides all over Ireland are, as they say of each other, "rare boys for romancing ;" and the Dublin

boys beat all the rest. The traveller does not need to be reminded that he must exercise, too, some discretion about admitting the fares which carmen charge : he has, no doubt, had sufficient experience already on that subject. London cabmen contrive now and then to make mistakes about distance : Liverpool cabmen have the reputation of being (as they doubtless are) the greatest cheats of the fraternity in England : but both these are mere novices and bunglers compared with their Dublin brethren. Pat does it with such a grace—so coolly and civilly, as well as broadly ! It is hard if he does not, either by barefaced assertion or blarney, get something more than his due. One we hired the other day from one of the railway-stations, may serve as an example. After our ride, we put into his hand the exact fare. "Sure now," said he, looking from the coin to the giver with a comic stare, as if unable to contain his astonishment, "sure now, your honour'd never be so offering *this* to a poor man ?—look at the long ride yez been having now : by dad ! it's above four hours and a half you have been driving about !" Thinking we had him tight enough for once, we said, with all the mildness we could muster, "Haven't you made some mistake in reckoning the time ?—the train came in at eleven, and see, it is not quite twelve yet !" But Mike, without the least discomposure, answered, "Why then, it's some sort of mistake I must be making ; but this is a rare nate horse for going,—and, anyhow, it's a mighty long way yez have bin :" and then he proceeded to enumerate the distances, which, according to his reckoning, came to almost his four hours' work ; winding up, as he put on his most persuasive face, with—" Yer honour's a better scholar than I am : just put them together, and —give me whatever you plaze ; for bad luck to me for ever if it shall be said Mike Casey took a dirty advantage of sich a free-spoken honourable gentleman, anyhow—poor as he is !"

The result of an Englishman's rapid examination of Dublin will probably be that it is larger, grander, more modern, and less English in appearance, than he anticipated. At least, that was our impression of it. Dublin is, in form, a decided "tendency to circularity." The diameter is about three miles ; the 'Circular Road' by which it is nearly surrounded is somewhat under eight miles in extent. The population of the city is above a quarter of a million. The river Liffey runs due east and west through the city, dividing it into two nearly equal portions. Old Dublin, which contains the castle and the two cathedrals (and which Mitchell described as the stronghold of Young Ireland), occupies the western portion of the southern half : the remainder of the city is comparatively modern. In the old part the streets are narrow, the houses mean ; but in the modern part—that is, in the chief part— the streets are broad and straight, the houses of fair size and well built, and the public buildings, which are numerous, generally of commanding appearance, both from their extent and architectural character. All the streets are thronged with passengers ; and if there is a smaller number of coaches and of carts than in London, there appears to be a much larger proportion of cars; which are indeed so numerous, and in such general request among all classes, that one is led to believe that in Dublin everybody makes a point of riding who has sixpence in his pocket to pay for a 'set-down.'*

Besides the broad, well-built, and thronged streets, there are several very large squares, surrounded by handsome mansions. The river, in its passage through the city, is confined within thick granite walls, and is crossed by nine bridges, below the first of which it is crowded with ships and steamers, moored along the quays. The whole conveys the impression of a noble, a wealthy, and a busy city. So long as he keeps to the main thoroughfares, the visitor is full of admiration of Dublin; but as he extends his peregrinations, he soon becomes aware that it is encircled with an undue proportion of wretched, poverty-stricken, and unwholesome streets and alleys, which do, indeed, not merely surround the city, but, at every turn, force their way up into the very heart of it.

We cannot give even a cursory view of the history of Dublin, as we have done in noticing other cities and towns. The history of Dublin is too intimately blended with the history of Ireland to allow of its being told without running to greater length than our space permits, and trenching on matters we wish to avoid. Its epochs, its changes, and its fortunes, are involved with all the great and small events of the national story. Yet the history of Dublin would be an interesting theme in the hands of one who, while master of his subject and able to treat it without party spirit, could also reanimate the past, and restore to present times the Dublin of old. Strange have been its changes, and curious would be its domestic history. The Town of the Ford of Hurdles (for so native historians translate its Celtic name of Bally-ath-cliath); the Eblana of Ptolemy; the Dubh-lynn, or Black-pool of somewhat later times, must remain hidden in the dim mist that envelopes all the early history of the land of Erin; and even the Four Masters, were they to return to earth, would hardly be able to dissipate the obscurity. What was its condition in the glorious days of Brian Boroimhe, or of Malachi of the Collar of Gold; or in the gloomier days of Strongbow, and later Saxon conquerors, we can scarcely expect or desire to learn; but as we descend the stream of time clearer pictures become visible. Till recently, the very houses spoke of the influence of the English spirit which prevailed in the reign of queen Elizabeth.† Hints as to its state in the succeeding century are not wanting. Then come abundant notices of the Dublin in which Swift lived and ruled. How remarkable was the state of society

* A drive direct from any part of the city to any other part, without alighting on the way, is called a 'set-down;' and the legal fare for it is only sixpence—which, as the car carries four passengers, is enough to tempt those who do not like walking.

† See Whitelaw's 'History of Dublin.'

there half a century later, may be seen in the 'Sketches of Ireland Sixty Years ago:' and what it was before and after the Union is told in many a grave volume and scattered memoir. That well-abused event unquestionably wrought a vast alteration in the Irish metropolis. When Parliament no longer assembled there, the 'notables' ceased to make it their residence; and the tone of manners gradually changed: yet the city itself suffered no decay, but has rather gone on steadily increasing in size and population, and improving in appearance: may it continue to increase also in prosperity.

We will now undertake to look a little more closely at the city. The main streets, we have said, are of striking appearance. The two grand thoroughfares are the Quays, as the roadway by the Liffey is called, which, as was mentioned, runs east and west, through the centre of the city; and Sackville and Grafton Streets, which run at right angles to the quays, or north and south. There are several other streets hardly inferior in importance to these, and many more that are in nowise remarkable: altogether the city is said to contain 800 streets,—but we should think the number overrated.

Sackville Street deserves all the admiration which the citizens bestow upon it. It is one of the noblest streets in the kingdom. Its unusual width—120 feet throughout—imparts to it an air of majesty which the style and arrangement of the houses, and also of the buildings which terminate the vista in each direction, are, on the whole, well calculated to sustain. But it is not so rich in public edifices as some other streets, and perhaps its great width is an inconvenience to foot-passengers, while it certainly makes the houses, though really lofty, appear to want elevation. Near the centre of Sackville Street stands the Nelson Column,—one of those erections which the perversity of architects and committees have so superabundantly inflicted on the memory of our great naval hero. On the top of this, as on all these pillars, the unlucky admiral is perched, like another St. Simon, for the edification and contemplation of rooks and skylarks; he is beyond the ken of human eyes, unless assisted by a good telescope. The column is Doric; the shaft, which is fluted, is, with the capital, about eighty feet high; it stands on a pedestal about thirty feet high; the podium on which the statue is placed is twelve feet and a half high. Nelson himself is thirteen feet high, and his height from the ground is about 125 feet. We can say nothing as to the sculpture, for we were unable to make it out, but certainly the column (though in itself as little to be commended as that in Trafalgar Square) assists in giving an appearance of dignity to the street. It presents an imposing central object for the eye to rest upon, and prevents the sort of straggling unconnected look which the two sides of an extremely broad street have a tendency to exhibit. Standing, too, as it does, at the junction of the long line of Henry and Earl Streets with Sackville Street, it is seen conspicuously from many points. Close by the Nelson Pillar is the Post Office, a very handsome building, which was erected, in the year 1817, from the designs of Francis Johnston. It has a frontage of about 220 feet, is 150 feet in depth, and fifty feet high. The chief feature is a fine hexastyle portico, of the Ionic order, which is eighty feet wide, and projects over the footpath. The pediment is surmounted by a statue of Hibernia in the centre, with others at the extremities of Mercury and Fidelity. The building itself is constructed of mountain granite, the portico of Portland stone. Architectural critics may doubtless find some imperfections in the style, but to an ordinary observer its appearance is at once simple, dignified, and substantial.

One of the most favourite points of view, to which the citizens lead a stranger in order to show the interior of the city to advantage, is Carlisle Bridge. From it you look along the Liffey on one hand, full of ships, the quays alive with a busy and noisy multitude, the road bordered by goodly buildings, the chief of which, the Custom House, serves as a crowning grace to the picture. On the other hand, the Liffey, as it winds gently between its broad, granite embankments, is seen crossed by several bridges: the quays, though little used for commerce, present abundant signs of activity; numerous public buildings and churches are visible wholly or in part; the classic dome of the Four Courts rises high above the meaner structures; and in the extreme distance are the wooded heights of Phœnix Park, crowned by the Wellington Testimonial. Northward is Sackville Street, with its column and stately buildings, the distance being terminated by the Rotundo. Southward, D'Olier Street and Westmoreland Street diverge, each affording more than commonly pleasing effects of street architecture. But perhaps Grafton Street, or College Green, the very centre of the busiest part of the city, where the magnificent fronts of Trinity College and the Bank are seen in combination, presents the most striking appearance to the stranger. We have selected College Green for an engraving, (Cut No. 1), because, though perhaps less striking than Grafton Street, it is more adapted for a wood-cut. The equestrian statue in the front is the celebrated statue of William III., which was the object of so many party contests, both with pen and shillelagh, in the more pugnacious days of "ould Ireland."

The Bank is the building which Swift has celebrated in his terrible verses, entitled 'The Legion Club.'

> "As I stroll the city oft, I
> See a building large and lofty;
> Not a bow-shot from the college—
> Half the globe from sense and knowledge;
> By the prudent architect
> Placed against the church direct,—
> Making good my grandam's jest,
> ' Near the church '—you know the rest."

In other words, it is the old Irish Parliament House, where, before the Union, the Irish representatives

> "Sat in grand committeé
> How to plague and starve the city."

The original House of Parliament was erected early in the eighteenth century; but being found too small, was subsequently greatly enlarged; it was completed in the form in which it now appears in 1794, at a cost of £95,000. After the Union, being no longer required for legislative purposes, it was sold to the Governor and Company of the Bank of Ireland for the sum of £40,000, and an annual rent of £240:— and by them it will doubtless be held till that fine morning when O'Connell's oft-repeated prediction shall be fulfilled, and Erin see her chosen sons once more assembled in College Green. On the whole this is the finest building in Dublin, and one of the very finest in the kingdom. It is far grander than the Bank of England—forming, instead of a number of ' pretty bits' like that much-praised pile, a consistent and magnificent whole. In form it is nearly a semicircle. The grand front looking on College Green consists of " a noble colonnade of Ionic pillars raised on a flight of steps, and ranged round three sides of a spacious quadrangular recess in which is the court-yard. The colonnade supports an entablature and cornice of the same order, surmounted by an attic. In the centre of the recess projects a fine portico of four Ionic columns, sustaining a tympanum, in which appear, in bas-relief, the royal arms; while the apex is ornamented with a colossal statue of Hibernia, supported by Fidelity on the western, and Commerce on the eastern points. Circular screen walls behind columns, surmounted with an entablature and cornice, run from each extremity of the central pile, and connect it with the eastern and western fronts. The former of these, facing College Street, is a beautiful Corinthian portico of six pillars, the tympanum of which is surmounted by a figure of Fortitude, with Justice on the one side and Liberty on the other. The western portico is Ionic." (*M'Glashan's ' Dublin.'*) The architect employed in the enlargement and completion of the building was Gandon, to whose genius Dublin owes so much of its splendour. Since its conversion into a bank the interior has of course undergone an entire change—except the House of Lords, which yet retains very much of its original appearance. In the recess which was occupied by the throne, now stands a statue of George the Third.

Trinity College is also a noble pile; worthy of the metropolitan university. To Cantabs and Oxonians, who are so accustomed to associate Gothic architecture with collegiate edifices, it is perhaps at first sight a little disappointing; while in the eyes of pragmatic mediæval ecclesiologists it is an abomination. We confess if it were to do again we should prefer Gothic to Grecian for such a building, but we are well content to take it as it is—and rejoice that a classic style being chosen, so fine a building is the result.

Trinity College was founded in the 34th year of the reign of Queen Elizabeth (1592), under the title of the ' College of the Holy and Undivided Trinity, near Dublin.' This title it still retains, though it is to all purposes a university—and more correctly styled, as it often is, Dublin University. The original found-

1.—BANK AND TRINITY COLLEGE, DUBLIN.

ation consisted of a provost, three fellows, and three scholars. As increased by various augmentations and benefactions, it now consists of the provost, seven senior fellows, twenty-three junior fellows, with ten fellowships recently founded by the college, the various professors and teachers, seventy-five scholars, and thirty sizars. The number of students generally averages about 1,400. If it cannot exhibit a roll of scholars rivalling those of Oxford or Cambridge, it has a list of which it may well be proud.

The grand front of Trinity College is turned towards College Green. It is about 300 feet long, and three stories in height; the order is Corinthian. The centre consists of a pediment supported by four columns; the wings are terminated by pavilions, which are ornamented with coupled pilasters, and raised a story higher than the rest of the front. Altogether the effect is rich and stately. The large quadrangle, in which are the chapel, the library, the refectory, the theatre, and lodgings for the fellows, is of noble proportions, being 570 feet long by 270 feet broad. It is consequently much larger than the quadrangles of any of the English Colleges; Trinity College, Cambridge, being 334 feet long, by 325 feet where widest; and Christ Church, Oxford, 264 feet by 261 feet. But though the several buildings are sufficiently imposing, it, to our thinking, has by no means the same venerable collegiate air as either of those we have mentioned. The next quadrangle, Park Square, which is 280 feet by 194 feet, is recent and common-place. The third quadrangle is commonly known by a name of unpleasant sound and associations—Botany Bay: both these are chiefly appropriated to apartments for the students. Beyond these quadrangles there is the College Park, a pleasant piece of ground of about twenty acres, planted with trees, and containing the magnetic observatory and school of anatomy building; it is open to the public. There are also gardens for the fellows. Several of the buildings deserve inspection. The chapel, which is on the north side of the great quadrangle, is a neat edifice, Corinthian in style, the architect of which was Sir William Chambers. The interior is handsomely fitted up: the choir is celebrated: the choral service is open to the public. The library is a very handsome building, three stories high. The façade, which is 270 feet in length, is built of mountain granite, and has a very fine effect. The principal room, a magnificent apartment, extends nearly the whole length of the building, being 210 feet long, forty-one feet broad, and forty feet high. In front of the presses which contain the books, is a series of busts of eminent men both ancient and modern. The books in this room are above 110,000. In a room beyond is another very valuable collection called the Fagel Library, from having been purchased of a Dutch family of that name: it consists of about 18,000 volumes. The library contains a celebrated collection of manuscripts, some of which are of great value; admission to it is only granted for a special purpose. Corresponding in size and style with the chapel is the theatre, which is worth visiting for the portraits it contains of several

of the more eminent scholars of Trinity College; and also for a very elaborate monumental group, in memory of Provost Baldwin. It consists of several figures, and is much admired: the sculptor was a native artist, Mr. Hewetson.

On the south-side of the great quadrangle is the refectory; a building which every one familiar with the English colleges will be likely to turn to with some interest. But it is disappointing. In collegiate edifices, classic dining-rooms seem but poor substitutes for the noble old Gothic halls. This, for example, (not to speak irreverently,) reminds one but too forcibly of an English provincial assembly-room. However, it is a fine room, and of ample proportions, being some seventy-five feet long, by thirty-five wide, and as many high. The portraits form its chief attraction; among them the most noteworthy are those of the Fox and Pitt of the Irish House of Commons,—Grattan and Flood.

Perhaps, however, the room which will most interest the ordinary visitor is the Museum. The collection is a very general one; there are minerals, fossils, antiquarian relics, South Sea and Indian idols, weapons, and garments, and so forth. But the portion which will chiefly attract the stranger is the collection of early Irish antiquities, which is varied and tolerably extensive,—too much so for us to touch upon here.

Supposing the visitor to be interested in these remains, we strongly advise him not to neglect, while in Dublin, to visit the Museum of the Royal Irish Academy, which is just by the College, i. e., in Dawson Street, opposite the Provost's House. The Irish Academy was founded towards the close of the last century, "for the study of polite literature, science, and antiquities," to quote the terms of the Act of Incorporation. The study of Irish archæology, and the collecting of Irish antiquities, have been from the first the most prominent features of the Institution. The results are shown in the publication of many elaborate memoirs, and in the contents of the Museum. This is by far the largest and finest collection of Celtic remains in the world. Many of the specimens in gold, silver, and the less precious metals are both "rich and rare." They consist of torques, and other personal ornaments; reliquaries, crosiers, patens, and other articles connected with religious purposes. There is also a goodly store of weapons in bronze, and iron, and stone, some curious bronze horse-bits, trumpets, and other matters, that speak of warlike service. In the library is a choice collection of ancient Irish manuscripts.

From the Academy the visitor should, in order to complete his examination of Irish antiquities, proceed to the house of the Royal Dublin Society in Kildare Street. The building itself will repay the visit. It is a very handsome one; originally it was the residence of the Duke of Leinster, from whom it was purchased by the Society in 1815, for the sum of £20,000. The objects of the Dublin Society, as stated in its Act of Incorporation, are much more various than those of the Irish Academy. It was founded in 1731 "for the

Improvement of Husbandry, Manufactures, and other useful Arts and Sciences." From the Irish Parliament the Society received an annual grant of £10,000; from the Imperial Parliament it only receives half that sum. From the variety of subjects to which the Society directs its attention, there is a considerable diversity of objects to be seen within its walls. The Museum occupies several rooms. In natural history it is especially rich; but a mere mention of it will suffice here: the enormous Irish elk, which is the chief feature of this part of the collection, is a remarkably fine specimen; but specimens of it are now to be met with in England: that at the British Museum, or at Cambridge, will perhaps be familiar to the reader. The Irish antiquities, which chiefly led us here at this time, deserve careful inspection. An examination of these collections of remains, found so abundantly in Ireland, will not fail to give rise to much curious speculation, and perhaps lead to further inquiry into a subject full of interest, though comparatively little known to Englishmen. But we must hasten on. One object of the Dublin Society was the promotion of the Arts, and here may be seen some of the productions in painting and sculpture of the pupils who have attained eminence. Of living artists, Sir Martin Archer Shee, the President of the Royal Academy, and Mr. Behnes, the celebrated sculptor, may be mentioned as old pupils of the Society. A room is set apart for a collection of casts from the Elgin Marbles, &c. There is also an Agricultural Museum, containing models of farmhouses, cottages, and other objects connected with the science. Besides these, there is a good library. Altogether, an hour or two will be well employed in examining the rooms. Certain days are set apart for the admission of the public to the different departments; but any part, or the whole, may at any time be seen by strangers visiting Dublin upon presenting their cards. This very considerate and handsome arrangement, we ought to mention, is also adopted at Trinity College, the Irish Academy, and other institutions in Dublin. But it is only just to add, that everywhere in Dublin the stranger meets with the greatest courtesy and readiness to afford him all proper facility.

But it is time to visit the vice-regal abode, and the older part of the city—which, indeed, ought to have been done before, as they seem to be fairly entitled to precedence in any account of Dublin. The Castle is situated at the end of Dame Street,—the prolongation westward of College Green. In passing towards it, the famous equestrian statue of William the Third, the object of so many a battle, will of course be noticed. It is of bronze; but when the Corporation of Dublin was thoroughly 'Orange,' they used to have it always newly painted against the 1st of July; and on that morning it was sure to be adorned with orange ribbons. The opposite party, of course, also daubed it,—but not with orange paint; and then there was a fight. The unlucky king has had, in the course of the century and a half that he has stood there, to endure an abundance of maltreatment, from both friends and foes; but as the feeling on both sides appears to be losing its intensity, it is to be hoped that the hero may be permitted to anticipate future Julys, without dread of losing sword, or nose, or obtaining a new coat of paint. The position of the statue is shown in the woodcut. Dame Street has one or two good buildings, and some large and handsome shops.

Cork Hill, on which the Castle stands, is the highest ground in the city; but it is so built upon that the exterior of the Castle cannot be seen as a whole, which, however, need excite no regret. The site was, no doubt, chosen with a view at once to defend and command the old city, which extends westward from it. The erection of the original castle commenced early in the thirteenth century; it was completed in 1220. The present castle is almost wholly modern; and, as an architectural object, as poor and unsatisfactory as can well be conceived. A large gateway, on which is a statue of Justice, leads to the Upper Castle Yard—a quadrangle, 280 feet long by 180 feet broad, in which are the state-apartments and official residence of the Lord Lieutenant, which occupy the whole of the south side and part of the east; while the apartments of the Chief Secretary, the Dean of the Chapel Royal, and other officers of the household occupy the rest of the Court. The state-apartments, as will be supposed, are not wanting in splendour. The Presence Chamber, which contains the throne, is a handsome room, and fitted up in a costly manner: the throne is extremely rich. The Council Chamber contains portraits of all the Lord Lieutenants since the Union. Other public rooms are also more or less noticeable: but the finest of the state-apartments—and, in truth, the only one that is particularly worth going to see—is St. Patrick's Hall, a noble room, eighty-two feet long, forty-one feet broad, and thirty-eight feet high, with galleries at each end. The ceiling is divided into compartments, which are painted with subjects connected with Irish history.

In the Lower Castle Yard (Cut, No. 2,) are the Bermingham or Record Tower, and the Chapel Royal. The Bermingham Tower is the only part of the Castle which is at all ancient; alone, it is not very picturesque, or of much interest; but, from its height, it serves to indicate the site of the Castle from the suburbs. As its name intimates, it is now used as a depository for the state records. The Chapel Royal is a very elaborate, but not particularly successful, example of modern Gothic. It consists merely of a choir: its dimensions are seventy-three feet long by thirty-five feet broad. At the eastern end there is a large perpendicular window; on each side are seven buttresses with crocketed pinnacles. Around the exterior is a good deal of carving: among others are the heads of the entire series of English kings. The sculpture over the northern entrance is a curious fancy: the head of St. Peter is placed above the door, and over it the head of Dean Swift! The interior is extremely elaborate, and rather striking in effect; but it hardly sustains a close examination. Every part is highly ornamented; but like the groined roof, all appears imitative plaster-

1.—LOWER CASTLE YARD.

work, instead of the good old free hand-carving of real Gothic churches. All the windows are filled with stained glass. The galleries are distinguished by having crimson-curtained thrones in the midst: that on the south side is for the Lord Lieutenant,—the opposite one is for the Archbishop of Dublin. The viceroy generally attends the service on Sunday mornings, and the chapel is usually crowded.

The Lower Court is a large quadrangle, 280 feet by 220 feet; but there is little to be noticed in it. In it are the ordnance-office, the arsenal, and the armoury, in which, among its other contents, are 60,000 muskets. In the Castle, too, are the head-quarters of the Metropolitan Police. A guard of both horse and foot soldiers remains constantly on duty at the Castle, which, from the number of soldiers and policemen about it, contrasts rather curiously with our London palaces.

On Cork Hill, near the entrance to the Castle, is a building called the City Hall, formerly the Royal Exchange. It was erected in 1769, from a design by Thomas Cooley, the celebrated native architect; and it is universally admitted to be one of the most graceful buildings of the kind in existence. It is a square of about 100 feet, surmounted with a dome, and has three fronts. The principal front consists of a noble portico of six Corinthian columns, which stand on a high basement and support an enriched entablature and pediment. The interior is even more elegant than the outside, and should be seen. In the area are several statues.

There is little in the old city besides the cathedrals

to attract the visitor. Though older than in the other parts, the houses are not ancient; and the oldest of them have suffered too much from decay and reparation to be in any way noteworthy. And as there is no antiquity to attract, neither is there any picturesqueness: but there is squalid misery almost past conception. A few of the streets are tolerably wide; but by far the greater number are narrow, and many are without thoroughfares: all seem given up to the very poor, and those who supply them with provisions and other necessaries. That the dirt and odour of these streets are endured in these days of sanatory reformation is quite surprising. The household dirt is perhaps too sacred to be interfered with; but the streets, one would think, might be kept clean, and the refuse, if permitted to be thrown in them, at least occasionally be cleared away. Yet, dirty as the streets are, the stranger must be of resolute nerves who does not speedily take to the middle of them, in order to escape from the vicinity of the houses. If the visitor should attend the cathedral service on Sunday morning, it would (if he can put up with some few "sights and sounds and scents vexatious") be worth while to come half an hour before the time for a stroll through this locality. There is, of course, no Sabbath quiet here: the shops are open, and more than commonly busy,—especially the spirit stores and old clothes shops. The

"Jolly lads of St. Patrick's, St. Kevin's, Donore,"

have done with early mass, and are now beginning to grow a little lively, if not uproarious. Beggars abound (for beggars appear, on Sundays, always to seek alms in the poorer localities), and are trying every means to obtain a trifle. We, a few Sundays back, heard three or four families of them singing emigrant and other begging songs along these streets and the wretched streets on the north and west sides of the city. Altogether, there is something as striking in the noise and activity of the streets of Dublin as in the quiet and comparative desertion of those of Edinburgh.

If the dwelling-houses of the old city are not very old-looking, it is otherwise with the churches. St. Patrick's Cathedral is very old, and looks older. The style is early English, and it is nearly uniform. But it is far inferior in beauty of detail, as well as in general character and size, to many English cathedrals in which the same style prevails. It is cruciform, with a lofty but not very elegant tower, and a plain spire. The dimensions are: length, 300 feet; breadth, eighty feet. On the whole, the exterior is chiefly remarkable for a certain rude massiveness of appearance. The interior is much finer, and has recently undergone very extensive repairs. The nave was formerly in a dilapidated state, and the stone roof entirely gone; but a thorough restoration having been effected, it now forms an object of antiquarian interest, and possesses much grandeur of effect. The floor is raised above the bases of the columns. The choir is lofty, and of fine proportions; and though not to be compared with the choirs of most English cathedrals, has much to interest the admirers of ecclesiastical architecture. The arches of the triforium, some of the windows, and the capitals of the columns, are very beautiful. In the choir are the archbishop's throne, the stalls of the chapter, and those of the knights of St. Patrick, over each of which are suspended the helmet, sword, and banner of the knight who occupies it.

In the nave and choir are several monuments that command attention. The largest and showiest is that to the Earl of Cork,—one of those strange, huge, sculptural combinations of several stories, which were fashionable in the 17th century; it is a rather remarkable and striking specimen of the class. There are also monuments of several archbishops, and some of other distinguished persons. The monuments which are the chief attraction, however, are three mere mural tablets,—but they bear the name of Swift, and suggest many recollections connected with his history. One, a plain slab of black marble, affixed to a pillar on the southern side of the nave, marks the spot where the remains of Jonathan Swift were deposited, and contains the terrible inscription, of his own writing,—" Ubi sæva indignatio ulterius cor lacerare nequit!" On the adjoining pillar is another tablet, to the memory of " Mrs. Hester Johnson, better known to the world by the name of Stella, under which she is celebrated in the writings of Dr. Jonathan Swift, dean of this cathedral." The other monument to which we referred is in the choir, and is to the memory of the celebrated Duke Schomberg. It was erected by Swift, who wrote the bitter epitaph. George I. was so much displeased with the reflections cast by it on the descendants of Schomberg, that he took public notice of it, declaring that " the Dean of St. Patrick's had put up that monument out of malice, in order to stir up a quarrel between himself and the King of Prussia," who had married Schomberg's granddaughter. " It caused," say the biographers of Swift, " an irreconcileable breach with the court."

Christ Church Cathedral is situated some little distance north of St. Patrick's and nearer the Castle. It is the older building of the two, but it has been so often altered and repaired as to retain little of its original character. Nor is it in its present state either grand or picturesque, externally; while the interior has little of the venerable solemnity we are accustomed to expect in a Gothic cathedral. Some time back it was thoroughly ' repaired and beautified;' it is therefore in nearly as good a state as that of St. Patrick's, but it will not afford the same kind of gratification to the general visitor, or the student of Gothic architecture. It is commonly visited by strangers who admire the cathedral service, on account of its fine organ and the choir, which is sometimes said to be the best in Ireland. But we were very unlucky in the two services we attended, for the singing was more slovenly and the conduct of the boy-choristers far more irreverent than it was ever our mishap to witness in any other cathedral or chapel choir,—and that is saying a good deal. There are some ancient monuments of considerable interest in Christ Church, and numerous modern ones. But we need not make a longer tarryance.

It will be as well, perhaps, to notice the other ecclesiastical edifices before turning to another subject. Dublin is divided into twenty parishes, and in addition to the churches which belong to them, there are also several chapels-of-ease. Very few of the churches are ancient, and none of those are very remarkable. St. Audoen's, near the Corn-market, though only a fragment of the original church, is one of the most beautiful examples of Gothic architecture in Dublin,—and it contains some curious old monuments. St. Michan's, on the opposite side of the Liffey, is noteworthy as the burial-place of many who have gained a name in the recent history of Ireland. But several of the churches, which are quite uninteresting in themselves, have memorials that will be looked upon with more or less respect. One of the poorest, for instance, St. Anne's, in Dawson-street, contains monuments in memory of that sweet singer, Mrs. Hemans, and of Cæsar Otway, whose descriptions of Irish scenery have done so much to attract attention to the beauties of the country and the condition of the peasantry. Most of the modern churches are of the Greek or Roman orders of architecture. Some of them are admirable specimens of the adaptation of the classic forms to Christian churches. The finest is St. George's Church; it is situated in Hardwick Place, at the northern extremity of the city, —a rather out-of-the-way locality, but it will repay the journey. It has in the principal front a very fine tetrastyle Ionic portico. The steeple, which is about 200 feet high, displays much originality as well as good taste, and combines with the Grecian temple-architecture very much better than is usual with such incongruous objects as steeples. The architect was Francis Johnston, and it is one of his best works.

The Roman Catholic churches and chapels are very numerous; they are, of course, all modern, and, like the churches of the Established Church, they are commonly 'classic' in style. The prevalent Gothic feeling is only now finding vent in the new churches of both communions which are rising in the suburbs. One Gothic Catholic Chapel, however, may be pointed to, St. Michan's, in Anne-street, as, though far from perfect, a very pleasing and ornamental structure: it is built entirely of mountain granite. The most important of the Roman Catholic places of worship are the Church of the Conception and St. Andrew's Chapel. The former, often called the Metropolitan Chapel, is a magnificent structure; the style is Grecian Doric; the principal front has a massive hexastyle portico raised on a platform; the apex and extremities of the pediment are surmounted with colossal figures of the Virgin, St. Patrick, and St. Lawrence O'Toole. The south side also presents an elaborate frontage to the street. The interior is divided into a nave and aisles by a series of columns, which support an arched roof. The eastern end terminates in an apsis, from which the altar, a costly structure of white marble, stands detached. Altogether the appearance of the interior is very imposing, especially if seen during the performance of high mass. This chapel is said to have cost £40,000. St. Andrew's Chapel is situated in Westland Row, close by the terminus of the Kingstown Railway. This, like the Metropolitan Chapel, is a Grecian Doric structure. It is cruciform, and of spacious dimensions, the nave and choir being 160 feet long, the transepts 150 feet; the breadth and height are twenty feet. But the front of the chapel is prolonged at each end by the priests' houses, and thus forms a Doric façade, 160 feet long. On the pediment is a colossal statue of St. Andrew. The effect of the exterior is by no means good. The interior is less heavy. " The walls are divided into compartments with Grecian Doric pilasters. The grand altar consists of four massive pillars of Giallo Antico, which support a pediment similar to the Lantern of Demosthenes at Athens. The tabernacle and sarcophagus are of Italian marble; over the former is a fine group of figures, representing the Transfiguration; they are the work of our celebrated Irish artist, Hogan."— (M'Glashan.) St. Paul's Chapel, Arran Quay, and that of St. Francis Xavier, Upper Gardiner Street, are both very elegant structures.

If the stranger spends a Sunday afternoon in Dublin, he might visit one of the Catholic cemeteries, in order to see an Irish funeral—or, at least, saunter along the road to witness the funeral procession. Here are two of them. The first is evidently a 'grand' one. A hearse with six horses (not black ones) and white feathers leads the way. Next come three or four mourning coaches, each drawn by two horses. Then follow some fifteen or twenty hackney-coaches, all filled with 'mourners:' after which succeeds an almost interminable train of outside-cars (we count above fifty), each having its full complement of six passengers —men, women, and children—not a bit of black to be seen on the back of any one of them: the men, and some of the women, smoking their short pipes,—the 'boys' making fun with the girls, and all talking and laughing in full concert. The next procession is a shade less grand, but still a 'dacent' one. First comes the coffin, carried by men in their ordinary clothes; next the chief mourners on foot, but without cloaks or bands, and in many-coloured garments; and then come all the 'friends' of the deceased, a ragged band, mounted on some thirty or forty cars, every kind of finery and rags mingled together, and, if possible, more jovial than those in the other procession. Alongside of each, and bringing up the rear, is a motley assemblage on foot. To these funerals every one who in any way knew the deceased is invited, and all go, in order, as they phrase it, "to show respect." The custom seems ingrain; but recent misfortunes show how urgent distress will break through every custom. We were struck by the contrast presented by a funeral which we met, a few days later, in one of the poorer districts of the interior of Ireland. A plain deal coffin lay, without any covering, on a little donkey-cart, and one old woman walked beside it. We fancied that it was merely a coffin being conveyed to the house of the deceased person; but, on inquiring, found that it was, in truth, a poor fellow being carried thus unhonoured to his last earthly home.

We will now take a stroll along the Quays, which, as yet, we have only seen from Carlisle Bridge. The Liffey, as has been said, flows in easy windings quite through the centre of the city. The stream is confined within granite walls, which form a series of excellent quays, along which there is on each side of the river a clear footway, from Carlisle Bridge to King's Bridge. Indeed, the Liffey has rather the appearance of a grand artificial canal than a river. Between the quays and the houses is, on each side of the river, a wide roadway. Thus, there is here a feature which no other city in the kingdom possesses—a broad open thoroughfare, three miles long, with a fine river flowing through the midst, spanned by 7 bridges, and some noble structures along the sides. Not only should it be an ornament to the city, but, as it is a tidal stream, it ought also to contribute to its salubrity. Very far otherwise must it be,—as every one knows who has spent a summer's day in Dublin. Into the Liffey the sewerage of the city is turned; and as when the tide ebbs the bed of the river is left exposed, the most unwholesome vapours ascend and impregnate the entire vicinity. How the citizens can endure so pestiferous a stench is inconceivable. Every one admits and laments the evil; but you are told that no system of flushing the river has yet been suggested which promises to be successful, and therefore—patience.

The lower part of the river is devoted to commerce. Along the quays ships of large size are moored, chiefly

3.—THE CUSTOM-HOUSE, DUBLIN.

emigrant and other vessels which trade to America and the colonies; colliers and coasting craft. But there is also a sprinkling of foreign ships. On both sides of the river there are docks; those by the Custom-house and those of the Grand Canal, are extensive, but there are very few vessels in them. From nearly all the ships lying out, and loading and discharging their cargoes in the not very wide river, the quays are very crowded, and there appears to be much more commerce than there probably is: but the shipping trade has the appearance of activity. It is, by the way, a curious sight just now to see the eager swarms that surround the emigrant offices on Eden Quay.

On the north bank, a short distance below Carlisle Bridge, is the Custom-House,—an isolated building, of far higher architectural rank than its London name-sake, and probably than any other of the kind in the world. It was commenced in 1781, and completed in 1791, at a cost of above half a million sterling. The architect was James Gandon. It is 375 feet in length, and 209 feet in depth. All the four fronts are highly enriched; but the chief front is, of course, that which faces the river. (Cut, No. 3.) The river front consists of a centre and wings, with an advanced tetrastyle portico of the Doric order. The tympanum contains a bas-relief, representing the Union of England and Ireland. On the attic are statues of Neptune, Plenty, Industry,

and Mercury. A noble cupola rises to the height of 125 feet, and is surmounted by a colossal figure of Hope. The north front is scarcely inferior to the southern, though less ornamented: on the attic above the portico are statues of Europe, Asia, Africa, and America. The interior is also admirable: the great room, especially, is a very handsome apartment. But this magnificent building is on far too colossal a scale for the Customs of Dublin; indeed, of late, it has been found to afford ample room for the offices of the Commissioners of Excise, of Stamps, and of Records; of the Board of Works, the Poor-Law Commissioners, Army-Pay, and several other Government Boards; and then verge enough for Geological and, we believe, other museums —in short, it is now something like what Somerset House would be, if one could fancy that edifice removed to Thames Street and incorporated with the Custom-House.

Towards the other end of the quays, just above Richmond Bridge, is another of the buildings which add so much to the grandeur of the city—the Four Courts. Our engraving (Cut, No. 4,) will serve to show its general appearance and save the necessity of description, for which we are becoming somewhat straitened in space. The Four Courts were commenced in 1786, from a design by Cooley, the architect of the Royal Exchange; but he dying while the works were

4.—THE FOUR COURTS, DUBLIN.

in progress, the completion was entrusted to Gandon, who made some alterations in the design. Within these few years there have been considerable additions made to the original pile. The entire structure is very large, having to afford accommodation for the courts of law, and offices connected with them. The grand front extends along King's Inns Quay for nearly 500 feet. The central building, which contains the four courts of Chancery, Queen's Bench, Common Pleas, and Exchequer, has a very beautiful portico of six Corinthian columns, with statues of Moses on the apex, and Justice and Mercy on the extremities of the pediment; and above ascends the large and graceful dome. Altogether this is generally considered to be one of the very finest as well as most important buildings in Dublin.

The great hall of the Four Courts is a very beautiful circular apartment, sixty-four feet in diameter, with a Mosaic flooring of concentric circles. In the centre is a statue of Truth on a pedestal, of which nothing better can be said than that it serves for a gaslight. Round the hall are eight entrances, leading to the courts and passages; between them are coupled Corinthian columns. An entablature surmounts these, running all round the hall, above which is an Attic pedestal. In panels over the entrances are bas-reliefs, representing William the Conqueror establishing courts of justice; the signing of Magna Charta; Henry the Second granting the first

charter to Dublin; and James the First abolishing the Brehon law.

The interior of it must not be overlooked, if the stranger be so fortunate as to spend a morning in Dublin in term time. As you enter the circular hall (a singularly beautiful one), instead of hearing the sort of quiet hum that greets you on entering Westminster or Guildhall, you are half-stunned by a confusion of voices worthy of Babel, and jostled to and fro in a crowd rivalling that of the Stock Exchange. In the passages men and women and boys are hawking tapes, and knives, and all kinds of small wares that lawyers need; and cakes, and pies, and fruit, and almost every variety of refreshment that lawyers or suitors could manage to swallow amid such a tumult. Within there is a perfect army of barristers, whether briefless or briefed, all as merry as grigs, cracking jokes on the right and left with learned brothers or unlearned clients, or assembled around some famous wag who is keeping them in a constant roar of laughter. The attorneys, and witnesses, and lookers-on, all appear bent on mirth, and laugh and talk with heart and voice heartily. Gravity seems by common consent banished from the outer court of Themis. In the inner temple, and in the presence of 'my lord,' there is of course something more of quiet and seriousness. If 'Counsellor Butt,' or some other favourite be addressing the bench and jury, there is silence deep enough; but if an unlucky witness is 'tabled,' you are almost sure of some amusement. An Irish barrister seems to adopt a much more 'free and easy' style in examining a witness than an English one, and poor Pat, falling into the same familiar vein, is certain to be led into some ludicrous mistake, or contradiction, or strange absurdity.

There is another building connected with law, the King's Inns, which is worth visiting, though it is some distance off, and rather out of the way. We may conveniently reach it by Capel Street, taking, *en route*, the City Sessions House in Green Street, and the adjoining Prison of Newgate, both solemn and sombre edifices, and passing on till we come to the Linen Hall, a building which deserves a moment's attention. It is an immense pile of six large courts, and contains 575 apartments. It was erected at a period when Dublin was the emporium of the Irish linen trade: now that trade is almost wholly transferred to Belfast, and the hall is comparatively deserted. Though the only inns of law in Dublin, they occupy a situation almost 'out of town,' and wear a very secluded air. The building is a large and very pleasing one, and if not ro striking as some others in the city, it exhibits much richness of effect, especially in the chief front, which consists of a fine central archway of granite, surmounted by a handsome Doric portico, above which, and somewhat retired, rises an octangular cupola. The wings are two stories in height, and surmounted by pediments. In each wing is a handsome doorway. The office for registering deeds and the Prerogative and Consistorial Courts are within the building. The hall is a very handsome room. Close by the Inns is the station of the Mullingar Railway; and not far distant is St. Mary's Church; both interesting buildings, and, with those we have just described, amply sufficient to repay a walk to this end of the city. From this locality we pass into Rutland Square, in which are several fine mansions. The most distinguished is Charlemont House, on the northern side, called Palace Row. It is a princely mansion, retired from the square, and detached from the other mansions. The interior is highly worth visiting, having a fine library, a statue gallery, and some remarkably fine pictures, including a Rembrandt and a Titian. On the southern side of the square we see the Rotondo, with its fine colonnade and cupola. From hence it is but a short distance eastward to Montjoy Square, which is handsome and regularly built. Next we pass down Gardiner Street, one of the finest in the city, terminated strikingly by the northern front of the Custom House. But we must stop midway, and pass in, on the left hand, to the central establishment of the Board of National Education. The front consists of two massive granite buildings with Grecian façades, and contains board-room, library, and other apartments. The model schools, male and female, are in the rear, behind which are fine exercise ground and gardens. A visit to the schools will well repay the expenditure of half an hour.

The most striking recent additions to the architecture of Dublin are the railway stations; and they are quite worthy of the high character of the civic buildings. This Mullingar, or Midland Great Western Railway Station, is a very striking structure. The long Ionic arcade, which has just been completed, is an exceedingly chaste design; it is constructed of a choice kind of mountain granite, which adds much to the effect. From this station there is a good view of the city. The terminus of the Drogheda Railway, close by the Custom House, is in the Italian Palazzo style, with a lofty central tower. It is a graceful building, but hardly so appropriate or characteristic as the others. The principal front is of Wicklow granite. The terminus of the Dublin and Kingstown Railway has no architectural pretensions. But the handsomest railway terminus that we have seen in any part of the kingdom is that of the Great Southern and Western Railway, near King's Bridge. This is the railway that we hope to conduct our readers along, on the way to Killarney, in our next Part. The station is a very large building, of the Italo-Corinthian order; the façade is highly enriched, and the style is carried out in the *tout-ensemble* and in the details with excellent taste. It is constructed entirely of the beautiful Wicklow mountain granite, exquisitely wrought and dressed; a material which, now it is quite fresh and clean, has quite a brilliant effect when seen under a bright sun.

Not far from this station is one of those excellent institutions which are so numerous in Dublin. This one is the Royal Hospital, which stands on the site of an ancient priory of the Knights Templars. The hospital is a noble building, erected from a design by Sir Christopher Wren. Near the terminus is Steevens's Hospital,—a noble institution, founded by Miss Steevens in 1720, and augmented by Dr. Steevens with a legacy of £60 a-year. Another edifice in this neighbourhood, though of no great elegance, will be regarded with interest when its name is mentioned—it is St. Patrick's, or, as it is more commonly called, Swift's Hospital, the institution which Swift, apparently with a painful foreboding of his own fearful malady, founded and endowed for the reception of lunatics and idiots:—he gave, as he said, with a levity that appears to have been put on, to conceal the keenness of his feelings on the subject:

> " He gave the little wealth he had
> To build a house for fools or mad,
> And showed, by one satiric touch,
> No nation wanted it so much."

If we had space, we might mention other charitable institutions; as it is, we can only say that they are very numerous, and of almost every kind, in Dublin; and many of them are on a large and liberal scale. The charity of the inhabitants of Dublin has always been munificent; and it is exercised as well privately as through public institutions.

It would be a great oversight to omit noticing the squares of Dublin; but we can only mention them. The chief is St. Stephen's Green—the largest square in Europe. It is an English mile in circuit. The central area is laid out and planted, and contains an equestrian statue of George II. The houses around are large and lofty—many of them are noble mansions. Among the most noteworthy are the residences of the Archbishop of Dublin and of the Lord Chancellor; the Dublin University, Stephen's Green, and United Service Clubs; the College of Surgeons and Museum of National Industry are also here. Next in size to St. Stephen's is Merrion-square; which is, however, only about half as large. The houses here are uniform in appearance, spacious, and lofty.

DUBLIN EXHIBITION OF NATIONAL INDUSTRY.

"These are the gifts of Art, and Art thrives most
When Commerce has enrich'd the busy coast;
He catches all improvements in his flight,
Spreads foreign wonders in his country's sight,
Imports what others have invented well,
And stirs his own to match them or excel.
'Tis thus reciprocating, each with each,
Alternately the nations learn and teach;
While Providence enjoins to ev'ry soul
A union with the vast terraqueous whole."

COWPER.

THE Industrial Palace of Dublin, which is now displaying its collected results of skilful enterprise and mechanical ingenuity to admiring thousands, is in many respects a more attractive and interesting object than its great prototype of '51, which was constructed in Hyde Park. Apart from the wondrous novelty, the originality of conception, and the rapidity of completion which characterized the *Palais Paxton*, as our lively neighbours choicely designated the great structural feature of the age, the Temple of Industry, now exhibiting its treasures in Dublin, presents to the spectator as large an amount of instructive development and skilled enterprise as its gigantic precursor did in the capital of the empire. Indeed, for exhibitional purposes, it is superior in several respects; for its form of structure, its arrangement for the admission of light, and its compact expression of purpose, which are the leading essentials in buildings of this kind, are more artistically developed than they were in the Hyde Park Exhibition of '51.

The Dublin Exhibition presents a tripartite front, which forms the eastern termination of the structure, consisting of a centre and two side halls of minor proportions, and, when viewed externally, has anything but an agreeable appearance. At the first *coup-d'œil*, indeed, the elevation in its whole breadth presents the features of a dinner service on a large scale. The principal halls appear like huge dish covers, the one in the centre towering above its companions with almost ludicrous proportions, which disturb, for the moment, the otherwise pleasing sensations arising from an exterior view of the structure. Let the reader, however, enter the building, and the first glance of its internal arrange-

ments will amply compensate for any external defect. The central hall forms a grand temple of 425 feet in length by 100 feet in breadth and 100 feet in height, with semicircular bayed extremes, the whole being covered by a semicylindrical roof, constructed upon fourteen gigantic terminated trellis ribs or arches, which form single spans of 100 feet each across the hall. The spherical extremities of the roof are constructed upon four semi-arches, concentred with the last grand arch at each end. The lateral halls running parallel with the centre hall, or nave, have squared terminations, and are each 325 feet in length by 50 feet in breadth and 65 feet in height, with roofs to correspond with the larger hall, from which they are divided by passages of 25 feet in breadth. The symmetry in elevation of the side halls is preserved by an addition of like proportions to the passages, which, being divided into compartments, renders the classification of exhibited articles comparatively easy. Above those compartments and passages are spacious internal galleries, which run the length of the building, and afford an increased space for exhibition; these also serve as agreeable promenades, the ascent to which is by means of transverse selfsupporting staircases of uniform design, which admirably harmonize with the character of the structure. The light is admitted from above, and in so subdued a form and volume that every object appears in its proper relief and in its most pleasing aspect. This mode of lighting structures for exhibitional purposes is deserving of imitation, and is most ingeniously devised. The Fine Arts Hall is 325 feet in length and 40 in breadth, forming a noble compartment for the exhibition of its choice treasures; and the Machinery Court has 450 feet in length and 50 in breadth for the display of its mechanical ingenuity. The Auxiliary Halls, which necessity has demanded since the original suggestion of the project, consist of two corridors forty feet in width, which extend round the house of the Royal Dublin Society, under whose immediate direction the whole affair is placed, and upon whose lawn the superstructure is raised. These corridors unite with a large circular building erected in front of the society's house in Kildare-street, which connects the north and south portions of the main structure with the refreshment saloons, and affords an uninterrupted promenade through the entire building.

The external gallery, running round the front of the building facing Merrion-square, is a prominent feature of this splendid structure, and commands a singularly delightful view. This gallery is supported by slender but solid pillars, of light and elegant design, and forms a pleasing architectural ornament to the facade. In addition to this it is a useful and convenient means of communication between the principal galleries. It also forms a pleasant promenade, from its commanding a view over the eastern portions of the city, and being perfumed with the white and black thorn, which are thickly planted in Merrion-square.

The plan of the building provides (in the shape of galleries, ground floors, side spaces, refreshment and retiring rooms, with the necessary offices) for 147,704 feet of flooring, and 87,000 feet of wall space; but the additional structures just mentioned will add to the provision 60,000 superficial feet of flooring and counter space, and 37,000 feet of wall space. A more definite idea, however, of the extent of the building may be acquired, when we state that the counter space alone forms a continuous line of more than six miles in length, and that the wall space is equivalent to five miles of shop windows without any interval, and admits of a display of goods to a height of six feet from the lower part of each window.

On entering the building, at the main avenue, the eye of the spectator is at once arrested by the finely-proportioned roof, whose arched ribs present series of concentric spans of extreme beauty, and by the uniform and mellowed diffusion of light, which presents every object in its natural proportions. This we esteem one of the greatest results of the whole structure. Wandering on, without any precise design, through the varied objects which present themselves, the attention of the spectator is directed hither and thither as though there were no fixed point whence the most striking view of the structure might be taken, or whence the eye might range over the largest space with effect and advantage. At length, however, the mind becomes fatigued with gazing on objects as though it were lost in a maze, and quietly settles down to examine them with something like a fixed and definite intention to comprehend their nature and the purport of their being submitted to its examination.

In this tone and temperament the spectator may follow, we will presume to say, with advantage and instruction, especially if an economy of time be a desideratum, this brief but condensed sketch of the varied contents of the Exhibition, which is the result of more lengthened details in other leading and responsible quarters.

The contributions from the United Kingdom are divided into thirty classes, which comprehend almost every branch of industrial enterprise and every material that can be operated upon by human ingenuity. The exhibitors, for the most part, are grouped together according to the character of their contributions or the nature of their productions. In the Colonial and Foreign Departments a similar plan has been adopted, which renders the inspection of the objects comparatively easy.

The articles exhibited on the floor of the central hall, apparently placed without design, are also intended, as far as possible, to direct the visitor to similar contributions in the lateral halls and in the intersecting avenues. The banners, again, which are displayed in the various parts of the building, indicate the positions of the different classes of objects. With their indications, therefore, the visitor may easily comprehend the general internal arrangement of the building, and examine with facility any particular portion of its contents, to which either his taste or inclination may chance to lead him. The circular panels, near the springs of the arched roofs, will likewise serve as a guide to the spectator, as the banners and devices of the several towns and countries are painted upon them immediately over their respective contributions.

The first object of immediate interest to the industry of Ireland that strikes the eye is the geological survey of Dr. Griffiths, whose elaborate and minute delineations completely establish the vast resources of her mineral wealth. This survey is the result of forty years' labour; and the only fault, connected with so valuable a contribution, is, that it is placed too high. The reduced map, however, which immediately adjoins it, is a most explanatory aid to its singular contents. Passing down the centre avenue, after noticing a bell of remarkable tone and fine quality of metal, your attention is directed to two Sikh guns, which are singular for the strength, the mechanical skill, and the ingeniously wrought metal, which they display, whatever may be their peculiar quality in other respects. Turning, however, from the symbols of war and destruction, your eye immediately falls upon the group of the *Three Graces*, by Baily, which has all the purity, chasteness of feeling, and almost unearthly atmosphere about it, which his refined chisel can so easily impart to the softer portion of the human race. On the right of this exquisite piece of art stands the statue of *Spartacus*, in bronze, which is copied from the original in the garden of the Tuileries. In some respects it is ably executed; the muscular development is perhaps a little too exaggerated—a common fault with French sculptors, who are sadly afraid that their figures should appear natural, even under a passionless temperament of mind; therefore a defect of this kind ought scarcely to be noticed in the representation of an individual who must be supposed, from his character and position, to be in the highest possible state of excitement.—Disposing of the sculpture, which is mainly standing in the grand avenue, in as studied a manner as our brief space for description admits, we direct the visitor's attention to the cast from *Eve at the Fountain*, the well-known *chef-d'œuvre* of modern sculpture, to the *Tired Huntsman*, and to the busts of Lords Gough and Brougham, and Sir John Herschel, by the same artist, who deservedly stands at the head of his profession. The *Eve* of Macdowell is well known; so also is the *Sabrina*, by Marshall, both possessing peculiar merit, though of a totally different nature. The statue of Her Majesty, by Marochetti, is a commanding figure, though too large for the space assigned to it; so also is the figure of *Innocence*, by Foley, which, however, attracts from its gentleness rather than from the quality the preceding work displays. The busts, which are crowded most ridiculously throughout the whole avenue, we must pass over. There is one, however, in the Fine Art Department, which is well deserving of notice, from the combination of opposite qualities it exhibits. We allude to the bust of the Empress of the French, by Jones, which is full of intellectual expression of a high order, and of a singular melancholy combined with determination in the character of that expression. Altogether it is an able work of art, however temporary circumstances may have imparted to it an additional interest. The several contributions from the Antiques are also deserving of remark; many of them indicate the highest excellence in sculpture. There are, moreover, some singular groups of modern execution, which purport to be the production of a Spaniard, and which are stated to have been the property of Napoleon, when in the zenith of his power; they are in most instances roughly executed, but occasionally display considerable delicacy in parts. Their singular feature, however, is a rich masterly power of grouping, for which quality alone they are deserving of a study. These four groups are placed immediately under the *Dais* at the end of the principal nave, and are surrounded with myriads of objects of a similar nature as regards material, but much inferior in point of art. An exception to this remark must be taken, in drawing attention to the *Greek Slave*, by Power—a figure which attracted so large a share of public attention in '51. The *Hercules wrestling with a Bull*, by Kriesmann, is more gigantic in size than in expression; nevertheless it seems to indicate that the practical and the ideal were nearly allied in the author's mind at the time of its execution. The small cast, from the celebrated *Horse and Tiger* of Kiss, is worthy of attention; so, also, are the two beautiful figures in the Belgian Department by Fraikin, the *Captive Cupid*, and *Psyche calling Cupid*, both of which are expressive of the most graceful tenderness. The first we remember in the Exhibition of '51. A *Daughter of Eve*, by Bell, is an interesting illustration of the Negro character; and if there be such gentle creatures, so modestly timid a race amongst the "ebony images" of God's creation, there surely is a large amount of grievous wrong to lay at the feet of those who have kept them so long in debasement and oppression. The figure, though in the comparatively unyielding metal of bronze, is soft and delicate in its expression, and appeals, with affecting humility, to the compassion of the spectator. The *Tired Water Carrier*, by E. E. Papworth, is a poetic conception, and most truthfully carried out.

But we must here close our desultory sketch of the sculpture contributions. To do justice, however, to this section of the Exhibition, we cannot omit calling attention to the statue of Wm. Dargan, Esq., the spirited originator of the undertaking. The catalogue here, happily, comes to our aid; and let those who contemplate the representation of that energetic individual, standing with a commanding attitude in the nave, peruse the following verses:—

"Those features so massive, that forehead immense,
     Prove the block forms the head of no blockhead;
What a face full of talent, and goodness, and sense,
     Has that man with his hand in his pocket.

"That hand holds no hard, sordid gripe of his gold,
     For the good of mankind he'll unlock it;
For science and art thousands freely are told
     By this man with his hand in his pocket."

The statue is executed by Jones, and will be finished in marble when the subscriptions are sufficient for that purpose. The expression of the features is bold, impressive, and determined, and the natural easy way in which the characteristics of the original are depicted, especially with the hard thrust in the pocket, is singularly but by no means offensively expressive.

Retracing our steps, in the central nave we have the electric telegraph, contributed by the Company, which, with another in the southern gallery, is occasionally worked, and is useful to transmit messages when required. The one most generally used is owned by Messrs. Smith, the active news agents, and frequently affords amusement to the visitors by its mysterious movements. In immediate proximity to this object, a group of the Serpentine Marble Works of Cornwall are exhibited, which, from their extreme polish and singularly fine grain of marble, attract universal attention. The elegant and tasteful shapes of the objects also deserve notice, many of them being executed in the best style of ornamental art. The next object of mark is the Terra-cotta fountain from Glasgow, which is neither so artistically arranged nor so skilfully designed as the one lower down in the nave, from the foundry of Val Dosne, in France, and which is the tasteful production of M. Andre, of Paris; nor does it equal the contribution from the Coalbrook Dale Company, which is playing opposite to the large refreshment room, so ably served by Poulson, the Gunter of Dublin. The only fault to be found with the last-named fountain is, that the simplicity of colour is not uniform, the green and yellow of the reptiles writhing round the stem marring strangely its otherwise classically designed outline, and its excellence of execution. The Jaquard Looms, three of which are employed in weaving poplins, are naturally attractive objects. The ingenuity of the process of manufacture they display, both in the cards which form a portion of the figure woven, and also in the apparent complication of the threads and wires which communicate with the cards, had puzzled many an uninitiated eye, and taxed the initiated attendant, almost *ad nauseam*, to explain them. Some rather eloquent structures, containing a medley of contributions from the lace, the silk, the poplin, and the worked-muslin departments of manufacture, are the next prominent features in the main avenue, and have, according to their respective merits, their peculiar admirers. The structures are decidedly ornamental additions, especially the one bearing the name of James Forrest, which contains lace goods of almost every kind, and in the most beautiful quality that it is possible to manufacture. A case of bog-oak carvings forms a characteristic feature in the Exhibition, irrespective of the merit displayed in both the designs and the execution of the objects. The pianofortes fill a large space in the nave as well as in the southern gallery, and consist of contributions from all the leading manufacturers both in England and Ireland. The Irish, it is necessary to remark, are remarkably fond of music, and patronize a piano, when their patronage cannot even be extended to articles of greater domestic utility. The trade in these instruments is therefore comparatively large in Ireland, which will account for the great show which is made by most of the good makers. Price, the patent candle manufacturer, has a most tasteful structure, exhibiting his peculiar excellence in that article ; and Benham and Sons exhibit a series of grates, fire-irons, fenders, and other objects of domestic use which are highly creditable to their taste and judgment, especially as regards arrangement.

Ascending the Dais—one of the most interesting features in the building, whence the eye can radiate in every direction over the ground-floor of the Exhibition, and discern distinctly each object in the great nave—a silver group, called a *Fountain Temple, with Portraits of Horses, the property of Her Majesty*, designed and composed in the style and spirit of the Alhambra, is well worthy of examination. The fine piece of metal art exhibits the peculiar excellence we have attained in the manufacture of silver, and reflects the greatest credit upon the Messrs. Garrard, from whose house it emanated. The temple is composed of bright and frosted silver, with portions enamelled or gilt, and represents a covered fountain, with Arabs leading horses to water. The horses are portraits of presents from different sovereigns to Her Majesty ; and appear, from their symmetrical beauty, to be truthfully sketched. The clustered columns and the high springing arches resemble the central portico of the Palace of Lions ; and the roof, with its double stage, the pinnacle, and the central dome, are in perfect unison with the most ornamental character of Moorish architecture. The grouping of the men and horses affords a view from every side ; and the action of each figure, moreover, forms a distinct feature, which imparts an additional interest to the whole composition. Altogether it may be designated as the leading if not the most beautiful feature of the Exhibition, from its combination of the highest taste and the most skilled manipulation of a precious metal, with an originality of conception in the design. Adjoining this exquisite work of art are two racing cups, of more than ordinary richness in sculptural work. The one represents the Emperor's Plate, and is designed by Macarthy, and the other the Goodwood Cup, both contributed by the late Lord-Lieutenant, the Earl of Eglintoun. From this point may be seen to advantage Chance's Lighthouse, which formed so prominent a feature in the Hyde Park Show. This lighthouse, with its dioptric apparatus, and its catadioptric zones, is constructed according to the system of Fresnel. The lamp in the centre of the apparatus is on the moderator principle, and consists of a burner with four concentric wicks, throwing its light with immense power to a distance of even fifty miles, when the weather is clear. The large *Equatorial Telescope* of Grub is equally prominent, and purports to be an instrument constructed with improved clock-work, and carrying an achromatic telescope of twelve inches clear aperture, with a focus of twenty feet. And the Coalbrook Dale contribution, a little further on, displays its usual excellence in castings and other ornamental iron-work. To the right of this instructive display, the Messrs. Houldsworth exhibit their rich manufacture of silk damasks in almost every possible variety, and also

with improved effect. In this contribution may be viewed a singular epitome of manufacture—worsted damasks, yarn-dyed damasks, printed satinets, and table covers, consisting of silk, worsted, and cotton, sometimes mixed together : in other samples a single material is used. Here, also, are a collection of fabrics for furniture and ecclesiastical decorations, embroideries by patent process on cloth and satins, which admit of varied application ; an entirely new fabric called guipurette, which is exceedingly effective in appearance, and has both sides alike, so that no lining is required when it is used. The silk medallions for covering chairs, the bordered satins and terrys, with the brocatelles and damasks, make up a contribution of certainly the richest and most varied, if not the newest, in the textile fabric department. The electro-plating skill of Messrs. Elkington is elaborately displayed in the several objects which make up their singularly artistic contributions ; and the group of bronzes, though heavy as compared to the French, denote that we have made great progress in that branch of art-industry. The silver work of Dublin, which is highly creditable to her skill, is largely represented by Waterhouse and Acheson, both of whom exhibit objects of tasteful design and highly-finished manipulation. The group of *Michel and Satan* is remarkable for the purity of the frosted silver—a difficulty which is rarely overcome, for that process of working the metal is apt to generate a dull and leaden appearance. The same remark may be applied to the group of Wilkinson, which is beautifully electrotyped ; the frosted portion of the silver appearing of the clearest and whitest hue. Battam and Son have enriched the Exhibition by a contribution of vases, in imitation of the Pompeian art ; and, though not so light, the style and character of the decoration is equally subdued, and perhaps a little more tasteful than the antique. The next objects of more than ordinary attraction are two angels in bronze, from the Berlin Art-Foundry. They are modelled with great feeling and in the choicest style of art, and the metal has a more than ordinary expression here, being of a darker green, and throwing out a bolder relief, than those in the French department, which are shaded up to a yellow tint. With a passing notice of a set of powerful metal reflectors, some choicely designed carpets on each side the organ, a bell of fine tone, and a glance at a couple of pianofortes from Mr. Cadhy's London Factory, which have just been placed in the nave, and which, from the originality of construction displayed in their manufacture, are deserving of more than a passing remark, we must invite the reader to an inspection of the side avenues, which exhibit their respective treasures of art and industry.

On the south side of the building the contributions of Germany, France, and Belgium, may be seen with both pleasure and instruction, each having its special excellence. After glancing at the richly-filled case of Rhenish manufacture of velvets and silks, the visitor's attention is directed to the bronze productions of Berlin, which in many respects are equal to the French. Amongst these the statuettes of the Electors of Brandenburgh, executed by the galvanic process; a group of fox and ducks; the prize representing the four seasons and the ages of man, composed, modelled, chiselled, and inlaid with silver, by Vollgold; and a small copy of the *Hercules and the Bull* are remarkably expressive, and denote a highly advanced stage of art-excellence. The objects in Terra-cotta are equally interesting. The china, the pipes, the prints, and the wood-carvings display their peculiar excellence, and deserve more space than we can devote to their description.

From the Zollverein we pass to the French contribution, which fills a large space, is tastefully arranged, and appears highly effective in every department. The Sevres china alone is a study for those who delight in the tasteful and elegant in material objects, and present phases of art which few can justly appreciate, from the exquisite and long-studied nature of its execution. The bronze productions are exceedingly beautiful both in design and execution, and singularly varied in the character of their illustration—for the art of France seems vastly comprehensive in its range, and skilfully studied in its delineation. To particularize amongst so much excellence is perfectly needless. The visitor, indeed, need scarcely be directed towards it. The Gobelin Tapestry and the Aubusson Carpets display their peculiar richness with great effect; and in tone of colour, in character of design, and in exquisite manipulation, they are certainly unequalled in the whole range of art manufacture. The leading attraction, however, in this department, to the multitude especially, is a group of characters in clay, which is extraordinary for its illustration of humour. The artist seems to have revelled in his highly-gifted genius, when he passed these several objects through his hands; and there is so wicked a spirituality in the expression and character of each position of the group, that the mind of the spectator instantly assents to the power and originality of the conception displayed throughout the whole composition. A candelabra of rare construction, and singularly chaste in its character of ornamentation, is also deserving of notice in this department. Indeed throughout the whole of this contribution the exquisite taste and refined execution of our lively neighbours is most amply developed.

The articles in oxidised silver, in this department, are curious, and, like other novelties, will enjoy their hour of fashion. So also will the enamelled jewellery, the jaspar tazzæ, and other objects of a tasteful and decorative kind, in which the art-genius of France is so prolific. The clocks and lamps are equally expressive of her subdued and highly-cultivated taste, which hits the newly-attained medium between over-charged ornamentation and sparsely-decorated utility.

On leaving this department for the Belgian, the attention of the visitor will be drawn to a panel of decorative paper-hangings (comprising twenty-two frames), which represents a landscape and figures in colour, executed with artistic skill rarely equalled. It is a study of itself.

The Belgian contribution displays the peculiar

excellence of that industrious people. A chimney-piece in statuary marble is a beautiful work of art, the *relievi* in every part being worked out with the most careful precision. The colour of the marble is also worthy of notice, and must have been cut from a block of rare and pure grain. The Chinese bird-cages are singular and ingenious objects of ornamentation; and from the novelty of construction, apart from the material of which they are composed, attract general attention. The window-blinds, painted on muslins, are deserving of a remark or so, the colours being curiously infixed on the surface of that slender fabric. This branch of industry might be cultivated to advantage in England, as she abounds in the material itself, possesses artistic skill equal to Belgium, and is by no means inferior to the precise chemical knowledge required for its completion. The tapestry-work is more antique than artistic in design, and certainly inferior to the French in being worked out. Nevertheless it is amply entitled to an inspection from the observant visitor. There appears, to our taste, too much green throughout the work; yet there is plenty of space for a contrast of colours in delineating the several objects represented in the illustrations. The guns and pistols are the finest specimens, as regards finish, of Belgian manufacture. Their qualities, however, must be tested before any definite opinion can be given upon them. In ornamentation they are equal to the French; but in hue of metal and goodness of workmanship, certainly inferior to the English. Nor do they handle with that telling effect which characterizes the best makers of the latter. The printed floor-cloths, cotton, flannel, table-covers, and the several samples illustrating the process and progress of oil-cloth manufacture, will attract, as they deserve, the keen and observant eye of the visitor who may be more particularly interested in these several branches of industry. Nor are the samples of hemp and peeled flax, the copal varnish for carriages, and the superior qualities of starch for getting-up laces, less entitled to observation. The flax-thread for the ground-work of Brussels lace is minutely examined, as that branch of industry is materially extending in Ireland. The twist or throw of the thread, irrespective of the carefully-prepared material, is slightly harder than the same numbers in England, but not so truthfully spun, which arises from the excellency of our machinery, both for hackling and spinning. The samples of white and half-white window glass, and the cylinders of the same material, will also be minutely examined; for the race between Belgium and England, since the repeal of the duty, has been severe in the manufacture of glass. Belgium for some years has excelled France in the manufacture of plate-glass, and we have annually imported large quantities of that article ourselves. Now, however, the case is somewhat different, the English makers equalling in most respects the best of the Belgian. On the whole, this department, though limited and unpretending, is usefully interesting, and highly suggestive to the practical eye of the visitor.

The Irish fisheries claim the attention of the spectator, immediately on the left of the preceding department. Here we have fishing tackle of every kind in use in Ireland, which furnishes a rare subject of industrial study. To the initiated the following brief enumeration of articles may not be uninteresting. Green hemp and Manilla lobster lines, tarred hauzlin, yacht marlin, trawl line, salmon twine, and herring netting in abundance, and apparently of the most carefully-prepared condition, are exhibited. Then we have Ball's haddock *snowding*, fine cod and Baltic *snowding*, rod lines, landing nets, eel cockell, and tackle lines of almost every weight, from three-fourths to three pounds. In addition to these varied articles for fishing in calm and troubled waters, the denizens of the deep are entrapped by the several weirs, of which there are models presented for the instruction of the observer; by the harpoons, and grains, and spears; by the albicore hooks; by nets of every conceivable form and every possible application, whether out at sea, or the waters of the interior lakes, or in the streams which communicate with both. Boats, models of river-fixtures, and apparatus for hauling bay-nets, make up the contribution, which, especially as regards Ireland, is in every view interesting and instructive.

The visitor at this point will experience a curious transition, the objects of the western world of industry being exchanged for those of the eastern, and demanding a new train of thought for their inspection. As the eye curiously wanders over the *Japanese Department*, each object seems familiar to the sight; and the idea for a time fills the mind that we are in company with our old friends the Chinese, or rather we are looking at objects and articles which seem identified with the habits, the character, and the custom of that singular people. A closer inspection, however, will quickly undeceive the visitor; and if his eye be tutored to the examination of objects of industry, there will be little difficulty in discovering a rarer quality of workmanship in the manufacture of these objects, and a wider range of industrial art, which imply that the community who encourage the exercise of these qualities must be proportionately advanced in civilization. Here are certain objects also of a novel construction, which suggest a new development of thought and a new phase of social existence. Nor is the material, in some instances, less curious in its application for such purposes. Branches of industry, too, which were esteemed exclusively European, and were of comparatively recent invention, appear familiar to the Japanese. In these instances the mind of the visitor is naturally awakened from the even tenor of its thought, and launched into a sphere of speculation, the limits of which are almost beyond human capacity to measure. Our remarks, however, upon this highly interesting contribution must necessarily be limited, and simply corroborative of the preceding indications. First, then, the objects of *Japanned* material, which originated with the ingenious people whose industry we are now contemplating, and to whom we have applied in a substantive form the very name as a mark of designation. These objects are both numerous and beautiful. In most instances they suggest the uses to which they are applied, and appear to have been brought to their present perfection, both in form and excellence of material, by a series of transitions, which is the common characteristic of art-industry throughout the entire world and amongst all people. The Japanese could not have jumped at a leap to the newly-shaped, and, in several instances, elegantly-formed dishes and tea-pots, which are in common use amongst them. Nor could they, by analogy, have acquired that exquisite manipulation of materials, which is so manifest in several objects, without a series of developments which the skilled application of labour alone can produce. Let the visitor range his eye, for example, over the japanned dishes in the contribution; and if he be conversant with that kind of work amongst ourselves, standing as we do A 1 *in this respect*, he will quickly perceive that the Japanese display a more exquisite touch than we can pretend to. The principal object aimed at in japanned articles is to work up the material, consisting mostly of paper, either whole or in a pulpy state, to as close, compact, and homogeneous a state as possible, in order that it may receive the highest possible polish, appear light and smooth as glass, and be impervious to crack or any other surface disfigurement. In all these respects the Japanese are evidently a-head of us, and it is scarcely possible to conceive, without actual observation, that such perfection could be attained in manufacture. Nor are they less backward in elegance of design, especially in objects of domestic use, than in excellence of workmanship. We shall simply cite two other examples of the ingenuity of this little known but ingenious people. On one of the banners may be discerned silk ribbon streamers; but these ribbons are *watered*,—a process in the manufacture of silks of which the French claimed the invention about forty years ago. To water a ribbon or piece of silk, a metal roller is required with the figure of the wave engraven upon it, and other appendages which indicate considerable ingenuity. All these requisites the Japanese possessed antecedent to the presumed discovery of the French, and executed quite as effective, if we except the *moire-antiques*, which our lively neighbours have recently introduced to the world of fashion. Again, we have a couple of storks in bronze, in the form of candelabra. This branch of art belonged, almost exclusively, to the French until a recent period. The moderns borrowed the idea from the Greeks and Romans, several of whose productions were found in the ruins of Pompeii and elsewhere. These objects of art were mostly cast, and the only difference discernible is in the nature of the metal. But a new idea struck some modern artist, of comparatively recent date—whether a native of France is not clearly ascertained—namely, to grave over the casting with his tool, so as to touch up the leading points of his figure with more sharpness than a casting can possibly give.

The graver has been used but very few years in Europe, and was considered, and justly so, as an advance on ancient art. But while we were gratulating ourselves in Europe on the superiority to which we had attained as compared to the backward and barbarous East, the Japanese were in possession of precisely the same excellence, though it is possible they may never have seen a single remain of ancient art to suggest, if not to dictate, the necessity of it. The storks to which we allude, upon examination, are found to be cast, and graved up in the wings and back, in order to give them a finished imitation of nature, precisely as though they had been under the hands of a modern artist. In addition to these interesting objects, there are coins of singular form and extraordinary size; those in gold varying in circular pieces from a quarter of an inch in diameter up to five and six, which have more the appearance of golden pancakes on a small scale than coins of the Japanese realm. Wooden types, bankers' notes, porcelain of exquisite beauty and lightness; daggers, spears, and swords, whose steel seems of the highest quality, from the peculiar purple hue by which the best modern metal is described; manufactures in silk and other materials of rather a singular application; palanquins, oscritoires, lamps, and stoves, equally illustrative of the habits of the people and of their mechanical excellence; and, above all, views on screens, which denote that the Japanese artist is far beyond his Chinese neighbour in the art of perspective, and even in the proportions of drawing; the umbrellas and musical instruments, several of the latter being of singular forms; the gongs and drums; the personal ornaments of men and women of rank, and the uniform of their soldiers—we must leave to the inspection of the visitor, and content ourselves with simply calling attention to them. This department will well repay a minute investigation, and is suggestive certainly of the most singular, if not of the most instructive, train of thought; and the habits of a people, as indicated by isolated objects, both social and political, little known to us, cannot fail to furnish a subject of both a singular and instructive nature.

The balance, scales, and weights furnish an insight of Japanese customs, which is equally interesting as that of their manufactures. Here we see at a glance the minute division of the standard of weight which obtains amongst them; but without the cipher to the characters impressed upon the several symbols, it is useless to substitute a relative comparison with our own. The shape of the weights, however, is deserving of notice, as it admits of their being used with facility; and the reader has only to imagine a compressed parallel opide, with its larger sides bent in, and its shorter curved out, to have it present to the eye. These weights are made of a compound metal, in which copper seems to prevail, and the denomination of each is marked in characters upon the surface. The balance and scales are made of brass, and appear to be hung with great nicety of bearing. The articles used in the celebration of religious ceremonies are similar to those of the Chinese; but the pack of cards, which numbers one hundred, and is divided into separate series, with distinct marks, would puzzle a European gamester to

divine their application. The box of coins, in gold and silver pieces, is equally significant, and just as inexplicit as the cards. The gold pieces are twenty-nine in number, and vary in size from a parallelogram, whose diagonal is half an inch in length, to one measuring five inches. The largest coins in gold, however, are more of an oval than of a rectangular shape, and are valued at sixty pounds sterling each. Their precise use, in the monetary arrangements of the Japanese, it would be difficult to divine; for they are evidently too large for ordinary circulation, at least according to European conceptions of money-changing, though purses in common use in Japan are fully capable of receiving them. The silver pieces are more minutely divided, which clearly indicates that the circulation of commodities, amongst the community who use them, admits of greater activity. It is in poor and over-populated countries that a minute division of coinage generally obtains. All these coins are impressed with their appropriate values; and the characters expressive of those values are not engraved upon the largest, but impasted with a black material, as though it were lacquered upon the precious metal. The others appear to have been stamped with a die. The bank-note is a curious feature in money affairs. It is about one-third the size of a Bank of England note, cut longitudinally; and its "promise to pay," or whatever may be the true definition of its printed characters, covers the surface from top to bottom. This note is made of thin, wiry, and apparently glazed paper, similar to that used by the Chinese in the linings of tea chests, and appears capable of bearing a good deal of wear and tear. The purses are numerous and curiously formed, the material and embroidery indicating the rank and bearing of those who require their use. Some of them are as large as a lady's reticule; others as small as those in use with us. The types cut in wood denote that the Japanese are by no means backward in the art of wood-cutting, however inferior they may be to Europeans in other respects.

Such is a general though brief review of this interesting Exhibition, which redounds so honourably to the credit of the sister kingdom. The world has often heard of "great days for Ireland," but we know of none more entitled to that designation than that which saw the consummation of an undertaking commenced and carried out wholly by Irishmen, and calculated to increase, in an immense degree, the industrial resources of the country. This great work has been accomplished at the sole risk of Mr. William Dargan, one of the great captains of industry peculiar to our æra, and whose name will be ever worthily connected with his country's history. In carrying out his views he has been most ably assisted by Mr. P. C. Roney, whose energy, admirable temper, command of languages, and indomitable perseverance, have enabled him to surmount all difficulties, and to produce the successful result witnessed by myriads.

We shall now conclude in the words of Lord Granville, which were appropriately addressed to the élite of Ireland at the grand inaugural dinner given by the Mayor of Dublin to commemorate the auspicious occasion:—

"Before the building for the Exhibition in Hyde Park was opened," said his lordship, "an eminent French architect came to us, and expressed his admiration of the building, and of the manner in which the work had been carried out. He criticised some of the details, but he ended by saying that the thing which struck him with the greatest admiration and astonishment—and which was a thing utterly unknown in France and other European countries—was, that there should be found private contractors able to carry out such works, relying solely on their own private means. I believe it is, even in England, a modern innovation, that we find men undertaking such enormous works as they do now; and I can say this, that at the time of the Exhibition of 1851, when funds were comparatively wanting, it was an English contractor, furnishing the example of a grant of £50,000, which enabled us to obtain further grants that took us successfully to our object. And now I find, on coming to Ireland, another instance of a similar result, effected by one of the same class of men, who from industrious habits and enlarged operations have arrived at the greatest possible liberality of feeling. He (Mr. Dargan) had displayed unexampled generosity and munificence in contributing, to the extent that he had done, money and time towards the accomplishment in view."

THE ENVIRONS OF DUBLIN.

The environs of Dublin are, in parts, very beautiful: by means of the different railways the more celebrated spots within a few miles of the city may be easily reached. Our first stroll shall be westward—we can return by the train. Phœnix Park adjoins the city; and is at once an ornament to it and a most important benefit to the inhabitants. It occupies an area of some eighteen hundred acres, and is nearly seven miles in circumference,—being one of the largest and finest public parks in the Empire. The surface is in places undulated; but there are no hills. It is pretty well planted: though an open space is left sufficiently extensive for reviews on the grandest scale. In this park is the Lord Lieutenant's Lodge—a large and handsome mansion, with a considerable domain attached. Opposite to it is the Chief Secretary's Lodge. The Wellington Testimonial, which is so noticeable an object from the city and suburbs, stands in this park, at no great distance from the entrance.* It is a plain

* The stranger in Dublin will find the hand-book published by M'Glashan, entitled 'Dublin and its Environs,' a convenient and sufficient guide. We compared many of its notices on the spot, and found them to be very faithful: and we have been a good deal indebted to it in drawing up this sketch.

but massive granite obelisk, mounted on a pedestal, which is raised on an elevated platform: the height of the obelisk is 205 feet. On the sides of the obelisk, from base to summit, are inscribed the victories of the duke: the sides of the pedestal are intended to have bassi-relievi of the chief battles. A lofty insulated pedestal in front is intended to bear an equestrian statue. The Duke of Wellington, it will be remembered, was born in Dublin; and the citizens, proud of their fellow-townsman, erected this testimonial, in honour of him, at a cost of £20,000, which sum was raised by a public subscription. From the mound on which the Testimonial stands a remarkably good view of the city is obtained. Nearly all the principal buildings are visible, and the open country is seen beyond. A similar, but rather more extensive, view is that from the eminence just beyond, on which stands the military Magazine known as Wharton's Folly, and which Swift made the subject of one of his latest epigrams:

"Behold a proof of Irish sense!
  Here Irish wit is seen:
When nothing's left that's worth defence,
  We build a magazine."

It is the kind of wit of which there has been too much in Ireland. While speaking of the general view of Ireland we may mention that the most extensive prospect (though more distant than this) is to be seen from Dunsink Hill, about three miles north-west of Dublin: it embraces not merely the city, but the noble bay of Dublin and the heights of Killiney. There is a road across the park, which leads by Observatory Gate to Dunsink Hill: the Observatory is on the hill. We must just mention, before leaving, that the gardens and menagerie of the Zoological Society are in Phœnix Park.

Quitting the Park by Knockmaroon Gate you come upon the Liffey, where flowing along a narrow but rich valley it is quite a picturesque stream. On either hand the banks form lofty uplands; those on the south are clothed with luxuriant foliage. Forwards are seen the heights of Woodland, the beautiful demesne of Colonel White. The northern slopes are for above a couple of miles entirely covered with plantations of strawberries; from them the city is supplied, but all the fruit is not sent into the city. The Strawberry Beds, as the whole tract is called, are one of the notable places of the vicinity of Dublin. During the season this is a favourite resort of holiday-makers, for whose accommodation there is a number of permanent spirit and refreshment huts built along the road-side. But Sunday is the day on which the Strawberry Beds are chiefly visited; and in fact there is a 'strawberry fair' held here every Sunday afternoon during the whole of the strawberry season, and for some time after the fruit has disappeared—indeed it is continued till Donnybrook fair, (August 26), which famous festival terminates the summer holidays in Dublin county. It is worth while for one observant of popular habits to come here for once, in order to obtain a notion of Pat's style of enjoyment. Besides the permanent houses, there are erected for the occasion numerous booths, with painted signs, such as 'the King of the Brook,' 'the Old Harp,' &c.; flags are suspended from some, and the entrances are decorated with evergreens. From three in the afternoon—when the business of the day, confession, and perhaps 'a burying' or two, have been duly attended to—the 'boys' begin to flock hither, and continue to do so more and more till the close of day. The *fun* does not fairly commence till about six or seven o'clock. Then every booth is crowded; and the road is thronged with a noisy multitude. The day's supply of strawberries is by this time exhausted, but whiskey and porter make amends, and are in sufficient demand. At the further end of each booth boards are laid down for dancing on, and fiddlers or pipers are provided. Dancing begins early, and is prosecuted vigorously. On the boards Pat is in all his glory—especially if he have a pretty partner; and it is quite surprising to see what neat-looking lasses attend these places: many of them are pretty, quiet, modest girls, and neat and trim in their dresses, yet they will be dancing along with sottish dirty fellows, who have not a sound garment upon them;—but generally the Irish girls are much superior to the men of the same rank. The Irish dance is something national. An Irishman seems by dancing to work himself into a state of excitement much as an Indian does. As he warms the dance quickens, till Pat grows half delirious—of course, that is, if he has had a due allowance of whiskey. The fiddlers ply their elbows as quick as grasshoppers, but are quite unable to keep time with the wishes of the dancers, who seek to quicken them by some sufficiently odd expressions. "Arrah then move faster wid you, darling,"—"Go it, my boy, go it, more power to you: Och then get along if you love me: Och now go it, Dan—go it like blazes, and may the Almighty favour you!"—were some of the exclamations we noted.

Outside the booths there is a noisy crowd, composed of every variety of 'the finest pisantry.' Irish joking abounds, and the visitor must put up with his share of it. At every turn in the road may be seen an eager group clustered round a keen-looking rascal, who is sitting on the ground with a board on his knees, upon which a leather thong is coiled, while he is challenging one and another to try his luck. It is the old English game of 'pricking the girdle,' but it holds the place at Irish fairs and races of the English pea-and-thimble game: it is just as deceptive and as fraudulent, but the stakes are commonly pence instead of half-crowns. The game seems always to find plenty of players. But not the least curious part of the spectacle is the vast number of beggars who are assembled. As very few 'respectable' people go to these strawberry fairs, it is evident that the ordinary frolicers must give alms plentifully to attract so many mendicants: and a close look at the peasantry in any part of Ireland will evince that this is one of the causes of the overwhelming amount of mendicancy. The poorest will give if he have anything to give—and receive if he have not. Mendicancy is not looked on as degrading: even those who would themselves rather suffer than beg, are quite ready to bestow on the beggar while they possibly can.

Of course Pat cannot jig and tipple whiskey without exhibiting as the result a little superfluous liveliness; but on the whole there does not seem to be very much quarrelling at these strawberry fairs, though there is a good deal of noise. Of shillelagh-work we saw little, and were told that there is seldom much now. Once these fairs were somewhat 'riotous assemblages;' but that section of Young Ireland which attends them has grown pacific—is tired, it may be, of physical-force doctrines—or overawed perchance by the number of policemen about. Be the cause what it may, the strawberry fairs are now pretty orderly; the police, too, clear out all the booths at half-past nine. But they cannot be visited without it being seen that they are a great evil: and it is impossible to loiter about at one for a few hours, without the feeling being deeply impressed on the mind that the reckless improvident habits of the lower classes of Irishmen are in truth almost more than a 'second nature,' and that the task of elevating their moral as well as physical condition is a most difficult one—a feeling, by the way, which everything that is seen of them in country as well as in town, at home or abroad, only serves to intensify. Yet this is the task that every Irishman seems emphatically called on now to address himself to with heart and soul. An entire social regeneration is the thing needed;—a mighty labour, and not to be accomplished by talking or fighting!

Continuing along the river-side by Woodlands, Lucan is soon reached. The whole of this part is extremely pleasant, and will afford much to interest those who have time sufficient to wander awhile about. The beautiful grounds of Woodlands, and those of Lucan House, in which are some ruins of a castle, are open to the stranger. Leixlip, a couple of miles further, is a decayed town, slovenly-looking, but picturesque: around it there is much fine scenery, and in the neighbourhood are many objects of interest. The chief attraction is the waterfall, or rather rapid, known as the Salmon Leap. In a fine ravine, the Liffey rushes over a ledge of bold black rocks, and then forces its way among massive detached fragments, that lie scattered along its bed. Leixlip Castle, which stands on the southern bank of the Liffey, is an ancient edifice, and forms with the foaming river a fine picture. About four miles from Leixlip is a place familiar by name to every one—Maynooth College. The buildings form three sides of a quadrangle, the principal front of which is 400 feet in length. In the neighbourhood there is some very fine scenery: Carton, the extensive demesne of the Duke of Leinster, is especially celebrated. If the stranger visit Maynooth, he can return to Dublin by the Mullingar Railway: if he direct his steps southwards, he can return by the Great Southern and Western line. The nearest station from Leixlip on this line is at Celbridge, not far from which is Marley Abbey—or, as it is now called, Celbridge Abbey—where resided the unhappy Miss Vanhomrigh, Swift's Vanessa. In the grounds are still pointed out some of the laurels which she used to plant against the visits of the Dean. The first station from Dublin on this Great South Western Railway is at Clondalkin, a place that certainly should be visited; it is about five miles from the city. The name of the town is derived from that of a church, Cluain Dolcain, which is said to have been founded here by St. Mochua early in the seventh century. Clondalkin was once a bishop's see. Of its monastery only a few traces of the walls are discernible. But there is here a very perfect specimen of that curious Irish edifice the Round Tower. This one has a rather peculiar basement, and it is crowned with a conical roof. It is about ninety feet high, and fifteen feet in diameter; the entrance is about ten feet from the ground. The interior may be ascended by means of steps, which have been fixed for the purpose. We need not stay to puzzle over the purposes of these buildings, as we shall have another opportunity of speaking of them. The village of Clondalkin is a decent Irish village: with a parish church, Catholic chapel, monastery, and national school. In the neighbourhood are extensive limestone quarries.

On the northern side of the city, and only about two miles from it, is the secluded, half-decayed village of Glasnevin—interesting from its associations, and worth visiting on its own account. The village lies partly in the valley of the Tolka, whence it climbs up Glasnevin Hill. In the valley on the south side of the river is the Botanic Garden of the Dublin Royal Society, some thirty acres in extent, varied in surface, and admirably arranged and stocked. The conservatory and hothouses have a fine display of exotics; and on the lake there is a good collection of aquatic plants. In this garden is the house in which Tickell the poet dwelt during his abode in Ireland. Addison was a frequent visitor; and here, as at Oxford and Eton and some other places, his favourite walk in the grounds is pointed out, and is still called 'Addison's Walk.' Tickell's house is now the residence of the Professor of Botany. A house on the higher ground of Glasnevin is that in which Dr. Delany, Swift's friend, dwelt. Swift spent a good deal of his time at Delville House; and Addison, Sheridan, and Parnell, are among the other celebrated persons who were in the number of Dr. Delany's guests. Glasnevin House is the residence of the Bishop of Kildare. Clermont, the National Deaf and Dumb Institution, near this, is well worth visiting.

Along the line of the Drogheda Railway, or northeast of Dublin, are some noticeable localities. On the left is Marino, the handsome mansion of the Earl of Charlemont. In the grounds is the Casino, a miniature Doric temple, designed by Sir Robert Chambers, and constructed in a very costly style. In it the Earl used to unbend, in company with Grattan, Flood, Curran, and other eminent Irishmen of his day. Clontarf (where is the first station) is a spot famous in Irish history: here it was that Brian Boroimhe, the Alfred of Ireland — "You remember the glories of Brian the Brave?"—fought, on Good Friday, 1014, his last and greatest battle with the Danes under Sitric. Maelmora, the subordinate king of Leinster, had joined with the enemy; but Brian gained a glorious victory over their combined forces. Brian and his son Murogh both fell in the battle, and a great number of their nobles with them, but the victory was perfect. Clontarf is a modern Gothic castle of mingled styles: it stands on the site of an ancient one, and is believed to indicate the battle-field. The castle is, from its position, a striking object in the landscape, and commands a wide and beautiful prospect. There is fine scenery here, along the shore, looking over the bay; but we must proceed to another famous place— 'the big Hill of Howth.' "The peninsula of Howth, or, as it is generally termed, the Hill of Howth, is one of the most remarkable features in the vicinity of Dublin. It forms the northern entrance to Dublin Bay, is about three miles in length by two in breadth, and lifts its rocky summit 563 feet above the level of the ocean."—(Fraser.) The surface is greatly diversified; and from various parts of it are many most picturesque prospects of the coast and country beyond. Especially fine is the view of Dublin, with the splendid Bay and the estuary of the Liffey in front, and the Dublin Hills in the distance. From the northern slopes the little island called Ireland's Eye is seen to great advantage, as well as the coast towards Malahide; while from the tongue of land on which the Baily lighthouse stands are obtained some most striking views of the wild and precipitous rocks in which the promontory terminates seaward. In the little village of Howth there are some vestiges of an old abbey. Howth Castle, close by, is the seat of the Earls of Howth: only a tower remains of the original castle. Howth Harbour was constructed from the designs of Rennie: it was commenced in 1807, and completed in 1832, at a cost of above £420,000. It was intended for a harbour of refuge, and for the mail-packet station; but in consequence of its silting-up, and the accumulation of sand at its mouth, it is not available for either purpose, and is, in fact, nearly useless. As may be supposed, from its peculiar and characteristic beauty, the Hill of Howth is a favourite resort of the citizens. Holiday parties are constantly made to it, and there are good hotels, and ordinary tea-gardens, where all may disport themselves according as their tastes or pockets prompt them. In the summer, a steamer makes daily excursions from Dublin; and this is a very pleasant way of reaching Howth. The sail down the Liffey and along the Bay is a delightful one.

If the visitor have time, he might continue along the coast by the Strand and Portmarnock to Malahide. Or Malahide may be reached at once by the railway: Malahide station is nine miles from Dublin. The chief attraction is the Castle, a large and magnificent though somewhat incongruous pile, the seat of the Talbots, to whom the demesne was granted by Edward IV. Some portions of the building are ancient; but the greater part is modern. The interior is both splendid and interesting, and it contains some good pictures: it is permitted to be seen on any day but Sunday. Close by it is a ruined church; the grounds are very picturesque. Malahide is a straggling fishing village; and an Irish fishing village is always "a thing to admire at." A very fine hotel and two handsome terraces have been recently erected. About two or three miles distant is the old town of Swords, famous in Irish chronicles, and worth visiting for its antiquities. These are; first, extensive remains of the archiepiscopal palace : next, the vestiges of the chapel of a monastery founded here in 512 by that famous saint, holy St. Columb, and of which the scarce less famous St. Finian was the first abbot: and, finally, there is a round tower—one of the rudest of those strange structures : it is seventy-two feet high, and fourteen feet in diameter. The old town of Swords is a very poor place—to Saxon eyes it seems a wretched one ; but then it is none the less picturesque. About three miles north of Swords, at the village of Lusk, is another round tower.

The Dublin and Kingstown Railway will enable visitors to see the south-eastern suburbs of Dublin with great facility. This line skirts the southern coast of Dublin Bay, and as it affords a series of beautiful sea-views, it is in much favour for short pleasure runs. It is only fair to say that the Company do their best to make these excursions agreeable. The second-class carriages are comfortably cushioned ; and a commodious kind of open carriage is provided for those who wish to view the scenery ; the seats in these are cushioned, and there is a covering overhead. It is so seldom that Railway Companies do anything to render travelling agreeable to any other than first-class passengers, that it ought to be noticed when it does happen. There is another excellent thing on this line : the Company have constructed near several of the stations very convenient bathing-places ; and second-class tickets are granted every morning throughout the summer, which entitle the holders to ride from Dublin to any station they please, have a sea-bath, and return for eight-pence. Bathing places are also provided at some distance from the others, for the use of ladies, at the same charges. The bathing-tickets later in the day are charged a somewhat higher price.

On the way to Kingstown there are several stations, but we cannot stay at either ; Kingstown will occupy as much time as we have to spare. The town itself is nought : it is a new town, a good deal frequented as a watering-place by the Dublin citizens ; and the houses are what might, in such a place, be expected. Kingstown is not the original name of the place. It was formerly called Dunleary, from there having been here, say the topographers, a dun, or fort, in which dwelt Leary, king of Ireland, about the middle of the fifth century. Be that as it may, here was a little dirty village called Dunleary, with a small harbour, at which George IV. landed on his visit to Ireland in 1821. The visit half-crazed the good people of Ireland ; and among other of the methods of eternizing their gratitude which they adopted, was that of erecting an obelisk on the spot where he stept ashore, and changing the name of the place, which, on account of the con-

struction of the new harbour, was promising to become a town of some importance, into Kingstown. The new town has left old Dunleary, however, rather on one side. Kingstown Harbour is the chief feature here : it was commenced in 1817, when the failure of that at Howth became palpable. Rennie was employed to make the designs and superintend the construction. It is formed by two immense piers, which incline towards each other so as to leave an opening seaward of 850 feet. The western pier is 4950 feet long,—the eastern, 3500 ; they enclose an area of 251 acres, being one of the largest artificial harbours in the kingdom. Frigates and Indiamen of 800 tons burden can ride in the harbour ; at the wharfs vessels of heavy tonnage can discharge their cargoes at any state of the tide : but the harbour is not found to be as useful as was anticipated. The entrance is so wide and so ill-placed, that during easterly gales vessels within the harbour are unable to keep their anchorage : it should be observed, however, that it was part of the original plan to have the entrance protected by a breakwater. Some £700,000 are said to have been expended in the construction of the harbour ; but the expenditure has extended over thirty years. The eastern pier forms an admirable parade, and affords the residents and visitors abundant amusement : the seaward prospect is a noble one ; the view of the bay is very fine ; the harbour has generally a goodly number of vessels of all sizes, including a great many yachts, whose evolutions are always attractive ; and it is the place where the packets embark and disembark their passengers. At the end of the east pier is a lighthouse, which, at night, displays a revolving light. The railway-station, a rather stately building, is close against the harbour.

On summer evenings the band of one of the regiments stationed at Dublin generally adds to the liveliness of the scene by performing popular airs on the jetté. Of the numerous villas and terraces seen bordering the strand, or scattered over the heights inland, it is needless to speak. The whole distance from Dublin is thickly sprinkled with them, and some are of considerable pretensions. A ride of a mile and three quarters on the Atmospheric Railway will bring the tourist to Dalkey. There is not much to be seen in the village itself ; but it has some historic celebrity, and the vicinity is attractive. In early times this was an important neighbourhood ; and in order to defend it, and afford protection to the shipping, there were seven castles built along the coast. Three of these castles (or rather forts) are yet in part remaining at Dalkey, one at Bullock, and another at Monkstown. There are also at Dalkey some remains of an old church. Just off Dalkey Point is a little island, of about twenty-five acres area, which is separated from the mainland by a sound about 300 yards wide. Dalkey Island was formerly the scene of an annual assemblage of Dublin citizens,—sometimes to the number of 20,000,—whose proceedings were recorded in a 'Dalkey Gazette,' issued on the occasion, and are still referred to at due length in the local histories and guide-books. The object of the

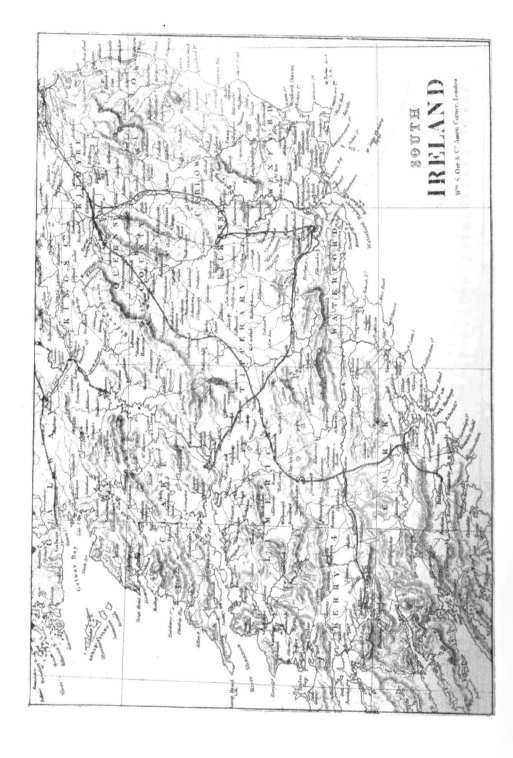

SOUTH
IRELAND

Wm S. Orr & Co. Amen Corner, London

meeting was to elect and crown a sovereign of the island. The King of Dalkey and Emperor of the Muglins was assisted in the government of his island by a prime minister, an archbishop of Dalkey, an admiral, a general, and other ministers and officers ecclesiastical, civil, and military. The election was conducted with due solemnity, and after the coronation a sermon was preached by the archbishop; the whole affair was carried through with much relish. It appears to have been some such an annual revel of the cockneys of Dublin as was indulged in by the cockneys of London in the election of their 'Mayor of Garratt;' the chief difference being that while the Londoners were content with a magistrate, the Dalkeians, loftier in their notions, would have a monarch. But their ambition was their ruin. The government of the King of the other island became alarmed at the increase of their number, and suppressed the meeting. The King of Dalkey was compelled to abdicate, and the King of England reigned alone. Dalkey Island was taken possession of by the British sovereign, and is still occupied by a British garrison,—two or three of the coast-guard,—who are its only inhabitants.

Now let us climb this hill: it gave us a pleasant greeting as we came over the sea, and it seems as though it would afford us a cheerful welcome on the summit. We will not linger by the way. From the new brick-and-mortar work about the lower slopes we gladly escape. The name of yonder village has so Italian a sound, raises such visions of soft blue skies, and Arcadian scenes, recalls such poetic fancies, that we must avoid it, lest the reality be too discordant. Let Sorento be unseen. Nor will we now go to look after the quarries which supplied the granite for the construction of yon harbour. Killiney Hill is worth ascending. We are not five hundred feet above the sea, but we have a prospect that might lead us to fancy we were a thousand. How beautiful from this height is that glorious Dublin Bay! Howth stands out majestically in the serene ocean, and from it the varying coast sweeps round in a splendid curve to the base of the hill on which we are standing. Streams of silver dash across the dark blue water as the light breeze plays gently over it. White sails glitter in the sunshine; one and another dark hull moves steadily along, leaving behind it a stream of yellow smoke. And there a tall-masted emigrant ship is working slowly out of the Bay, bearing with it how many hopes and fears—blighted prospects, young imaginations! Let us look another way. Here is a view of soft smiling valleys, and wooded slopes, of rich demesnes, handsome villas, cultivated fields, enough to charm away gloomy fancies. And here again, if we turn northwards, is another beauteous scene over this fine Killiney Bay away to Bray Point; inland across a country bounded by the Mountains of Wicklow—a tract we ought long ere this to have been rambling over. Let us away.

WICKLOW.

There are many other spots in the immediate vicinity of Dublin whither we might conduct the reader, but we leave them unvisited, for we have stayed already so long as to leave but too little time for a sufficient examination of the beauties of Wicklow. We shall pass through the more celebrated parts of this beautiful county without much regard to the order of the route, taking the several spots as we can most readily reach them in a careless ramble at a little distance from the coast to Arklow, and thence back by the mountains which occupy the middle of the county. As there is no railway in Wicklow, it may not be amiss to say a few words as to the means of conveyance. Of course the best way to see a district such as this is to walk over it: much of it cannot be well seen in any other way. Along the main lines of road there are a good many coaches and vans, which run at very low fares, and are serviceable even to the pedestrian, in enabling him to get over some of those uninteresting or dreary spaces which intervene between the more important points. All, or nearly all, the Wicklow and Wexford conveyances go from one office in Dublin, and it will be well to call at this office, which is situated in Harry Street, to learn the lines of route, and the times, which are frequently being altered. By a little contrivance, and without much expense, these vehicles will enable any one whose time is limited to two or three days, to pass through much of the most beautiful scenery, and to visit the most famous spots. It will only be necessary to fix on two or three stations where the coaches pass, and from them there will be little difficulty in reaching the places which are out of the coach-road, either by walking or hiring a car. Cars are kept at almost every inn of any size (and there is sufficient traffic to support an inn in almost all the larger road-side villages); they are let at sixpence or eightpence a mile, and there are few or no turnpikes. Indeed the usual way of seeing Wicklow is by hiring cars from place to place; and there is only the objection to it, that a great deal is of necessity overlooked which is most characteristic of the country and the inhabitants.

BRAY AND THE DARGLE.

Bray must be our starting-point. It is situated on the Bray river, which here divides the counties of Dublin and Wicklow, and, as it stands on both sides of the river, it belongs in part to each county; but Bray proper belongs to Wicklow. It is about thirteen miles from Dublin. Bray, as the centre of a beautiful district, is a place of great resort; and being but a short distance from the sea, it is also much frequented as a watering-place. The town itself is a long straggling one, consisting of a principal street, and several lesser streets and fragments of streets diverging from it or connected with it—for it is not very easy to explain the arrangement of an Irish country-town, even when like this it belongs to the more respectable class. The town is built on very irregular ground, the houses are anything but uniform, the church stands on a lofty bank, lifting its tower high above the rest of the buildings, hence its general appearance from a little distance is picturesque : as you ascend the river towards it, and it is seen backed by the Sugar-loaf Mountains, it is eminently so. Bray has little trade, less manufacture, and just the shadow of a fishery : but one way and another it is tolerably prosperous. It has a population of 3000 souls. In order to keep the visitors in good temper, the natives curb their own inclinations and keep it comparatively clean ; and that there may be no cause of complaint left, it possesses one of the best hotels in all Ireland.

Bray is the centre of one of the richest and loveliest districts on this side of the island. The natural features of the county too are not, as in too many other parts, disfigured by the frequent signs of the deep misery of those who dwell among them. It is as fair, and in appearance nearly as flourishing, as many of the happiest spots in England. All around are the mansions and demesnes of the nobility and gentry of the county, and the villas of the wealthier merchants and professional men of the metropolis. Many of these are celebrated on account of their owners, and many on their own account. Nothing can well be more delightful than some of them, and it is a very pleasant way of spending a day to ride or stroll from one to another under good guidance. Among the more famous of them is Kilruddery—a noble mansion, belonging to the Earl of Meath, standing within a demesne of surpassing beauty. Kilruddery is a modern mansion of the Elizabethan style : not far off is Hollybrook, a mansion of the Elizabethan age. Adjoining Kilruddery is the demesne of Bray Head, which is also worth visiting. The fine promontory of Bray Head, being some 800 feet above the sea, affords a splendid sea view, as well as one of much richness inland. On the other side are St. Valerie, the seat of the Hon. P. Crampton, one of the most charming places in Great Britain ; Old Connaught, where the wisest and wittiest of the present generation have delighted to assemble around the hospitable board of Lord Plunkett ; and very many others which—are they not written in the Guide-books of the county ? If the stranger have time and inclination, he may visit some one or other of them, and he will generally find that the more beautiful grounds are freely opened to him.

The lion of all this district is the Dargle, a spot to which almost every one who visits Dublin is carried, whatever other spot be left unvisited. The Dargle is only an abbreviation of its proper name, which is the Glen of the Dargle,—it being really a glen of somewhat over a mile in length, through which the river Dargle flows. Nature has indeed been lavish of her favours here. For the whole way the streamlet winds between lofty and precipitous rocks, whose sides are clad with the most luxuriant foliage. In places, the banks ascend to an altitude of above three hundred feet, and with the trees that bend forward from them towards the opposite sides, steep the deep abyss in an intensity of gloom that might well have suggested its native name of the Dark Glen. But then there are broad open dells, where the bright sun sends down its rays through the leafy screen and lights up the depths of the hollow, glancing hither and thither from rock to rock, just by a touch gilding one mossy fragment and casting its neighbour into a deeper shadow, making the waterbreaks to glitter as with countless gems,—and in a word producing that sunny spot a picture such as a fairy might have wrought, who, having been looking at one of Creswick's paintings, was tempted to try how such another would appear if executed with Nature's own materials. A good footway is carried through the glen along the summit of the north bank, which enables you to see it very conveniently ; and at all the places where there are scenes of superior beauty or grandeur a seat is placed, an opening is cut, or some other such silent intimation given. From some of these stations the appearance of the glen is of exceeding beauty ; from some, too, there is much of a gloomy grandeur,—but the general character of the glen is that of surpassing loveliness. One of these resting-places, where the bank is of the greatest height and steepness, is known as Lover's Leap ; a name it is said to have received from —— : but we made a sort of promise not to be repeating these legends, and our fair readers will readily imagine for themselves the remainder of this one ; in which there are, of course, a gentle lady and a tender youth, love that does not run smooth, and a good deal more that we have forgotten, but which they will easily recall or invent. We make no doubt that their versions will be quite as veritable as those written in the books, or told by the guides,—no, not by the guides, for there is no guide attached to the place, and stranger guides are not permitted to enter the Dargle ; a very excellent arrangement, by the way, for you are thus not merely left to wander about at will, but saved from the intrusion of some nonsensical piece of information, or silly story, when you would be hearkening only to the voice of the woods and the waters, and the song of the birds ;—but we are running off from the subject with which we commenced, and so we return to the Lover's Leap. And now we are there again, just let us beg you to notice what a rich and charming view there is along the glen. The other principal station is known as Rock View, and it has the advantage of not only yielding a beautiful prospect of the Dargle, but also of the country above and beyond it. (Cut, No. 5.)

The mansion of Powerscourt, with the beautiful demesne of which it is the centre, forms a conspicuous object in the mid-distance, while the lofty ridge of Kippure closes the prospect. But the Dargle is equally fine if viewed from below. There the stream, foaming along its stony channel, forms the central feature, and with the rocks and trees, with all their sombre shadows and rich colouring for their accompaniments, makes pictures such as poet or painter would in vain attempt to embody.

The Dargle, as has been hinted, is private property and enclosed. The west bank belongs to Lord Powerscourt, the opposite to Mr. Grattan. Admission is always granted upon application at the lodges, at either

5.—THE DARGLE.

end. It is best seen by entering at the southern end,—the upward course of the stream presents bolder and more varied features, and the distant prospects are finer. In any case it is better to go quite through the Dargle, than, as is often done, to go part of the way and return: some choice views are sure to be lost if either end be left unseen.

Powerscourt is the most important seat in this part of the county: it can only be seen upon procuring an order from the agent of Viscount Powerscourt. It is a large but rather plain building; the interior has some very splendid apartments. The demesne is of great extent, of most varied character and extreme beauty. The territory of Powerscourt extends over 26,000 acres. That part of it called the Deer Park, lying some miles south of the mansion, contains some very grand scenery, and is much visited. In it is a very celebrated waterfall, formed by the Dargle (or, as it is called by the natives in its upper course, the Glenisloreane), which,

after a course of some two or three miles from its source in Crocken Pond, here throws itself over a rocky steep some three hundred feet high. After storms, or when there is much water in the river, it must form a noble cataract; but when we saw it there was very little water, and its grandeur was much diminished. The Douce Mountain, which is the highest of the mountains in this neighbourhood, being 2384 feet above the sea, and which forms so conspicuous and imposing an object in the surrounding scenery, is often ascended from this waterfall.

Tinnahinch, Mr. Grattan's seat, is the mansion which was purchased for £50,000 by the Irish Parliament, and presented to the celebrated statesman Henry Grattan, (the father of the present proprietor), "as a testimony," to borrow the words of the vote, "of the national gratitude for great national services." It is a plain substantial mansion, but delightfully situated, and the estate is a very fine one. There are a couple of other demesnes situated on the Dargle that are permitted to be seen, and are a good deal visited—Charlville, the seat of the Earl of Rathdown, and Bushy Park.

GLEN OF THE DOWNS; DEVIL'S GLEN.

Again renewing our journey southwards from the Dargle, we soon reach the village of Kilmacanoge—a collection of poor and slovenly cabins, with a very large and showy new Union-house. Thence we pass the base of the isolated conical mountain called the Sugar Loaf. This mountain, which is 1651 feet above the sea, has received the epithet of Great, to distinguish it from the Little Sugar Loaf, 1120 feet high, which rises on the borders of Kilruddery, some miles to the north of its greater namesake. Though neither of the mountains is much like a sugar-loaf (as sugar-loaves are made now-a-days), they are, as seen from some points, singularly like each other. The Great Sugar Loaf is a conspicuous object over a wide range of country, from standing, as we said, quite isolated; and hence, also, it commands a wide and splendid prospect from the summit.

A little further and we enter another of the more famous of the many beautiful glens which distinguish this county. The Glen of the Downs is an opening between two mountains of a very grand and romantic character. The ravine is a mile and a half long,—a little streamlet brawls along the midst; the mountain sides rise abruptly, sometimes to a height of five or six hundred feet, the space between them varying from one hundred to a hundred and fifty feet. The long mountain ridge on the right is called the Down Mountain, whence the glen has received the name. Beautiful as this glen is, it must once have been very much finer. A very good but formal coach-road has been carried along the bottom; and the hill-sides have been in parts disfigured by stiff regular plantations. In places, however, the natural woods, or some that have assumed the character of natural woods, prevail, and, climbing about the rugged crags and slopes, produce a rich effect. The finest views of the Glen of the Downs from the road are in a northward direction, when the opening is filled by the peak of the Sugar Loaf Mountain.

But the glen should also be seen from above. At the southern end of the left bank is Belle Vue, the seat of P. Latouche, Esq., of whose demesne that side of the glen and the heights above form a part. Admission is readily granted to the grounds. From them there is a splendid view along the glen and over the country beyond. When the sun is sinking below the hills, and all the lower parts of the ravine are in the deepest shade, while the slanting rays are gilding the summits, and over a rich expanse, broken and bounded by the peaks of numerous mountains, the lengthening shadows are slowly stretching, and a thin hazy vapour is creeping up the hollows, the whole scene puts on an air of grandeur and of beauty whose charm is irresistible.

The village that is seen a little way out of the road on the left after quitting the glen, is Delgany. It is worth stepping aside to see. The situation is very beautiful, and the views of the village are very picturesque and pleasing, as well as those from it. Moreover, it wears an aspect of comfort that is quite refreshing, after becoming inured to the almost total want of it that is so frequently in these Wicklow villages. Delgany is, we believe, a good deal resorted to as a summer abode—which of course to some extent explains its neatness of appearance; but it is more satisfactorily explained when you are told that there have been some generations of good and considerate resident landlords.

The next village on the road, Newtown-Mount-Kennedy, is the centre of some much-admired scenery. The places which are usually visited, are the demesnes of Altadore and Glendaragh on the west, and Mount Kennedy and Woodstock on the east. There is no doubt much that will amply repay the leisurely visitor; but we must not linger among them. Newtown village is a long and populous, but by no means attractive place, and there is a sad array of mendicants waiting about ready to fasten on the stranger, or to surround the doors of the coaches which stop there.

Ashford Inn, or the Inn at Newrath Bridge, might very well be taken as the centre from which to make two or three excursions, and also to enjoy a little fishing. The chief attraction here is the Devil's Glen,—the great rival of the Dargle and the Glen of the Downs. Like the former, it is a long narrow pass, or rather a deep cleft, formed, as it would seem, by the parting asunder of the living rock. But the Devil's Glen is larger than the Dargle, and more stern and sombre in character. This, indeed, is what characterizes it, and the preference will be given either to it or to the Dargle according as the more strictly beautiful or the sterner aspects of Nature are most in unison with the taste and the feelings. The Glen of the Downs is of quite another character, and cannot be properly compared with either. Along the narrow bottom of the glen the river Vartry forces its way around and over the massy fragments of rock that fill the channel, and rushes sparkling and foaming along as if impatient of the hindrances to its progress. The sides of the glen rise up rugged and precipitous. On the one hand is a luxuriant hanging wood; the other is bare, but the more pleasing from the contrast of its gray crags to the verdure opposite. At the end of the glen is a noble waterfall—the Vartry pouring over the black rock in one sheet, and falling at once a hundred feet into the dark pool below. The Vartry has at all times a much larger volume of water than the Dargle, and the fall is always a very striking one—none the less so from the absence of foliage; when the river is in flood it is said to be exceedingly grand. The glen of the Dargle is wanting in this feature: and Powerscourt Waterfall, though so much loftier, is certainly not comparable with this in grandeur. The views from the banks above the Devil's Glen are very fine,—but the Dargle is finer.

There is another very pleasing glen in this neighbuurhood, a few miles north of Ashford—Glen Dunran. It is two miles long, narrow, and finely wooded. It must not be compared with the more famous one we have been visiting, but it is a lovely spot.

Close by Ashford is the classic demesne of Rosanna, the property of D. Tighe, Esq. Here it was that the charming Irish poetess, Mrs. Tighe, wrote the beautiful poem of 'Psyche.' The grounds are especially famous for their magnificent trees. These impart to it a stateliness such as few of the Irish parks possess, and not many English ones surpass. It is said in Curry's 'Handbook for Ireland,' that "this well-wooded demesne contains among its venerable trees some of the finest old oaks and Spanish chestnuts in the country." Many of them would dignify one of the finest parks in Kent. Along the road which passes the demesne they form an almost matchless avenue. One noble patriarch stands out quite apart in the road,—to the no small danger, as it would appear, of coaches travelling that way, but certainly adding much to the picturesque beauty of this bit of road.

Before quitting this locality, let us add that the river Vartry, after it leaves the Devil's Glen, and being joined by two or three small affluents, expands into a good-sized stream, passes by Ashford and Newrath, and soon approaches the sea. But here a sandbank has formed and prevented its egress: the river, in consequence, has expanded to the right and left, making a narrow lagoon, two miles in length, which is known as Broad Lough, at the southern end of which, by the town of Wicklow, a mile and a half below its original outlet, it flows into the sea. The sandbank is called the Morrogh.

WICKLOW: ARKLOW.

Wicklow, though the county and assize-town, is a miserable-looking place. It has a rather considerable corn-trade, and a few small trading vessels; but else it appears to have little commerce of any kind, and to be altogether a neglected locality. The town and the people seem alike disheartened: even the fishery is not looked after. There is not much to be seen in the town. Of the old castle there are a few unimportant vestiges remaining on a steep rock, which projects into the sea by the entrance of Broad Lough. It bears the name of the Black Castle. There are also some remains of the Abbey which was founded here in the reign of Henry III. These, with a doorway of the old church, are all that remain to attest the former consequence of the town, or to recall the recollections of its history.

Nor is there much of beauty in the town, or its immediate vicinity, to attract the stranger; and it is, therefore, seldom visited. It is, indeed, almost only noteworthy as an example—unhappily not a rare thing to meet with—of an old decayed Irish town. But so looked at, it may be regarded with some interest; and there is something in the appearance of the people and their houses, and cabins also, noteworthy. The

heights about Wicklow afford some fine sea views; and the bold bluff promontory of Wicklow Head, with the lighthouses, is a feature that a painter of coast scenery would stay to sketch. All along here, and round to Wicklow, the coast is a drifting sandbank; as dreary and unhappy-looking as a coast-line well can be. And the country inland between these towns is hardly better. Wicklow is much resorted to in the bathing season.

From Wicklow to Arklow, the tourist has the choice of several roads—that most usually selected is by Genealy, Rathdrum, Avondale, thence to Castle Howard and "the Meeting of the Waters," by Avoca and Shelton Abbey. The coast road is, however, the shorter, and is not without its attractions, presenting at intervals some fine views of the shore, and bold sea scenery. There is an intermediate line, which, however, we would not counsel the tourist to attempt, as it is very precipitous, though passing through some fine scenery.

Arklow is now a much more important town than Wicklow. It is the most populous town in the county. At the census of 1841 there were 6,237 inhabitants in the parish of Arklow, of whom 3,254 resided in the town. It is situated on the estuary of the Avoca, at the southern extremity of the county. Between the town and the sea there is a wide strip of coast, a drifting sandy waste, only relieved by the "dunes," or hillocks of loose shifting sand. The haven is in good part filled with sand, and of little use except for boats and very light vessels. Along the creek is a gathering of poor clay cabins, called the Fishery. The town itself, or at least the business part of it, stretches up a slight ascent nearly parallel to the river, but not close to it. The river is crossed by a long rude bridge of eighteen arches, and on the Wicklow side of it there are a few poor-houses.

Arklow has at different times been the scene of some stout contests. The castle, the chief object of the assailants, was built in the reign of John, and was dismantled by Oliver Cromwell. The last time Arklow was made a battle-field was as late as 1795. The "rebel army," under the guidance and command of Father Murphy, had surprised and taken Wexford, and now, above 20,000 strong, determined to march upon Dublin. Flushed with success, they summoned Arklow to surrender; but there was in it a stouthearted garrison of 1,600 men, commanded by General Needham, who had no thoughts of yielding. The rebels succeeded in forcing their way into the lower part of the town, which they set fire to and destroyed. In the upper town the fight was protracted till nightfall, when the insurgents were repulsed with fearful loss. Father Murphy was among the slain. Had they not been checked at Arklow, it is believed the misguided men might have reached the capital.

There is not much that is characteristic or interesting in Arklow. Of the castle there is a mere fragment left: it stands at the end of the town, against the barracks. The church is a large and substantial modern pile. There are no other public buildings that call for remark. The houses generally, in the principal street, are respectable; there is a good inn; and there must be some amount of business. But there is an unhappy listlessness hanging about the place, which is very uncomfortable. Once, Arklow had an important and prosperous fishing-trade; and there is still a large number of fishing-boats belonging to the town. But the fishing has greatly fallen off. The herrings—the fish chiefly taken—are said to have left the coast. The night we stayed there, however, there was a very large take of them; and that there is a ready market for them was proved by the fact that the whole quantity was purchased at once by a person from Liverpool, who was here with a small vessel, on 'the look out.' Indeed, we strongly suspect that if some English spirit could be infused into the Arklowites — Liverpool or North Country energy, and South Coast skill—the fishing would be again as of yore, or better. Improvement is sadly wanting here. The Arklow boats are clumsy half-decked things; and the nets are hardly half the size of those used by the Brighton or Hastings crews. The boatmen, too, would cut an odd figure beside the bluff many-jacketed Deal or Hastings fishermen. It would do an Arklow man some good to go to one of these places, or to Brighton, for a month or two.

The houses in the principal street, we said, are generally respectable; but then the rest are mostly very poor. The Fishery is the worst part. There all the houses are mere clay cabins—many of them with one window, and not a bit of garden, or even yard, and all that were looked into were dark, miserable, almost without furniture, and very filthy: yet we were assured at Arklow that the poor there are "comparatively well off."

The country west of Arklow is not often visited by the tourist; nor is there very much to reward him. Yet perhaps a journey by Croaghan Kinsella to Aughrim, and thence up the glen toward Lugnaquillia, would repay the pedestrian; the roads would hardly do for cars. On the slopes of Croaghan Kinsella is passed the celebrated Wicklow Gold Mine: "our Lagenian Mine," as Moore has it—

> "Where sparkles of golden splendour
> All over the surface shine;
> But if in pursuit we go deeper,
> Allured by the gleam that shone,
> Ah! false as the dream of the sleeper,
> Like Love, the bright ore is gone."

This is nearly true now, but there was a time when it was regarded in a very different light. There had for some years been a vague report current that gold had been found in this neighbourhood; when, "in the year, 1796, a piece of gold, in weight about half an ounce, was found by a man crossing the Ballinvalley stream, the report of which discovery operated so powerfully upon the minds of the peasantry, that every employment was forsaken, the benefits of agriculture abandoned, and the fortunes of Aladdin, or Ali Baba, were the great originals they hoped to imitate. Such infatuation," continues our author, "called for the interference of

Government; and accordingly a party of the Kildare militia were stationed on the banks of the rivulet, to intercept the works and break the illusion:"—which, by the way, seems rather an Irish method of employing soldiers. They might occupy the "diggings" and intercept the works, but think of a regiment being ordered to "break the illusion!" However, the illusion was broken somehow. The same writer says, that "during the short space of two months spent by these inexperienced miners in examining and washing the sands of the Ballinvalley stream, it is supposed that 2,666 [which is a mighty nice calculation] ounces of pure gold were found, which sold for about £10,000." Having driven off the gold-finders, the Government undertook to open mines; and the works were carried on till 1798, when all the machinery was destroyed by the insurgents. The works were renewed in 1801; but being found not sufficiently productive to repay the expenses, were eventually discontinued. "The quantity of gold found while the stream-works were under the management of Government, appears to have been inferior to that collected by the peasantry, amounting to the value of £3,675 7s. 11¼d." (*Wright: 'Scenes in Ireland.'*) Evidently the Government workers, with all their machinery, were very unlucky, or Croaghan's stock of gold was soon exhausted; or perhaps there was some mistake in counting up the 2,666 ounces. It is mentioned in Curry's 'Hand-Book of Ireland,' that "a London Company had been engaged in streaming for gold, as it is termed, for these two years past . . . . but the results were not such as to induce them to proceed." A few labourers, it is added, continued to be employed by them without any regular superintendence; "a fixed sum being paid for whatever gold they may find." Even this casual searching is now discontinued; but there yet prevails a lingering belief among the peasantry, that there is still gold in Kinsella, and only the 'lucky man' is wanting. Many an anxious look, we doubt not, is turned on the brook when it has been 'roarin' in spate;' but we fear, as one of the peasantry of whom we had been asking some questions oddly said, "it will never touch California."

Croaghan Kinsella is nearly 2,000 feet above the sea, lifting his head high above his neighbours for miles around. The summit commands a prospect both wide and magnificent. The little town of Tinahely has nothing to lead the wayfarer aside. It was destroyed by the rebels in 1798, and has been rebuilt in a neater style than usually prevails in such sequestered places; there is an inn which will afford accommodation, if that route be taken. Aughrim, which lies in the route we pointed out, is quite a mountain village, rude and poor, but very picturesque:—a collection of stone and clay cabins by the river's side, and backed by bare mountains. Glen Aughrim, which commences here, is in its way very fine. There are no soft cultivated slopes, but, instead, a genuine wild mountain glen, a swift stream running along the bottom, the vast mass of Croaghan Moira rising full in front. The road continues beside the Aughrim river to Aughavanagh Barrack. For some time the giant of the Wicklow mountains, the lofty Lugnaquillia, has been directly before us, and here its huge form blocks further progress forward. The road on the right will lead to Drumgoff Bridge, where there is another barrack—another of the many erected after the insurrection; the road is a portion of what is called the 'great military road,' it having been constructed on the same occasion, in order to open a way into this wild mountain district. At Drumgoff Bridge the rambler will find something more pleasant than a barrack—a very comfortable hotel. The ascent of Lugnaquillia (not very often made) is best made from the road between Aughavanagh Barracks and Drumgoff. The ascent is by no means difficult, except at one precipitous point. A guide can be had, if desired, at Drumgoff inn. Lugnaquillia is 3,039 feet above the sea; and 2,500 feet above the bottom of the valley. On the summit is a sort of cromlech, known as Pierce's Table. The prospect is said to be unmatched from the mountains of Wicklow—but the visitor will be fortunate who meets with a suitable day for it. Even when all is clear on the summit, it is very seldom that the plains and the extreme distance are free from mist.

Drumgoff Bridge crosses the river Avonbeg, which rises among the mountains some miles higher, and after flowing through Glenmalure, unites with the Avonmore at the celebrated Meeting of the Waters. That part of the glen which is above Drumgoff is inconceivably grand. But then the grandeur is that arising from the savage majesty of Nature. There is nothing of the placid or beautiful here. All is sterile, desolate; forbidding, as it would seem, the presence of man. But man has been here piercing into the very heart of the mountains. The lead-mines are extensive and productive. Indeed the glen itself is said to owe its name to its mineral treasures—Glenmalure signifying the 'glen of much ore.' High up the Avonbeg precipitates itself over a long rocky shelf, and forms the Ess Waterfall. Immediately below Drumgoff the glen is hardly less grand, and it assumes gradually, as it descends, a gentler character. But the proper way to see it through its whole extent is upwards, and it can be conveniently so visited from Wooden Bridge in the Vale of Avoca. From Drumgoff the road to Laragh and Glendalough exhibits to great advantage this portion of the Wicklow Mountain range.

THE VALE OF AVOCA.

The route we have just indicated has its attractions for the lover of the wilder and grander scenery; but that we are now to speak of delights every one. It is the Llangollen of Ireland.

On leaving Arklow, the proper course for tourists lies through the demesne of Shelton Abbey. There is a high road, but the Earl of Wicklow very liberally permits the stranger either to walk or drive through his grounds, and accordingly he will do well to avail him-

6.—VALE OF AVOCA—SECOND MEETING OF THE WATERS.

self of the privilege, and save seven miles of dull road. Shelton Abbey is the most celebrated mansion at this end of Wicklow. It is a modern gothic structure of very ornate character. The situation is low, but as much has been made of its capabilities as possible. The grounds are of great extent and of great beauty, though not kept in as good condition as in English parks where the owner is resident. Some of the roads too, on the outskirts of the demesne, are bordered by lines of beeches, which form rich umbrageous avenues, with pleasant peeps between. From the grounds of Shelton, you may pass into those of Ballyarthur, the seat of E. S. Bayly, Esq. These are especially worth visiting. The house is not large, but plain and substantial, like a moderate-sized old English manor-house. The grounds afford shady walks, with delicious prospects : one immediately behind the house is especially worthy of note. Ballyarthur seems, in short, one of the most enjoyable residences in all Wicklow : just the house and grounds one might wish for—if one had Fortunatus' Cap—as a resting-place in these our later days.

From Ballyarthur we pass into the famous Vale. Wherever the English language is read, the beauties of the Vale of Avoca are known ; and so long as music married to sweet verse finds admirers, its loveliness will be verdant :

" There is not in the wide world a valley so sweet
    As that vale in whose bosom the bright waters meet."

The Vale of Avoca is indeed extremely beautiful. It is a cheerful open valley, several miles long, nowhere closing into a glen, nor expanding so as to leave the opposites sides unconnected, but gently widening as it descends ; it is everywhere a delightful companionable dale. The Avoca flows along the midst with a still quick current, but never disturbing the placid character of the scenery. The hills on either hand are lofty, varied in surface and in outline, and presenting new and always pleasing combinations at every turn. The valley is now thickly covered with rich dark masses of foliage, and presently sprinkled over with single trees, or detached groups, of light feathery form. Sometimes the trees climb the mountain sides ; at others the slopes are only covered with bright verdure, and again they are bare, rugged, and precipitous. And yet with all this beauty the stranger is apt at first to question whether it be equal to its fame. The bard of Erin has stamped on it the title to such superlative loveliness, that the vision which has been formed of it can hardly be realized. It is forgotten that he has associated with its natural charms a moral claim on his admiration :

" Yet it was not that Nature had shed o'er the scene
    Her purest of crystal and brightest of green ;
  'T was not her soft magic of streamlet or hill,—
  Oh ! no—it was something more exquisite still.

  'T was that friends, the belov'd of my bosom, were near,
  Who made ev'ry dear scene of enchantment more dear ;
  And who felt how the best charms of Nature improve
  When we see them reflected from looks that we love."

With such associations and feelings to heighten her beauties, we too might admit the pre-eminence of Avoca.

The spot we have now arrived at is the ' Second Meeting of the Waters,'—sometimes said to be that Moore has celebrated ; but this is evidently an error, as the poet has himself in a note to the passage explained his allusion to be to the confluence of " the rivers Avon and Avoca ;" whereas this is the meeting of the Aughrim and the Avoca. This is a charming scene. Not alone have we here the meeting of the rivers, but of the glens also, many and lovely. And then the views both up and down the vale are full of beauty. While here, too, the visitor should, if possible, ascend the heights of Knocknamokill, for the sake of the wider prospect not only down the vale but over Arklow to the sea. (Cut, No. 6.)

This Second Meeting of the Waters is otherwise called Wooden Bridge ; close to the bridge is the chief resting-place of tourists. Wooden Bridge Hotel is said to be, " with the exception of Quin's, at Bray, the most generally frequented by tourists of all the Wicklow houses of entertainment." (Curry's ' Hand-Book of Ireland.') Higher up there is another tourist's house, the Avoca Inn.

Ascending the vale some way, and having passed Newbridge—a very pretty spot—quite a new feature opens in the landscape. The mountain sides are for some distance literally riddled with the works of the copper mines. These are the Ballymurtagh and Cronbane mines, the most extensive and valuable copper-mines in Wicklow : the Cronbane mine has yielded nearly 2600 tons of copper ore in one year. The quantity raised is not now so great, but there are yet above a thousand men employed in the two mines. It cannot of course be said that the works add to the beauty or even picturesqueness of the scenery, but the strange scarification of the mountain sides, the apparently almost inaccessible spots in which some of the working gear is placed, and the enormous slow-moving water-wheels, certainly give a very peculiar and striking character to it. An iron tramroad is carried from these mines to Arklow haven.

The First Meeting of the Waters, (Cut No. 7,) that which Moore has sung of, is even more beautiful than the other, and the general prospect of the vale more impressive. The Avonbeg has rolled down from Glenmalure a rapid mountain stream ; the Avonmore* is gentle and placid as a lowland river. All around—along the valley, in the water, and on the heights—is luxuriant foliage. The hills are bold and lofty, their

* We asked a countryman the meaning of these names : " Sure, then," said he, "Avon is a river, and beg (which he pronounced big) is little : and more"—is more little! " Ah ! no—more is great ; and so it is just the great river and the little river." Moore was mistaken in speaking of the meeting of " the rivers Avon and Avoca." On the maps they are written as we have said, and we were assured they are so called there : they take the name of Avoca after their confluence, and retain it, as we have seen, to the estuary at Arklow.

sides well covered with trees; gray crags protruding from leafy canopies, or soft sunny slopes of brightest verdure. On either side other valleys open and exhibit fresh beauties. In the distance are mountain summits clad in aërial hues, and the higher grounds are equally delightful. It is as sweet a spot wherein to spend a summer with good company as even a poet could desire.

The castellated mansion seen on the hill is Castle-Howard, the seat of Sir Ralph Howard—a modern structure, more eminent for its noble site than for its beauty. The views from it and from the grounds are, as will be readily imagined, of surpassing beauty. Our way onward lies along the Vale of Avon; the tourist may pass through the demesne of Avondale, which is three miles long, and very charming, with the Avonmore winding through the midst the whole distance. Thence he passes by Rathdrum, and along the road which keeps above the Avonmore to Laragh. There is another road from the Meetings Bridge to Rathdrum along the higher grounds by Castle-Howard, which, though perhaps not so beautiful as that through Avondale, is shorter, and affords wider and very fine prospects.

GLENDALOUGH.

Very striking is the first glimpse of Glendalough. You proceed from Laragh up a mountain road, which appears to have an outlet only by a narrow pass at the further end; but a slight turn brings before you first a few rude cottages, then a round tower, which rears its tall head beyond, with apparently several ruined buildings spread around it; and as a back-ground is a dark hollowed coomb, formed by perpendicular rocks of great altitude, which then fall back into mountain slopes. It is not till you are nearer that the lakes become visible:—unless, indeed, you ascend the hill-side somewhat—a point from which as good a general conception of the whole glen, and lakes, and antiquities, can be obtained as anywhere. (Cut, No. 8.)

Long before you get near the ruins a crowd of beggars has beset you, intreating alms by the recital of every kind of distress; others beg you to purchase fragments of rock or crystal. Next come some two or three wild-looking fellows, who each assures you that he is the best possible guide, and no other knows anything in comparison with him, and, moreover, he won't deceive your honour with any false lies at all. You will do well to escape from the annoyance by selecting one; let him lead you round to all the sights, tell you all the legends, induct you into St. Kevin's Bed, and persuade you, if he can, that you are one of the knowingest gentlemen and best walkers he has been along with in all the years he has been there: submit to it all patiently, and you will then be left to stroll about in quiet and at leisure afterwards and see things for yourself. Some of the books have recommended particular guides; and the men themselves boast of the great folks and fine writers they have conducted. " And it's myself that was Mrs.

Hall's guide, God bless her! and more power to her, and many a good word she has bestowed upon me therefore," says one; while another claims Sir Walter Scott, and a third is content with Mr. Fraser. On the whole, there is not much choice between the three, for just so many there are. We tried two, and gossipped with the third, and moreover climbed into St. Kevin's Bed, and therefore are privileged to speak authoritatively. We would just as soon credit one as the other; their power in fabling appearing, as far as we could judge, nearly balanced—the older one had the larger store and more experience, but the younger was the more vivacious.

The name is suggestive of the character of the place; Glen-da-lough, is the glen of the two lakes. The lakes lie in a deep hollow between immense mountains, whose sides rise bare and precipitous from the valley to the height of some three or four hundred feet. The further end seems entirely closed in, but there is a narrow and almost impassable ravine, down whose rugged bed the Glencalo, the chief feeder of the lakes, forces its way. The other stream which supplies the lakes has to leap over a lofty wall of rock, forming a waterfall, called from it the Poolanass. The glen is about three miles long; the upper lough is a mile long, and nearly a quarter of a mile wide. It is around this lough that the wilder features of the glen are combined; and nothing hardly can be finer or more sublime than the scene from its bosom as night is setting in, and heavy storm-clouds are gathering over the mountain summits, and thin gray mists are creeping along the sides of the cliffs which rise in frowning blackness at once from the water, and the deep purple waves are curling up and lashing menacingly against the boat, as the wind sweeps along in a hollow prolonged sough.

It is here that some little height up the rock is the famous Bed of St. Kevin. It is a hole piercing into the rock far enough and large enough to admit two or three persons at a time. Here it was that the famous St. Kevin retreated, in order to escape from the persecutions of love and the allurements of the world. The reader of course knows the legend—all the world knows it—as told by Moore,

> " By that lake, whose gloomy shore
> Skylark never warbles o'er;
> Where the cliff hangs high and steep,
> Young St. Kevin stole to sleep:
> ' Here, at least,' he calmly said,
> ' Woman ne'er shall find my bed.'
> Ah ! the good saint little knew
> What that wily sex can do!"

The rest it is needless to repeat. Since St. Kevin so ungallantly hurled the fair Kathleen from his chamber into the deep waters below—and it is fourteen hundred years ago—every lady who has ventured there has borne a charmed life, for so the good saint in his remorse prayed it might be. More than a few fair ladies have tested the charm in our day by scrambling into the Bed, and all have returned in safety. But besides

7.—VALE OF AVOCA—FIRST MEETING OF THE WATERS.

the immunity purchased at so costly a price by that Kathleen, there is a living Kathleen here, as guardian angel of the rock, whose whole care is to avert all chances of a mishap in the adventure. This Kathleen is unhappily not so lovely as her namesake, but she has (what is of more importance here) a strong hand and a steady foot. She lives in a dog-hole of a cabin up among the rocks, and gets a living by helping all hardy adventurers into St. Kevin's bed. She has been here, she says, for above thirty years. The scramble into the Bed is certainly rather a rough one, and it looks dangerous, as you have to crawl along a narrow ledge of rocks which overhangs the water: but the danger is merely in appearance; by the assistance of the guide, and the help of Kathleen's hand at the critical point, the least skilful climber might get up without difficulty. Inside the cave are numerous names and initials of those who have accomplished the feat: among others, Kate will point out that of Sir Walter Scott, though it is not easy to decipher it. Scott's ascent into the Bed is told by Lockhart, in a letter printed in the 'Life.' The danger, he says, has been exaggerated; "Yet I never was more pained than when, in spite of all remonstrances, he would make his way to it, crawling along the precipice. He succeeded, and got in; the first lame man that ever tried it. After he was gone, Mr. Plunkett told the female guide he was a poet. Kathleen treated this with indignation, as a quiz of Mr. Attorney's. 'Poet!' said she: 'the devil a bit of him; but an honourable gentleman: he gave me half-a-crown.'"

There is a marvellously fine echo in this glen. One of the guides, a man of Stentorian voice and leathern lungs, chaunts, in a delectable sort of slow sing-song, that might be heard a mile almost, Moore's legend of St. Kevin, and the echo rings it out again to the last syllable clear as a bell. Pat then shouts a heap of nonsense, adds some Irish, and winds up with an Hibernian 'Och, arrah!' All this is duly returned, and the Irish is done as sharply, and the brogue hit off as nicely as though native to it.

The Seven Churches, as the ruins are called (and oftentimes the whole place is so named from them), are at the lower end of the glen. They consist chiefly of what is called the cathedral; of the chapel of the Virgin; a church, with a turret at the end, which is commonly called St. Kevin's Kitchen: these, with some other remains of buildings, and the vestiges of several stone crosses, are, with a round tower, contained within an enclosure which is still used as a grave-yard. Other ruins of churches are to be seen within a short distance. Why such buildings, and so many of them, should be placed in a spot like this, seems quite unaccountable; but there is evidence that there was an ecclesiastical establishment here in the fifth or sixth century, and that it was several times plundered and devastated in succeeding years. Glendalough was early constituted a bishopric, and it so continued till it was united with the see of Dublin: even now the full title of the Metropolitan is Archbishop of Dublin and Glendalough.

The ruins are remarkable, and have been the subject of much inquiry. We cannot afford space to enter

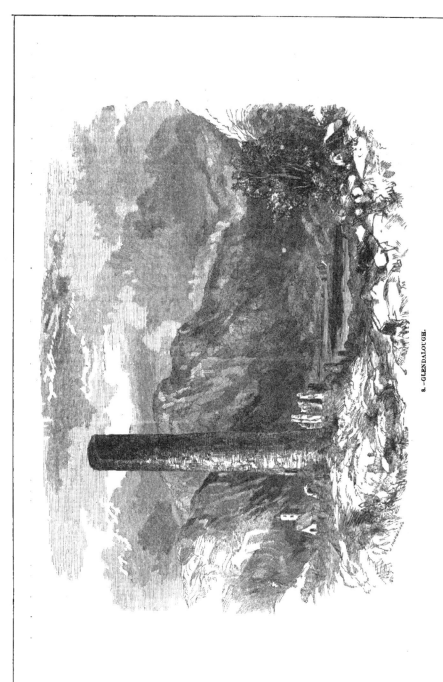

8.—GLENDALOUGH.

into an examination of them,—and indeed to attempt to do so would involve an amount of antiquarian detail that would be quite out of place here. We may just notice in a few words the Round Tower, as that is a kind of structure always regarded with curiosity. This tower is fifteen feet in diameter at the base, and tapers very gradually to the summit; it is 110 feet high. Originally it was crowned by a conical roof, but that is gone. The entrance is by a narrow arched doorway, the bottom of which is eleven feet from the ground. The upper windows are very narrow. It is constructed of rubble stones of different sizes, but arranged in regular courses. The question, What could these towers have been intended for? has always been a hard problem for antiquaries. Many solutions have been proposed, but none is yet admitted as demonstrable. It has been suggested that they were beacons, dwelling-places for anchorites, sepulchres, and many other things even stranger than these, till some were ready to believe, as an Irishman hinted, that they were just built " to puzzle posterity." The opinion that seemed most to prevail among the learned was, that they were ' Fire-towers,' where the sacred fire was kept alive : and it has been said that this opinion is countenanced by vague traditions still existing among the peasantry. But since the publication of Mr. Petrie's Essay on the Round Towers of Ireland, that hypothesis is less stoutly maintained, and there is a growing belief that they were erected by the Christian ecclesiastics who were settled in Ireland at a very early period. Mr. Petrie thinks they were intended to serve at once for keeps, or places of security from marauders, and for belfries. That they were meant to serve as strongholds we have very little doubt. Their position, too, always in connection with an ecclesiastical establishment, would seem to indicate that they were used as places of refuge by the ecclesiastics. The character and style of construction of the buildings prove, as we think, that they are of a later date than the worship of Baal. In a word, we believe that they were certainly the keeps of religious establishments; but of their other use or uses we are not so well satisfied. Mr. Petrie has laboriously and with great acumen investigated the matter, and he is convinced that they are belfries; and his opinion is entitled to the greatest respect.

If the visitor is disposed to stay here a day or two to examine these various objects at leisure, and to explore the neighbourhood (which is very grand), he will find decent accommodation at the little inn just by the church. It is well to spend a night here. The gloomy lake, grand as it appears in the day, becomes infinitely more so as the sun is sinking behind the hills, just glancing upon their summits, and leaving in deepest gloom the glen and the lakes. Having stayed at night in the glen as long as we could discern an object, we resolved to see it by the earliest dawn in the morning. Long before the sun we were there, and truly the spectacle that greeted us was a glorious one. The atmosphere was charged with a heavy mist, which settled low and thick in the glen ; but by-and-by the

sun began to touch with a straggling ray upon the loftiest points, and then as the effect of his beams became felt, the mists seemed to sink into the gloomy hollow, a darker and heavier shadow settled on the valley, the mists steamed upwards, just catching as they ascended a momentary glance of the sun, and then vanishing ; the tops of the precipices became tenderly illuminated—and suddenly the glen was spanned by a rainbow that seemed melting into the tinted haze that clung about it. All the forms of the hills and cliffs and lakes were there, but all evanescent. It was one of the marvellous pictures of Turner changed into reality. The visitor may not see it thus, but he may see it under some equally grand effect of sun and shadow.

Lough Dan and Lough Tay, two of the largest of the Wicklow lakes, are usually visited from the Round-wood Inn at Togher,—a house much frequented by tourists, on account of its serving as a convenient centre from which to visit, besides Luggala and the Loughs, the Devil's Glen and the Seven Churches. But we may proceed to the Loughs direct from Glendalough. The way thither is by the rough mountain road which at Laragh turns northward behind the barracks. As there is a meeting of roads at Laragh, the pedestrian must be careful not to take the wrong, which it is very easy to do, as the right one hardly looks like a road, and one or two of the others seem to lie nearly in the required direction. Laragh, we may remark in passing, is a rude, poor village, but not unpicturesque ; and its cabins and their inhabitants would supply some good studies to a sketcher.

At Oldbridge, just at the foot of Lough Dan, will be seen a small farm-house with an uncommon cheerful English ' well-to-do ' aspect ; here a boat may be hired to carry you over the Lough : it is only by means of a boat that Lough Dan can be properly seen. Lough Dan is not very large, being only a mile and three quarters long, and nowhere half-a-mile across: but it is set within a frame of rugged mountains, which impart to it a sufficiently wild character. Slieve Bukh is its boundary on the eastern side, the Scar Mountain on the west, while directly in front rises the broken peak of the lofty Knocknacloghole. From the comparative narrowness of the Lough and its winding course, it has somewhat the character of a broad, still river. The sides of the mountains, except at the Oldbridge end, are bare, rugged, and steep. Masses of blue crag project boldly from among the furze-clad wastes and the broken and scattered grassy slopes, where a few sheep find scanty pasturage. As you sail in the morning over the black water, while the mists are slowly breaking away from the mountain sides, all seems to wear an air of desolate majesty.

In order to visit Luggala you land where the Avonmore enters the Lough ; but you should not land without first rowing to the head of the lake, as that is perhaps, the very finest part of it. Let us add, for the sake of Waltonian tourists, that although the trout are not large, there are plenty of them in Lough Dan, and some good fishing may be had there. A narrow winding valley, about two miles long, with the Avonmore flowing through it, lies between Lough Dan and Lough Tay. We will not stay to describe this pleasant vale, but we must, in passing, call attention to the spirited improvements that are being effected by the owner of this tract of country. The whole valley is being drained, the river turned into a more direct course, and an excellent road has been formed along the pass. We rejoice to say that improvements of this nature are now very generally carried on in Ireland.

Lough Tay (Cut, No. 9) is much smaller than Lough Dan, being less than a mile long, and nowhere half a mile across, but it is more compact and lake-like, and it is generally regarded as the more beautiful. We confess to not sharing in this opinion. But Lough Tay is certainly very beautiful. It is encircled by lofty mountains, which in places rise almost precipitously from the water. The extensive plantations however take off much of the natural grandeur it would otherwise possess; and the prevalence of spiry firs not only destroys the beauty which foliage might impart, but very materially injures the picturesqueness of the scene. Lough Tay lies wholly within the extensive and beautiful demesne of Luggala, of which it is of course the chief feature.

From Luggala, the Military Road will lead, by way of Sally Gap, to a couple more of the Loughs that are among the notabilities of Wicklow: they are well worth visiting. The road will afford some noble mountain views. From some of the heights on either hand, which may easily be ascended, will be seen a long range of mountain summits, their peaks rising in grand perspective behind each other, and displaying as they recede the richest aërial effects. These mountains are entirely desolate. In the maps they are marked as the "uninhabited mountains." So wild, desolate, and little known were they, that after the rebellion in 1798 a number of the rebels were able to maintain themselves among them for some years, under the leadership of one Dwyer. It was not till the Military Road was constructed through the district, after the outbreak in 1803, that there could be said to be any road over these mountains. This wild pass of Sally Gap, where we now are, Wicklow Gap, and Glenmalure, were the only practicable entrances.

The Lough Brays (or Breagh) lie both of them high up among the mountains, the one being 1,423 and the other 1,225 feet above the sea. Both lie in deep glens, and both are very fine. Upper Lough Bray is the lonelier, and perhaps the grander; the Lower Lough is the more cheerful. The scenery around both is exceedingly beautiful. After visiting the Loughs, the pretty village of Enniskerry will be the object to be attained; and Glencree might be seen on the way. Then from Enniskerry, by the Scalp, to Dublin.

There is another route through which we intended to lead the tourist. That, namely, from Laragh or Glendalough up Glendassan, by Wicklow Gap, and along the desolate mountain roads to Polaphuca Waterfall, and thence to Blessington, returning in another direction. But we do not recommend it unless our wayfarer have a superabundance of time on hand.

9.—LOUGH TAY.

THE LAKES OF KILLARNEY.

Some ·ti·me has past since we saw Killarney ; but every succeeding day and night brings it more distinctly to our vision. We looked upon those lakes and mountains with slight book-knowledge of them ; we lost no enjoyment in the dreary labour of note-taking ; we made no passing thoughts (sweet or bitter) prosaic, by attempting their registry. But Killarney, in its graceful and solemn aspects, in sunshine or in mist, will be to us "a joy for ever."

> "Ah ! that such beauty, varying in the light
> Of living nature, cannot be pourtray'd
> By words, nor by the pencil's silent skill ;
> But is the property of him alone
> Who hath beheld it, noted it with care,
> And in his mind recorded it with love."

We have not alluded to "bitter" thoughts unadvisedly. An eloquent and philosopical French writer has described the *physical* contrasts which the neighbourhood of Killarney presents :—"On approaching the Lakes of Killarney, and halting near the Abbey of Mucruss, we look upon two scenes essentially different. On one side, uncultivated fields, sterile bogs, monotonous plains,· where feeble rushes and consumptive pines gloomily vegetate, wide stretches of heath, intersected here and there by low rocks,—this unvarying aspect, destitute of all beauty in its wildness, proclaims only the poverty of Nature. It is impossible to imagine a more barren and desolate tract. But on the other side, a totally different prospect bursts on the view. At the foot of a chain of mountains, of gracefully varied outline, separated from each other by a succession of charming lakes, are spread rich and fertile plains, green and smiling meadows, forests, gay with ferns and verdant undergrowth ; here, cool shades, secret grottos, mysterious caverns,—there, wide vistas, bold summits, an unbounded horizon ; —the margin of the silver streams covered with luxuriant shrubs,—everywhere, abundance, richness, grace,—everywhere the extraordinary accident of Nature at once most beauteous and most fruitful. Thus, at one and the same time, two aspects present themselves to the eye which are absolutely opposed—here the perfection of abundance, there the extremity of barrenness."

But the "bitter" thoughts have their source in feelings kindred to the analogy which M. Gustave de Beaumont sees in this his picture of Killarney. He says, "IT IS THE IMAGE OF IRELAND." The physical contrasts are here somewhat overcharged ; but the contrast that forces itself upon our mind, between the exquisite loveliness of the inanimate creation and the debased condition of a portion of the noblest of God's works that we trace here and all around, mixes up the people mournfully in all remembrances of the scenery. The great question of the condition of Ireland is not to be understood in a rapid transit through a small portion of the country ; but he that has looked upon any of the more afflicted districts of that land with his own eyes, however imperfectly, is in a better position than before to weigh the mass of evidence, embarrassing and contradictory as it is, as to the extent, and causes, and possible remedies, of Ireland's great social disease. Happily for Ireland, something has been done, since the period to which we allude, for her amelioration. From the misery in which the visitation of Heaven had prostrated her she is at length arising. The chastisement, if severe, has been wholesome. A new spirit of energy and of industry has been infused into her, and already this beautiful region, as well as many another locality, is giving evidence of regeneration that fills us with hope for the future.

The journey from Dublin to Killarney is accomplished now in less than nine hours. The Great Southern and Western Railway carries you a hundred and forty-five miles, from Dublin to Mallow, in six hours and a half, and thence by the new railway to Killarney in about two hours more. There are many objects of interest to be seen along the line ; yet what can we see worth recording in the rapid and monotonous transit by the iron road ? We first roll on through a tolerably fertile country, not badly cultivated, but presenting few remarkable objects. The Wicklow mountains linger in our view, with no rivals to break the monotony of the level. We pass through the Curragh of Kildare, and then gaze upon the ruined Cathedral and the mysterious Round Tower by its side. Now and then we descry a mansion on a hill slope, with fair plantations and smiling meadows, and a hamlet at its feet that we might fancy the abode of peace, did we not know what Irish hamlets for the most part are. In the distance is the famous Rock of Dunamase, crowned with the ruins of the castle of Strongbow, the great English earl, who won the fortress, not by the strength of his arm, but by marriage with the daughter of Mac Murrough, king of Leinster. It is strange that, with these marriages and intermarriages, in the early times of the conquest, there should have been six centuries of hatred between the Celt and the Saxon. Saxons and Normans became one race in a century or two. But the Rock of Dunamase may solve the mystery. The wars of conquest were succeeded by the wars of religion ; the castle of Strongbow was battered into ruin by the cannon of Cromwell. We ride on, through large tracts of peat moss ; but the distance is varied by the bold outlines of the Slievebloom and the Devil's-Bit mountains. It is a bleak country, with occasional patches of fertility. There are towns about the line,—most with small trade, some dilapidated, all somnolent. They have to be awakened by the inevitable course of agricultural improvement,

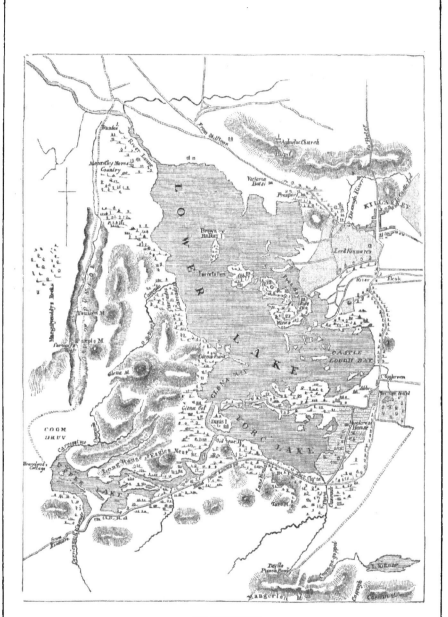

MAP OF KILLARNEY.

which, we rejoice to say, is already everywhere apparent through the country. At a hundred and seven miles from Dublin we reach the Limerick junction. Some twenty miles beyond is Kilmallock, the stronghold of the great Desmonds. Thirteen miles further, and we are near Buttevant, the land in which dwelt Edmund Spenser,—where

" Mulla mine whose waves I whilom taught to weep,"

still flows,—where the Castle of Kilcoleman still exhibits a blackened ruin, telling of fire and slaughter rather than of the immortal ' Faery Queen.' From this we pass through very picturesque scenery, becoming more beautiful till we enter the valley of the Blackwater, and the train rests at Mallow.

If one had an hour or two to spare, it could not be better employed than in a stroll, not through the town of Mallow, but in its beautiful vicinity. The grounds of the Castle (the seat of Sir C. D. Norreys, Bart.) are open to the stranger, and a charming walk leads along the Blackwater. Ballyelles is also a fine demesne, and lies at the opposite side of the river. From Mallow we proceed by train to Millstreet, a distance of about twenty miles. On either side adjacent to the town are pretty villas and fine mansions, and the country wears the aspect of civilization and culture. Midway in the journey, upon the southern side, runs the range of hills known as Mount Hillary ; and just before we reach the Millstreet station we get a charming glimpse of the demesne and Castle of Dreshune (the seat of Henry Wallis, Esq.), close to the line. From this point the beauty of the scenery increases ; in front are seen the Clara and Cahirbarnagh Mountains, beyond which rise the conical summits of ' the Paps,' and in the far distance at length emerge from the clouds the lofty serrated ridges of the Reeks. And now we reach the picturesque scenery around the Flesk river. Mangerton shows his head on the left, then the Torc Mountain, wooded to its base, and Flesk Castle ; and so we reach the terminus at Killarney. There are now several excellent hotels here, and one can scarcely go astray in the selection. The Victoria is exquisitely situated on the northern side of the Lower Lake, where we can testify to the most attentive of hostesses. Nor will the Torc View, or the Castle Lough, we believe, be found inferior to the Victoria. Then there is the Muckross, and others ; so let us haste to some one of them, where we shall be sure of a welcome that makes us at home in a moment. And then for dinner in right earnest.

A gray evening. In the constant twilight of June

1.--AGHADOE.

2.—INNISFALLEN.

we can dimly trace the outline of the mountains long after sunset. Thin clouds float slowly beneath their heads, and seem almost to kiss the Lake. The moon is climbing the sky, " with how sad steps." Ever and anon the quiet water is bright with one long silver streak. But how small the lake looks ; how close seem the mountains. Islands! they appear no bigger than buoys! Will the morning light give breadth and grandeur to the scene?

He who would see the beauties of this lovely region thoroughly to advantage should make up his mind to early rising. Of this we felt convinced the first moment our eyes fell on the vales and mountains that environed the lake. We yielded our hearty accord to the advice of the "old traveller," whose "week in the South of Ireland" we fortunately had procured. "Up with the lark! Nature loves not sluggards: to them she shows not her matutinal loveliness. Turn on your pillow if you will after day-light, but then you shall not see the sun lighting up the tops of the far-away Reeks, or the shades in the recesses of the Purple Mountains and the Toomies, nor the clouds flinging their flying shadows on the hill sides and over the glistening waters. Up, we say, with the lark, and make acquaintance with Killarney." Well, that you may thus " rise with the lark," go " to bed with the lamb," as the old saw has it.

Our first night's repose was at the Victoria, and the sun had scarce raised his head above the horizon ere, following his good example, we raised ours from the

1.—WATER-CARRIERS.

pillow. We rose refreshed and vigorous, as if the fresh buoyant air that comes from the mountains was already transfused through and invigorating our frames. We rose, threw back the shutters, opened the window of our chamber, and looked out. Broad day, bright and beautiful! The Lake lay in beautiful repose, with the sun lighting up its western side, and the shadows of Innisfallen and Ross stretching far away into its waters. At some half mile from the Victoria Inn there is a considerable hill, upon which stand the remains of the Church of Aghadoe. (Cut, No. 1.) It is the most accessible eminence from which we can obtain an adequate view of the Lower Lake. As I dressed, the scenery grew upon my vision, and became every minute more familiar and more appreciable to me. And at length, when I stood for a moment to take a last view ere quitting the room, I involuntarily exclaimed—

Yes! Killarney *is* magnificent!

> " In the distance Heaven is blue above
> Mountains where sleep the unsunn'd tarns."

On the opposite shore of the lake beneath us, gigantic hills, clothed with magnificent timber to the water's edge, with " cloud-capp'd " heads, Toomies and Glena; rising over these, the glowing Purple Mountain and the mighty Reeks ; the Lake studded with green islands; every variety of outline—every combination of colour. Let us away, and look into the inmost bosom of this enchanting region! A boat!—a boat!

This is, indeed, a " trim-built wherry," and a fitting crew—four " boys," with frank Irish faces, that will light up under a joke. They had hard times not long ago. Colonel Clarke, in his examination before the Lords' Committee, a few years since, on the operation of the Irish Poor-Law, told a sad tale :—" This last summer the unfortunate state of the country entirely deterred persons from visiting Killarney; and so far from benefit being derived there, I was informed that the proprietor of the Victoria Hotel was a dead loser of £1000 by the season. . . . . . I believe there were a great many boatmen thrown out of business. The visitors were so few at Killarney last summer, that, in fact, there was nothing doing of any sort." Happily, this state of things no longer exists, and the Killarney boatmen have abundant work. Gerald Griffin has described them, in ' The Collegians :'—" Them watchers arn't allowed to dhrink anything while they're upon the lake, except at the *stations :* but then, to make up for that, they all meet at night at a hall in town, where they stay dancing and dhrinking all night, till they spend whatever the quollity gives 'em in the day. Luke Kennedy (that's this boy) would like to save, if he could; but the rest wouldn't pull an oar with him, if he didn't do as they do. So that's the way of it. And sometimes afther being up all night a'most, you'll see 'em out again at the first light in the mornin'."

At the helm of our boat sits what is here termed " a bugle." John Spillane, one of the sons of a famous sire, was our musician and our steersman. He

quietly told us what we were going to see ; and when we saw it had no superfluous raptures to bestow upon the " *genius loci*,"—an excellent fellow, from the beginning to the end of our four days' experience. Our crew, till we became better acquainted, were silent and reserved. We had a very light infliction, throughout our stay, of what Gerald Griffin describes as " the teasing of the guides, and the lies of the boatmen." Innisfallen! Coleridge says, " Expectation is far higher than surprise;" and who has not had " expectation" raised by the name of Innisfallen ? We pulled through a heavy swell from the west, which gave us some faint notion of the occasional dangers of the Lower Lake, and soon neared the famous islet. There it rests—one mass of brilliant green on the bosom of the dark wave. As we come nearer and nearer we trace the exquisite forms of its woods, in all their wondrous variety of foliage, dropping to the water's edge. One gleam of sun to light up the brilliant mass,—and then a mist creeps down from the mountains, and Innisfallen is in her tearful mood. (Cut No. 2.) Half an hour's ramble, in spite of mist or shower, o'ercanopied by elm and ash as we tread the dewy greensward, or looking out from some little bay, bright with holly and arbutus, over the bright lake—and we leave Innisfallen—happily without knowing that some of the trees have been cut down since a lady tourist first visited it, and that she last saw it " with soreness of spirit :"

> " Sweet Innisfallen, fare thee well !
> May calm and sunshine long be thine :
> How fair thou *wert* let others tell,
> While but to feel how fair is mine !"

And now our little craft is steered across the Lake, that we may land at O'Sullivan's Cascade. O'Sullivan, and more especially O'Donoghue, will soon be " familiar in our mouths," when our boatmen become talkative—but not as yet. We land at a little cove, and find ourselves in a thick covert, treading upon soft moss, as we ascend a gentle hill. Gradually the path grows narrower—the plash of waters fall on the ear— a rapid rivulet is beneath, dashing through the underwood—and at length we stand before the solitary Fall. Here is no basin where the troubled waters may rest in their course, as at the Lower Fall of Rydal. The torrent rushes on, hiding itself in the green banks, as if glad to escape from noise and light, into silence and mystery. This is indeed a charming Fall—severe in its beauty—unspoiled by art—especially solemn now the mist is on the hill. Here the botanist may revel in the search for plants which belong only to the West—mosses and ferns little known in our southern woods and water - courses. Bree's Fern (*Lastræa Recurva*), according to Mr. Newman, is the admiration of botanists in the neighbourhood of Killarney ; and at O'Sullivan's Cascade he observed it in the most graceful and beautiful luxuriance. To the unscientific eye, the prodigality of growth exhibited by these feathery forms—dark purple stems, contrasting with the brightest green of the crisped leaves—is sufficiently striking. The foliage around us is quivering with approaching steps. We look about expectantly. But no

"Satyrs and sylvan boys are seen,
Peeping from forth their alleys green."

Two emaciated little girls, preternaturally pallid, have watched the arrival of the stranger, and are come to offer their gleanings of the woods—a hart's horn—a wild nosegay. Poor wretched children—all mirth of childhood is vanished from their faces. In the mountain-hovel where they crouch, there has been grievous want. They have become acquainted with the bitterness of life very early. And we are pleasure seeking! We are surrendering ourselves to all sweet thoughts and influences! "The sunshine of the breast" is driving out all remembrances of fear and trouble. But now, when we think of that quiet place in the luxuriant woods, the faces of these poor children still haunt the spot, and make us sad. We understand now, when we read the evidence of a resident in the county of Mayo, the exact meaning of his words:

"Will you describe the condition of the infants and young children?"

"They look very bad indeed: they seem almost like animals of a lower class; they are wasted and wan."

There is direct testimony that in the Killarney district this terrible indication of the ravages of famine is too apparent. A competent witness speaks of "the wretched emaciated appearance of the children." Other tourists will see these very children; and, perhaps, will come home and talk of Irish beggary. "Take physic, Pomp." May these heirs of misfortune live to see brighter days! May they, escaped from pinching want, surround the stranger, as he was wont to be surrounded, with smiling faces, unheedful of naked feet or scanty drapery—such a group as Ireland has often shown to the delighted artist—joyous and graceful in the simple labours of happy poverty! (Cut No. 3.)

We run up the Lake under the shadow of Glena, and look back lingeringly upon Innisfallen. There is the little ruined oratory which gave us shelter from the passing shower—a relic of the abbey which existed, according to the 'Annals of Innisfallen,' twelve centuries ago. The material works of the monks have perished, but their higher labours tell of ancient learning and its isolated civilization. The 'Annals' have been translated and printed as recently as 1825;—one of the original copies is in the British Museum. No one of the population speaks of the humble labourers in the arts of peace who dwelt here for ages; and whose records, combined with those of their country, come down to the fourteenth century. But the memories of the barbarous chieftains who once ruled over these lakes and mountains in devastating power, linger still in music and legend. One of the records in the 'Annals' is to this effect:—"Anno, 1180; this abbey of Innisfallen being ever esteemed a paradise and a secure sanctuary, the treasure and the most valuable effects of the whole country were deposited in the

hands of the clergy; notwithstanding which, we find the abbey was plundered in this year by Maolduin, son of Daniel O'Donoghue. Many of the clergy were slain, and even in their cemetery, by the Mac Carthys." But the O'Donoghue, whose legends are associated with every island of these lakes, and of whom we are now beginning to hear unceasingly, was (at some dateless period) the lord of Ross—brave and wise, beautiful and generous. Unfortunate, of course, he was, so one of the islands is O'Donoghue's prison;—a mighty leader of chivalry, so another is O'Donoghue's horse;—learned, and therefore a rock must be O'Donoghue's library;—jovial and hospitable, so a cave is O'Donoghue's cellar. On every May morning he is seen gliding over the lake on a white steed, and he has a palace under the waters, whence he issues to gladden the eyes of many who have actually beheld him. Philosophy has discovered that the appearance of the O'Donoghue is an optical illusion, and that the boatmen do not wholly palm their stories upon the credulity of the stranger. Such an illusion, if we may venture to say so, is the spirit which is just now attempting to raise up a nationality out of Celtic remains, and Irish literature. The antiquities of every country are full of instruction, and Irish antiquities especially so. They tell of past ages of feudal barbarism; but these are associated with the song of the bard and the learning of the priest. On every side there are ruined castles, dilapidated abbeys, mysterious towers, cairns and cromlechs. Most wisely has the hand of taste and public spirit interfered to prevent the lamentable desecration of all these objects which had been going on for many a year. Translate the old popular songs, cherish the native music, search into the ancient annals of the country—but let not the men of ability and various knowledge who are labouring at this good work believe that a true nationality is to be founded upon the memories of the times which preceded the English conquest. We may be prejudiced; but to us it appears little better than the weakness of a false enthusiasm to lament over the decay of the Irish language; and to stigmatize the efforts to disseminate the use of English, as a tyrannous and selfish policy. Upon what do our Englishmen found their nationality? Not upon the legends of Arthur, or the victories of Athelstan—the learning of Eadmer or the verses of Cædmon. We read the Saxon war-song of the battle of Brunanburgh with antiquarian delight,—but when we hope to be "free or die" we think of "the tongue which Shakspere spake." In our view, the true Irish nationality had better be raised upon the great names in literature of Swift, and Berkeley, and Burke, and Goldsmith, and Edgeworth, and Moore, and a hundred other illustrious, than upon the relics of the old bards, pagan or Christian;—and one lesson from the real civilizer, "the man who makes two blades of corn grow where one grew before," is to our minds more precious than all the dreams of the barbaric splendour of the Mac Murroughs and O'Neals, and all the glories of the hill of Tara.

The shower is of short duration. We have seen

the mountains in their misty sublimity, and now the woods are glittering in the passing sun-light, and towering to the soft blue sky in their unrivalled verdure. We are near enough to the base of the mountain to see distinctly the character of that sea of woodland which stretches up to its gray summit. It is not composed of tiny shrubs, but of tall trees, infinitely varied in their summer tints—and at the water's edge is the bright arbutus, itself a tree in these regions. We are steering towards the little cove, at the head of the Lake—and now we land at the loveliest of pleasure houses, planted under these embosoming woods in a garden rich with "flowers of all hues." There is another cottage, too, where the stranger will find a welcome. Provident has the good hostess of the Victoria been for our comforts—and there is a piece of epicurism to be gone through, for which even the best sauce of Soyer would be "wasteful and ridiculous excess"—salmon fresh from the lake, broiled upon arbutus skewers before a peat-fire. Charming Glena! We must come again to loiter in thy quiet walks. We can never be sated with thy peacefulness. We have no tourist's desire to be moving on and seeing more. We envy the statesman of whom they told us, that, coming here in an autumn afternoon, and lingering too long, the lake was suddenly lashed into fury by the rising wind, and he was compelled to stay all night in the sheltered cottage. But we must go. The bugle summons us from our reveries. We have the Torc Lake to explore, before the sun sinks behind the Purple mountain.

Look, reader, upon the map of the Lakes, and trace our course, for it is scarcely to be made intelligible without such help. Starting from the bay at Glena, there is a narrow inlet to the Torc Lake between Dinis Island and the Peninsula of Mucruss. But there is another way by which that Lake is entered—the broader channel on the west side of the island. The continuation of that channel leads to the Upper Lake— a river scene, five miles in extent. The passage round Dinis Island into the Torc Lake is something so peculiar in its beauty, that we scarcely know how to convey a notion of its characteristics. Some of the creeks of the Thames above Windsor, and more especially a close passage between Henley and Marlow, are eminently beautiful. There the osiers lose their formality amidst banks of sedge and beds of water lilies—and the unpollarded willow drops gracefully into the silent stream, unruffled except by the leap of the chub or the plunge of the kingfisher. But here the common river-trees are scarcely to be recognized in their exceeding verdure. The channel is not difficult because of rush or weed,—but huge masses of rock form narrow eddies where the boat can scarcely glide, and then shelve off into sheltering basins for the lilies. But the ferns! It is impossible to conceive of the beauty of a close river whose banks are completely fringed by the noble Flowering Fern, the *Osmunda Regalis*—(a latinized Saxon name, of which *mund* signifies strength)—a fern exquisite in its grace, and gigantic in its proportions. Those formal rushes of our southern streams, how can we tolerate them, when we have seen the immense ferns of Dinis o'erarching the little river with their pendulous heads,—sheltering

4.—TORC LAKE.

legions of water-fowl who seem to be fearless under their emerald canopies. Scott, it is said, had no word of praise for these Lakes and Mountains, he was thinking of Loch Lomond and Loch Awe. But when he was here he exclaimed, "*This* is worth coming to see!"

The sun is westering as we enter the Torc Lake. We are in the most profound solitude. Scarcely a breath of wind creeps over the waters. We gaze in silence on the noble mountain from which the lake derives its name; when the mellow notes of Spillane's bugle for the first time soothe and gladden us. Over the water floats the tender air of 'Eileen a Roon'—the gem of Irish music five centuries ago—plagiarized into 'Robin Adair' in Scotland—naturalized in France, by Boieldieu. Ever and anon a slight echo returns some emphatic note. And then, with a natural courtesy, one of our boatmen sings an Irish air at our request: it was a pastoral song, wild and melancholy. A writer of taste, Mr. Edward Walsh, has translated many of these popular ballads, which appear to have been chiefly produced in the last century. Many of their favourite images seem to be derived from the scenery of these regions: "The enamoured poet will lead his love over the green-topped hills of the South or West, will show her ships and sails through the vistas of the forest, as they seek their retreat by the shore of the broad lake. They shall dine on the venison of the hills, the trout of the lake, and the honey of the hollow oak. Their couch shall be the purple-blossomed heath, the soft moss of the rock, or the green rushes strewn with creamy agrimony, and the early call of the heath-cock alone shall break their slumber of love." We go coasting round the Lake; we see the distant Torc Waterfall—a pencil of light; we listen to other songs and other bugle-notes; and, steered into one of the caverns of the rock, learn that we are in O'Donaghue's wine-cellar,—a fitting place for one "cup of kindness" with old and new friends. And now for a long pull homeward. (Cut No. 4.)

A brilliant morning! Away with the libellers of Killarney—the praters about perpetual showers! Could it be the Irish LOVER who wrote these vile unpatriotic lines on his country's climate?

> "The rain comes down
> The leaves to drown,
> Not a gleam of sun to alloy it;
> From my heart I wish
> I was but a fish,
> What a glorious place to enjoy it.

5.—THE GAP OF DUNLOE.

" No light is on
Old Mangerton,
And Tore I cannot make out, sir ;
What need to roam,
When, nearer home,
You've a fine cascade from the spout, sir ?"

At any rate *we* are lucky. Here is a glorious morning
for a ride through the Gap of Dunloe, and the boat to
meet us at the head of the Upper Lake.

The road which leads along the northern bank of
the Lower Lake, till it falls into the Laune river, is a
quiet and picturesque road, with few traces of extreme
poverty. The little fields are well cultivated, and the
wretched hovel is seldom seen. We reach the Laune
Bridge ; below us is a rapid stream, very tempting to
the angler ; before us the Gap opens its ponderous
jaws. Through a wild and boggy country we gradually ascend a mountain road. We have to pass round
the shoulder of a rock, and at the angle stands a
tidy woman, waiting for the travellers, with her jug
of goats'-milk. We turn the rock, and ascend the
Gap :

" The abrupt mountain breaks,
And seems, with its accumulated crags,
To overhang the world."

It is curious how tourists differ in their estimation
of particular scenes. Inglis says, " The Gap of Dunloe
did not seem to me to be worthy of its reputation : it
is merely a deep valley ; but the rocks which flank
the valley are neither very lofty, nor very remarkable
in their form ; and although, therefore, the Gap presents many features of the picturesque, its approaches
to sublimity are very distant." Mrs. Hall calls it, " a
scene rarely paralleled for wild grandeur and stern
magnificence ; the singular character of the deep ravine
would seem to confirm the popular tradition that it was
produced by a stroke of the sword of one of the giants
of old, which divided the mountains, and left them
apart for ever. Its deep gloom oppresses the spirits
with exceeding melancholy." These wide differences
of opinion probably proceed from the different aspects
under which a scene is viewed, and the varying moods
of mind produced by those varying aspects. What is
beautiful in the noonday sun is solemn in the misty
evening. We passed through this chasm in a bright
July morning ; the Loe was rushing down its rocky
bed ; on the right the Reeks lifted up their heads to
the blue sky,—even the topmost peak ; on the left,
the Purple Mountain blushed in the glowing light.
We halted at a spot where Spillane vanished into a
deep dell, and then rose such a wild bugle strain,
repeated in the most delicious softness by the rocks
around, that the whole scene was one of enchantment.
We thought of Shelley's noble translation of Faust,
in which the images of beauty and sublimity are so
gloriously mingled :

" But see, how swift advance and shift
Trees behind trees, row by row,—
How, clift by clift, rocks bend and lift
Their frowning foreheads as we go.

The giant-snouted crags, ho ! ho !
How they snort, and how they blow !
Through the mossy sods and stones,
Stream and streamlet hurry down,
A rushing throng ! A sound of song
Beneath the vault of Heaven is blown !
Sweet notes of love, the speaking tones
Of this bright day, sent down to say
That Paradise in Earth is known,
Resound around, beneath, above
All we hope and all we love
Finds a voice in this blithe strain,
Which wakens hill, and wood, and rill,
And vibrates far o'er field and vale,
And which Echo, like the tale
Of old times, repeats again."

There is a charming description in ' The Collegians'
of the view looking down the Gap, from the Purple
Mountain. We would rather trust it than our own
rapid impressions :—" Although the day was fine, and
sometimes cheered with sunshine near the base of the
mountain, its summit was wrapped in mist, and wet
with incessant showers. The scenery around was
solitary, gigantic, and sternly barren. The figure of
some wonder-hunting tourist, with a guide-boy bearing
his portfolio and umbrella, appeared at long intervals,
among the lesser undulations of the mountain side ;
and the long road which traversed the gloomy valley
dwindled to the width of a meadow foot-path. On
the opposite side of the enormous ravine, the gray and
misty Reeks still raised their crumbling summits far
above him. Masses of white mist gathered in sullen
congress between their peaks, and, sometimes floating
upward in large volumes, were borne majestically
onward, catching a thousand tints of gold and purple
from the declining sun. Sometimes a trailing shower,
of mingled mist and rain, would sweep across the
intervening chasm, like the sheeted spectre of a giant,
and present to the eye of the spectator that appearance
which supplied the imagination of Ossian with its
romantic images. The mighty gorge itself, at one
end, appeared to be lost and divided amid a host of
mountains tossed together in provoking gloom and
misery. Lower down, it opened upon a wide and
cultivated champaign, which, at this altitude, presented
the resemblance of a rich mosaic of a thousand colours,
and afforded a bright contrast to the barren and shrub-
less gloom of the solitary vale itself." (Cut. No. 5.)

Echoes again ! but not the echoes of music. There
is a poor man with a cannon, who produces mimic
thunder at a shilling a shot. The report goes
brattling and ringing up the mountain sides in varied
tones. We ride on till we cross the lonely bridge
over the Loe, and ascend to the extremity of the
gorge. And now there is indeed a scene. We look
over " The Black Valley " through which lies our
road ; the Upper Lake is beneath us—a basin amongst
the mountains. All around us is unmistakeably grand.
The long valley of mingled rocks and greensward—
the stream which flows through it into the Lake,—
mountains which shut out the world—one way to

enter, the gorge which we have left,—one to retreat, the Lake which seems to have no outlet. At the top of the Pass we came up with two Englishmen. They were millwrights from Newcastle who had been working in the interior, and had come a long distance to see Killarney on their way homeward. Honoured be their noble curiosity. A great Poet—one we must all reverence—has argued that the love of fine scenery is an acquired taste, and belongs only to highly cultivated minds;—and so Grasmere is no proper place for a Manchester weaver. Such notions come of seclusion from the world. It is the privilege of the times in which we live that the glories of our own land are rendered accessible to those of very humble means; and the interchange of thoughts between the artisans of one district and another, would do far more to destroy prejudices and cultivate good will, than the confined observations of the rich pleasure-seekers, who seldom come in contact with the people. These worthy men went home, we have no doubt, with improved hearts and understandings;—better satisfied with their own lot, and more ready to make some sacrifices for relieving the wants of others.

As we approach the Lake the road becomes more difficult; but the sure-footed ponies step briskly amongst the stony lumps that lie in the path, and instinctively avoid the frequent bogs. We come to an iron grating, in a rude wall, which turns on its rusty hinges, and admits us into a smiling demesne. Here the river runs between gentle banks, in flowery meadows:

> " Cultured slopes,
> Wild tracts of forest ground, and scattered groves,
> And mountains bare, or clothed with ancient woods,
> Surrounded us; and, as we held our way
> Along the level of the glassy flood,
> They ceased not to surround us; change of place,
> From kindred features diversely combined,
> Producing change of beauty ever new."

The Poet of 'The Excursion' from whom we quote, has done so much to make us all love his Lakes and Mountains, that, for his sake, we might wish that the railway whistle should never sound over Windermere: but for the sake of our fellows we heartily rejoice that it does so sound; and more especially glad are we that Killarney can now be reached by common men. There is nothing grander in these kingdoms than the Upper Lake, over which our boat is now gliding. The mountains seem to have their feet in the deep waters;—they rise sheer up on every side. Gray islands spring abruptly from the bosom of the deep. Then, again, there are island rocks surmounted with the greenest of trees,—and on some the arbutus attains a size that is altogether wondrous. (Cut No. 6.) But we must see this Upper Lake again:

> " Too solemn for day, too sweet for night."

We are now in "The Long Range "—that beautiful channel which terminates at Glena. We are nearing the far-famed 'Eagle's Nest.' But before we make a sudden turn round the point of the channel at its base, we must land, while the most marvellous echo of Killarney is awakened. The bugle calls. One echo, full,—another, faint;—another, fainter;—another, imperfect;—another, bothered;—original echo;—repeat, imperfect. This is Mr. Crofton Croker's catalogue, accompanying his musical notation, of the echoes of the Eagle's Nest. The day was not quite favourable to the effect, so we lost some of this wonder. But the cannon! Alpine thunder could not be more sublime: one crash,—a peal,—another—and another—silence—then, far away, a solemn roll,—dying into low murmurings in the extreme distance. Inglis has truly and beautifully said of these startling effects, " our imagination endues the mountains with life; and to their attributes of magnitude, and silence, and solitude, we, for a moment, add the power of listening, and a voice."

The Eagle's Nest is a pyramidal rock, rising without a break from its base. At a distance, with the giant mountains hanging over it, the Eagle's Nest appears of no marvellous elevation. Even when we float beneath its shadow, it is difficult to imagine that it is three times the height of Saint Paul's. We have been surrounded with none but large objects, and the eye has lost its accustomed sense of height and distance. The pencil cannot make such proportions intelligible. (Cut No. 7.)

Below the Eagle's Nest is a passage through which a laden boat is not very safe to pass, according to the boatmen. To shoot the Old Weir Bridge is a feat, and it is quite proper to keep tourists out of the way of danger. We land, therefore, and let the boat glide through " at its own sweet will," bearing only our fair companion, who, with all womanly sympathies and refinements, has too high a mind to fear imaginary dangers. Once more on the lovely Dinis River, and then into the Lower Lake, and across to Ross island.

Our space is too limited to allow us to digress much into history, or the history of Ross Castle would be worth relating. Erected by one of the early Donoghues, it was the last stronghold in Munster which defied the cannon of the Parliamentary Ironsides. Ludlow laid siege to it in 1652; and by some wondrous exertion conveyed boats to the Lake with the intention of attacking it on the side where an enemy could scarcely be expected. The garrison surrendered with little resistance—alarmed, it is said, by the remembrance of a prophecy, that Ross should fall, when war-ships should sail upon the Lake. As Innisfallen is associated with the ancient religion of these beautiful regions, Ross is in the same way allied to all records and legends of the feudal power, which once held undivided sway over these waters. Beneath this embattled tower the spirit-stirring bagpipe once summoned the mountaineers together at the call of 'The Eagle's Whistle,' and 'The Step of the Glens,'—the marches of the O'Donoghues, which still may be heard in hall or bower, " stirring the heart as with a trumpet." Froissart has a striking picture of such chieftains as those who sat five centuries

6.—UPPER LAKE.

ago in the halls of Ross. It is the narrative of Sir Henry Christall, who was taken prisoner by the Irish in the time of Richard II.—married the daughter of his captor—and coming back after many years to English society, was sent to attend upon the kings who had submitted themselves to England, and were detained in a sort of honourable captivity in Dublin :

" The king my sovereign lord's intent was, that in manner, countenance, and apparel of clothing, they should use according to the manner of England; for the king thought to make them all four knights : they had a fair house to lodge in in Dublin, and I was charged to abide still with them and not to depart; and so two or three days I suffered them to do as they list, and said nothing to them, but followed their own appetites. They would sit at the table and make countenance neither good nor fair. Then I thought I should cause them to change that manner. They would cause their minstrels, their servants, and varlets, to sit with them and to eat in their own dish, and to drink of their cups ; and they showed me that the usage of their country was good, for they said, in all things (except their beds), they were and lived as common. So the fourth day I ordained other tables to be covered in the hall, after the usage of England, and I made these four kings to sit at the high table, and their minstrels at another board, and their servants and varlets at another beneath them, whereof by seeming they were displeased, and beheld each other and

would not eat, and said how I would take from them their good usage, wherein they had been nourished. Then I answered them, smiling to appease them, that it was not honourable for their estates to do as they did before, and that they must leave it and use the custom of England, and that it was the king's pleasure they should do so, and how he was charged so to order them. When they heard that they suffered it, because they had put themselves under the obeisance of the king of England, and persevered in the same as long as I was with them ; yet they had one use which I knew well was used in their country, and that was, they did wear no breeches ; I caused breeches of linen cloth to be made for them. While I was with them I caused them to leave many rude things, as well in clothing as in other causes. Much ado I had at first to cause them to wear gowns of silk furred with minever and gray ; for before these kings thought themselves well apparelled when they had on a mantle. They rode always without saddles and stirrups, and with great pain I made them to ride after our usage."

It is pleasant to contrast the frank fellowship of the native kings towards their minstrels and servants, with the formal etiquette of the Anglo-Norman court. There were nobler feelings in these despisers of " gowns of silk furred with minever," than in the luxurious Richard. Two centuries after, Sir John Harrington saw the great rebel, Hugh Tyrone, and wondered at the love of his retainers. If the old brotherhood were kept up, there is no mystery in the matter. The young O'Neals, the sons of Tyrone, wore velvet jerkins and gold lace, and the father made the "witty godson" of Elizabeth read him some cantos of his translation of Ariosto; but the followers of the earl were unspoiled in their fidelity by any refinements of luxury or knowledge:

"The earl," says Sir John Harrington, "began by debasing his own manner of hard life, comparing himself to wolves, that fill their bellies sometime, and fast as long for it. * * * * Other pleasant and idle tales were needless and impertinent, or to describe his fern-table and fern-forms, spread under the stately canopy of heaven. His guard, for the most part, were beardless boys without shirts; who, in the frost, wade as familiarly through rivers as water-spaniels. With what charm such a master makes them love him I know not, but if he bid come, they come; if go, they do go; if he say do this, they do it."

But we are lingering too long amongst the traces of old manners, as we lingered, till the sun was setting, in the exquisite gardens of Ross Island,—looking out from paths beauteous with every shrub and flower that art has here acclimated or nature strown, upon the mountains on which the mists are gathering, and driving fast before a gusty wind. Our steersman is impatient,—and he has cause. "The boys" pull with a will through the waves, which now heave like a troubled sea. We have passed in a quarter of an hour from serene beauty into stern grandeur. How solemnly now sleeps Innisfallen in her watery bed; Glena looks frowning; the Lake is black, beyond all imaginable blackness of water—black in its vast depth, and beneath the gloom of the gathering clouds. Welcome the friendly shallow of the point on which our boat at last is stranded.

Now, that we have seen these Lakes under very favourable circumstances, and can judge in some degree of their claims to surpassing beauty, let us compare our own impressions with those of two very competent but essentially different observers. Inglis, acute, cau-

7.—EAGLE'S NEST.

tious, rarely elevated beyond the point of calm satisfaction; Wilson, the most tasteful and discriminating of enthusiasts. It is true that we have been only two days, as yet, amongst these wondrous scenes;—but we have had rare opportunities of weather—all appliances at hand—and not an hour lost. We agree to the utmost extent of admiration with our two authorities.

And first Inglis :—" Although the lakes of Killarney are three in number, yet they are all contained in one mountain hollow; and certainly there is not, within the same compass, anything in England presenting the same concentration of charms. There is infinitely greater variety at Killarney. In form, and in the outline of its mountain boundaries, the lower lake of Killarney is decidedly superior to Winandermere: and though the head of Ulleswater presents a bolder outline than is anywhere to be found in Killarney, yet it is upon this outline alone that the reputation of Ulleswater depends. Elsewhere than at Patterdale, the lake scenery is tame; and the same may be said of Winandermere, which, towards the lower extremity, is almost devoid of attraction. On the contrary, throughout the whole chain of lakes, there is a variety at Killarney; tameness is nowhere to be found: and I cannot think that the somewhat nearer approach to sublimity, which is found at the head of Ulleswater, can weigh in the balance against the far greater variety in the picturesque and the beautiful, which Killarney affords. It would be unfair to compare the lakes of Killarney, with Winandermere,' Keswick, and Ulleswater; for these are spread over a great extent of country; whereas, the lakes of Killarney are all contained within a smaller circumference than Winandermere: but even if such a comparison were to be admitted, Killarney would outvie the English lakes in one charm, in which they are essentially deficient. I mean the exuberance and variety of foliage which adorns both the banks and the islands of the Killarney lakes. Such islands as Ronan's Island, Oak Island, Dinis Island, and Innisfallen, covered with magnificent timber and gigantic ever-greens, are nowhere to be found amongst the English lakes. I think it will be gathered from what I have said, that I accord the preference to Killarney."

Christopher North, in the passage which we are about to quote, is more brief than in his previous summing up of the characteristics of the English and Scotch Lakes; but he is not in the slightest degree less emphatic when he thus bursts out. He is looking from Mangerton, whither we shall lead our reader before we part :

" What a panorama! Our first feeling was one of grief that we were not an Irishman. We knew not where to fix our gaze. Surrounded by the dazzling bewilderment of all that multitudinous magnificence, the eye, as if afraid to grapple with the near glory—for such another day never shone from heaven—sought elief in the remote distance, and slid along the beautiful river Kenmare, insinuating itself among the recesses of the mountains, till it rested on the green glimmer of the far-off sea. The grandeur was felt, far off as it was, of that iron-bound coast. Coming round with an easy sweep, as the eye of an eagle may do, when hanging motionless aloft he but turns his head, our eyes took in all the mighty range of the Reeks, and rested in awe on Carran-Tual. Wild yet gentle was the blue aërial haze over the glimpses of the Upper Lake, where soft and sweet, in a girdle of rocks, seemed to be hanging, now in air and now in water—for all was strangely indistinct in the dim confusion—masses of green light, that might be islands with their lovely trees. But suddenly tipt with fire shone out the golden pinnacles of the Eagle's Nest; and as again they were tamed by cloud-shadow, the glow of Purple Mountain for a while enchained our vision, and then left it free to feast on the forest of Glena, till, wandering at the capricious will of fancy, it floated in delight over the woods of Mucruss, and long lost among the trembling imagery of the water, found lasting repose in the stedfast beauty of the sylvan isle of Innisfallen."

With this passage in our minds we close our second day, with hopes of a bright sky for Mangerton tomorrow.

For two days we have been sequestered on the bank of the Lower Lake, in the profound quiet of our hotel. The Killarney beggars find no admission here. The only signs of Killarney life are the two patient women who sit all day at the hotel-door, offering their knickknacks of the arbutus and the bog-oak. It is time we saw something of the population; so we will walk to Mucruss on our way to Mangerton.

A pretty road of a mile leads to Killarney. We pass the unfinished cathedral, begun, from the design of Pugin, some four or five years ago, and left as it is through failing means. At a distance on the hill is a noble asylum for pauper lunatics,—and, somewhat nearer, the Union Workhouse—a large fabric. Within this Workhouse all is order and cleanliness. At the time of our visit to Killarney the Guardians had additional buildings for in-door relief,—the whole capable of accommodating 2,800 persons. The Union, it appears, is admirably managed; the Guardians have had no assistance from Government; out-door relief has been administered, not to the able-bodied, but in extreme cases of widows and children. And yet, although a stern necessity was driving the able-bodied fast into the Workhouse, there were causes in operation which kept out many even when famine was at their door.

The Mucruss Hotel, which we pass on the road to the Mangerton Mountain, is in some respects more advantageously situated than the Victoria. It commands no view of the Lakes, but it is close to the charming walks of the Mucruss Peninsula. A glance at the map will show all the advantages of this position : these walks extend for miles; and the natural beauties of this peninsula, dividing the two lakes, and commanding the finest views of the scenery of each, have been improved by admirable taste. Mucruss Abbey

3.—LOWER LAKE, LOOKING OVER MUCRUSS DEMESNE.

9.—MUCRUSS ABBEY.

10.—TORC WATERFALL.

is a beautiful ruin: many parts are in good preservation. In the cloister is a most remarkable object—a magnificent yew-tree springing up from the centre, its spreading branches forming a graceful roof to the arched walls. The trunk of this tree rises up to a greater height, without a limb, than we have before observed in any of these vegetable memorials of long past generations. Its girth is inferior to many of our English yews. The east window, seen through the pointed arch of the chapel, is very perfect. Within are some tombs and monuments, ancient and modern. The Abbey stands amidst the most luxuriant groves,—the vivifying power of nature cherishing the perishable works of man,—and clothing decay with ever-springing beauty. (Cut, No. 9.) Torc Waterfall is within a walk of Mucruss (Cut, No. 10); but we reserve that for the last look of Killarney!

We mount our ponies. The ascent to the mountain is very gradual—a bare and dreary road. On we go without any striking views for a mile or two, till the way gets steeper and more rugged. Company begin to gather about us. There is the regular Irish guide, who springs up at every turn of a road which leads to sights. We soon get rid of him. But the mountain-girls, with their goat's milk and potheen, are not so easily disposed of. The troop gathered thick and fast at every step of the ascent; no persuasions could induce them to let us proceed in peace. Great want was not apparent,—or it was hidden under their bright shawls, worn as gracefully as if arranged by the most tasteful of tire-women.

For a mile or two in the channel of a torrent, and we at length from Mangerton look over the Lower Lake. Magnificent was the view—glorious was the day. But our trusty Spillane urged us forward, for he saw the mist gathering in the distance. We have hurriedly passed the hollow in which lies the famous tarn, "The Devil's Punch Bowl," and are nearing the summit. Severe is the cold, even in the sun of a July day. Now rest. We have given Wilson's description of the scene, and how can we attempt to embody our own impressions. For the first time we saw the Atlantic: there it sparkled, over the shoulder of one of the distant cluster of mountains. Why is it, that one glimpse of the great highway of the world raises the spirit far more than the open prospect of the narrow seas?

"There is a magnet-like attraction in
These waters to the imaginative power
That links the viewless with the visible,
And pictures things unseen. To realms beyond
Yon highway of the world my fancy flies."
CAMPBELL.

But the near mountains—they lie around us. The light falls on one, the shadow on another,—they seem to heave and swell like the vexed ocean. A mist creeps over some summit far below us, and then plunges into the glen;—up another craggy steep rises the mist from the valley, and hovers about till it mingles with the upper clouds. The Lakes seem to wash the bases of these giant forms that close us in from all the outer world, except where the Kenmare river brightens to the south, and the great sea to the west. The monarchs of the solitude seem to look down upon the beauty at their feet, solemn and sad, whether in glimmer or in gloom. We heed not their names, as they are repeated in our ear—Carran-Tual, Purple Mountain, Toomies, Glena, Tore, Drooping Mountain, Cahirna, Ierc, Sugar-Loaf. We regard not their comparative elevations. Carran-Tual is a thousand feet higher than Toomies, and six hundred feet above where we stand. They all seem to dwell close together in glorious companionship, and the equality of brotherhood. And yet Carran-Tual is eight miles away; though it seems as if the eagle could wing his flight from one top to another as easily as the swallow skims from Innisfallen to Ross. But the mist is gathering, and we must descend. We send our ponies down before us;—for we have a path to tread in which our own feet will best serve us.

We descend not far. We have crossed the sinking bog on the crest of Mangerton, and look down a steep declivity into the glen in which lies the Devil's Punch Bowl. It is a melancholy place, amidst high rocks—the tarn " which never plummet sounded," dark as

winter; cold as ice, they say, though Charles Fox swam across it. We sit down under the shelter of a rude stone wall. We have sandwiches and potheen—and there are clear springs not far off. One of the women that followed us up the mountain suddenly appears at our side. She sits down. With a mournful cadence she sings one of her native songs. " Her voice is sweet, is soft, is low." Another, and another. Her store is exhaustless. She gave us some little argument to explain her ditties. They were unquestionably the pastoral ballads of a mountain peasantry. One was a dialogue, similar, perhaps, to that which Mr. Walsh has given in his " Irish Popular Songs :"

" Oh! if thou come to Leitrim, sure nought can us sever,
    A phlur na m-ban doun óg !*
Wild honey and the mead-cup shall feast us for ever,
    A phlur na m-ban doun óg !
I'll show thee ships and sails, through the vistas grand,
As we seek our green retreat by the broad lake's strand,
And grief would never reach us within that happy land,
    A phlur na m-ban doun óg !

* Flower of brown-hair'd maidens.

11.—THE BLACK VALLEY.

To Leitrim, to Leitrim, in vain thou wouldst lead me,
    Duirt plúr na m-ban doun óg!
When pale hunger comes, can thy melodies feed me?
    Duirt plúr na m-ban doun óg!
Sooner would I live, and sooner die a maid,
Than wander with thee through the dewy forest glade,
That thou art my beloved, this bosom never said,
    Duirt plúr na m-ban doun óg!"

We again mount our ponies. A ride of two hours brings us back to the Victoria.

A night is before us, such as we cannot forget. Gansey, the famous piper of Killarney, gives us the pleasure of his company. A venerable man, blind ;— a man of real genius—a gentleman. All the old traditionary music of Ireland is familiar to him. He has his modern ballads for those who want an ordinary pleasure : but if he have "audience fit though few," he will pour out strain after strain, wild and solemn, gay or pathetic, with a power that seems like inspiration. Never heard we such effects from one instrument, since the days of Paganini's violin. Midnight was passed before we ceased to listen, enraptured, to

    " Many a bout
Of linked sweetness, long drawn out."

One more day at Killarney—and then, farewell ! How shall that day be passed by us ? In perfect repose. One of our companions has gone to perform the difficult feat of ascending Carran-Tual. We are to meet him with the boat long before sun-down, at the head of the Upper Lake. We are true to the appointment. There is one with us watching for him with some anxiety ; but the scene is so glorious that anxiety can scarcely find a place even in the breast of a loving wife. The mountains are lighted up with all the most gorgeous hues of heaven. The full moon is up—we wander on, far away from the lake, through the Black Valley. (Cut No. 11.) Solemn and more solemn grow the shadows of the mountains. The sun is altogether gone. Then the rocks begin to put on mysterious forms. Not a sound falls upon the hushed air. A footstep ! one of our friend's guides is come to beg us yet to wait. It was a needless message. But that poor guide—he has fallen in his rough descent, and is badly wounded. Fear then begins ; but at length the wished-one comes, worn out, but safe. He has beheld sights from Carran-Tual which we would see ourselves, if we were a few years younger.

And now, one sight that all Killarney visitors should behold, if possible, at the risk of some inconvenience— a row of twelve miles, under the light of the summer moon. As we came up the Lake, four hours ago, we marked every form of hill and island. They are now all blended in one faint tint, when

    " A sable cloud
Turns forth her silver lining on the night;"

or suddenly touched with the partial light of the full orb, which renders them even more indistinct in the unshadowy splendour. In the evening glow we saw

the heron fishing. The owl now flaps by us, startled. We rest under Glena ; and there, in the deep silence of midnight, we hear the mountain echo to the bugle in a voice which seems unearthly. A night ever to be remembered.

Farewell, at last, to Killarney. The car is ready that is to bear us to Kenmare. Our way lies by the new road—a great work, unsurpassed, perhaps, in these islands for its picturesque character. It passes close by Torc Waterfall, which we stop to view. It climbs the mountain, and cuts through the rocks, heedless of obstacles. This is the way by which tourists reached Killarney when the readiest passage was from Bristol to Cork. We are not sure that it is preferable to coming by the railway from Mallow, and gradually finding out the beauties of the Lakes. Here they are revealed. The first impression of the scenery at the exquisite points of view which this road offers must be ineffaceable. But we are satisfied to have won a growing delight, instead of being struck mute with a first admiration.

Such an admiration—speechless wonder—is the view of Glengariff and the great arm of Bantry Bay, which presents itself from the grand road recently completed from Kenmare. We passed through that town ; saw the improvements which a benevolent landlord may effect in his district ; saw dwelling after dwelling on the hill-sides, which contrasted happily with the ancient mud cabin : and passing through a long tunnel, such as railroads have made us familiar with, rapidly descended the road which leads to Glengariff. And then that prospect !—Mountains — bays — islands — and the great Atlantic rolling placidly in to kiss a shelvy shore.

Glengariff—the glen itself—must remain unvisited. No heavier clouds ever descended on Ireland than those which fell at Glengariff when we rose on the morning after we left Killarney. Well, Otway has well described it ; and our readers will have no regret in missing our own description :

" I do not know how to begin, or where to take up, or in what way to put forth the dioramic conception I have in my mind's recollection of this delightful glen. Mountains—why you have them of all forms, elevations, and outlines. Hungry Mountain, with its cataract of eight hundred feet falling from its side ; Sugar-Loaf, so conical, so bare, so white in its quartzose texture ; Slieve Goul, the pathway of the fairies ; and Esk Mountain, over which I was destined to climb my toilsome way. Every hill had its peculiar interest, and each, according to the time of the day or the state of the atmosphere, presented a picture so mutable—or bright or gloomy, or near or distant—valleys laughing in sunshine, or shrouded in dark and undefined masses of shade ; and so deceptive, so variable were the distances and capabilities of prospect, that in the morning you could see a hare bounding along on the ranges of those hills, that, at noonday, were lost in the gray indistinctness of distant vision. Then the glen itself, unlike other glens and valleys that interpose between ranges of mountains, was not flat, or soft, or smooth—no meadow, no morass, no bog—but the most apparently-tumultuous, yet actually regular, congeries of rocks that ever was seen. Suppose yon the Bay of Biscay in a hurricane, from the west—suppose you the tremendous swell, when the top-gallant mast of a ship would be hid within the trough of its waves—and now suppose that by some Almighty fiat all this vexed ocean was arrested in an instant, and there fixed as a specimen of God's wonders in the deep. Such you may suppose Glengariff. It appears as if the stratifications of the rock were forced up by some uniform power from the central abyss, and there left to stand at a certain and defined angle, a solidified storm. And now suppose, that in every indenture, hole, crevice, and inflexion of those rocks, grew a yew or holly; there the yew, with its yellow tinge; and here the arbutus, with its red stem and leaf of brighter green, and its rough, wild, uncontrolled growth, adorning, and at the same time disclosing the romantic singularity of the scene. I know not that ever I read of such a place, so wild and so beautiful." (Cut No. 12.)

In that morning of tremendous rain we take our seats in a covered car, to pursue our journey towards Cork, by Macroom. Not one feature of the scenery to be descried except the river, by the side of which the road for some time runs. But after two hours' travel we at length come to a wonder, which such a day as this raises into sublimity. The Pass of Keimaneigh has been described by Otway, as it appeared to him under brighter circumstances:

" This deep and extraordinary chasm which Nature has excavated through these mountains, and which, within these last ten years has been taken advantage of in order to make an excellent road between Macroom and Bantry, is really one of the most picturesque things in Ireland. It is well worth a journey to see its rocks and precipices—its cliffs clothed with ivy, and, here and there, interspersed through the masses of rocks, old holly and yew-trees, and occasionally an arbutus; and then its strange and sudden windings—you look back, and you cannot find out how you got in—before you, and you cannot imagine how you are to get forward. You might imagine that the Spirit of the Mountains had got you into his stronghold, and here you were impounded by everlasting enchantment. Then! the surpassing loneliness of the place,—

' I never
So deeply felt the force of solitude.
High over-head the eagle soared serene,
And the gray lizard in the rocks below
Basked in the sun.' "

But when we were hemmed in, for about a mile, by the mighty chasm, we saw neither the yew, nor the holly,

nor the bright arbutus,—no cliffs clothed with ivy looked smilingly down upon us. We saw only a double wall of rocks, down whose sides torrents were dashing at every step,—cataracts that hissed and foamed as they rushed over the steeps, whose tops were one a sea of mist. This Pass of Camineagh was the scene of a strange affair in 1822, when the Rockites were in insurrection. As the soldiery passed through the defile, the "boys," who were hidden amidst the rocks, suddenly loosened an enormous mass which they had quietly undermined, and down it came into the glen—blocking up the defile. They were a moment too late. The soldiery had gone by; and their plan of overwhelming the loyalists by superior numbers was effectually frustrated by their own act. The rock which had fallen was an impassable barrier.

There is another route from Bantry to Cork, through Bandon, which is a very interesting one, and, now that the railway from Cork to Bandon has been opened, it also possesses the advantage of saving time. This route leads the traveller through some fine wild upland country, and thence down a very picturesque pass, into Dunmanway, a populous and thriving village, beautifully situated in an amphitheatre of hills, just at the foot of the heights which here form the frontier of the mountain district of the south-west of Ireland. From Dunmanway the road proceeds for several miles along the lovely river Bandon, whose brown transparent waters wind so pleasantly among the grassy knolls. Spenser's residence, Kilcoleman, was not so distant from this as to prevent his making acquaintance with the scenery, and he has celebrated

" The pleasant Bandon crowned with many a wood."

These woods have, however, disappeared, having from time to time fallen beneath the stroke of the woodsman's hatchet. Approaching Bandon, the scenery, which was wild and pastoral, diversified with hills and dales, assumes a more cultivated character. Then comes Castle Bernard, the residence of Lord Bandon, skirting which the road runs, and you get, now and then, some sweet peeps of woodland scenery, through which the river at intervals gleams; and so into the town. Bandon is situated on the river of the same name, and occupies the declivities on both its sides. Its population, with the suburb of Roundhill, is about 9,000; and it returns one member to Parliament. It has two parish churches, one convent, a Scots church, and two endowed schools. Once at Bandon, the railway is the fate of the tourist. What can we ever see in railways, save flitting glances of beauties that should be lingered over to be rightly estimated? We step in, then, to the carriage, steam away over the lattice bridge, traverse the great Chetwynd Viaduct, stop at Inneshannon; go on again, getting a peep at Frankfield and Mount Vernon, and at length reach the terminus at Cork.

12.—GLENGARIFF.

CONNAMARA.

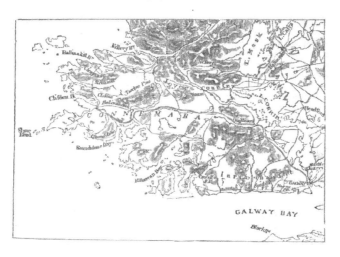

We have grouped Connamara with Killarney in the same section of 'The Land we Live in,' for two reasons. In the first place, it appears to us that there is great hope for Ireland in the development of the vast resources of this district. Connaught, in the times of religious persecution, was assigned as the place of banishment for the non-conforming Catholics—a place which was profanely associated by the intolerance of puritanism with that more desolate region to which fanaticism would consign all those who differ in points of belief. It would accord well with the better spirit of our own times, if Connaught were to become a place in which capital might find its employment, and labour its refuge from the worst of tyrannies—the land tyranny. To *plant* Connaught was the ambition of a great statesman ; and it will be planted,—whether by individuals or corporations, is little matter. Secondly, Connamara is full of glorious scenery ; and now that Ireland is again claiming her proper share of a laudable curiosity, Connamara will open her noble bays, and lakes, and mountains, to the gaze of the stranger.

No one, accustomed to the associations which group themselves around commercial and maritime affairs, can look at the Shannon and the portion of Ireland spread out beyond it, without a desire to penetrate the future, and see what Providence holds in store for this remarkable country. The noble river acts as a line of separation, extending nearly north and south, through so long a distance as to form a very significant boundary between Connaught and the other provinces. This has been regarded, however, by the rulers of Ireland, in past times, as a boundary in a sense which we may hope will now pass away. " It is singularly illustrative," says Sir Robert Kane, in his ' Industrial Resources of Ireland' (a work replete with valuable information), " of how little reflection was devoted to Irish subjects —of how slightly the true and only means of consolidating a people by giving them common habits of industry, of sociality, and of traffic, was thought about in relation to this country, that the Shannon was for so many generations looked upon as a useful barrier and defence against the uncivilized tribes who dwelt beyond its boundary. The cost of maintaining in good repair the various fortifications at what were called the passes of the Shannon, was defrayed with pleasure ; but the idea of rendering fortifications useless, of erecting the bulwarks of the state in the hearts of the inhabitants by fostering their industry, by encouraging their commerce and agriculture, and promoting their education, did not occur to the statesmen of that epoch."

The counties which are cut off from the rest of Ireland by the Shannon—Clare, Galway, Mayo, Roscommon, Sligo, and Leitrim—are among those whose misery has most frequently been brought under the notice of England and Englishmen during the last few years. A portion of Galway is that to which we are about to call the reader's attention.

It is impossible to glance over the wonderful maps of the Ordnance Survey of this part of Ireland, without a saddened feeling for the present and a hopeful one for the future. We say *wonderful* maps; for seldom has there been such another display of mapping as this celebrated Survey presents. Take the county of Galway, for instance—the one which contains the Connamara district. Here we find no less than 137 large sheets devoted to this county, on a scale of six inches to a mile; while the Index Map, in which the whole county is represented in one sheet, is quite a triumph of minute engraving. Although on a scale of only one-third of an inch to a mile, this index-map presents the natural and social features with astonishing fulness.

One of the most striking entries on this map, both for its frequency and the tale which it tells, is " Castle in ruins." This entry is not met with so repeatedly in Connamara as in the portions of Galway county farther to the east; but it is to be encountered even in that region of rugged beauty. Eastward of the town of Galway, however, the " Castle in ruins" meets the eye so frequently in the map that the attention is forcibly arrested by it. How old are these ruins? What was the state of the people when those castles were built? Was English conquest or internal discord the cause of the ruin? Such are the queries that suggest themselves to the mind. So far as the *names* are concerned, nothing can be more thoroughly Irish than these ruined castles—Kilroge, Kilcoritan, Clogh-moyle, Cloghballymore, Cloancurreen, Ballynaman-tragh: such names tell much more of the Celt than of the Anglo-Norman.

But when, leaving these relics of man's work, we transfer our attention to the natural features of Conna-mara, it is difficult to imagine that such a country will always remain as it is—a social and commercial blank. What a chain of lakes! what a coast line! A short line of about seven miles will connect the eastern extremity of Killery Harbour with the western extre-mity of Lough Mask; and thus we have formed a northern boundary to Connamara, all but seven miles consisting of coast-line. Then a straight line of two miles is all of land that intervenes between the south of Lough Mask and the north of Lough Corrib; and this latter noble lake stretches southward till it pours its waters into the river Corrib, which itself finds an embouchure in Galway Bay: thus is an eastern boundary given to Connamara, of which all but two miles consists of water. As to the western and southern boundaries, they are wholly formed by the sea. We may therefore say that this large district—measuring, perhaps, forty miles from east to west by twenty-five from north to south — differs from an island only by the occurrence of two isthmuses, of seven and two miles respectively: as viewed upon a map, it is a peninsula, and as a peninsula we shall treat of it. Strictly speaking, and in relation to the ancient divisions of Ireland, Connamara is comprised within . narrower limits than those here

marked out; for the peninsula contains three ancient divisions—Joyce's Country in the north-east, Jar-Connaught (or West-Connaught) in the south-east, and Connamara all that lies westward of those two divisions. In this narrower sense, Connamara would be pretty accurately bounded on the east by a line drawn from the inner part of Killery Harbour to the inner part of Kilkerran Bay; and the district thus marked out would extend from twenty to twenty-four miles in each direction. But the physical and indus-trial features of the peninsula are independent of these local divisions; and we shall continue to give the name of Connamara to all that lies westward of the two noble lakes. These lakes, containing nearly seventy thousand acres of water-surface, and entering into the Atlantic by a river which passes through the county town—ought to effect great blessings for Ireland some day or other. Then there are in addition an almost incalculable number of smaller lakes spread over the peninsula, but more thinly in the southern than the northern half. This, too, is a district where the coast-line presents such a series of inlets and harbours as is not easily to be paralleled elsewhere. The word Connamara is said to mean " land of bays." Beginning at Killery Harbour, with its many coves and inlets, we pass round a jetting promontory and find ourselves in Ballynakill Harbour, which throws out its manifold arms into the land in various directions. Then occur Claggan Bay, Streamstown Bay, Kingstown Bay, Clifden Bay, and Mannin Bay—all of which serrate the extreme western margin of the peninsula, and in front of which are numberless small islands washed by the Atlantic. Next, bending round south and east, we pass in succession the Bays of Bunowen, Ballyconneely, Gorteen, Roundstone, (Cut, No. 13), and Cleonile,—a series which ends in the deep inlet of Berbragh Bay. The minor bays of Ard and Mweenish, which next occur, are followed by the magnificent harbour of Kilkerran, whose deepest inlets have distinctive names of their own. From Kilkerran Bay the coast proceeds pretty regularly from west to east, ending at the town of Galway, and forming the northern side of Galway Bay; this line of coast is marked chiefly by the inlets which form Casheen Bay, Coonawilleen Bay, Kiggaul Bay, Greatman's Bay, and Cashla Bay, and by the island of Gorumna.

The best information which we possess concerning Connamara, and the source whence most subsequent writers have derived their principal details, is con-tained in the late Mr. Alexander Nimmo's Report on that district. Commissioners were appointed by the Crown, early in the present century, and soon after the Union of Ireland with Great Britain, to examine the bogs of Ireland, with a view to the suggestion of such plans as might facilitate their reclamation. The labours of the commission lasted several years, and did not terminate till 1814. The commissioners employed ten eminent engineers, and a large staff of surveyors, to examine and survey the bogs; and the separate reports of these engineers are full of valuable details concerning Ireland and its latent capabilities. They minutely surveyed, examined, and measured no less than 1,013,358 acres of bog land; while there were separate examinations, not professing to enter into so much detail, of three other districts in Wicklow, Erris, and Connamara; containing together about 387,000 acres of bog, and 355,000 acres of mountain peat soil. Mr. Nimmo, Mr. Lovell Edgeworth (the father of Maria Edgeworth), and Mr. Griffith, were among the most eminent of the engineers employed.

The Connamara district — considered as including the whole of Galway county westward of Loughs Corrib and Mask—is one of the most uncultivated in the whole of Ireland. The quantity of arable land seems, at first glance, not to exceed one-twentieth of the whole area; but the process of reclamation will give a more and more favourable ratio in this respect. Where cultivation has made the greatest progress on the south shore of Lough Corrib, the arable or dry land is interspersed with extensive tracts of naked limestone rock of a most desolate aspect; and it appears to be only after incredible labour, that a few patches of soil have been torn from the general waste. Nevertheless—as if in encouragement and reward for whatever labour and capital are bestowed on this region of wildness—such is the fertility of these spots, and the value of the pasture among the limestone, that this land, even including rock, produced at the time of Mr. Nimmo's examination a rent of fifteen shillings per acre, and where tolerably cleared, was rented as high as in any part of Ireland.

The other parts of the district are principally bare moors, consisting of various depths of bog, upon a bottom of primitive rock affording little soil; but several strings or beds of limestone run through the district, and are distinguishable by the verdure and cultivation which have taken place in their vicinity.

Mr. Nimmo estimated the population at 30,000. It is now supposed that the number must have exceeded that limit; but taking the estimate as he gave it, he states that half of the inhabitants are in Connamara proper, one-third in Jar-Connaught, and one-sixth in Joyce's Country; that nine-tenths of the inhabitants of Connamara proper are settled along the sea-shore; that in Jar-Connaught the inhabitants reside either on the sea coast, or on the northern slope of the hills next to the limestone country; and that the upland part of Joyce's Country is quite uninhabited. But in these details, and in the statement of total rentals, the lapse of nearly forty years has in all probability introduced wide differences.

Before any reclamation of bog land commenced, 57 per cent. of the whole area of Connamara consisted of mountain and upland pasture, 34 per cent. of bog, 7 per cent. of arable land, and 2 per cent. of limestone-rock. A formidable picture this, with only one acre in fourteen deserving the name of arable land! Yet Mr. Nimmo was impressed with the conviction that there are certain facilities about and around Connamara which might render the improvement and cultivation

of the district more hopeful than in many other waste lands of the kingdom. These facilities presented themselves to his mind under the forms of *climate, aspect, coast-line*, and *geological formation*.

First for the climate. It is decidedly mild. Snow is little known even in the hardest winters. The cattle are never housed; for the mountains in the north, and the great variety of surface, afford considerable shelter. The least favourable features are wet summers and strong west winds.

Next for the aspect. Although Connamara may be deemed in some sense mountainous, it is not an upland country like Wicklow. At least three-fourths of Connamara proper is lower than 100 feet above the level of the sea; and this low level must have an undoubted influence on the prospective vegetable fertility of the district. Jar-Connaught rises from the shore of Galway Bay, in a gently sloping plain, to about 300 feet, at the upper edge of which there are some hills of about 700 feet, and beyond them a low limestone country extends to the edge of Lough Corrib. Joyce's Country is, in every respect, more mountainous and wild.

In respect to sea-coast, nothing can well (size being considered) be more magnificent than this peninsula. After reading Mr. Nimmo's remarks thereon, a reader must lack hope indeed who cannot look forward to a day of prosperity for the district—far-distant, perhaps, but not the less certain and cheering. "The district is nearly surrounded by the sea on the south and west, and by the great lakes Mask and Corrib on the east—the latter navigable into the town of Galway, and could easily be made so to the sea. Various great inlets penetrate the district, so that no part of it is distant four miles from existing navigation. There are *upwards of twenty safe and capacious harbours*, fit for vessels of any burden; about twenty-five navigable lakes in the interior, of a mile or more in length, besides hundreds smaller. The sea-coast and all these lakes abound in fish. The district, with its islands, possesses no less than 400 miles of sea-shore. On Lough Corrib it has fifty miles of shore; so that with Lough Mask, &c., there are, perhaps, *as many miles of shore of the sea or navigable lakes as there are square miles of surface.*"

In respect to the geological features, there are extensive bands of calcareous sand round the coast in almost every bay; there are numerous beds of available limestone adjacent to almost all of the navigable lakes; and there is bog-peat which will furnish an inexhaustible supply of fuel.

Taking in conjunction the above four groups of circumstances or conditions, Mr. Nimmo remarks:— "On the whole, it appears to me that the improvement of this district, so far from being difficult or hopeless, is a thing highly feasible; and if vigorously but steadily pursued, is likely to meet with fewer obstructions and greater ultimate success than, perhaps, in any other part of Ireland."

In respect to the fitness for agricultural purposes, Mr. Nimmo arranges the peninsula into four parts—

the Limestone Field, the Granite Moor, the Middle Division, and the Northern Division. The Limestone-Field lies principally between the town of Galway and Lough Corrib, and along part of the western shore of the lough. It is a triangular nook, forming the western edge of the great limestone-field of Ireland. Much of this limestone-rock is bare; but on its edges are many very fertile spots; the hollows are mostly filled with bog. Other patches of limestone are interspersed with other rocks in various parts of the peninsula. The Granite Moor forms the southern part of the peninsula; it contains no limestone, but is partially covered with bog of various depths. There is a large supply of shell or coral-sand in the bays on the coast, which might easily be applied to the manuring of this moor; and there is abundance of red sea-weed, equally applicable to such a purpose. The Northern Division contains no limestone or calcareous matter; but it is so deeply indented by Loughs Corrib and Mask, that no part of it is distant more than three miles from some spot whither lime may be brought by water-carriage. The great drawback to this division, at the time of Mr. Nimmo's examination, was, that there was neither a single road fit for a wheel-carriage, nor a single bridge over a stream or inlet, in the whole of this portion of the peninsula. The Middle Division, the last of the four portions into which Mr. Nimmo divided the peninsula in respect to agricultural capabilities, contains numerous veins or beds of limestone, so situated that almost every farm within that tract has either limestone upon it, or within half a mile of it. Many of these lime-rocks are also situated on long and deep lakes—a circumstance which gives a facility of transport that may at some future time become of the greatest importance.

The industrial processes which were carried on in Connamara at the date of Mr. Nimmo's examination, are interesting to note, because they mark the early stages of a course of labour which may, perhaps, lead to prosperous results in future years. One employment was that of cutting sea-weed for manure, or collecting that which is at every tide cast ashore. Two or three boat-loads of sea-weed, of about six tons each, were usually applied as manure over an acre of potato ground. The weed was usually sold at half-a-guinea a ton. The rotation adopted at the farms at that period was frequently as follows:—one year of potatoes raised on sea-weed; one year of oats or barley; four or five years of natural meadow; and then potatoes manured with sea-weed, as before.

Among those things which have to some extent checked the productive labours of Connamara is the decline in the use of *kelp*. Since the wonderful progress of chemistry, which has led to the manufacture of soda from common salt, the obtaining of the same alkali from kelp has been almost discontinued; because the lowest price which would keep the poor kelpers from starvation is still higher than that at which soda can now be purchased. Kelp used to be made by burning sea-weed, and soda by purifying the kelp.

Experience, however, has shown that it is more profitable to employ sea-weed as manure for the improvement of the wastes, than to manufacture kelp, even at remunerating prices.

The hopeful anticipations of Mr. Nimmo with respect to the harbour and water-power of Connamara have already been touched upon; and we find that he was not less hopeful with respect to its bogs:—

" I am perfectly convinced," says he, "from all that I have seen, that any species of bog is by tillage and manure capable of being converted into a soil fit for the support of plants of *every* description; and with due management, perhaps the most fertile that can be submitted to the operations of the farmer. Green crops, such as rape, cabbages, and turnips, may be raised with the greatest success on firm bog, with no other manure than the ashes of the same soil. Permanent meadows may be formed on bog, more productive than on any other soil. Timber may be raised, especially firs, larch, spruce, and all the aquatics, on deep bog; and the plantations are fenced at little expense. With a due application of manure, every description of white crops may be raised upon bog; and I know no soil from which they can be extracted without it. There is this advantage in the cultivation of bog, that any species of soil will act as a manure to it: even the siliceous sand of Renvill having that effect; but this admixture of foreign soil, though highly beneficial, is not essential to the improvement of bog; fallowing and manure, such as dung or lime, will convert the bog-stuff itself into a soil, and extract large crops from it; so that there is nothing desperate in the cultivation of bog upon a basis of rock."

Those travellers—few and far between—who have visited Connamara since the date of Mr. Nimmo's examination, are invariably struck either with the latent capabilities not yet developed, or with the fine scenery which portions of the peninsula exhibit. Sir Robert Kane, in the work before quoted, passes in review the sources of power which are presented by the rivers and lakes of that country. When he comes to speak of that province which contains the district of Connamara, he says:—" The province of Connaught is that which deserves most attention in relation to its navigable lakes. Its soil is not inferior to that of the rest of Ireland; some of the sweetest pastures and most productive lands are found within its limits. Its coasts abound with fish; its mountains are rich in ores; its people are willing to work, and travel hundreds of miles seeking for work, even at a rate which only allows them to sustain existence. Yet that province is the reproach of Ireland and the by-word of Great Britain. Its population is relieved by charitable subscription from recurrent famines. Little more than one-half of its area has been made available for cultivation; and it is but a few years since its interior was first rendered accessible to industry by the formation of proper roads."

Mr. Inglis, whose 'Tour through Ireland' about fifteen years ago, was a means of bringing many beauties of that country before the notice of English readers, shared in the general opinion of the capabilities of the Connamara district. "At Maam," he says, "one is forcibly struck with the advantages which would be opened up to this district by the extension of the navigation of Lough Corrib to the sea. Fine slopes of reclaimable land border the deep stream that, at the distance of half a mile, flows into Lough Corrib; and the same boats that would carry to market the produce of the cultivated land, would bring from the bay of Galway sand, sea-weed, and lime to be laid upon the yet unimproved wastes." The same thought seems to have repeatedly occurred to the mind of Mr. Inglis, during his journey through Connamara. "It was impossible," he says, while progressing on foot from Maam to Clifden, "to cast the eye over the vast inclined plains of bog-land, skirted by fine water levels, which seemed to invite draining, without feeling a conviction of the immense capabilities of this part of Ireland; and seeing, in prospective, these vast tracts bearing abundant produce, and the chain of loughs carrying that produce—on the one side to Lough Corrib and Galway Bay; and on the other to Birterbuy Bay, or one of the other bays which lie to the westward." Again, the following remarks suggest irresistibly the future which *must* be destined for this remarkable peninsula. "There is perhaps no part of Ireland so well adapted for experimenting on waste lands and reclaimable bogs as Connamara. No part of Connamara is more than six miles from some sea-bay, or lake having communication with the sea. If there were good roads in all directions, this length of land-carriage would not be great; but even this distance would be much diminished by improving and connecting the navigation of the chains of lakes which extend through every part of Connamara."

Besides the industrial associations connected with this district, there are many scenes of great beauty. The Killery, for instance, is a beautiful and remarkable boundary to Connamara on the north. It is a narrow deep inlet of the sea, extending far up into the country, and bounded on both sides throughout its whole extent by a range of mountains nearly as elevated as any in Ireland, and of very picturesque forms. The inlet is not above a mile across. In several spots the mountain boundary rises abruptly from the water; but there are many clefts and hollows which reveal more elevated peaks beyond, and show the extent of the range. Those who have visited both regions say that there is nothing in the British Isles which approaches so near to the character of the Norwegian *Fiords* as Killery—a deficiency of dark-foliaged timber being the chief drawback from the comparison.

The Rev. Cæsar Otway, who published several works relating to the topography of the north-west of Ireland, speaks of Lough Corrib as "a noble sheet of water, here and there studded with islands—some large and fertile, others rugged rocks; some embattled

13.—ROUNDSTONE BAY.

with the ruins of an old fortress; some made holy by the crumbling remains of a still older church, where some Culdee made his desert,—a disciple of Columba, or Fursey, or Fechin, his retreat. If such a lake as this were in Scotland, or indeed anywhere else in Europe, it would be covered with steam-boats and yachts, and there would be hotels and accommodations on its shores, and a county as rich if not richer than Cumberland, would be opened out, and planted, and built on."

One of the most extraordinary scenes of this extraordinary peninsula is displayed at the isthmus between Loughs Mask and Corrib. The waters of the former flow into the latter at the town of Cong; but no river or stream is to be seen in the maps, and the existence of any communication appeals rather to the ear than to the eye. The flow is in great part subterraneous. The rocks have been tunnelled during the lapse of ages by the waters which came from Lough Mask and some smaller lakes towards Lough Corrib. Well may Mr. Otway, after such a description as the following, claim for Ireland the attention of those who love wild scenes of beauty and grandeur :—" Cong is certainly a rare place—it might be called the Irish Arabia Petræa; but there is this great difference, that our place of stones is also a place of rivers of waters. For here, amongst hills of stones and valleys of stones, you hear the rustling sound of streams through a multitude of holes, and gullies, and caverns; where waters are now appearing and then disappearing, until all at once they burst forth from under the rock, and form a rapid river, rushing to Lough Corrib, larger than the Liffey. It certainly is a singular sight. To the left of the village you see a strong and turbulent stream gushing through salmon and eel weirs, as it flows with all its turbulent eddies to the lake; then you look to the north, south, east, and no river is seen, nothing but the great gray ridges of limestone; you look closer, and you see enormous springs turning at once some great mill-wheels with the impetuosity and force of their waters as they rise from the earth; and while those springs start up and boil in all directions around you, as you do not know whence they flow, so you do not understand whither they are tending."

The western districts partake less of the beautiful than the eastern; but even here there are scenes which drew forth from Mr. Inglis no small amount of admiration. After speaking of the road from Roundstone to Clifden, which seems to be bare and desolate, he thus records his opinion of the north-western part of the peninsula :—" I do not hesitate for a moment to say, that the scenery in passing from Clifden to the Killeries and Leenane is the finest in Ireland. In boldness of character nothing in Killarney comes near to it; and although the deficiency of wood excludes the possibility of a competition with Killarney in picturesque beauty, I am certainly of opinion that the scenery of this part of Connamara, including especially the Killeries, which is in Joyce's Country, is entitled to rank higher than the more praised (because better

known) scenery of Killarney. I would not be understood as saying one word in disparagement of Killarney, which, in the combination of forms and colours, is not to be surpassed; but in speaking of Killarney, I think I ventured to observe that no approach to sublimity was to be found; and as, in the part of Ireland of which I am now speaking, there are undoubted approaches to the sublime, with all of the picturesque besides that depends upon form, I think these ought to weigh heavier in the balance than that softened beauty which at Killarney is created by abundance and variety of wood, and consequent splendour of colouring. I know that a far stronger impression was made on my mind in this journey than by anything I saw at Killarney. Be it known, too, that this is a country of lakes—lakes with as fine mountain boundaries as are to be found in the three kingdoms."

Chiefly through the exertions of Mr. Nimmo, a road has been made entirely round the peninsula, beginning at Galway, and winding sufficiently near to the sea and the lakes to open up those districts to the tourist and (what is better to the capitalist. There is another road extending across the district from south-east to north-west. The road to Ballinahinch passes close by the southern slope of the remarkable group of mountains called the Twelve Pins; and among these mountains is now quarried a green marble so beautiful, that it only waits to be better known in order to find a ready market. These Twelve Pins form a striking nucleus to a striking district. They stand in the very centre of Connamara, and occupy an area six or seven miles square. It is supposed that the name *Pin* is here a corruption of the Scottish *Ben* or mountain; but be this as it may, the mountains, about a dozen in number, are placed in two opposite rows, inclining together at the ends so as to enclose a kind of oval valley. The chief among the mountains are Knockannabiggen, Bengower, Benlettery, Derryclare, Bencullagh, and Benbaun; these vary in height from 2400 to 2000 feet; the others average about 1800 feet. (Cut No. 14)

Mr. and Mrs. Hall, in their work on 'Ireland,' give the details of some information which they received concerning the Connamara marbles, from the proprietors of one of the marble works in Galway town. The quarries in question are situated on the shores of Lough Corrib; and they were discovered in the following way :—An Englishman was exploring the country for minerals, useful rather than ornamental, when he chanced to discover a stone of fine texture, which, on being polished by a mason, was pronounced to be marble of a fine jet colour. He was unable to work the quarry for want of means; but two brothers of the name of Ireland made an arrangement with Sir Valentine Blake, the proprietor of the estate on which the marble was found, to export some blocks of it to London. This occurred about the time when Mr. Nimmo was making his examination. The marble-merchants soon appreciated the beauty of the material;

and ever since that time the black marble of Galway has had numerous admirers and purchasers. The entrance-hall and grand staircase of the Duke of Hamilton's palace near Glasgow, are formed of this beautiful material. The right of quarrying is at the present time leased to certain capitalists, who have extensive stone-working machines at Galway. The process of obtaining the marble is simply as follows :— The men first remove a covering of limestone, about twenty-five feet in thickness ; it lies in beds or layers from one to two feet thick, and requires blasting with gunpowder to ensure its removal. The black marble, thus exposed to view, lies as flat as a billiard-table, in successive layers varying from six to fifteen inches in thickness. There are joints or fissures in these layers, which greatly facilitate the process of quarrying ; wedges are driven into the fissures, and a few blows suffice to separate a complete block—for the different layers seem to be easily detached. Some of the blocks or slabs procured in this way are as large as twelve feet long by ten wide. The black marble here spoken of is a wholly distinct material from the green marble of the Twelve Pins. A visit to the mineralogical gallery at the British Museum will enable us to see a specimen of this beautiful green marble, in the form of a table presented by Mr. Martin, of Galway.

The family of the Martins in Connamara were formerly the owners of a greater number of acres than any other family in Ireland. If the resources of the country were fully developed, the estate would be of enormous value ; but the wealth of mountain and bog is of a prospective character. Colonel Martin, the representative of the family thirty or forty years ago, is said to have endeavoured to put the Prince Regent out of conceit with the famous "long walk" of Windsor, by saying that the avenue which led to his hall-door was thirty miles in length. The pleasantry was true to this extent, that the whole distance of thirty miles from Galway to Ballinahinch lay within the Martin estates, while the road from the one to the other stopped short of the mansion, beyond which there was little else than rugged paths. Ballinahinch is the name of a barony, a lake, a rivulet, a village, and a demesne ; and the whole form the head-quarters of a family which once possessed almost regal power in this wild region : indeed the title of "king of Connamara" has been given almost as much in seriousness as in joke to the representative of the family, by the native Irish around.

But this great estate, like many other great estates in Ireland, has passed from its ancient proprietors. The whole of the Martin estate has been sold, and is now principally in the possession of the Law Life Assurance Company. "Humanity Martin," as the proprietor of these vast estates was called, on account of his persevering exertions for the prevention of cruelty to animals, forgot to extend his humanity to the two-legged animals of his own country ; and the squalid misery which his heartless neglect entailed, superinduced

a fearful retribution on him and his family. Whatever regret one may feel, at the sudden reverses that have thus ruined an ancient family, it is impossible not to be sensible of the vast social amelioration which the transfer of those estates is sure to effect in these wild and hitherto most neglected districts. Indeed the change is in many places already apparent. Many English settlers have found their way into these regions, and have brought with them their spirit of enterprise, industry, and love of comfort and order. Miss Martineau, in a recent visit to this district, observing upon the visible improvement, says, "This was noticeable in the neighbourhood of the mansion lately called the Martins' Castle ; and pleasant it was to see neat, white cottages upon the hill sides, each with its 'stooks' of oats beside it."

Another of the centres of power in this district is Clifden, the residence of the D'Arcys, one of the small number of proprietors of Connamara. Clifden is almost at the south-west corner of the district. In 1815 it consisted of one single house : it now contains several hundred. In the former year its site and a large extent of surrounding country yielded no revenues whatever to its proprietor : it now yields several thousands per annum. In 1822 roads were commenced, eastward from Clifden to Ballinahinch and Oughterard, and northward to Westport ; these were the forerunners of the town ; and an excellent quay, built by Mr. Nimmo at the inner extremity of Ardbear Harbour, gave to the incipient town the means of exporting and importing produce. The formation of this town did not involve any actual outlay on the part of Mr. D'Arcy ; he offered leases of plots of ground on advantageous terms, to whoever was inclined to build ; many availed themselves of the opportunity, and the result has been favourable both to lessor and lessees. This town of twenty seven years' existence now boasts of its gothic Parish Church, its Roman Catholic Chapel, its two public schools, its dispensary and workhouse, its three streets of tolerable houses, its import trade from Liverpool and even from America, its trade in curing and exporting herrings, its grain market, its breweries, distilleries, and corn-mills, and its corps of fishermen. The bay on whose shore it stands is so completely landlocked as to constitute a favourite rendezvous for the government cruisers. Mr. D'Arcy has built a beautiful castle at Clifden, in the midst of a scene of natural grandeur—mountain and sea coast forming component parts — not easily surpassed in Ireland. There was one piece of flat unsightly bog ; but this has been drained and converted into a lawn in front of the castle. Clifden is in every sense a valuable example, to show what may yet be done in the industrial regeneration of Connamara.

Of Joyce's Country, it is doubtful whether so much will be made as of Connamara proper, on account of the bareness of its mountains and its lesser proportion of sea-coast. Its inhabitants are nearly all Joyces— who have the reputation of being the tallest and largest men in Ireland. "Big Jack Joyce" was for many years a well-known giant among a race of giants. Mr. Inglis met with a young Joyce, seventeen years of age, who measured six feet three inches—not exactly "in his stockings," for he had none. The Joyces of Joyce's Country, and the Flynns of Connamara, have for ages had a sort of hereditary faction-feud. Will the present generation see such feuds die out?

The best route for the tourist from Galway is by Oughterand to Clifden, which can be accomplished either by public conveyance, the Mail, or Bianconi's car, or, better still, by hiring a vehicle. With the exception of an occasional glimpse at Lough Corrib, and one or two seats of resident gentry, and old castles, there is not much to interest or attract. Approaching Oughterand the aspect of the country improves; and while it is not less picturesque, it is more cultivated. Shortly after passing Lemonfield, the seat of George O. Flahertie, Esq., we reach the town, which is extremely pretty, with some good edifices.

Thence to Clifden the road mounts through a singularly wild region, and lake succeeds lake in quick succession, amid dreary bogs and wild marshes. At length "the half-way house" is reached. Beyond this is Lough Ourid, along whose northern shore the road winds, while to the right are seen the range of the Mamturk Mountains. Next comes Glendalough, with Ben-y-Gower towering in front; and so on by Ballinahinch to Clifden through bold mountain scenery. From Clifden to the Killeries, by Kylemore, is a delightful drive: and Salrue should not be left unvisited. Thence to Maume is as wild and grand as can well be imagined. If time permits, by all means visit Cong; if not, you can back to Oughterand. Thus an excellent notion of the physical features of this interesting region may be formed by the intelligent tourist. None others will gain much wherever they go.

14.—THE TWELVE PINS, LOOKING OVER CLIFDEN.